BOOKS PUBLISHED BY FREDERICK ELLIS

(New Hardbacks)

Buy Direct – USA, UK, AUSTRALIA – 20% Discount
Free Shipping – Pay with PayPal

Contact - frederick659@yahoo.com

Retail Prices Below

Hardbacks

Author - Jack London

$36.75…………...WAR OF THE CLASSES

$36.75…………JOHN BARLEYCORN

$33.75…………THE PEOPLE OF THE ABYSS

$34.75…………JACK LONDON ON THE ROAD

$44.75…………Martin Eden

$35.75…………THE ASSASSINATION BUREAU, LTD.

$36.75…………THE IRON HEEL

$34.75…………ESSAYS OF REVOLT

Author – Bruno Traven

$32.75…………GENERAL FROM THE JUNGLE

$38.75…………THE DEATH SHIP

$35.75…………THE REBELLION OF THE HANGED

$34.75…………THE WHITE ROSE

$34.75…………THE BRIDGE IN THE JUNGLE

$34.75…………MARCH TO THE MONTERIA

$37.95...............THE TREASURE OF THE SIERRA MADRE

Author - Frederick Ellis

$19.75................THE OAKLAND STATEMENT (softcover)

Author – Mao Tsetung

$39.75.................QUOTATIONS FROM CHAIRMAN MAO TSETUNG

Author – Upton Sinclair

$33.75.................OUR LADY

$44.75.................OIL

$39.75.................THE JUNGLE

$32.75.................THE FLIVVER KING: THE STORY OF FORD-AMERICA

$35.75.................ONE HUNDRED PERCENT: THE STORY OF A PATRIOT

$34.75…………….THE SECRET LIFE OF JESUS

$34.75…………….THE MONEYCHANGERS

$35.75…………….MENTAL RADIO

$35.75…………….THE MILLENIUM

$35.75…………….A PERSONAL JESUS

$36.75…………….PROFITS OF RELIGION

$34.95…………….THEY CALL ME CARPENTER: A TALE OF THE SECOND COMING

$53.75…………….DRAGON'S TEETH (1943 Pulitzer Prize Winner)

      Author – Thomas Paine

$38.75…………….COMMON SENSE & THE RIGHTS OF MAN & THE AGE OF REASON

$33.75…………….THE AMERICAN CRISIS

      Author – Karl Marx

$40.75…………….DAS KAPITAL

$33.75……………..THE COMMUNIST MANIFESTO & WAGES, PRICE AND PROFIT

$32.75……………..WAGE-LABOUR AND CAPITAL & VALUE, PRICE AND PROFIT

Author – W. E. B. Du Bois

$34.75……………..THE SOULS OF BLACK FOLK

Author – Eugene Debs

$35.75……………..WALLS AND BARS

$54.75……………..DEBS: HIS LIFE WRITINGS AND SPEECHES

Author – Jean-Jacques Rousseau

$34.75……………..THE SOCIAL CONTRACT

Author – John Reed

$37.75……………..TEN DAYS THAT SHOOK THE WORLD

$36.75……………..INSURGENT MEXICO

Author – Antonio Gramsci

$33.75................THE MODERN PRINCE AND SELECTED WRITINGS

    Author – V. I. Lenin

$35.75................THE STATE AND REVOLUTION

$36.95................FIGHT AGAINST STALINISM & IMPERIALISM: THE HIGHEST STAGE OF CAPITALISM

    Author – John Dewey

$35.75..................HOW WE THINK & EDUCATION AND EXPERIENCE

$37.75..................INDIVIDUALISM OLD AND NEW & LIBERALISM AND SOCIAL ACTION & A COMMON FAITH

$39.75................DEMOCRACY AND EDUCATION & FREEDOM AND CULTURE

    Author – David Ricardo

$37.75..................PRINCIPLES OF POLITICAL ECONOMY AND TAXATION

    Author – Thomas Jefferson

$34.75................BIOGRAPHY OF THOMAS JEFFERSON & THE LIFE AND MORALS OF JESUS OF NAZARETH

Author – Emma Goldman

$35.95.................ANARCHISM AND OTHER WRITINGS

Author – Rosa Luxemburg

$32.95.................REFORM OR REVOLUTION & THE MASS STRIKE

Author – Leon Trotsky

$35.75................THE REVOLUTION BETRAYED

Author – John Stuart Mill

$33.95.................ON SOCIALISM & THE SUBJECTION OF WOMEN

Author – Friedrich Nietzsche

$34.75................BEYOND GOOD AND EVIL

$40.75.................THE BIRTH OF TRAGEDY & 75 APHORISMS & THE ANTI-CHRIST

Author – John Quincy Adams

$33.95.....................THE AMISTAD ARGUMENT & THE STATE OF THE UNION ADDRESSES

Author's – James Madison. Alexander Hamilton and John Jay

$40.75....................THE FEDERALIST PAPERS

Author – G.W. Friedrich Hegel

$43.75.....................THE PHILOSOPHY OF HISTORY

Eugene Debs

DEBS:

HIS LIFE WRITINGS AND SPEECHES

Published By Comrade Frederick Ellis
6015 S. Virginia St.
Reno, Nevada 89502

ISBN 978-1-934568699

ABOUT THE PUBLISHER

Frederick Ellis, born in 1936, is a direct descendant of Nicholas Gilman, a delegate from New Hampshire to the Constitutional Convention and later a US Senator. Nicholas's brother was the 2nd Governor of New Hampshire serving six two-year terms.

Frederick grew up in Vermont and New Hampshire, graduated from Villanova University, Philadelphia with a degree in Economics. After service with the US Army (Artillery Sgt.) he started his first business, an independent insurance agency in Freeport, IL.

It wasn't long before the civil rights movement gained strength and Frederick, a Roman Catholic, became an activist in the open housing movement as a businessman without much support from his fellow business friends, actually hostility. As the 1960's progressed Frederick became involved with the anti-poverty movement as the founding treasurer of the NW Illinois Community Action Agency. And in 1968 became one of the two candidates to the Democratic Convention pledged to Gene McCarthy.

In 1971, Frederick sold his agency and with his wife and 4 children moved to Oakland, CA. Soon after that he became the Campaign

Manager for George McGovern in Berkeley. He was then asked to be a member of Congressman Ron Dellums Executive Committee and was elected to the Alameda Democratic Central Committee and to the Board of Directors of OCCUR (Oakland Citizens Committee for Urban Renewal). In 1975 became President of the MGO Democratic Club, the largest in Oakland.

It wasn't long before he formed the Jack London Democratic Socialist Club and joined Michael Harrington's DSOC (Democratic Socialist Organizing Committee) and NAM (New American Movement). In the mid 1980's he returned to graduate school and gained an MBA in Finance. He began to grasp the concepts of Karl Marx, especially 'the surplus value of labor'.

He left the country in 1996 at age 60 and headed for Costa Rica and lived in San Jose for 8 years then moving to Granada, Nicaragua for 2 years (a great supporter of the Sandinista movement). Then headed back to the USA with his Nicaraguan Rama Indian wife to the USA landing in Dubuque, IA and got the idea to publish left political books, philosophy and psychology. Then on to Denver for a couple of years and finally settling in Reno, NV (The biggest Little City in The World) in 2009. He is now a Anglian Catholic, a Marxist and a Democratic Socialist.

He is a believer in 'hard money' and is a gold/silver analyst and trader. His present dream is to reopen 'The New Harold's Club' in the center of downtown Reno in an vacant older 2 story building with table games and bars only (no slots) giving the best odds in Reno, have his employees start a new union – Casino, Hotel, Restaurant Workers Community Union Local 17 and within 5 years sell the casino to the employees.

A special WEB site is uptonsinclairinstitute.com with the 11 volumes of Upton Sinclair's World's End – Lanny Budd series is discounted at 30% with free shipping.

DEBS:

HIS LIFE, WRITINGS AND SPEECHES

WITH A DEPARTMENT OF
APPRECIATIONS

AUTHORIZED

1908
THE APPEAL TO REASON
GIRARD, KANSAS

Copyrighted, 1908
By The Appeal to Reason

NOTE.—Copyright protection is taken upon this volume for the sole purpose of protecting the work of Comrade Debs from prejudicial misuse by pirate Capitalist publishers, and will not be invoked against Socialist and Labor publications and Comrade publishers, they giving us notice.—Appeal to Reason.

PRESS OF
GEO. G. RENNEKER CO.
CHICAGO, ILL.

Contents

	PAGE
BIOGRAPHY	1 to 76

WRITINGS—

Where Daisy Sleeps (Poem)	77
How I Became a Socialist	79
Outlook for Socialism in the United States	85
The American Movement	95
Unionism and Socialism	119
Socialism	143
Reply to John Mitchell	157
The Federal Government and the Chicago Strike	181
You Railroad Men	207
The Growth of Socialism	227
An Ideal Labor Press	239
Childhood	243
The Crimson Standard	245
Roosevelt's Labor Letters	247
Labor Omnia Vincit	253
Open Letter to President Roosevelt	257
December 2, 1859	262
The Martyred Apostles of Labor	263
Mother Jones	269
John Brown, History's Greatest Hero	271
Martin Irons, Martyr	273
Thomas McGrady	277
Looking Backward	283
Labor Day Greeting	289
Proclamation to A. R. U.	291
Flea and Donkey	296
Eye to Eye	296
Stopped the Blacklist	297
Prince and Proletaire	301
Revolution	305
Vive la Revolution	307
Arouse, Ye Slaves	309
Growth of the Injunction	313
What's the Matter with Chicago?	319

SPEECHES—

Liberty	327
Prison Labor	345
The Socialist Party and the Working Class	357

CONTENTS

	PAGE
Craft Unionism	375
Class Unionism	401
Revolutionary Unionism	427
Industrial Unionism	445
Golden Wedding Anniversary	467
The Issue	473

APPRECIATIONS—

Mr. Debs an Artist in Expression	495
From Woodstock to Boise	495
Here Comes a Man	498
Without Guile	499
Eugene V. Debs as an Orator	499
Lincoln, 1860—Debs, 1894	501
Eugene V. Debs, Incarnate Spirit of Revolt	504
A Companion of Truth	509
Greater Love Hath No Man	512
Agitator and Poet	512
A Love Shared by Lincoln and Debs	512
A Righteous Cause Must Win	513
Loves Inter-racial, Pan-human Language	514
Sincere to the Core	515

Illustrations

Photogravure of Eugene V. Debs	Frontispiece
Debs' Birthplace	13
Debs' Present Home	29
Katherine Metzel Debs	45
Theodore Debs	61
Marguerite Marie Debs	77
Comrades	93
Debs' Library	109
Debs and His Little Girard Comrades	125
Debs' Cell at Woodstock	180
Corridor in Jail at Woodstock	186
Scene at Woodstock upon the Liberation of Debs	194
Debs Reception in Chicago After His Liberation	200
Woodstock Jail	334
Liberty Enlightening the World	509

THE THIRD REVOLUTION

The publication of this volume is not of Comrade Debs' seeking. When approached upon the subject several months ago he stated that he did not suppose that he had accomplished enough to make a book, and it was only after much persistent urging that he snatched the time from his busy labors to correct and revise the original proofs of his Writings and Speeches, and the argument he finally yielded to was that this work would multiply his usefulness to the Socialist movement by as many copies as may be distributed.

The *First American Revolution* accomplished the overthrow of the rule of the English King in the Colonies, the extinction of all rule by inheritance, and the abolition of the proprietary charters to privileges in America which had been granted to favorites and legatees of the British Crown. The movement very early established the precedent of the "boycott" of "unfair" products when the Boston Tea Party by strategy boarded the ships of the English merchants and dumped their cargoes into the sea. Nor was the period without its "undesirable" citizens, whose memories loyal Americans delight to revere.

The Civil War, or the *Second American Revolution*, accomplished the overthrow of a fundamental principle in the Federal constitution as interpreted by our highest judicial authority, in the Dred Scott decision, and the abolition of a special form of slavery or property in black human beings.

The Socialist Movement, or the *Third American Revolution,* has for its accomplishment the overthrow of private property in social wealth, machinery and land, and the abolition of the Wage System, a form of general slavery whereby men profit and grow fat out of the hunger-enforced labor, and hence out of the *lives* of others.

It is no strain of words to say that in the extinction of Wage Slavery a modified state of war even now obtains, and not so very modified at that. We need not the tinsel and glitter of soldiery, nor the clash and clangor of arms to constitute war, but if we did, was it not but yesterday we heard the tread of troops in Colorado? And today, what is it we hear from the South but a fusilade upon the striking miners of Alabama? And tomorrow may we not hear the ripping, whirring sound the Gatlings and Maxims make?

But aside from the open battle, a struggle far more brutal and inhuman, wages bitterly. The poor are warred upon, plundered and ravished. Our children famish and die at the machines of the Capitalist Class, and our wives, our widows and our daughters are torn from us and prostituted to uses abject and unmentionable. What more do we wish to make it war, and what more must we suffer?

This book, every line of which is a labor of love, is the property of The Third Revolution, and as such is dedicated to the Wage Slaves of the world who smart under the crack of the Hunger Whip. BRUCE ROGERS.

Girard, Kansas, August 1, 1908.

BIOGRAPHY

And there's 'Gene Debs—a man 'at stands
And jest holds out in his two hands
As warm a heart as ever beat
Betwixt here and the Jedgement Seat!"
                —*James Whitcomb Riley.*

Life of Eugene V. Debs

By Stephen Marion Reynolds

The life of Eugene Victor Debs is so complicated and entwined with the dominant thought and action of his time, and he has so persistently, with conscious purpose, touched and impressed it with primal vigor, integrity and energy as will make a distinct and lasting work, not merely upon the institutions of this country, but upon the future welfare and development of all the peoples of the whole world.

This is an age of rare vitality, and of swiftly changing variety of events.

There is growing every hour a new consciousness of the purposes of BEING, and there is such healthy, hearty, emphatic enthusiasm in it all as promises vast changes and uplift for humanity.

The converging streams of races are now neighborly and accessible; superstitions are being overthrown, and The People are being prepared; and,

"When the materials are all prepared and ready, the architects shall appear. I swear to you the architects shall appear without fail. I swear to you they will understand you and justify you, O Peoples of the Earth! The greatest among them shall be he who best knows you and encloses all and is faithful to all. He and the rest shall not forget you, they shall perceive that you are not an iota less than they. You shall be fully glorified in them."

Before the battles for freedom, there have always appeared the writers, the orators, the artists, and the singers; Rousseau, defining the "Logic of Liberty;" Tom Paine, calling for freedom from the king; and Patrick Henry, as large as his times, fearlessly announcing new doctrines to take the places of decadent ideals; Lincoln and others pleading for the chattel slave; and in our time, multiplying voices crying aloud for complete freedom from wage-slavery, subtlest and meanest of all forms of human bondage.

We could not have had Appomattox without the conditions that made a Legree and Uncle Tom, and then came Harriet Beecher Stowe to reveal them to the world. We have had our Franklin, Jefferson, Lincoln, patriots, statesmen, abreast the light of their times. Now we have "so-called statesmen" who "talk" and "fiddle while Rome burns" and the army of the hungry and unemployed increases.

If we trace the poems and the orations we find the poets and the orators, and back of them the conditions that filled their souls with songs and eloquence and gave them power to utter the longings of the human heart. These poets and the orators, the true advocates that speak for the people, seem to see from some high mountain a vision in the lonely hours, when their eyes are unbound, the Deity passing by, leaving commands to be obeyed. These are those who are lifted above themselves as witnesses of the panorama of progress that the unseen hand unrolls; thus only can we account for sweet poems from bitter poets and words of love from the hateful things in life. We then understand why Jesus drove the money changers from the temple and said words of doom to the generation of vipers, and condemned in unmistakable words the greed for wealth.

Foremost among the architects of the present day, striving to build up "Industrial Democracy," to emancipate man from economic servitude, appears the architect DEBS, knowing that the materials are ready and consciously serving and building for his brothers, the intended ideal "Kingdom on Earth" for man to rule and dominate at last for himself instead of his masters; bribes, menaces, the entreaties of his friends, all exhausted in the vain endeavor to move him from his firm and resolute will.

No one now attempts either.

He stands a towering rock of hope to the down-trodden and outcast workers of the world.

In field, shop, mill, mine and factory, on the railroads and on the ships of the seas his name is synonymous with devotion, love, sacrifice and unswerving integrity to the workers and their cause. Even the outcast rich admire "The Unpurchasable" and fear him with a reverence that means much for their future, too, if they could but understand how all-inclusive are his labors to abolish classes and class struggles; for he appears in this age pointing steadily and with unblinded vision to the paths of industrial peace, plenty and human brotherhood.

He comes to bring to all that nameless power, that something which one involuntarily feels when in the presence, actual or ideal, of a genuine, strong, true, vital man; such a man remains with those he meets and when he departs leaves the permanent things of life and love with them and they live forever in the imperishable marks and indications of uplifted manhood.

The life of such a living, growing man cannot be written by even his most intimate associates, for he is but an expression of the yearnings of the people, a voice of the proletariat, an embodiment of their needs.

If his physical life should end the task would be even more difficult. So tangible and inspiringly vital is his complete physical, mental and spiritual presence. He has personally touched more lives than any other living man.

No man has ever written more personal letters, throbbing with the ascending song of life, clearly revealing the inner and spiritual processes of growth, than this comrade whose acknowledged conscious kinship to the manifestations of the universe does not end with the sponge on the rock, nor with the highest and most perfect forms of human and God-like life.

Whoever has taken his magnetic hand has never forgotten the experience, but has, for the time at least, ceased to note any serious or passing disagreements and has been conscious of standing in the presence of a fearless searcher for Truth.

The man that comes crying a message in the wilderness and pointing to the inevitable farther heights to which humanity must ascend, meets misunderstanding, insult and rejection, but he is "The Darling of Tomorrow," when the heights are reached and the risen races run to mark the fields of battle with the pathetic monuments of regret and of grief.

Some day, when perhaps his letters are published, or when the stories of his unselfish, loving life are known to the emancipated workers of the world, their tears of joy and appreciation will wash out the shame of contemporary ignorance and neglect.

It may be that he will be an exception and yet live to see the summits reached and "freedom for all" accomplished. This is not improbable, for he is young and strong, growing and in step with the life-giving growth in intelligence of the workers. These are the days of quick growth and development. Electric wires on land and under the seas are everywhere. The voice may be heard over the distant mountains and even without wires, the thoughts and feelings of mankind are transmitted. Moreover there is something wonderful, as yet little understood, in the illuminating power of "Class Consciousness," seeming to unify the intents and purposes of men and simplifying the hitherto strangling problems of progress; compelling all forces to move resistlessly in the forward direction of freedom.

Even obstruction and resistance are harnessed for advancement, plainly revealing that there is an approaching change for better things, that men recognize, even while they deny and resist.

It is not long ago since he was born—November 5, 1855—in a lowly cottage,* No. 447 North 4th Street, Terre Haute, Indiana. The Democratic party had only begun its descent into decadence and vain protest. The now missionless and moribund Republican party had not yet been born, but there were signs in the Republic of its begetting and pregnancy. There were signs of impending crises in the affairs of masters and chattels. The long-continued struggle for the abolition of chattel slavery, that began with the first chattel slaves in America, culminated in cruel fratricidal war while he was yet a tender child. That period had a formative influence upon him, for there was noise and strife and pain in all this section of Indiana; soldiers encamped and wounded men in hospitals and prisons, and fierce debates and sounds of victory and of defeat.

His father, Jean Daniel Debs, and mother, Marguerite

---
* Illustration page 13.

Betterich Debs, natives of Alsace, had many stories to tell to the children at the fireside of France and her joys, sunshine, shadows and sorrows. The father was intimately acquainted with all of French history and had a most complete library of her history. He was upright, loving and lovable; the mother wise and gentle; both intimate companions of the children, and were familiarly called "Dandy" and "Daisy."

FAMILY RECORD.

BORN.

Jean Daniel Debs was born at Colmar, Alsace, France, December 4, 1820.

ON A SAILING SHIP.

Jean Daniel Debs left Colmar for America November 10, 1848, and arrived at New York January 20, 1849.

Marguerite Marie Betterich left Colmar for America August 7, 1849, and arrived at New York September 11, 1849.

MARRIED.

Jean Daniel Debs and Marguerite Marie Betterich were married in New York City September 13, 1849.

LOCATED.

They left New York for Cincinnati, Ohio, September 30, 1850; left Cincinnati for Terre Haute, Indiana, May 20, 1851; left Terre Haute March 24, 1854, returning to New York and locating in Brooklyn (Williamsburg, L. I.,); left Brooklyn September 25, same year, returning to Terre Haute and locating there permanently.

CHILDREN.

Ten children were born to them, of these six are living.

*Theodore, the only brother, well known as an ardent Socialist and tireless worker for the cause, has always been and is very close and very dear and helpful to "Gene" in all his work. There are four sisters and only a few years' difference in the ages of all of them; they make the ideal family group. The father did not long survive the mother, she departing this life April 29, 1906, and he following her November 27, 1906.

---
* Portrait page 61.

This family grew up where there were no jealousies and where love was not only felt, but expressed in acts of service and of sacrifice. Sincere affection gives insight, intuition, understanding, and equips for service and shuts out greed and degrading ambition for place and power.

The stories of his childhood and few school years are replete with human interest and would take much space to fully record. From the beginning, the law of his life was work, but he was equally zealous in all the plays and sports of childhood. There were many children and much to do to support them, so his school years were short and ended with his graduation, with credit, from the Old Seminary School in Terre Haute, where the Indiana State Normal School now stands. In May, 1870, he began to work for the Terre Haute & Indianapolis Railroad Company (now Pennsylvania System) first in the shops and later as a locomotive fireman.

He worked continuously until October, 1874. The mother could not conceal the tears of fear in her eyes when, with lantern in hand, he kissed her to go out over the unballasted prairie railroad. So when he was offered a position by Herman Hulman, of the Hulman & Cox grocery house at Terre Haute, he accepted and filled all requirements until September, 1879, when he was elected city clerk. He served in that office four years. He had joined the Brotherhood of Locomotive Firemen when it was first organized at Terre Haute. He had organized the Brotherhood of Railroad Brakemen, now the Brotherhood of Railway Trainmen; had helped to organize the Switchmen's Mutual Aid Association, the Brotherhood of Railway Carmen, the Order of Railway Telegraphers and other labor unions, and at the Buffalo convention, in 1878, he was made associate editor of the Firemen's Magazine, and in July, 1880, was appointed Grand Secretary and Treasurer, and Editor and Manager of the magazine, serving in the former capacity until February, 1893, and in the latter capacity until September, 1894.

At the time he took charge of the affairs of the Brotherhood of Locomotive Firemen the order had only 60 lodges and $6,000 debt. In a short time he had been able to add 226 lodges and had wiped out the debt. No such demonstration of love and pathetic regret had ever been known in a national gathering of citizens as that which was shown to him when the order, after having exhausted all efforts of persuasion, reluctantly accepted his resignation from these offices of the order. When he resigned from these offices he was receiving $4,000 per year. It was at the Cincinnati convention, 1892, he tendered his resignation, which was unanimously refused; he was unanimously re-elected to all the offices previously held. He again tendered his resignation and insisted upon its acceptance, with the frank statement that "organization" should be broad enough to embrace all the workers, and that he desired and proposed to give all his energy to the building up of such an organiaztion. The convention unanimously voted to give him, as a mark of appreciation, $2,000 for a trip to Europe, for rest and enjoyment; this he declined. Finally, after unyielding insistence, his resignation from the several offices was accepted, taking effect as above stated.

With the assistance of a few others he organized at Chicago, in June, 1893, The American Railway Union, and his salary was fixed at $75 per month. During the last two years of the organization's existence he drew no salary at all. His further motives for his action in resigning from the Brotherhood of Locomotive Firemen to organize the A. R. U. cannot be better told than in his own words uttered by him at the time:

"I do this because it pleases me, and there is nothing I would not do, so far as human effort goes, to advance any movement designed to reach and rescue perishing humanity. I have a heart for others and that is why I am in this work. When I see suffering about me, I myself suffer, and so when I put forth my efforts to relieve others, I am simply working for myself. I do not consider that I have made any sacrifice whatever; no man does, unless he violates his conscience."

GREAT NORTHERN STRIKE.

April 16, 1894, a circular letter was issued to the members of the A. R. U. containing a scale of wages paid on the Great Northern Railroad. This scale showed that the Great

Northern Railroad never did pay such wages as other Pacific grand continental lines. According to this scale train despatchers were receiving $80 per month; freight conductors, $78; freight brakemen, $42 to $53; engineers, in some cases, only $2.80 per day; inspectors, $35 per month; operators, $37.50 to $41.50; roundhousemen, a dollar a day; trackmen, a dollar a day, and truckmen, a dollar a day. The cheapest board in Butte, Montana, was $26 a month.

The Great Northern sent out a cipher dispatch to remove all spirited men and to gather together all available men to take their place. The A. R. U. gained knowledge of this step on the part of the Great Northern and decided to call the employes to quit on very short notice. Enclosing this circular letter issued from the Butte City, Montana, headquarters of the A. R. U., the directors closed their appeal to the men in the following words:

"We need your financial and moral support everywhere. It is the greatest strike the world has even seen. Give us your moral and financial support through the general office at Chicago. Act quickly. See if we cannot break the chains that are being forged to reduce us, not only to slavery, but to starvation."

Before ordering the strike the following letter, dated April 13, was sent out:

"To C. W. Case, Gen'l Manager of the Great Northern Railway:

"Sir: I am instructed by your employes to say that unless the scale of wages and rules of classes of employes that were in effect prior to the first cut made August 1, 1893, are restored and switchmen at Great Falls and Helena receive the same pay and schedules as at Butte and the management agrees to meet the representatives of the employes at Minot not later than ten days hence and formulate schedules accordingly, all classes of employes will quit work at 12:00 o'clock noon this 13th day of April."

The notice was only six hours and the employes had no apologies to make in this respect. No reply being received before the hour set, the order to strike was given. Mr. Hill, on receiving information of the walk-out of his employes, issued a notice expressing the wish that faithful employes would remain, making general promises of promotion usual in such cases. The A. R. U. held revival meetings at all points on the line of the Great Northern and membership increased by the thousands.

On the 22d of April Mr. Debs and Mr. Howard addressed a large gathering of railroad men at St. Paul and added 225 members to the A. R. U. Beaten at every point, Mr. Hill called for a conference. The purpose of that conference on Mr. Hill's part was to close up somebody's eye. His business success has been largely bottomed on that characteristic. Those acquainted with Mr. Debs had no fear of the result. Mr. Hill wound up the lengthy conference by proposing arbitration. This was refused by Mr. Debs. Mr. Debs saying at the conclusion of the conference these words:

"Let me say that we do not accept the proposition. Efforts have been made ever since this trouble started to divide the organization and make trouble between the Union and the Brotherhoods. I understand such to be the policy of this company. Now if the other organizations represent the men, let them set your wheels turning. Our men will not go back to work. My idea is that in raising the question of representation you have sought to evade the issue. We presented the terms upon which we would go to work. I am authorized to say that we will settle on these terms and on no others. This grievance is a universal grievance and all the men are united in this action. It will be to no avail to attempt to divide us into factions. If wages are not restored you can no longer have the service of the men. For the past week we have restrained the men from leaving your employ. Now, understand me that I am too much a gentleman to make a threat and I do not mean this as anything but a plain statement of fact, but if there is no adjustment, those men will withdraw from your service in a body. They are convinced that their demand is a just one. If their request is not complied with," continued Mr. Debs in slow and measured tones, "they will, without regard to consequences, continue this struggle on the lines already laid down and fight it out with all the means at their command within the limits of the law.

We understand your position; you understand ours. We will not withdraw from this conference. We shall be in the city several days and shall be glad to receive any further communications from you."

Mr. Hill was not slow in understanding and the world knows the facts about this great victory, won with peaceful methods.

MR. DEBS' RETURN HOME AFTER THE A. R. U. VICTORY, MAY 3, 1894.

(*From the Terre Haute Express.*)

Mid soul-stirring music and the joyous shouts from the lips of 4,000 of his friends and neighbors, men, women and children, Eugene V. Debs, President of the American Railway Union, was welcomed home last night, care-worn and weary, from his 18 days' struggle for victory in the Great Northern strike.

Mr. Debs marched with the people, refusing to enter the carriage provided, and in the park near the Terre Haute House he delivered the following address:

"Gentlemen, my friends and neighbors: From the depths of my heart I appreciate and thank you for this demonstration of your confidence and respect. I had not the remotest idea that on my return to my native city such a magnificent demonstration awaited me.

"As a rose-bud yields to the tender influences of a May shower, just so does my heart open to receive the expressions of gratitude and esteem from you, my friends and neighbors. I have, as you are aware, just returned from the Northwest, the scene of trouble on one of the greatest railroad systems in the country. The contest on the Great Northern system has no parallel in the history of railroad trouble. From the hour the strike commenced the men were united; they stood shoulder to shoulder—engineers, firemen, brakemen, conductors, switchmen, and even the trackmen and freight handlers, who are generally first to suffer, stood up as one man and asserted their manhood.

"One of the remarkable features, very remarkable, in the contest, was the good feeling which prevailed during the 18 days of the strike, and the good feeling lasted during the trying and anxious hours of arbitration. I am glad, my friends, to be able to say to you tonight, that in all those 18 days there was, from one end of the Great Northern road to the other, not a single drop of human blood spilled. The American spirit of fair play was uppermost in the minds of the manly men who were involved in the trouble, and their fight for wages was conducted without rowdyism or lawlessness. The reduction on the Great Northern Railway was without cause. In resisting it, the employes met solidly organized capital face to face, and man to man, and for 18 days not a pound of freight was moved and not a wheel turned, with the exception of mail trains. As a result of this unification, this show of manliness and courage on the part of the employes, they gained 97½ per cent of what they claimed as their rights. The arbitration of the differences was entrusted into the hands of 14 representative business men of the Twin Cities, with Chas. Pillsbury, the merchant miller prince, as chairman. The preliminaries leading up to that memorable meeting of arbitration covered many weary hours, but once in session and facing the great question of wages of thousands of men, these 14 men, all of whom were men of capital and employers of labor, reached a verdict in one hour, a verdict for the employes, by which $146,000 more money will monthly be distributed among the deserving wage-earners than would have been had they not stood up for what they knew to be justly theirs.

"My glory, my friends, consists in the gladness which I know will be brought into the little cottage homes of the humble trackmen among the hills in the West. I can almost see the looks of gratitude on the faces of these men's wives and little children. In all my life I have never felt so highly honored as I did when leaving St. Paul on my way home. As our train pulled out of the yards the tokens of esteem, which I prize far more highly than all others, was in seeing the old trackmen, men whose frames were bent with years of grinding toil, who receive the pittance of from 80 cents to $1 a day, leaning on their shovels and lifting their hats to me in appreciation of my humble assistance in a cause which they believed had resulted in a betterment of their miserable existence.

"The American Railway Union does not believe in force except in the matter of education. It believes that when agreements and schedules are signed there should be harmony between all. It believes and will work to the end of bringing the employer and employe in closer touch. An era of closer relationship between capital and labor, I believe, is dawning, one which I feel will place organized labor on a higher standard. When employer and employed can thoroughly respect each other, I believe, will strikes be a thing of the past. For as Mr. Hill, President of the Great Northern, said to me at the conclusion of the arbitration conference, 'You have fought a good fight and I respect you,' and I answered, 'Mr. Hill, if this shall be your policy I will give you my word of honor that in future your road will be engaged in no more such trouble as has just terminated.' This strike is not without its fruit and will result in much good all along the line. I hope to see the time when there will be mutual justice between employer and employes. It is said the chasm between capital and labor is widening, but I do not believe it. If anything, it is narrowing down and I hope to see the day when there will be none.

"What has occurred tonight seems to me like a dream, a revelation. You are all too generous, honorable, magnanimous, and my heart rises to my lips in receiving this demonstration from you, my neighbors, from the people of my home, where I was born and have grown from childhood to manhood. A look into the recesses of my heart only can show you the gratitude I have no words to express. I can only assure you my eternal friendship and loyalty. With my heart on my lips I thank you, my friends—honorable men, lovely women, and little children. Had I the eloquence of an Ingersoll I could not express the happiness, the long life and success I wish you one and all. Once more, with gratitude trembling upon my lips, I bid you all good fortune."

THE PULLMAN STRIKE.

In June, 1894, the great Pullman strike was fought and won, but victory was turned into defeat by the Federal administration using the courts and the soldiers to imprison the

DEBS' BIRTHPLACE, TERRE HAUTE (See Page 4)

leaders and crush the strike. The railroad corporations then resolved to annihilate the A. R. U. Debs was indicted for various crimes, the railroad corporations demanding that he be prosecuted for conspiracy, treason and murder. Many predicted that he would be hanged. He was imprisoned several times and served six months in Woodstock Jail for contempt of court. While serving at Woodstock, he was taken daily to Chicago, a distance of 55 miles, under escort of two deputy sheriffs, where he was being tried for conspiracy and other crimes, but when the prosecution learned that Debs and his attorneys were in possession of the secret proceedings of the Railroads' General Managers' Association and that they had a number of witnesses to testify as to who had committed the crimes charged to the strikers, the trial was abruptly ended on the plea that a juror had suddenly been taken sick. No effort has ever been made to impanel another jury and so far as the records show, the juror is still sick, and the cases ended by evasion and subterfuge on the part of the Railroad Corporations.

Debs was kept 18 months in the jurisdiction of the court by postponements and various pretexts, calculated to prevent him from re-organizing the A. R. U., and when finally released, the railroad corporations put detectives on his track and for two years they followed him, and whenever he organized the men they were discharged, as were many who even recognized him or who were suspected of having any sympathy with his work or for him personally. He saw that it was vain and hopeless to reorganize the A. R. U. and that all the influence the corporations could combine were opposing it.

SOCIALISM DAWNING UPON THE LABOR LEADER'S MIND.

The Great Northern strike, the strike of the A. R. U. in sympathy with the suffering workers at Pullman, the injunction and the proceedings for contempt, the imprisonment of Mr. Debs and his associate officers for contempt of court, the trial for conspiracy and many other events which will hereinafter be set forth in greater detail, developed the vision of the Labor Leader and turned his mind in the direction of political action to solve the wrongs of labor.

In a letter to the "Coming Nation," now the "Appeal to Reason," November 23, 1895, Mr. Debs first advocated the establishment of the co-operative commonwealth by the exercise of the ballot.

"Liberty, be it know, is for those only who dare to strike the blow to secure and retain the priceless boon. It has been written that 'Love of Liberty with life is given,' and that 'life without liberty is a continuous curse,' and that 'an hour of liberty is worth an eternity of bondage.' It would be an easy task to link together gilded periods extolling liberty until the mind weary with delight, becomes oblivious of the fact that while dreaming of security the blessings we magnified had, one by one, and little by little, disappeared, emphasizing the truth of the maxim that 'eternal vigilance is the price of liberty.'

"Is it worth while to iterate that all men are created free and that slavery and bondage are in contravention of the Creator's decree and have their origin in man's depravity? If liberty is a birthright which has been wrested from the weak by the strong or has been placed in peril by those who were commissioned to guard it as Gheber priests watch the sacred fires they worship, what is to be done? Leaving all other nations, kindred and tongues out of the question, what is the duty of Americans? Above all, what is the duty of American workingmen whose liberties have been placed in peril? They are not hereditary bondsmen; their fathers were free-born—their sovereignty none denied and their children yet have the ballot. It has been called 'a weapon that executes a free man's will as lightning does the will of God.' It is a metaphor pregnant with life and truth. There is nothing in our government it can not remove or amend. It can make and unmake presidents and congresses and courts. It can abolish unjust laws and consign to eternal odium and oblivion unjust judges, strip from them their robes and gowns and send them forth unclean as lepers to bear the burden of merited obloquy as Cain with the mark of a murderer. It can sweep our trusts, syndicates, corporations, monopolies and every other abnormal development of the money power designed to abridge the liberties of workingmen and enslave them by the degradation incident to poverty and enforced idleness as cyclones scatter the leaves of our forest. The ballot can do all this and more. It can give our civilization its crowning glory—the co-operative commonwealth. To the unified hosts of American workmen fate has committed the charge of rescuing American liberties from the grasp of the vandal horde that have placed them in peril, by seizing the ballot and wielding it to re-gain the priceless heritage and to preserve and transmit it, without scar or blemish to the generations yet to come.

> "Snatch from the ashes of their sires,
> The emblems of their former fires;
> And he who in the strife expires,
> Will add to theirs a name of fear,
> That Tyranny shall quake to hear."

March 22, 1899, a conference was held at 39 West 26th Street, New York, attended by a large number of representatives of scattered organizations having altruistic tendencies, with a view of organizing a new political party. Mr. Debs attended this conference and in reply to an address made by the chairman of the meeting, Mr. Debs said:

"I wish to be candid with the gentlemen present. I am a Socialist. I am one who believes in the co-operative ownership, not only of the means of production and distribution, but of this planet. Such an amalgamation as this proposed here cannot succeed, and if it did succeed it would mean the sacrifice of principle. I have tried to gather together men of various beliefs. I have tried the step at a time policy, I have been an opportunist, but after years of experience and work and agitation, gentlemen, I have finally landed on the bedrock of Socialism and from that I will not move."

Dr. W. S. Rainsford, rector of St. George's Episcopal Church, replied, saying:

"All great reforms have been the result of compromise. History proves that beyond question. I realize, as well as anybody else, the need of radical action, but I also believe that men of kindred sympathies must sacrifice personal opinions and stand together for the common good of all the people, hence I am happy to confess that in these matters I am an opportunist."

The Rev. Dr. Henry Frank said his experience told him that all the great men of today were Socialists, "the statesmen, the writers, the thinkers, and even the fashionably gowned and the jeweled members of the so-called better classes in their hearts are Socialists." It was not a question of principle as much as a question of program that must be decided upon.

George M. Pullman was summoned to give some testimony.

Mr. Debs, who seemed alone in his uncompromising opinions, replied that the results of the compromises spoken of are wage-slavery, such as the world never saw. He would rather have 10,000 Socialists with their faces to the storm and their teeth set, who knew what they wanted and who stood firm, than a million men of varying opinions held loosely together in the hope of making a step at a time. He said he did not care if victory could be given to such men tomorrow. They are not sufficiently well organized and until that was done all hope of lasting results were futile.

At the evening session Mr. Debs declined to vote on the resolution offered to hold the conference at Buffalo, reiterating his belief that the proposed conference will come to naught unless it comes out for bed-rock uncompromising Socialism.

The labor movement received its origin from low wages and over-work. Of the millions who are employed, only a few obtain fair wages. These constitute the *"aristocracy of labor."* They care nothing for the great majority whose wages are so low that under most favorable circumstances they are only able to barely live. The labor movement then has two supreme purposes in view,—first, the advance of wages all along the line; second, the reduction of the hours constituting a day's work. These purposes are fundamental, eliminate them and the labor movement disappears and labor organizations forthwith collapse. We hear much for and against labor in politics. Why so? Simply because laws have been enacted by which wages can be forced down and men compelled to work more hours than is good for soul and body. Who made these unjust laws? The old parties, Democrat and Republican, are both culpable. Does labor desire to continue such a policy? The universal answer is "no." Then why not vote for a party honestly committed to a policy which would enact just laws and honestly administer them? No rational reply can be made. The labor movement is based upon a few simple propositions,—more wages and a less number of hours for a day's work, which would inevitably result in better conditions.

In spite of the fact that during Mr. Debs' imprisonment in Woodstock Jail, he had read many books on the philosophy of Socialism, including Carl Marx's great work, handed to him by Victor Berger, who visited him for the purpose of interesting him in this great question, and in spite of the fact that he advocated the union of workingmen at the ballot box, he did not see at that time any way of incorporating social economics into political expression. He was still a democrat, fighting in the dark, but with the scales gradually falling from his intellectual eyes. He supported the candidacy of William Jennings Bryan in the campaign of 1896, believing, as millions did, that Mr. Bryan put man above the dollar, and that Mr. Bryan would truly represent the democratic instincts of the people and do all in his power to undo the wrongs heaped upon labor by Grover Cleveland. He did not advocate Mr. Bryan's election in any revengeful spirit against Mr. Cleveland, but in the hope that this fresh, young orator from the West would do all he could to emancipate the people from the thraldom of the money power.

MR. DEBS REFERS TO THE INJUNCTION IN HIS SPEECH THE EVENING OF HIS RETURN TO TERRE HAUTE, NOVEMBER 23, 1895.

"In our cases at Chicago an injunction was issued at a time when the American Railway Union had its great struggle for human rights and they were triumphant in restraining myself and colleagues from doing what we never intended to do and never did do; and then we were put in jail for not doing it. When that injunction was served on me, to show that I acted in good faith, I went to two of the best constitutional lawyers in the City of Chicago and said, 'What rights, if any, have I under this injunction? I am a law-abiding citizen; I want to do what is right. I want you to examine this injunction and then advise me what to do.' They examined the injunction.

They said, 'Proceed just as you have been doing. You are not committing any violence; you are not advising violence, but you are trying to do everything in your power to restrain men from the commission of crime or violating the law.' I followed their advice and got six months for it. (Laughter and applause.)

"What does Judge Lyman Trumbull say upon that subject? Judge Trumbull is one of the most eminent jurists the country has produced. He served sixteen years in the United States Senate; he was chairman of the Senate Committee on Judiciary; he was on the Supreme Bench of the State of Illinois; he has held all of the high offices but he is a poor man. There is not a scar nor a blemish upon his escutcheon. No one ever impugned his integrity. What does he say about this subject? To use his exact language he says: 'The decision carried to its logical conclusion means that any federal judge can imprison any citizen at his own will. If this be true, it is judicial despotism, pure and simple, whatever you may choose to call it.' When the trials were in progress at Chicago Mr. Geo. M. Pullman was summoned to give some testimony. Mr. Pullman attached his car to the New York train and went East, and in some way the papers got hold of the matter and made some publication about it and the judge said that Mr. Pullman would be dealt with drastically. In a few days Mr. Pullman returned and he went into chambers, made a few personal explanations and that is the last we heard about it. Had it been myself, I would have to go to jail. That is the difference. Only a little while ago Judge Henford cited Henry C. Payne, of the Northern Pacific, to appear before him to answer certain charges, and he went to Europe and is there yet. Will he go to jail on his return? Of course not. The reason suggests itself. If it were a railroad striker he would be in Woodstock instead of Berlin.

Governor Altgeld, in many respects the greatest governor in the United States, says: 'The precedent has now been established and any Federal judge can now enjoin any citizen from doing anything and then put him in jail.' Now what is an injunction? It has all of the force and vital effect of a law, but it is not a law in and by the representatives of the people; it is not a law signed by a president or by a governor. It is simply the wish and will of the judge. A judge issues an injunction; serves it upon his intended victim. The next day he is arrested. He is brought into the presence of the same judge. Sentence is pronounced upon him by the same judge, who constitutes the judge and court and jury and he goes to jail and he has no right of appeal. Under this injunctional process the plain provisions of the constitution have been disregarded. The right of trial by jury has been abrogated, and this at the behest of the money power of the country. What is the effect upon the workingmen and especially railway employes to bind them to their task? The government goes into partnership with a corporation. The workingmen are intimidated; if there is a reduction of wages they submit; if unjust conditions are imposed they are silent. And what is the tendency? To demoralize, to degrade workingmen until they have reached the very dead line of degradation. And how does it happen and why does it happen that corporations are never restrained? Are they absolutely law-abiding? Are they always right? Do they never transgress the law or is it because the Federal judges are their creatures? Certain it is that the united voice of labor in this country would be insufficient to name a Federal judge. If all the common people united and asked for the appointment of a Federal judge their voice would not be heeded any more than if it were the chirp of a cricket. Money talks. Yes, money talks. And I have no hesitancy in declaring that money has even invaded, or the influence, that power conferred by money, has invaded the Supreme Court and left that august tribunal reeking with more stench than Coleridge discovered in Cologne and left all the people wondering how it was ever to be deodorized. There is something wrong in this country; the judicial nets are so adjusted as to catch the minnows and let the whales slip through and the Federal judge is as far removed from the common people as if he inhabited another planet. As Boyle O'Reilly would say:

"His pulse, if you felt it, throbbed apart
From the throbbing pulse of the people's heart."

On January 1, 1897, Debs issued a circular to the members

of the A. R. U. entitled "Present Conditions and Future Duties," in which he reviewed the political, industrial and economic conditions and came out boldly for Socialism. Among other things he said:

"The issue is Socialism vs. Capitalism. I am for Socialism because I am for humanity. We have been cursed with the reign of gold long enough. Money constitutes no proper basis of civilization. The time has come to regenerate society—we are on the eve of a universal change."

When the A. R. U. held its convention at Chicago in June, 1897, he and its members favored political action, and the Social Democratic party was organized June 21, 1897, and this was the beginning of what is now known as the Socialist party of America.

GOVERNMENT BY INJUNCTION.

The year 1894 marks a great historical change in the attitude of laborers towards government, for it was during that memorable strike that the now famous injunction was used to cripple the efforts of the workers to improve their condition by the lawful methods of the general strike. The late and now great (?) Cleveland, in spite of the traditional fealty of the Democratic party to state sovereignty, over the protests of Governor Altgeld of Illinois, who declared that the state was amply able to protect life and property in its territory, sent Federal troops into Chicago and disorder followed, and the strike was lost and, as stated, its leader thrown into prison.

Government by injunction is today the "slogan" of both old parties, and their hypocritical utterances as to this issue are convincing the American working people that with the army as a police force government by corporations has taken the place of government by the people and the farmers exploited by the packers' and elevator and railroad interests, the miner snubbed everywhere by the coal barons and the vast and increasing army of the unemployed, young and outcast old men are now thinking in terms of political strike, rather than in terms of boycott and idle protest.

The hours of work are now short enough to the workers, and far too short to provide food, shelter and clothing for themselves and families in the midst of industrial stagnation, caused by exhausting the purchasing power of the producers of wealth through the blind greed of those who claim the right to take unto themselves the earth and its exhaustless resources for abundantly supplying the needs of all.

During the eventful years from 1894 to this epoch-making year 1908, the two old parties have come into closer resemblance, until now Mr. Bryan is found claiming that Mr. Roosevelt has adopted his ideas. He is not so insistent, however, on this point as he was a year ago, when he admitted that there had been great additions to the gold supply, hence more money, hence more work, and hence more prosperity. He is now assuming to be more critical of the present government policies of his Republican friends and promises to bring the depressed workers back into more abundant pastures of the clover kind. It is not strange that the dormant minds of the people are being awakened, for the workers are no longer so easily bewildered by the strange talk of "full dinner buckets" and "abundant money." On all these matters Debs has been heard by hundreds of thousands and his words of prophecy have been more than fulfilled and in every argument he based every prediction upon the iron law of industrial production and distribution of wealth. While he has, during all these years advocated the ballot, he has never forgotten the unanswerable reasons for down-trodden workingmen using the outworn weapons of the strike and all its weapons of boycott and persuasion, but the attitude had been that of the wise understanding and not of the blind approval of the blind leading the blind.

When the A. R. U. went to pieces it had legal obligations for more than $40,000. There was no personal obligation resting upon Mr. Debs in this matter, and yet, for years he wrote and lectured and helped to pay off the last penny of the debt, and to this day there is no unpaid obligation of the defunct A. R. U.

TRIAL FOR CONSPIRACY TAKEN FROM THE RECORDS.

On Tuesday, July 10, 1894, a special grand jury was impaneled in the United States District Court of Northern Illinois. Judge Grosscup charged the jury as to what is insurrection, conspiracy, etc., and the jury retired to consider such evidence as might be brought before it concerning the conduct of the American Railway Union strike. Edwin Walker, counsel for the Chicago, Milwaukee & St. Paul Railroad, had been appointed by Olney, Attorney-General under Grover Cleveland, special counsel to assist in this prosecution, and he and Attorney Wright, of the Rock Island Railroad, were in attendance. One witness was examined—E. M. Mulford, of the Western Union Telegraph Company—and contrary to all precedent, produced for the jurors copies of the telegrams which had been sent out from and received at the American Railway Union headquarters since the strike had begun. With no further perliminaries, the jury promptly indicted four American Railway Union officials, and within ten minutes after Judge Grosscup received the indictments four warrants were issued, and within an hour Eugene V. Debs, President; George W. Howard, Vice-President; Sylvester Kelliher, Secretary, and L. W. Rogers, Director and Editor of the "Railway Times," were under arrest. The official headquarters were raided. All books, blanks, papers and correspondence of the Union were seized, as well as all President Debs' private mail. The officers returned Mr. Debs' private mail the next morning by order of the court.

On July 17 the four were again arrested for contempt of court on petition of Special Counsel Walker, alleging violating of the restraining injunction which had been issued by Judges Grosscup and Woods. In this restraining order persuasion was charged as a crime and union labor was given notice that it could not use persuasion in order to better their conditions. The defendants refused to give bail and the four slept in Cook County jail, where they remained until Wednesday, July 23, when their attorneys moved to dismiss the contempt proceedings, as they were virtually for the same offense charged in the indictments and that no man could be tried twice for the same offense. Their motion was denied. The defendants pleaded for trial by jury and this was refused. Further hearing of the case was then postponed to accommodate Judge Woods until September 5. Later a supplemental information was filed in the contempt case to include the directors of the American Railway Union.

BIOGRAPHY.

AMERICAN RAILWAY UNION.

In the A. R. U. there were originally sixty-nine persons named in the omnibus indictments for conspiracy to obstruct the United States mail. Before the trial the government counsel entered a nolle pros. as to a number of the persons indicted, leaving the number January 8, 1895, forty-five. There were seven indictments against Debs, Howard and Rogers, and three each against the full Board of Directors of the A. R. U. Debs, Howard, Kelliher and Rogers were first indicted with James Mervin for conspiring to obstruct a mail train on the Rock Island Railroad, and were arrested by the Marshall and placed in the County Jail until the court admitted them to bail. The four leaders were under $25,000 bonds in all of the conspiracy indictments except the omnibus indictment. The defendant directors were represented by S. S. Gregory and C. S. Darrow, and Jno. J. Hanahan was represented by Thos. W. Harper, of Terre Haute. Edwin Walker, District Attorney General J. C. Black and his predecessor, T. E. Milchrist, represented the government.

Mr. Gregory, addressing the court, said:

"I stand ready to prove that one of the attorneys, who is here to represent the United States, has been retained as counsel for one of the railroads interested in this case,—the Chicago, Milwaukee & St. Paul. We object to his sitting in this case."

Mr. Walker said: "Part of this statement is true and part is not true."

Mr. Gregory asked that Mr. Walker be interrogated, but the court declined to interfere.

Of the twelve jurors chosen, eight were farmers, one an insurance agent, one a real estate dealer, one a dealer in agricultural implements, and one a painting and decorating contractor. The government was very careful to exclude workingmen from the jury.

Mr. Milchrist, in his opening speech for the government, said:

"Men have a right to strike."

Mr. Darrow replied in his opening address:

"If this is so, it ends this case, for no one but the evil genius that directs this prosecution believes these men did anything else. There is a statute which makes the obstruction of a mail car punishable by a fine of $100, yet no one had heard of the men who actually obstructed the mails during the strike being indicted under that statute. In order to make felons of honest men, who never had a criminal thought, they passed by that state to seize on one that makes conspiracy to obstruct the mails a crime punishable by imprisonment in the penitentiary. To hound these men into the pentitentiary is their purpose, yet they call this respect for law. Conspiracy from the days of tyranny in England down to the day the General Managers' Association used it as a club has been the favorite weapon of every tyrant. It is an effort to punish the crime of thought. If the government does not, we shall try to get the General Managers here to tell what they know about it. The evidence will show that all these defendants did was in behalf of the employes of that man whose name is odious wherever men have a drop of human blood—Mr. Pullman. No man or set of men or newspaper ever undertook to defend Mr. Pullman except the General Managers' Association, and their defense gives added proof of his infamy. These defendants published to all the world what they were doing, and in the midst of a wide-spread strike they were never so busy but that they found time to counsel against violence. For this they are brought into a court by an organization which uses the government as a cloak to conceal its infamous purposes."

It was shown in the evidence from hundreds of telegrams read to the jury, all signed by Eugene V. Debs, that he counseled abstaining from all forms of violence and keeping within their rights as workingmen. There were more than 9,000 telegrams sent out during the strike and all telegrams that were considered of any value to the prosecution were produced by Edward M. Mulford, manager of the Western Union Company. It was shown by the defense that Mr. Wicks, vice-president of the Pullman Company, attended the emergency meetings of the General Managers' Association in June. Why he was permitted to be present was not explained by the prosecution.

Mr. B. Thomas, president of the Chicago & Western Indiana Railway Company, was put upon the stand and testified in regard to the General Managers' Association,—that it was organized April 20, 1886; that the purposes were to consider matters relating to railway management and wages, and that the Association had acted as a unit in resisting petitions for the increase of wages. The witness further testified that agencies had been established by the Association for the purpose of hiring new men to take the places of strikers, and that the expenses of the Association were apportioned among the several roads composing it.

Mr. Darrow read from the minutes of a meeting of the General Managers' Association August 31, 1893, that a general combination of the railroad managers throughout the United States was desirable and a committee of five men was appointed to take steps to carry out this idea. It was also developed that the object of this combination was to regulate wages and make them uniform throughout the country.

From the minutes of the meeting of September 21, 1893, Mr. Darrow read a resolution to the effect that however much it was to be regretted, a reduction in the wages of railway employes generally had become absolutely necessary.

After the examination of the General Managers, Mr. Debs, president of the A. R. U., was called to the stand, February 6, 1895.

In this evidence Mr. Debs, in reply to questions, gave a brief history of his life from November 3, 1855. He testified that more than $4,000,000 passed through his hands during his term of office as secretary and treasurer of the Brotherhood of Locomotive Firemen. He gave a history of the labor development among railway employes up to the time of his resignation from the Brotherhood of Locomotive Firemen, and his uniting with the American Railway Union in 1892. He stated the object of the American Railway Union to be "A unification of *ALL* railroad employes for their mutual benefit and protection." Being asked what led to the formation of the Union and to his conviction that it was necessary to form such an organization, Mr. Debs replied, that the concentration of the smaller railroads into the larger in this country had been going on for the last 20 years, the smaller roads being gradually reduced into the larger; that the wages had been gradually reduced, and in substance stated that the concentration of the railroads logically compelled a closer union among railway workers, as they could not accomplish anything by striking along craft lines.

He further testified that at the time of the strike on the Great Northern Road there were about 150,000 members of the A. R. U.; that the strike commenced April 13, 1894, and lasted eighteen days, culminating in complete victory, peaceful and orderly, and the strike was called off.

He testified that he first learned of the Pullman trouble when he returned from St. Paul, May 5, 1894, and first learned of the strike at Pullman on May 11. He was asked if the strike was brought on in any way by his advice, and Mr. Debs replied: "No, it was done contrary to my advice. I first went to Pullman," said Mr. Debs in his evidence, "on the 14th of May after the strike occurred, and stayed there part of the day and an evening. I went again on May 18." Mr. Debs stated he investigated conditions at Pullman by inquiry among the employes and their families and also from other independent sources, including the Rev. Carwardine, who had been preaching in Pullman for three years. "The result of the investigation," said Mr. Debs, "was that I came to the conclusion that the Pullman Company was in the wrong; that wages had been unjustifiably reduced below the living point and that rents were much too high in comparison with what was charged for the same class of dwellings elsewhere." He was not permitted by the court to testify as to the conditions existing among the people at Pullman. Being asked as to the convention of the A. R. U. held in Chicago, he stated that it was held June 12, 1894, and that 425 delegates were present from nearly all the states in the Union, and that newspaper reporters were present at all meetings of the convention except one executive session, which was called to consider the financial affairs of the Order and nothing else; that telegrams sent and received by the A. R. U. were subjected to the examination of members of the press; that nothing was concealed. He said the convention voted $2,000 of the funds for the Relief Committee at Pullman and the money was paid over to them; that the convention voted a levy of 10 cents a day per capita; that that was not collected because of the strike that followed.

Mr. Debs stated that there were speeches made at the convention by several on the situation at Pullman and that subsequently a motion was made to declare a boycott against the Pullman cars at once and that railway men should not haul them. Mr. Debs said that as chairman of the convention he declined to entertain this motion, on the ground that it was a very important matter which should not be acted upon hastily or until every means of effecting an amicable settlement had been exhausted; that he suggested that a committee be appointed to try to settle the matter by arbitration and avert a strike and that such committee was appointed; that the committee reported Saturday, June 16; that the Pullman Company positively declined to confer with any representatives of the American Railway Union and would confer only with their own employes as individuals. Another committee, composed entirely of Pullman employes, visited Mr. Wicks, vice-president of the Pullman Company, and reported that he said the company had nothing to arbitrate, and that he regarded the strikers in the position of "men on the sidewalk, so far as their relations with the company were concerned."

The Rev. Mr. Carwardine, on the following Wednesday, addressed the convention, told of his experience during his stay of three years in Pullman, and particularly of his knowledge of the condition and surroundings of the people there. He said they were on the point of starvation and appealed to the convention in the name of God and humanity to act. He closed by saying that whatever was done must be done quickly.

Mr. Debs then told of a resolution to declare a boycott on the Pullman cars and the appointment of a committee to notify Mr. Wicks that unless he agreed to arbitrate the matter, the boycott would go into effect at noon June 26. This committee reported that Mr. Wicks still refused and preparations were then made to put the resolution into effect. He was asked if he or anyone else counseled violence or violation of law; he answered that nothing of the sort was advised by himself or any of the other speakers. He said, "Never in all my life have I broken the law or advised others to do so." His testimony was listened to with marked interest by the jury. After Mr. Debs' testimony had been completed Deputy Marshal Jones reported to the court that he had made diligent search for Mr. Pullman at his office and couldn't find him. He said that "nobody appears to know the exact whereabouts of that gentleman." Johnson, who occupies the honorable office of preventing distasteful callers from having access to his chief by demanding that they shall first be properly accredited to him by a piece of pasteboard, was brought to court and testified that he took Mr. Jones' card in as usual and that Mr. Sweet, Pullman's private secretary, carried it to the magnate's room and returned, saying his employer was not in. He testified in a straightforward manner that Mr. Pullman walked into his office in the usual manner at 10:30 in the morning and on his way passed through the reception room. After that, the factotum declares he never saw the head of the Palace Car Company.

FURTHER EVIDENCE AS TO CONDITIONS AT PULLMAN, BY JENNIE CURTIS.

She stated that the Pullman employes were indebted to Mr. Pullman $70,000 for rent at the time of the strike; that their wages had been insufficient to enable them to live and pay their living expenses. Mr. Debs was re-called and asked if he sent out an official order June 28, and he said he did; that the official order was given to the city newspapers and the Associated Press over his own signature. Mr. Debs read the manifesto, which had been referred to, and after counseling peaceful methods in all cases and a strict compliance with the laws, the manifesto concluded with these words:

"A man who will violate law is against the interests of labor."

More than 150 telegrams were read to the jury, signed by Mr. Debs, counseling peaceful methods and standing together if they wished to win.

The government attorneys did all they could to prevent such evidence being introduced. The government attorneys asked Mr. Debs what wages he was getting as a fireman in 1875.

DEBS' PRESENT HOME IN TERRE HAUTE

He said, "I began at $1 a night." He said, "I was afterwards paid by the mile."

Attorney Walker for the prosecution then asked Mr. Debs the following questions:

"Q. Your salary as president of the American Railway Union of $3,000 still continues, does it not?

"A. No, sir; I cut it off myself last September.

"Q. The purpose of your Union was to get the control of all the railroad employes in the hands of the American Railway Union, was it not?

"A. Yes, sir, under the limitations of the Constitution and By-Laws."

Mr. Debs was then asked if the Great Northern strike was a peaceful strike. He replied it was,—that no intimidation was used; that the company made no attempt to bring in new men; that there were no troops called out. The government attorney then asked:

"Q. You simply took possession of the road and held it?

"A. No, sir; we simply went home and stayed there.

"Q. There was no excitement?

"A. None whatever."

Mr. Debs was then asked the meaning of the word "strike." He replied as follows: "A strike is a stoppage of work at a given time by men acting in concert in order to redress some real or imaginary grievance."

The government attorney then said: "Mr. Debs, will you define the meaning of the word 'scab?'" He replied as follows: "A scab in labor unions means the same as a traitor to his country. It means a man who betrays his fellowmen by taking their places when they go on a strike for principle. It does not apply to non-union men who refuse to quit work."

February 8 it was again reported to the court that Mr. Pullman could not be found. Each day there was reported an additional disappearance of employes of the Pullman Company; first, Mr. Pullman was reported gone, then his private secretary disappears, and the court issues subpœnas against the great man's stenographers, whose services are so valuable that they are generally in attendance upon the head of the company throughout the entire year, but no sooner are the subpœnas issued and the officials are sent to serve them than the individual for whom they are intended are not to be found. The judge looked very grave and when he heard the news of these disappearances of witnesses that the defendants were trying to bring into court and the attorneys for the defense failing to get these employes, issued subpoenas for others around the Pullman buildings.

On convening court Judge Grosscup announced that "owing to the sickness of a juror and the certificate of his physician he will not be able to get out for two or three days. I think it will be necessary to adjourn the further taking of testimony in this case." General Black, for the prosecution, said he thought it would be possible to arrange that the proceedings be continued with eleven jurors. Judge Grosscup thought such proceedings would not be valid. Mr. Darrow, for the defense, proposed that the place of the sick juror should be filled and the case proceed after the evidence had been read over to the new juror. Long argument was then held and on Tuesday morning, the 12th of February, 1895, Judge Grosscup discharged the jury, and continued the Debs case to the first Monday in May. This was done over the objection of the defendants. They were confident of an acquittal at the hands of the jury and their confidence was justified by both words and actions of the jurors after they were discharged. As soon as court adjourned they shook hands with Judge Grosscup and then made a break for the defendant and their attorneys. For half an hour they held a regular levee, shaking hands and chatting most cordially with Mr. Debs and the other defendants. Counsel for the government were rather left to pose as wall-flowers. Mr. Debs was told by more than one juror that on the notions he held when he went into the jury box, five years in the penitentiary might not have been unexpected, but that since hearing the testimony, his notions were very different. Mr. Walker, attorney for the government, who was nearest the jury, remarked to one of them that now he was free to do so, by reason of their being discharged, he would like to shake hands with them. "We want to shake hands with the judge first," was the reply he got. Most of the jurors shook hands with the judge, then hastened to find

Mr. Debs, the defendants, and their attorneys. One or two jurors shook hands with the prosecution attorneys, but there was a decided heartiness in the demeanor of the jurors toward the defense. Mr. Debs and all of the defendants have ever since believed that the jurors were fair, candid and able and they did everything possible to have the case brought to a conclusion by the jury which had been selected and accepted.

The sudden termination of the Debs case left the question of whether Mr. Pullman was in contempt or not in the shape of unfinished business. Mr. Pullman afterwards said that he had had the grip, had aches in all parts of his body; his nerves were shattered and his heart affected, he had a bad taste in his mouth and felt a disinclination to engage in any physical exertion; made up his mind to go East; thought the trip would do him good; had his private car arranged, attached it to a train which was to leave February 5. He admitted that he was in the Pullman offices, as stated before.

Mr. Pullman has never been able, nor will he ever be able to make any other explanation of his evasion of the law and his failure to do justice to himself and the accused in this historic case.

It is now known that the General Managers' Association, disguised in the United States lion's skin, was the prosecution and that it had but one purpose and that was to break up and annihilate the American Railway Union, by sending the leaders to the penitentiary, not only to get them out of the way, but to warn other agitators not to interfere with the General Managers' Association's right to do what they pleased with the wages and hours of their employes and with the rates and charges for transporting the products of the field, the mine, the farm and the factory, or the persons of the people as they pleased. If Debs had fled on the day of the trial, as Mr. Pullman did, we would not yet have heard the last of such cowardly conduct.

The case was not called up in May, nor has it ever been called up, nor have the indictments ever been withdrawn. The Railway Managers knew whom they could call upon to enable them to carry out their purposes and they called upon the late Grover Cleveland and in violation of every principle of state sovereignty, he sent the U. S. troops into Chicago to do ordinary police duty and crush out the right of the oppressed workers to peacefully obtain a redress of wrongs. The principal actors in this human drama have changed positions and roles. The accused are remembered and idealized by the people and their accusers are as though they never had been, except for the paltry parts they played.

It was almost impossible for the American people to learn about the truth in this great case, because the railroads controlled then, as they do now, the press. Bribery, falsehood, untruthful news items were spread all over the country and many good people still believe that Debs was the monster of wrong-doing and that Pullman was a magnate whose rights as an employer had been unlawfully invaded.

SOME EDITORIALS IN CHICAGO PAPERS APPEARING DURING THE TRIAL FOR CONSPIRACY.

Editorial in the *Evening Press,* November 23, 1895, entitled: "The Liberation of Debs":

"In the face of facts developed yesterday, it is idle to say that Eugene V. Debs has lost the esteem of the masses. No such demonstration as was made in his honor yesterday and last night has been seen in this city in many years, if at all. Had he been the victorious soldier returned fresh from conquests instead of a convict liberated from prison, his welcome could not have been more spontaneous, enthusiastic, sympathetic. Whether Eugene V. Debs merited imprisonment in the Woodstock jail; whether Judge Woods in adjudging him in contempt of court did or did not debauch the constitution, are questions now under consideration. Rightfully or wrongfully, legally or illegally, Debs was sent to prison and after serving his sentence to the last hour, was discharged yesterday.

"Do all men who transgress the law go to prison? Is the judicial and military machinery of the United States set in motion every time a law is violated? Is the interference with interstate communication a greater crime than open, flagrant, overriding of the will of the people in statute expressed by wealthy individuals and corporations? These questions may be discussed and should be discussed by every man and woman and child who hold law and justice in esteem.

BIOGRAPHY. 83

"Not many months ago members of the cabinet, senators and congressmen conspired with representatives of the Sugar Trust to rob the people of millions of dollars. A secretary admitted before a congressional investigation committee that he introduced a representative of this gigantic sugar monopoly to law makers who would aid his cause. A senator confessed to having made money by dealing in sugar stocks when the sugar schedule was under consideration in the senate. The President of the Sugar Trust boldly declared his concern made a practice of giving hundreds of thousands of dollars to political parties to insure favorable legislation. In each instance law was transgressed, yet not a federal soldier was ordered out and not a man went to prison.

"The influence of the Standard Oil Company on courts and legislatures and congress is notorious. Judges have been corrupted and law makers bought by the mighty concern and not a soldier was ordered to arms or another prison cell occupied. Steam and street railway companies have bribed assemblies and councils and stolen public highways and lake fronts and the soldier boys slept on in their fortresses and the prison tailor had no calls for striped suits.

"The day must never come when there is no law. But it must come when Justice will rip the bandage from her eyes and see and call for the Havemeyers and the Standard Oil magnates and other transgressors of law, as well as for the Debses."

And now, July 22, 1908, as I write, the famous decision imposing a fine of $29,240,000 on the Standard Oil Company for violation of the laws of the United States is reversed by the same Judge Grosscup who handed the lemons to the striking workers and their leaders in 1894. Do you see?

"COULD NOT SERVE GEORGE M. PULLMAN."

"At the beginning of the afternoon session the attention of the court was called to the difficulty experienced in securing the attendance of George M. Pullman as a witness. Deputy Marshal Jones told the court he had not been able to get personal service on Mr. Pullman, though he was satisfied he was in the city. He had been to Mr. Pullman's office and the elevator boy had told him that Mr. Pullman was in his private room, but when he announced his business to Mr. Pullman's private secretary, the latter went to the sanctum of the sleeping car magnate and returned with the information that Mr. Pullman was not in, but was wintering in Saint Augustine, Fla.

"The Court looked very grave when this announcement was made and remarked that he would see the attorney for the defense in his chambers after court adjourned."—*Chicago Times*, Feb. 7, 1895.

* * * * * * * *

"ROOM FOR THE MAGNATE."

"The Court then adjourned on account of the absence of George M. Pullman, for whom a subpœna had been issued.

"Of course, adjourn a court to suit the convenience of George M. Pullman, who has grown decidedly since last July. He is now a magnate of the first class in the Republican party, and the Court in having presumed to subpœna him at all ought to have accompanied the service of the process with ample apologies for venturing, even in the name of the United States, to trespass upon the valuable time of a gentleman distinguished not only in his own, his native land, but also throughout civilization as the proprietor of perambulating lodging houses and stand-up whisky bars.

"Of course, a court ought to adjourn in order to consult the convenience of Mr. Pullman. Mr. Pullman himself had regard for his own convenience when, during all the trouble of last July, he remained in the East, while the militia and the constabulary force of Cook County guarded his property so effectively that not even a blade of grass was trampled down, not even a window was broken in all the establishments of the town that bears his name.

"He rose superior to the dictates of common humanity last July, and why should the dictate of a court affect him in February?

"It is absolutely essential that Mr. Pullman should be heard; why should not his Honor adjourn his court and bring its officers and the jury and the whole entourage to Mr. Pullman's palatial residence and let him have his say while he sips his chocolate?

BIOGRAPHY. 85

"Is it not a fault of the republic that the masses do not sufficiently consider the dignity of the magnates? They are superior beings. Ordinary processes of law are made for ordinary individuals. Magnate Pullman has all the dignity of a Chinese mandarin, and he ought not to be approached save with the obsequiousness of a subject of the Celestial Empire prostrating himself at the foot-stool of Chinese majesty."—Editorial, *Chicago Times,* February 7, 1895.

"THE MAGNATE."

"Magnate Pullman is still missing. His whereabouts seem to give no concern to his immediate attendants, but Judge Grosscup of the United States Court is showing some anxiety to learn where he is and why it is that he has not been served with a process calling him into court. An examination of Magnate Pullman's colored doorkeeper made by the Judge personally disclosed that he saw the magnate enter his office Monday at 10:30 o'clock, an hour after a deputy marshal called, but he has since mysteriously disappeared, and the marshal has been unable to locate him.

"Why this assumption of right to inquire into the personal movements of so great a man as Mr. Pullman? Ought we not, rather, anxiously unite in efforts to ascertain whether he is entirely safe, for if Magnate Pullman were to disappear into thin air, it is doubtful if the world would continue to revolve upon its axis and make its usual diurnal revolution. Human laws are made for the mass of mankind. Why should Magnate Pullman, who does not belong to the mass, but is a being apart, constructed of superior clay, be subjected to any such belittling regulation? Magnate Pullman keeps more bar-rooms in more states in the Union than any grog shop seller and employs more male chamber-maids than any other magnate in the bed-house business.

"The *Tribune* finds excuses for the magnate. It says: 'It is not strange that he should be unwilling to go on the stand and be questioned by Mr. Darrow, Mr. Geeting and the other lawyers for the defense. It is not pleasant for a person who is at the head of a great corporation, who has many subordinates and no superiors, and who is in the habit of giving orders instead of answering questions, to be interrogated by persons who are unfriendly to him, and who may put disagreeable inquiries which he has to reply to civilly.'

"That's it. Mr. Pullman is superior to the law. Like the king, he can do no wrong, and no processes can lie against him. The *Tribune,* however, we are bound to say, weakens a little, for it adds: 'Nevertheless, it is the duty of all men to appear in court when they are wanted there. The subpœna does not discriminate between persons. Furthermore, those who need the defense of the law the most, should be the promptest and the most willing to submit themselves to the occasional unpleasantness of the law, and should try to show that they believe all men are equal before the law.'

"How presumptuous to suggest such a thing to Magnate Pullman, who does not believe that all men are equal before the law. The *Tribune* further ventures to say that Mr. Pullman 'should have faced the music like a man.'

"There was some music here last June and July. It was music that never should have been played if Magnate Pullman had been like the ordinary run of human beings, but, being altogether an extraordinary creature, he waved his baton and the band began to play, but, far from facing the music which he himself had set in motion, he retired with a lawyer bodyguard to the East and viewed the concert from a distance of a thousand miles. Really, he had nothing to fear, for, as it turned out, not a single pane of glass in his marvelous town was broken by what he regarded as a fearful mob.

"The outcome of the present matter will be, of course, a demonstration that Magnate Pullman is a bigger man than the United States Court."—Editorial, *Chicago Times,* February 8, 1895.

"SHALL DEBS BE TRIED AGAIN?"

"Owing to the illness of one juror the conspiracy cases against Eugene V. Debs and his associates of the American Railway Union have come to a sudden stop. The propositions of the defense to continue the hearing of the case with eleven jurors, or to swear in a twelfth juror and proceed after the evidence already in had been read to him, were both opposed by counsel for the government and the railroads. As the matter now stands, a new jury will have to be impaneled and the whole thing gone over again, unless the Government decides to abandon the prosecution.

"It is exceedingly unfortunate that the present trial should have been interrupted in this unforeseen fashion. A judicial declaration upon the issues involved would have been of very decided value to all classes of society. As the evidence has been detailed day after day in the very full reports in the columns of the *Times,* the people have been able to gain a clearer and more exact idea of the incidents of the great strike than was possible in the moments of heated controversy last summer. It does not seem like over-statement to say that there was every indication that the defense would be successful. The charge of conspiracy had not, at the time of the abrupt termination of the case, been at all forcefully substantiated. Interviews with the released jurors establish the fact that they would have acquitted the defendants had the case been carried to its regular conclusion. It is credibly asserted that the prosecution has for some time apprehended such an outcome of the trial, and it was probably for this reason that the attorneys for the Government exercised their undoubted right to protest against continuing with an incomplete jury.

"In this situation the question arises whether the Government shall proceed further with this prosecution. Heavy expense is involved in it and it will consume much of the time of a court already overcrowded with business. It is just, too, to call attention to the fact that the defendants are poor men. The expenses of the defense thus far have been met by voluntary contributions from other poor men, who are in sympathy with the men on trial. There is obvious injustice in enlarging this financial burden by bringing these men again to trial.

"In the opinion of the *Times* enough has been done to maintain the dignity of the State in this matter. Further prosecution of Debs and his associates would look like persecution. The Government would better abandon the case forthwith."— Editorial, *Chicago Times,* February 13, 1895.

"WANT A TWELFTH JUROR."

"Then there was a consultation between Court and counsel as to what to do. To discharge this jury and commence all over again would occasion a waste of time and delay which neither Court nor counsel wanted to permit, if there was any possible way of avoiding it. However, counsel for the Government seemed more easily able to reconcile themselves to it than anybody else. There was a very strong impression in the courtroom that the Government counsel had conceived the opinion that the jury would not convict, and were not altogether sorry something had arisen to give them a chance for a new jury.

"General Black at first thought that they could proceed with a jury of eleven, if the defendants would agree. The defendants were ready to agree, but took the view, and Judge Grosscup shared it with them that such a stipulation would be a fatal error. Finally, General Black came to this conclusion himself. Then the defense made a proposition itself. This was in effect that the present jury be discharged and a new one at once impaneled, consisting of the eleven of the present jurors and a twelfth man; that for the benefit of this twelfth man the evidence already taken might be read over. In support of this proposition Mr. Gregory read a lot of authorities, some of them interesting in themselves, aside from any aid they might be in the present case.

"The proposition was talked about informally between the Court and counsel, and the more they talked about it the more feasible it seemed. But before it was finally decided on Judge Grosscup wanted to sleep over it. So he adjourned court until 10 o'clock this morning.

DARROW MAKES A MOTION.

"'In this case, your Honor,' said Mr. Darrow, when the court resumed at the afternoon session, 'we wish to make a motion in the event that the Court should decide that it is not competent to proceed with the eleven jurors, that the place of the sick juror should be filled and the case proceeded with after the evidence has been read over to the new juror, we think we have authorities on that point and we will present them to your Honor. The evidence could be read over and that would save the whole time that would be occupied in representing the case to the Court. If General Black admits this

BIOGRAPHY.

to be right, we would like to present these authorities to the Court.'

"'When the court adjourned after the conference in your Honor's chambers this morning,' said General Black, 'I made an investigation of the points involved and I found one authority upon the point which, it seems to me, settles the question. It is the case of Callan against Wilson, decided by Justice Harlan. In that decision the judge discusses the question as to the rights of trial by jury under similar circumstances to this case, touching particularly the right of trial in conspiracy cases, and holds that it is an inalienable right that there should be a trial by jury, which means a jury of twelve men. The authority is so conclusive that I must abandon my position.'"—*Chicago Times,* February 12, 1895.

A. R. U.

(An article in the July, 1908, number of the Journal of the Switchmen's Union.)

MR. CONNERS ON THE STRIKE.

Mr. Conners in speaking of the A. R. U. strike and E. St. John, at that time general manager of the C., R. I. & P. railway and chairman of the General Managers' Association, said that he denied that Mr. St. John broke the backbone of the strike; on the contrary, he so exaggerated the cause of breaking the A. R. U. that he was let out of his job soon after the strike and was practically wiped out himself as a railroad man.

It is true that Mr. St. John said to the General Managers in meeting assembled on the eve of the strike, these words:

"Gentlemen, we can handle the various brotherhoods, but we cannot handle the A. R. U. We have got to wipe it out. We can handle the other labor leaders, but we cannot handle Debs. We have got to wipe him out, too."

He closed this article in the following words:

"At the end of the strike the railroads proclaimed their triumph and the annihilation of the A. R. U. but the principle that the A. R. U. stood for still lives and is stronger and more in evidence today than ever, which goes to show that wrong never really wins a victory over right, and iniquity is never long triumphant. There have been many changes since that great struggle against slavery, degradation and privation. Some of the exploiters of labor prophesied the death of the labor movement and it was down and out for a time, but history has repeated itself. Labor unions have again become a power. They are stronger than ever. Many an honest working man and woman went hungry in 1894 for daring to rebel against the humiliating conditions that existed at Pullman. Many a Union man went to jail for disobeying the injunction judges, Grosscup, Woods and Taft, but today we find Pullman has passed to the Great Beyond, where all are supposed to be equal; Woods is dead; Cleveland is dead; Egan has disappeared to God knows where; Grosscup has been under indictment; St. John has passed into the Shadowy Valley, but Eugene Debs still lives, loved by his fellowmen because of his honesty, for his many sacrifices to the cause of humanity. The cause of the working class is still here and here to stay and will be crowned gloriously triumphant long after the oppressors and tyrants and all their fawning retainers have gone the way of flesh and passed from memory."

In the *Railway Times,* published at Terre Haute, January 1, 1895, appeared the following special notice:

"SPECIAL NOTICE."

"The general offices of the American Railway Union and the *Railway Times* have been removed to Terre Haute, Indiana. The directors having been sentenced to prison, the change was made so that the work of the Order could be efficiently and economically done during their confinement. The work of organizing and equipping the A. R. U. will be pushed with unabated vigor. Insurance and secret work will be adopted as soon as it can be done under temporarily trying circumstances.

"All correspondence should be addressed to Eugene V. Debs, Terre Haute, Indiana.

"TERRE HAUTE, IND., Jan. 1, 1895."

In the evening papers of the country appeared the following on January 9, 1895:

"DEBS DEFIANT—ISSUES AN ADDRESS TO THE AMERICAN PEOPLE FROM THE JAIL.

"WOODSTOCK, ILL.—Eugene V. Debs, George Howard, Sylvester Kelliher, Louis W. Rogers, William E. Burns, James Hogan and Leroy Goodwin are confined in the McHenry County Jail. Last evening, as he sat in what Cook County prisoners would call a palace, Mr. Debs issued a manifesto to the American people, which contains the following:

" 'In going to jail for participation in the late strike we have no apologies to make nor regrets to express. No ignominy attaches to us on account of this sentence. I would not change places with Judge Woods, and if it is expected that six months, or even six years in jail will purge me of contempt, the punishment will fail of its purpose.

" 'Candor compels me to characterize the whole proceeding as infamous. It is not calculated to revive the rapidly failing confidence of the American people in the federal judiciary. There is not a scrap of testimony to show that one of us violated any law whatsoever. If we are guilty of conspiracy, why are we punished for contempt?

" 'I would a thousand times rather be accountable for the strike than for the decision.

" 'We are, by chance, the mere instrumentalities in the evolutionary processes in operation through which industrial slavery is to be abolished and economic freedom established. Then the starry banner will symbolize, as it was designed to symbolize, social, political, religious and economic emancipation from the thraldom of tyranny, oppression and degradation.' "

The following invitations were issued for a reception in honor of Mr. Debs upon his release from Woodstock Jail:

MR. ....

Dear Sir: You are cordially invited to attend a reception to be tendered Eugene V. Debs on his release from Woodstock Jail, Friday evening, November twenty-second, at Battery D, Chicago, by the liberty-loving citizens of Chicago and vicinity, in testimony of their sympathy with Mr. Debs and his colleagues in their unjust and unlawful imprisonment and as an expression of popular aversion to judicial despotism and devotion to Civil and Constitutional Liberty.

J. D. MAYERS,
    Secretary, 405 Thirty-third
      St., Chicago, Ill.

J. H. SCHWERZGEN,
Chm. Com. of Arrangements,
133 Rialto Building.

The Reception Committee will leave this city for Woodstock on a special train from the Chicago and Northwestern railway depot at 2:30 p. m., Friday, November 22, for the purpose of escorting Mr. Debs to Chicago. If you desire to accompany the committee, kindly inform the chairman or secretary. Tickets for the round trip, two dollars."

As the time approached when Mr. Debs' term in prison would expire, November 22, 1895, great preparations for celebration were made throughout the country, particularly in Chicago. October 31, 1895, Mr. Debs wrote from Woodstock Jail the following letter:

WOODSTOCK, ILL., Oct. 31.

Thomas J. Elderkin,
    President Trade and Labor Assembly,
      Chicago, Ill.

Dear Sir and Brother: Your favor of the 20th inst. in reference to the reception to be tendered my colleagues and myself upon my release and the condition upon which the Trade and Labor Assembly of Chicago will participate therein has been received and noted.

I quote from your letter as follows: "Some say you advocate the abolishment of Trade Union theories, while others declare you are still a friend and strong advocate of Trade Unions. The question of a demonstration by the Trade and Labor Assembly upon the occasion of your release from jail November 22, rests upon your position toward Trade Unions, for if you still believe Trade Unions are adequate for the emancipation of the workingmen the Trade and Labor Assembly will cheerfully join in the demonstration."

Permit me to decline in advance any "demonstration" on the part of persons whose sentiments are represented in the foregoing proposition. If the Trade and Labor Assembly of Chicago can afford to make such a proposition, I cannot afford to consider it. For twenty-one years I have been defining my "position" in relation to Trade Unions, and on all proper occasions I have given full, free and unequivocal expression to my views, but I must respectfully decline to do so for a consideration, even though that consideration be in the form of a reception upon my release from a jail in which I have served a sentence of six months for my fealty to the principles of the very Trade Unions which now propose to interrogate me as to my "position" in relation to their interests.

The statement that I am or ever have been hostile to Trade Unions and that I am advocating or intending to advocate their "abolishment" is too palpably false and malicious to merit an instant's contention. There is, of course, a purpose in having this question raised at this time, but it is difficult for me to conceive that it emanates from a Trade and Labor Assembly. If it had its origin in the General Managers' Association or some kindred body, it would be in consonance with the fitness of things and I should readily understand it.

Permit me to say, therefore, that the proposed reception is in no sense a personal affair. I understand it to be tendered in recognition of the principles involved in the illegal and unjust imprisonment of my colleages and myself, and as voicing abhorrence of, and protest against, judicial despotism in the United States, which constitutional rights are cloven down in the interest of corporate wealth.

I have not asked for a reception and I am sure I have no ambition to be the guest of anyone who finds it necessary to place me on the witness stand and interrogate me as to whether I am his friend or his enemy, especially after serving six months in jail for advocating his rights and defending his interests. To make myself perfectly clear, if there are those who have any doubt as to my "position," then, so far as I am concerned, I advise them to take the safe side and stay away from the intended reception.

The charge that I have "changed my views" in regard to Trades Unions, which, as I am informed, prompted the action and attitude of your Assembly, is simply a pretext which will serve the purpose for which it was designed if it creates dissension, arouses a sentiment unfavorable to the reception and makes of that occasion a dismal failure. The reason for this is so apparent that it will readily suggest itself. I admit that my views are subject to "change," but not of the legal tender variety.

I beg to assure you that no discourtesy is intended, although if the Trade and Labor Assembly had intended a deliberate affront it could not have adopted a method better calculated to serve that purpose than by attempting to pillory me in public at this time on the question of my allegiance to Organized Labor.

I have the honor to subscribe myself, with best wishes,

Yours fraternally,

EUGENE V. DEBS.

While Mr. Debs was in Woodstock Jail he wrote a series of remarkable letters which were published in the daily press and these letters seem now, in the light of industrial development, to have been filled with prophetic vision. The following are a few quotations from some of his letters:

"It is time that Organized Labor should learn the power and the imperative necessity of a united ballot and in this is meant the ballot of all who work for their daily bread, without regard to color or sex. It is also high time that allegiance to parties who make laws for the protection of capitalists and the subjugation of labor should be abandoned and that men should be found to enact and administer laws for the equal protection of labor which creates the capital and carries forward all the industries of the world. In this unification of labor forces for the amelioration of conditions by constitutional and lawful methods, as are contemplated in political action, there is no need of interfering with Trades Unions or any of the numerous social and industrial organizations or encroaching in the slightest degree upon their province or functions. On the contrary, labor organizations would be indefinitely strengthened by such a policy. The proposition is so self-evident as to require no argument for its elucidation. Until that time comes, capitalism will be in power and have absolute control. Capitalism will make the laws and administer them, control the army, bribe the press, silence the pulpit and workingmen will pay the penalty of their ignorance and stupidity in abject slavery."

KATHERINE METZEL DEBS (See Page 57)

BIOGRAPHY. 45

DEBS' LAST NIGHT IN JAIL.

Eugene Victor Debs' last hour of imprisonment ended with the first second after midnight of November 22, 1895. He had gone to bed early and was sleeping soundly when the hours of bondage merged into the hours of freedom. He had his breakfast with the Sheriff and the Sheriff's family and then with his brother Theodore, in a cutter, he drove about Woodstock and called on the various friends he had made while he was in prison. He came in late for dinner. During the afternoon farmers in great numbers came into the town to see the parade of the Chicago working people who were to come out to greet him. School girls and boys, young men and young women and all sorts and conditions of people assembled at the station. The train was greeted with shouts when it turned the curve southeast of the town, and when Reichart's Band started up the street everybody in the whole town followed to the public square. The train had arrived at 5 o'clock. As the crowd marched toward the jail the released prisoner stood on the stone steps in front of the Sheriff's residence. A crowd of big, burly workingmen rushed up and took Mr. Debs in their outstretched arms.* The yelling and cheering was something remarkable. Dozens hugged and kissed him. Others simply felt for his hand and if it was no more than a touch they seemed to be satisfied and went away yelling. The crowd called "Lift him up so we can all see him." Instantly he was hoisted up on the shoulders of the men. After the crowd had partaken of coffee and sandwiches at the several restaurants in Woodstock, the Chicago Special was entered and from Woodstock to Chicago music, singing and cheering drowned the noise of the train. When the trains arrived at the Wells street Station in Chicago, more than 100,000 people blocked the streets and bridges in the vicinity of the depot. The streets were filled with mud and slush and a heavy rain was falling, but the crowd did not seem to pay any attention. Mr. Debs himself refused to enter the carriage hauled by six white horses and as he took his place in the parade he said: "If the rest walk, I shall walk. What is good enough for them is good enough for me."

* Illustration page 194.

Battery D was crowded to its utmost capacity and his speech delivered upon that occasion was scholarly, brilliant, beautiful. The following is the closing paragraph relative to his life in prison:

"In prison my life was a busy one and the time for meditation and to give the imagination free reign was when the daily task was over and Night's sable curtains enveloped the world in darkness, relieved only by the sentinel stars and the Earth's silver satellite 'walking in lovely beauty to her midnight throne.' It was at such times that the reverend stones of the prison walls preached sermons, sometimes rising in grandeur to the Sermon on the Mount. It might be a question in the minds of some if this occasion warrants the indulgence of the fancy. It will be remembered that Aesop taught the world by fables and Christ by parables, but my recollection is that the old stone preachers were as epigrammatic as an unabridged dictionary. I remember one old divine stone who one night selected for his text 'George M. Pullman,' and said 'George is a bad egg; handle him with care. If you crack his shell the odor would depopulate Chicago in an hour.' All the rest of the stones said 'Amen' and the services closed.

"Another old sermonizer who said he had been preaching since man was a molecule declared he had of late years studied corporations and that they were warts on the nose of national industries and that they were vultures whose beaks and claws were tearing and mangling the vitals of Labor and transforming workingmen's homes into caves. Another old stone said he knew more about strikes than Carroll D. Wright and that he was present when the slaves built the pyramids; that God himself had taught his lightnings, thunderbolts, winds, waves and earthquakes to strike and that striking would proceed with bullets or ballots until workingmen, no longer deceived and cajoled by their enemies, would unify, proclaim their sovereignty and walk the earth free men.

"I have borne with such composure as I could command the imprisonment which deprived me of my liberty. Were I a criminal, were I guilty of crimes meriting a prison cell, had I ever lifted my hand against the life or liberty of my fellowmen, had I ever sought to filch their good name I could not be

BIOGRAPHY. 47

here. I would have fled from the haunts of civilization and taken up my residence in some cave where the voice of my kindred is never heard; but I am standing here with no self-accusation of crime or criminal intent festering in my conscience, in the sunlight, once more among my fellow-men, contributing as best I can to make this celebration day from prison a memorial day, realizing that as Lowell sung:

> " 'He's true to God who's true to man;
> Wherever wrong is done,
> To the humblest and the weakest
> 'Neath the all-beholding sun,
> That wrong is also done to us;
> And they are slaves most base
> Whose love of right is for themselves,
> And not for all the race.' "

(*Quoted from the Chicago Chronicle, November 23, 1895.*)

The arrival of the train bearing the party with Mr. Debs, which was carefully awaited, was the signal for a mighty yell. The crowd on the platform started it and it was taken up by those who thronged the stairs leading down to the platform and those who were above in the street.* The cheering became deafening. When Debs appeared on the platform of the coach the cheers became a tumult of frantic yells. Those who were nearest the labor leader rushed to him and seized him in their arms and bore him from the car into the surging, struggling, pushing, cheering, yelling throng. Sitting on the shoulders of men and raised above the heads of the crowd, bareheaded and smiling, Debs acknowledged the salutes of the crowd, bowing and waving his hat. Whichever way the labor leader turned there was a fresh outburst of cheers but so great was the crowd that it remained wedged together. No one could move. The police cried in vain but they could hardly hear their own voices. They pushed and struggled and pleaded with those that were nearest them to make way but the crowd stood as an immovable wall. Those who were near enough reached out to touch the leader's garment and those who were not were madly striving to do so. The men who were bearing Debs on their shoulders had not gone ten paces from the car when they could go no farther. From every direction the crowd faced toward their

* Illustration page 200.

idol. Men cried for air and egress from the pressing mass, but no one heard them. The policemen were as powerless as everyone else. Could they have made themselves heard, they might have accomplished something. For twenty minutes there was not a move in the packed center. It was oppressive and suffocating and men were being crushed and trampled. The slender form of the man whose presence brought out the outpouring was all the while held aloft and safe from the crush. A smile was playing over his clean-cut features. His face was aglow with the triumph of the hour. It was only by the efforts of the policemen and the officers of the Trades Unions which were on the outskirts of the crowd that the jam was worked apart and got in motion. They succeeded in getting those who were on the street above to move back, then those who were on the broad stairway were forced upon the street, and finally the congestion on the platform below was gradually relieved; but it was far from being dispersed. Two policemen managed to fight their way to where the labor leader was held and they made a path for two more and the four policemen succeeded by their combined strength in making a way for Debs. Inch by inch they moved, pushing, struggling and almost beating the crowd until they gained the stairs. As they started up, twice the tide of the throng carried them back down to the platform after they had gained the first step. They struggled on and on up the stairs, the great mass swaying and sometimes retreating, and all the time and above all the mighty cheering went on. Never did men strive and struggle to so demonstrate their love for a fellowman just released from a convict's cell. Their's was no outward show alone. There was no sycophancy in them. Debs was borne on the shoulders of strong men all the way along the depot platform and up the stairs and along the street. When he reached the Wells street bridge he asked those who bore him to set him down where his old lieutenant, William E. Burns, who was also a prisoner with Debs in Woodstock Jail, had gotten near enough to speak to him. They halted then to form a line to march in order to Battery D.

More than fifty of the Labor Unions of Chicago were represented in the six coaches that went out to Woodstock to receive Mr. Debs. The procession that marched through the storm was composed of the members of every Trade Union in the city, wearing badges and marching in his honor.

COMMISSION APPOINTED BY THE GOVERNMENT TO INQUIRE INTO THE CHICAGO STRIKE.

In the hearing before the Commission appointed in September, Superintendent of Police, Mr. Brennan, stated that the acts of violence in the strike in Chicago were perpetrated by a lot of hoodlums and vicious people mixed with women and children. Fire Marshal Fitzgerald testified that he attended nearly all of the fires and was on duty at all the fires of any magnitude. He stated that there was no interference with the firemen at any time; the cause of the fires was due to the action of youngsters who lighted waste and other inflammable material and threw it in the cars where it would catch the woodwork. "I stopped a number of boys whom I saw doing such work. There was no interference attempted by railroad men. A number of railroad men helped the firemen pull an engine into position at Forty-fifth street and the Fort Wayne tracks. I did not ask aid at any time during the fires."

Mr. Miller, reporter for the *Chicago Tribune,* also testified that he had an extensive acquaintance among railroad men. He said: "The trouble was caused by hoodlums and toughs. In my reports I characterized them as hoodlums. Many of them were boys. Sobriety was the rule among the strikers." Mr. Miller said: "The speakers at the public meetings advised against violence or lawlessness. I believe they were speaking sincerely." The testimony of many other reporters was in the same line. Mr. Harding of the *Times* testified that there was comparatively little disorder at the Stock Yards, but that the newspaper reports contained the accounts of fights and riots almost every night. "Captain O'Neil of the Stock Yards police told me," said Mr. Harding, "that volleys of shots were fired by the soldiers or the militia every day or night, which, on investigation, proved to have no cause other than the desire to create excitement. A crowd would naturally gather, newspaper reporters would flock around and they would gather something to tell, to brag about in the papers. I know this is so from talks with the men themselves."

Mr. Debs was on the stand an entire day. His testimony in the following words brought out very interesting points which the Commissioners elicited by direct question. Mr. Debs said: "Government supervision would not answer the purpose of preventing strikes. No good could come from compulsory arbitration; that is a contradiction in terms. Even if some means of enforcing the decree could be devised, those against whom the decree was rendered would not be satisfied. The basis must be friendship and confidence. Government ownership of railroads would be better than railroad ownership of Government," said Mr. Debs. Mr. Debs stated that the railroads do not obey the decisions of the Interstate Commerce Commission. If they do not obey this Commission, he did not think they would be likely to obey the decisions of a court of arbitration, unless it suited their convenience.

Commissioner Worthington asked Mr. Debs, "What about strikes in other industries?" Mr. Debs replied, "The replacement of the wage system by the co-operative commonwealth could alone solve the problem; as long as a man is dependent on another for work, he is a slave. With labor-saving machinery, which term is now a misnomer, as it is really labor-displacing machinery, unrestricted emigration and ten men bidding for a job, wages are bound to go lower and lower. Capitalists instinctively feel their affinity. I want the working people to feel the same way. To illustrate—in the late strike we did nothing to interfere with the *Chicago Herald's* business, yet the *Herald* felt its kinship to the capitalists who owned the railroads and made unmitigated war on the railroad employes."

Commissioner Kernan asked Mr. Debs, "If such a unification of working people was accomplished, would it not have a dangerous power?" Mr. Debs replied, "A little power is more dangerous than great power. If you have 100 switchmen working in a yard and ten or twelve of them are organized, you will have a strike on your hands very soon. The unification of labor would mean the abolition of the wage system."

Chief Deputy U. S. Marshal Donnelly was one of the most interesting witnesses before the government, because his testimony proved that the railroads run the government. Mr. Donnelly said, "We had a regular force of men sworn in of

BIOGRAPHY. 51

between fourteen and fifteen hundred, and then we swore in 4,000 for the railroads. The government armed and paid the regular force and the railroads armed and paid the others. The first lot of men we got were a poor lot. We went on the street and got such men as we could. The better class of men said they wouldn't serve against the strikers. At first we didn't ask for any certificates of character or fitness. We received our instructions from Attorney General Olney. He told us to hire all the men we needed. The number we needed was decided on at conferences between the United States District Attorney and Mr. Walker, Special Assistant District Attorney, and attorney for the Chicago, Milwaukee & St. Paul Railway. The railroads would send in a batch of men, saying they were all right, and we gave the stars to the railroads and took their receipt for them. These railway deputies were not under our orders; they made their reports to no one except the chief detectives of the railroads. They derived their authority from the United States. All the violence I saw and the car burning was done by boys—tough kids."

U. S. COMMISSION HOLDS INVESTIGATION OF CAUSES OF STRIKE.

Mr. Debs said in his evidence in August, 1895, before the Strike Commission:

"It is understood that a strike is war, not necessarily of blood and bullets, but a war in the sense that it is a conflict between two contending interests or classes of interest. There is more or less strategy, too, in war and this was necessary in our operations in the A. R. U. strike. Orders were issued from here; questions were answered and our men kept in line from here."

The attorney, Mr. Milchrist, for the government in the conspiracy trial at Chicago in January, 1895, further said that it was lawful for Mr. Debs to order our members of the A. R. U. but not others. Mr. Milchrist said the A. R. U. had spent $3,000 on telegrams. Mr. Milchrist said the mails were tied up. "Certainly if the trains were tied up," he said, "the government is not prosecuting the defendants for an overt act, but simply for interfering with the United States mails. It was argued to the jury by Mr. Debs' attorneys the law was used against the defendants as an excuse for working oppression, as there was no telegram or written or verbal order shown to the jury urging violence or interference with the mails. Mr. Darrow said: "But when men strike for oppressions against others and jeopardize their own livelihoods for the sake of those whom they do not even know, it is so much above the ideals of the railroad managers that they think it is a crime."

There were many brilliant arguments, many sharp replies during the trial. There were many telegrams read to the jury. Here is an exact copy of one that was read and became a part of the record in the case:

"July 16, 1894.
"C. S. McAuliffe, Wisconsin.

"We have assurances that within 48 hours every labor organization will come to our rescue. The tide is on and the men are acquitting themselves like heroes. Here and there one weakens, but our cause is strengthened by others going out in their places. Every true man must go out and remain out until the fight is over; there must be no half-way ground. Our cause is gaining ground daily and our success is only a question of a few days. Don't falter in this hour but proclaim your manhood. Labor must win now or never. Our victory will be certain and complete. Whatever happens don't give any credence to rumors and newspaper reports.
"E. V. DEBS."

This was sent to forty points. Then the troops were called and then telegrams like this were sent over the wires:

"To call out the troops was an old method for intimidation. Commit *no* violence. Have every man stand pat. Troops cannot move trains. Not scabs enough in the world to fill places, and more help accruing hourly."

Out of 9,000 telegrams, 150 were read to the jury and they were always proper and called upon the men to commit no violence. Among them was the famous: "Save your money and buy a gun" telegram. This was sent under the Debs' half-rate frank, but as shown was not authorized by him or sent with his knowledge, and when the whole telegram is read it is seen to be very innocent and harmless. The jury seemed to be amused at the juvenile attempts to fasten acts of violence on Mr. Debs. One witness, Dennis Ryan, was asked if he heard anything about dynamite. He said the Great Northern strike was won by the men standing shoulder to shoulder; that they did not want violence. February 6 the Railroad Managers' minutes were put in the case. Several defendants were examined. It was shown that the Managers' Association had been preparing to have a strike, and Mr. Darrow read from their minutes dated August 31, 1893, a resolution declaiming it was desirable that a general combination of managers throughout the United States was desirable and that the wages of the railroad men were to be reduced and made uniform throughout the country. The resolution stated one of the hardest facts the managers had to contend with was the men would complain that they were not receiving equal pay to men on other roads doing similar work.

From the minutes of the meeting of September 21, 1893, a resolution was read to the effect that however much it was to be regretted, a general reduction in the wages of the men had become absolutely necessary. It was then shown by the defense that the Managers' Association had established agencies to secure men to take the places of those who seemed likely to strike. The number of men so employed was shown by the evidence of Mr. B. Thomas, president and general manager of the Chicago & Western Indiana Railroad Company. He further testified that the Association was first organized on April 20, 1886, and among its objects wage schedules were to be agreed upon and stood by, by the railroads.

Mr. Debs was called February 7 and gave his testimony clearly and without hesitation. The examination was conducted by Clarence S. Darrow. He testified that the object of the A. R. U. organization was the unification of *all* railroad employes for their mutual benefit and protection. The attorneys for the railroads tried hard to exclude many answers, but the court ruled them competent and Mr. Debs said there were several railroad organizations and they were at war with one another and had been for a long time. The same classes of men were eligible to different organizations and the Railroad Managers' Association played off these organizations against one another. The railroads took advantage of this fact and made contracts with one or the other organizations and these would operate to the disadvantage of the others.

"The concentration of the smaller railroads into the larger had been going on for 20 years, and there had been a gradual reduction of wages." These things compelled the idea of organization of the A. R. U.

The first strike was on the Great Northern and commenced April 13, 1894, and lasted eighteen days.

"I first learned of the Pullman strike May 11, 1894. It was done contrary to my advice. I investigated conditions at Pullman first May 4, 1894, and again May 18, 1894. I made an investigation among the Pullman employes and was helped by the Rev. Carwardine of Pullman. I came to the conclusion that the Pullman Company was in the wrong, that wages had been unjustifiably reduced at different times below the living point and that rents were much too high in comparison with what was charged for the same class of dwellings elsewhere. The Pullman Company owned the whole town of Pullman, streets, water works, houses and everything."

Newspaper reporters were admitted to all sessions of the convention held at Chicago June 12, 1894, except one where finances were considered. All telegrams were subjected voluntarily to the examination of the press reporters.

Mr. Debs then gave a resume of his speech at the convention and stated that in his speech he spoke in particular about the victory on the Great Northern having been a peaceful one. He then testified as to the conference held by the convention committee with Manager Wicks of the Pullman Company and the committee reported June 16, that the manager of the Pullman Company said they had nothing to arbitrate. He testified as to the speech made to the convention by Rev. Carwardine; that the Rev. Carwardine told of his three years' life in Pullman and that the men and their families were at the point of starvation. The convention voted $2,000 for the relief of the Pullman employes. A committee was appointed to notify the Pullman Company that unless arbitration was agreed upon by June 26 a boycott on Pullman cars would be ordered. He further testified that he had advised all committees coming to his headquarters to abstain from any acts of violence and in reply to a question put by the counsel, replied, "No, sir; never in all my life have I broken the law or advised others to do so."

His testimony was listened to with marked interest by the jury.

A. R. U.

In the Chicago strike the strikers were not responsible for the burning of the property of the railroads. It was not done until after the arrival of the United States troops. It was done then at the instance of the railroads because the railroads knew that without violence they would lose the strike. People who doubt this statement are referred to the reports of Chief Brennan of the Chicago Police, Hon. Carroll D. Wright, head of the Labor Bureau, and the reports of the governor of Illinois, and the report of the Special United States Commission that heard witnesses of all sorts in their investigation of the A. R. U. strike.

The substance of the report of the commission was as follows:

"The third smash-up comes from the commissioners appointed by Cleveland, who make their report to Congress, that the Managers' Association at Chicago who fought the A. R. U. threw the whole country into turmoil and dismay, stopped traffic and destroyed commerce, was an utterly illegal body. The twenty-four railroads, including the Southern Pacific, Atchison and Southern California, which so ruthlessly pursued the employes to crush and starve them are now pronounced to have had no 'standing in law.' And yet, they had the influence to bring into their support the Federal executive and army and navy and all the machinery and power of the Federal courts. The commission says: 'If we regard its practical workings rather than its profession, as expressed in its constitution, the General Managers' Association has no more standing in law than an old trunk line pool. It cannot incorporate because railroad charters do not authorize roads to form associations or corporations to fix rates for service or wages, nor to battle with strikers. It is usurpation of power not granted. In fact, this "usurpation" had extended everywhere by courts as well as Railroad Managers' Associations. The latter can be classed with the other cutthroat organizations of hirelings and Hessians, who for money will start out to kill any citizens at the order of the corporations—the Pinkertons.'"

The commission says: "An extension of the Association, as above suggested, and the proposed legalization of pooling, would result in an aggregation of power and capital dangerous to the people and their liberties, as well as to their employes and rights." And they might have added that with the aid of the Federal judiciary these twenty-four managers could have subverted the constitution and erected a despotism. The commission thoroughly endorses the legality of the actions of the A. R. U. and refutes the charge that they were guilty of violence or encouraging it. They say:

"It should be noted that until the railroads set the example, the great union of railroad employes was never attempted. * * * The refusal of the General Managers to recognize and deal with such a combination of labor as the American Railway Union, seems arrogant and absurd, when we consider its standing before the law, its assumption, and its past and obviously contemplated future action."

Another signal reversal of the position assumed by the United States courts in the Chicago cases came in the shape of a reversal by the Federal Court of Appeals in the opinion of Justice Harlan against the use of equity proceedings to punish railway employes by means of contempt in injunctions and especially that the act of July 2, 1890, was totally inapplicable. Another was in the opinion filed by Attorney General Olney, who practically reversed himself when he declared in his brief to the United States Circuit Court that the position taken by the receiver of the Reading Railroad was entirely illegal and unjustifiable in his notice to the men that he would dismiss all who remained members of labor organizations of railways. It controverts everything that has been done in the Chicago cases and in other Federal courts on the subject of the A. R. U. and other brotherhoods.

After the appearance of the report of the strike commission, Mr. Debs wrote the following letter to the *New York World*, in reply to some criticisms of the report of the commission:
To the Editor of the *World*:

The report of the strike commission is eminently fair and impartial and meets with the unqualified approval of not only the A. R. U. but of all people who believe in the American spirit of fair play and desire the enthronement of justice. The conclusions of the board are based on the testimony and both are presented with absolute impartiality. The result is a triumphant vindication of the American Railway Union and fixes the responsibility for the lawlessness, violence, arson and loss of life with the General Managers' Association, where it properly belongs. Any intimation that I wrote the report or any part of it, or that I had anything to do with its preparation, directly or indirectly, is totally and maliciously false. I simply rendered my testimony in open session and then and there my connection with the board ceased. I never met or corresponded with any member of the board, either before or after my testimony was given.

EUGENE V. DEBS.

Mr. Debs made his first political speech for the Democratic party in 1878. He was tendered the nomination for Congress by that party and declined it.

In 1885 he was elected to the Indiana legislature and ran on the Democratic ticket with the avowed purpose of securing needed legislation for the working class in general, and railway employes in particular. In was this year, 1885, June 9, he was married to Katherine Metzel,*—"Kate" he affectionately calls her. She is one of the noblest types of women. She was born in Pittsburg, but her parents were Kentuckians. She is in thorough sympathy with him on social and economic questions and aids him materially in his work. She is always ready to give him up to the Cause and in every way adds to his strength, helping to keep his vast correspondence in order

---
* Portrait page 45.

and all his books and papers are instantly accessible. No children have blessed their lives. A little nephew has his home with them and Gene is a lover of children and always has time for their companionship.

Gene is distinctively a "home man;" belongs to no social lodge or club, simply because he wishes to spend his evenings at home. The Sunday evenings are home meetings and three generations met Sunday evenings when father and mother were living. He said, "My father and I were boon companions,* and I tell you, I miss it when I cannot have my Sunday evening talks with him. When I am out traveling, every day seems alike, but when Sunday evening comes, I invariably feel something tugging at my heart strings."

He said, without hesitation, "The dominant influence in my life has been my 'mother.' Whatever of good there is in me I owe to her. Do you know," he said, "I care absolutely nothing for the praise or condemnation of the world so long as my wife and my mother think I am in the right."

PERSONAL DESCRIPTION.

He is tall, six feet, two inches; is slim, powerfully built; a fine head, proudly set above broad shoulders; long, full neck; face clear, finely cut, smoothly shaven; blue, deep, searching, inquiring, frank, open eyes; a smile, childlike and sweet, usually upon his face; sometimes sad, as sad as Lincoln's. He is plain, dresses plainly, neatly always; is rational, logical, epigrammatic; quick words fit his thoughts; incisive and unambiguous, they seem to flow to him from a vast, well-filled vocabulary. He quotes from the great writers and poets, is intimate with them all; speaks fluently, never hesitates, draws faultless word pictures, makes epigrams, plain, pointed and easily remembered; gestures almost only with the right hand, steps quietly, leans forward to his audience, poised and when speaking his eyes seem like the eyes of a painting—to look at each one everywhere in his audience.

In 1878 Mr. Debs met Wendell Phillips and Robert G. Ingersoll. Their great oratorical powers inspired him to study the power of speech to move men, and no American has been a more tireless student of literature and the art of expression

---
* Portrait page 93.

BIOGRAPHY.

than he. To the end of Mr. Ingersoll's life he kept up an intimate correspondence with him upon all vital questions and was greatly aided by Mr. Ingersoll's good advice and able suggestions. To further equip himself for speaking and debating, he became an active member of the one-time locally famous Occidental Literary Club, and was a live and aggressive member, writing great papers and acquitting himself in the highest manner in every debate.

His home library* is large and the books it contains are on all phases of human history, politics, government, philosophy, religion, poetry and the arts, and they bear the marks of having been intimately handled.

He is a great reader and he has a wonderful and most orderly lot of magazine articles which he has had bound in volumes; newspaper clippings arranged in scrap books of ready reference; letters carefully filed and indexed.

He has been heard before vast audiences at Chautauquas, colleges, opera houses, labor halls, mining camps, farmers' festivals, etc.

In Faneuil Hall, Boston, under time-honored custom, no seats are allowed; audience and speaker stand. This permits the largest possible attendance. At Mr. Debs' October speech, 1904, the old Cradle of Liberty was packed to the sidewalk. It would be a mistake to state that only laboring people are interested in his economic discussions. Business men are keenly awake to the fact that this subject is the question of our day. In 1899 Mr. Debs spoke before the Nineteenth Century Club at Delmonico's, New York, and drew some word pictures that stood out like living flames. He touched the vulnerable spots in his listeners that left impressions for life. He never needlessly offends. At Harvard, Ann Arbor and before the greatest educational institutions he has been heard by wonderfully appreciative audiences. At Harvard the students were tremenduously enthusiastic; at Ann Arbor the Professor of Elocution told his classes that they had never heard a more accomplished orator, and the demonstration that followed his address to the students in the vast university amphitheatre will never be forgotten by those having the fortune to have heard it.

---
* Illustration page 109.

The most prized memento of the great strike is a little note from Eugene Field, the Chicago poet, author of "The Little Boy Blue." It seems that the poet had advance knowledge that Mr. Debs was to be arrested and he drove to Mr. Debs' headquarters and as Gene was not in he left the note which read:

"Dear Gene: I hear that you are to be arrested. When that time comes you will need a friend. I want to be that friend. EUGENE FIELD."

From a letter from F. L. Thompson, Lansing, Mich., in *Lansing Tribune,* February 3, 1899, after hearing Mr. Debs' lecture on "Labor and Liberty:"

"I was pastor at Pullman some years ago and know the truth of all Mr. Debs said of that place. He might have said much more and still have been fully within the truth."

From hundreds of letters and telegrams that poured in upon Mr. Debs during the A. R. U. strike and while he was in prison are here given a few, to show how his strength was increased and his courage fortified by loving words from home and friends everywhere:

DEBS.

Now and then out of the veiled universe comes a friend. In that hour, and in oft-repeated hours during our lifetime, he is the builder and the bearer of our dearest thought.

Now and then History, in her long, wavering, stumbling, but ever forward course, gives us a Hugo, an O'Connell, a Phillips, and now at last, thank Heaven, a Debs.

Seeing such men, we can realize why Emerson and Whitman can forever have patience and hope, and look to the sure-coming of the bright days.

Debs greets us and our day is brighter,—sweeter. His every word is a story. Every word a song. Every word is the bearer of purest love. His tones are sweet like tones of bells. His tones are firm like bell-tones. Greeting us, Debs leaves with us a bit of himself which will not leave us while we live. Debs comes to us with greatest love,—and the greatest lover is the greatest man.

GEO. F. HIBNER.

THEODORE DEBS (See Page 5)

CAMDEN, Jan. 13, 1907.

Dear Brother: I know you are very busy. I don't want to crowd in. But I want to send you my love. There is always time for love. You are a man upon whom love has showered its darling gifts. Cherish them. They are worth while. They are all that is worth while. You have troubles. I know about them. But you have lovers, and the light is full in your face, and you are leading men on towards the fulfillment of man's noblest dream. I know that though sorrow comes you are still satisfied. A man with work in him, with love in him, may always be happy. He is always next the throne. Good-night.

TRAUBEL.

WOODSTOCK, ILL., Aug. 29, 1895.

Mr. Ed H. Evinger,
  Labor Day Committee, Terre Haute, Ind.

Dear Sir and Brother: I am in receipt of your esteemed favor of the 19th inst., in which you say: "We have been unable to get a representative labor speaker for our Labor Day celebration and the committee ordered me to ask you to write us a letter to be read on the occasion."

In responding to your request I am disposed to recite a page of what all Christendom proclaims "sacred history."

There existed some twenty-five hundred years ago a king clothed with absolute power, known as Darius, who ruled over the Medes and the Persians. He was not a usurper like Wm. A. Woods, the United States Circuit Judge. Darius was royal spawn. His right to rule was what kings then, as now, claimed to be a "divine right." All the people in Darius' empire were slaves. The will of the king was absolute. What the king said was law, just as we now find in the United States of America that what a United States judge says is law. Darius, the Persian despot, could imprison at will; the same is true of Woods, the despot. There is absolutely no difference. Do I hear an exception? Allow me to support my indictment by authority that passes current throughout the Republic. Only a few days ago the venerable Judge Trumbull, one of the most eminent jurists and statesmen America has ever produced, wrote these burning words: "The doctrine announced by the Supreme Court in the Debs case, carried to its logical conclusion, places every citizen at the mercy of any prejudiced or malicious federal judge, who may think proper to imprison him." This states the case of the officers of the American Railway Union in a nutshell. They violated no law, they committed no crime, they have not been charged, nor indicted, nor tried, and yet they were arbitrarily sentenced and thrust in jail and what has happened to them will happen to others who dare protest against such inhumanity as the monster Pullman practiced upon his employes and their families.

More than twenty-five hundred years have passed to join the unnumbered centuries since Darius lived and reigned, and now in the United States we have about four score Darius despots, each of whom may at his will, whim or pleasure, imprison an American citizen—and this grim truth is up for debate on Labor Day.

It will be remembered that during the reign of Darius there was a gentleman by the name of Daniel whom the king delighted to honor. The only fault that could be found with Daniel was that he would not worship the Persian gods, but would, three times a day, go to his window, looking toward Jerusalem, and pray. This was his crime. It was enough. The Persians had a religion of their own. They had their gods of gold, brass, stone, clay, wood, anything from a mouse to a mountain, and they would not tolerate any other god. They had, in modern parlance, an "established church," and as Daniel, like Christ, would not conform to the Persian religion, "the presidents of the kingdom, the governors and the princes, the counselors and the captains," or as in these later days the corporations, the trusts, the syndicates and combines, concluded to get rid of Daniel and they persuaded Darius to issue an injunction that no man should "ask a petition of any God or man for thirty days save of thee, O king"—and the king, a la Woods, issued the decree. But Daniel, who was made of resisting stuff, disregarded the injunction and still prayed as before to his God. Daniel was a hero. In the desert of despotism he stands forever:

BIOGRAPHY. 63

"As some tall cliff that lifts its awful form,
Swells from the vale and midway leaves the storm:
Though round its breast the rolling clouds are spread,
Eternal sunshine settles on its head."

But the bigots triumph for a time. The king's decree must stand, and Daniel, as a penalty for prayer, must be cast into the lion's den and the bigots, the plutocratic pirates and parasites of that period, thought that would be the end of Daniel. They chuckled as in fancy they heard the lions break his bones and lap his blood. They slept well and dreamed of victory. Not so with the king. He knew he had been guilty of an act of monstrous cruelty and in this the old Persian despot was superior to Woods. The king could not sleep and was so pained over his act that he forbade all festivities in his palace. In this he showed that he was not totally depraved. The king had a lurking idea that somehow Daniel would get out of the lion's den unharmed and that he would overcome the intrigues of those who had conspired to destroy him. Early in the morning he went to the mouth of the den. Daniel was safe. His God, unlike the Supreme Court, having found Daniel innocent of all wrongdoing, locked the jaws of the lions and Daniel stood before the king wearing the redemption of truth, more royal than a princely diadem. Then the king who had been deceived by the enemies of Daniel, the sycophants and the vermin of power, gave his wrath free reign and had them cast into the lion's den where they were devoured by the ferocious beasts.

History repeats itself. I am not a Daniel but I am in jail by the decree of the autocrat. I appealed from one despot to a whole bench for justice, and the appeal was unheeded. I and my associates were innocent. There was no stain of crime upon our record but neither innocence nor constitution was of any avail. To placate the corporations, the money power, the implacable enemies of labor, we were sent to prison and here alone, contemplating the foul wrong inflicted upon me and my associate officials of the American Railway Union, with head and heart and hand nerved for the task, I write this letter to be read on Labor Day to friends and neighbors in the city of my birth.

It is not a wail of despondency nor of despair. The cause for which I have been deprived of my liberty was just and I am thrice armed against all my enemies. To bear punishment for one's honest convictions is a glorious privilege and requires no high order of courage.

No judicial tyrant comes to my prison to inquire as to my health or my hopes, but one sovereign does come by night and by day, with words of cheer. It is the sovereign people—the uncrowned but sceptered ruler of the realm. No day of my imprisonment has passed that the bars and bolts and doors of the Woodstock Jail have not been bombarded by messages breathing devotion to the cause of liberty and justice, and as I read and ponder these messages and as I grasp the hands of friends and catch the gleam of wrath in their defiant eyes and listen to their words of heroic courage, I find it no task to see the wrath of the sovereign people aroused and all opposition to the triumphant march of labor consigned to oblivion, and as an earnest of this from every quarter come announcements that the American Railway Union is growing in membership and strength, destined at an early day to be, as it deserves to be, an organization, which by precept, example and principle will ultimately unify railroad labor in the United States and make it invincible. There is a mighty mustering of all the forces of labor throughout the country. Labor is uniting in one solid phalanx to secure justice for labor. When this time comes, and coming it is, peacefully, I hope no judicial despot will dare to imprison an American citizen to please corporations. When this time comes, and coming it is as certain as rivers flow to the sea, Bullion and Boodle will not rule in Congress, in legislatures and in courts, and legislators and judges and other public officers will not be controlled, as many of them are, by the money power. There is to come a day, aye, a labor day, when from the center to the circumference of our mighty Republic, from blooming groves of orange to waving fields of grain, from pinelands of Maine to the Pacific Coast, the people shall be free and it will come by the unified voice and vote of the farmer, the mechanic, and the laborer in every department of the country's industries.

I notice in your letter that you say: "We have been unable to get a representative labor speaker for our Labor Day celebration," and here let me say that on Labor Day all men who wear the badge of labor are "representative speakers"—not "orators," perhaps, as the term is accepted to mean, and yet orators in fact, from whose lips fall "thoughts that breathe and words that burn;" coming warm from the heart, they reach the heart and fan zeal in a great cause into a flame that sweeps along like a prairie fire. It has been the good fortune of labor to produce from its ranks men who, though unlearned in the arts or oratory, were yet orators of the highest order, if effect instead of fluency is considered. It is the occasion that makes the orator as it is the battle that makes the veteran. Mark Antony said, "I am no orator like Brutus," but when he showed Caesar's mantle to the populists of Rome and pointed out where the conspirators' daggers had stabbed Caesar, the oratory of Brutus paled before his burning words. And every man, however humble he may esteem himself, may on Labor Day hold up the Constitution of the United States and point to where the judicial dagger stabbed liberty to death, and make the people cry out for the re-enthronement of the constitution—and Terre Haute has a hundred such orators.

I write in the hurry and press of business. Before me are a hundred letters demanding replies. I pass them by to respond to an appeal from my home, and in fancy, as I write, I am with you. I am at home again. My father bending beneath the weight of many years salutes me. My mother, whose lullaby songs nestle and coo in the inner temple of my memory, caresses me—her kiss baptizes me with joy and as if by enchantment:

>"Years and sin and folly flee,
>And leave me at my mother's knee."

In this mood I write with the hope that the celebration at Terre Haute will inspire renewed devotion to the interests of labor, and with a heart full of good wishes, I subscribe myself,

Yours fraternally,

Dict. E.V.D.   E. V. DEBS.

TELEGRAM.

INDIANAPOLIS, IND., July 18, 1894.

To Hon. Eugene V. Debs,
    Cook County Jail.

My wife, my boys and myself give you our greatest love. The helpless world now acknowledges you, the whole world will crown you.   Devotedly,

FRANKLIN W. HAYS.

Received at Chicago.
    Dated Terre Haute, Ind., July 18, 1894.
To Eugene V. Debs.

Stand by your principles, regardless of consequences.

YOUR FATHER AND MOTHER.

RESOLUTION OF INMATES OF WOODSTOCK JAIL.

We, the undersigned, inmates of Woodstock Jail, desire to convey to you our heartfelt thanks and gratitude for the many acts of kindness and sympathy shown us by you during your incarceration in this institution.

We selfishly regret your departure from here into the outer world and scenes of labor. Your presence here has been to us what an oasis in a desert is to the tired and weary traveler, or a ray of sunshine showing thro' a rift in the clouds.

With thousands of others we rejoice and extend to you our most earnest congratulations upon your restoration to liberty.

Hoping you may have a long, prosperous and happy life, success in all of your undertakings, especially "The American Railway Union," we all join in wishing you Godspeed and beg to subscribe ourselves,
    Your friends,
        CHARLES E. ANDERSON,   PAUL WAMBACH,
        EDWARD MADDEN,   W. E. HORTON.
To Eugene V. Debs, Esq.,
    Woodstock, Ill., Nov. 22, 1895.

BIOGRAPHY. 67

DEBS AND THE POETS.

(*Clipping from New York Socialist, June 20, 1908.*)

An infallible instinct for heart-analysis appears to be an attribute of the poets. For the most part they possess an unfailing judgment of character-worth, and whomsoever they know well and call good is apt to be a pretty safe pilgrim to tie to. President Roosevelt, of vituperative vocabulary, may loudly denounce him as an "undesirable citizen," but when the poets with deeper discernment and prophetic vision pronounce him a "desirable citizen" they voice the sure verdict of the justifying years.

To Eugene V. Debs have the poets been especially kind, for in him have they recognized a kindred spirit. In him they have detected the true impulse of the brotherhood, concerning which no poet can well be deceived. They have found that his mind is a garden in bloom, and that his soul is filled with fragrance. So right blithely have they sung him of their best, and many of Fame's favorites have been proud to call him friend—they who "sit at wine with the Maidens Nine and the gods of the elder days."

It was James Whitcomb Riley who thus characteristically expressed himself concerning this beloved Apostle of Advancement:

"God was feeling mighty good when he created 'Gene Debs, and He didn't have anything else to do all day."

Another poet of world-wife fame—Eugene Field—who was extremely discriminating in his friendships and exceedingly sparing of compliment, said: "'Gene Debs is the most lovable man I ever knew. Debs is sincere. His heart is as gentle as a woman's and as fresh as a mountain brook. If Debs were a priest the world would listen to his eloquence, and that gentle, musical voice and sad, sweet smile of his would soften the hardest heart."

There have been paid to Debs enough tender tributes in verse to fill a large volume. At one time when Riley was confined to his room by illness, Debs sent him a bouquet of the poet's favorite flowers, which called forth the following appreciation:

THEM FLOWERS.

(To My Good Friend, Eugene V. Debs.)

Take a feller 'ats sick, and laid up on the shelf,
   All shaky, and ga'nted and pore,
And all so knocked out he can't handle hisself
   With a stiff upper lip any more;
Shet him up all alone in the gloom of a room
   As dark as a tomb, and as grim,
And then take and send him some roses in bloom,
   And you kin have fun out o' him!

You've seed him, 'fore now, when his liver was sound,
   And his appetite notched like a saw,
A chaffin' you, mebby, for romancin' round
   With a big posey bunch in yer paw.
But you ketch him, say, when his health is away
   And he's flat on his back, in distress,
And then you can trot out your little bokay
   And not be insulted, I guess!

You see, it's like this, what his weaknesses is,
   Them flowers makes him think of the days
Of his innocent youth, and that mother o' his,
   And the roses she used to raise;
So here all alone with the roses you send,
   Bein' sick and all trimbly and faint,
My eyes is—my eyes is—my eyes is—old friend,
   Is a-leakin'—I'm blamed ef they ain't!

And in the "Hoosier Bard's" poem "Regardin' Terry Hut," appears these lines:

   And there's 'Gene Debs—a man 'at stands
   And jest holds out in his two hands
   As warm a heart as ever beat
   Betwixt here and the Jedgment Seat.

The picturesque genius, Capt. Jack Crawford, renowned as "The Poet-Scout," wrote of Debs:

   The same old pard of long ago,
   The whole-souled 'Gene I used to know,
   With the love of Truth writ on Justice's scroll,
   With a woman's heart and a warrior's soul.

At a reception given to Debs by the Denver Press Club Walter Juan Davis recited these lines, written for the occasion:

DEBS.

It is not his craft or creed,
  It is not the winged word
That springs from his soul to his lips, at need,
  And, flying, is felt and heard;
But something down in us all
  That makes us respect the man
Who says unto great and small:
  "You've a right to do what you can;
You've a right to preserve and keep
  Such things as the gods gave you;
You've a right to your hours of sleep
  And the worth of the things you do;
You've a right to the million or dime
  That your brain or your brawn has won;
But not in the length of time;
  In the light of the moon or sun,
Have you a right to a thing
That you steal or wring
  From me or from any one.

In 1904 he made such a campaign as no other man ever endured. He began at Indianapolis September 1, and from that date traveled to New York, and thence to California, thence to Portland, Maine, thence to his home, Terre Haute, closing his campaign in his home city before an audience of several thousands, and at least 2,000 could not gain entrance. During this time he did not miss an appointment by even one minute. He spoke every day and some days two, three and even four times. The crowds were so great in the large cities it seemed impossible for him to enter or go from the building at the close of the meetings. On several occasions it became necessary to stop and speak a few minutes to the waiting thousands on the streets. He had gone alone during all this time except from October 17 to November 8, when from Chicago to Portland and thence to Terre Haute, Comrade Reynolds, of Terre Haute, was with him, assisting in all possible ways to lighten the heavy work.

Owing to the lack of funds of the working class party Mr. Debs had been attending to baggage, hotels, time tables, and the vast correspondence necessarily following him. The old parties had the noise, brass bands, Pullman trains, luxuries of every sort, torch-lights and plenty of money. The Debs meetings were held in the largest obtainable audience rooms in the larger cities and were paid for by tickets of admission, and these meetings in every case netted to the campaign fund of the Socialist party considerable sums of money, from which Mr. Debs received only the expenses of travel, which were not very heavy.

In spite of the facts stated, most of the great capitalist papers either ignored these meetings or belittled them, or flatly misrepresented them, but the people are quick nowadays to get the truth about these things and there will be more wonderful meetings in the campaign of 1908 than ever before known by a rising militant minor political party. Those who heard him, heard the polished American orator; those who agreed with him were strengthened and confirmed in their beliefs; those who came seeking Truth were moved by his oratory and convinced by his array of facts and unerring logic, in making conclusions from them, while those who disagreed were disarmed of prejudice and commended him as a sincere, earnest man.

In 1880 he persuaded Susan B. Anthony to speak in Terre Haute in a series of meetings advocating Woman's Suffrage, and with her he walked and stood the odium that ignorance and prejudice poured out upon that great human question, at that time not so popular as it now is, when 100,000 women may surround the Parliament of England and demand that the voices of women be counted in the rules of life that concern them and their children as it does men and their children.

Mr. Debs has always stood for equality of rights, equality of opportunity for men and women everywhere without distinction of race, religion, color, or sex, and no Socialist platform fails to clearly state its attitude upon these great vital questions. Search the old party platforms and you may find terms of evasion but not of real affirmation of these fundamental demands.

BIOGRAPHY. 71

Mr. Debs was nominated by the Socialist party for President in 1900, receiving 97,000 votes; again in 1904, receiving 409,000 votes; again in 1908.

Debs has said these immortal words to the working people:

"I am not a Labor Leader; I do not want you to follow me or anyone else; if you are looking for a Moses to lead you out of this capitalist wilderness, you will stay right where you are. I would not lead you into this promised land if I could, because if I could lead you in, someone else would lead you out. YOU MUST use your heads as well as your hands, and get yourselves out of your present condition; as it is now the capitalists use your heads and your hands."

To teach, to serve is his mental and moral mission. He seeks no place of power or profit,—did not want to be nominated either time for the presidency, but when the rank and file lead and order, he has never hesitated to obey, and he believes, with unquestioning faith and love for the people, that when they are educated and understand, they will peacefully and intelligently set government about its proper business,— the government of the forces of production and the same arrangements of distributing the things the people need, and must have, if they are ever to rise to complete physical, mental and spiritual freedom.

In closing this necessarily brief and meager biographical sketch of this true, living, loving and lovable man, true neighbor, really "desirable citizen," and unimpeached and unimpeachable representative and servant of the working class, I cannot tell in any better way of "Debs at Home" than in the little pamphlet I wrote in 1904. It needs no change. He has only grown every day in intellectual and spiritual stature, more wise, more patient, more uncompromising and unconquerably aggressive and more loving and lovable and, therefore, able more safely to teach the workers and more to be feared by the exponents of the rapidly-dying system of capitalism tottering to its inevitable grave, dying because it has served its period of usefulness, because it now hurts, degrades and humiliates all of the human family.

DEBS AT HOME.

Here, in Terre Haute, where "Gene" Debs lives, everybody

admires him. All who know him personally love him. He has no personal enemies; he has enemies, but they do not know him. He has none in Terre Haute. Many here would like to hang his ideas, but the man, the strong personality, the gentleness and cordiality of his greeting when he meets his neighbors and fellow-citizens, disarm all prejudice. Politicians here, as elsewhere, fear him, for they know that his intrepid soul knows and permits no intellectual fears, stoops to no intellectual prostitution. He is as open and fearless when called upon for an opinion upon any matters of local interest as he is when he assails the capitalist system.

I remember first seeing him in the editorial office of the Locomotive Firemen's Magazine. I was struck by his alertness and the unhesitating speed of his work, whether engaged in writing or arranging the details of printing, mailing or distributing the great mazagine among the thousands of workers who read and had profitable enjoyment from its pages. I next remember his home-coming after the A. R. U. had won the Great Northern strike. An immense throng met him at the depot with the Ringgold Band, drum corps and torchlights. They had a carriage for him, but he protested and took his place in the ranks with the men,—only a look of joy shone on his face, nothing of exultation; he was as unconscious of himself then as he seems ever to be and is. The shouts of "Welcome Home" seemed only to elate and inspire his soul to do more for the cause of labor. Then I remember (I was a Republican at the time) reading of the awful strike begun in Chicago in 1894. I shared with others in my ignorance in condemnation of the things reported from Chicago. I commiserated his confinement in jail at Woodstock but believed, as millions equally as ignorant as I was then believed, that the laws had been upheld. I know now the details of the wrongs that in the name of Law and Order were heaped upon the cause of labor then and understand the superb courage and patience of labor's greatest and most far-seeing leader,—Debs.

When he came from Woodstock Jail to Terre Haute it had been raining all day. Mr. Debs' train arrived at 7:00 o'clock. There were several hundred people at the depot, among them

200 miners with the Coal Bluff Band. Escorted by the band he walked to his home, a few squares from the depot. There he found his aged father and mother, and they clung to him, kissing him again and again. After he had had his supper he was escorted to the Armory through the rain, along the route blazing with Roman candles. After the enthusiastic cheering and greeting had subsided, Mr. Debs made a short speech to the audience and afterwards he was kept busy shaking hands with his friends.

I do not know much of those long, fallow years when he went deep into the movement of things. I became a Socialist in 1899, entirely uninfluenced and alone. I emerged and found myself and a new life, a new outlook, and stand now serenely, knowing that the end of capitalism is in sight and the day of better things is certain.

I feel yet the throb of his heart in his great, strong hand when I told him I had taken my place on the side of the Barricades, where the cause of labor must soon entrench itself. From that time I have seen him intimately at all hours of the day, under all circumstances, and found him always sure in knowledge of the future, with unlimited faith in humanity and never once faltering. I know unnumbered things he has done for the "A. R. U. Boys,"—know he has gone to their personal assistance, not only with inspiring sympathy but with substantial help. His mail often brings him words of courage and good cheer from those who have come into the light with him, and these are the things that go deepest to his heart. He keenly suffers with the workers in all their industrial battles, but sees now only the greater lesson to them he himself learned in the A. R. U. strike. In that strike he learned that labor was powerless with the courts, the laws, police, the military and every power of government in the hands of capital, and always ready to weaken, if not destroy, unions, unionism and union leaders. He often speaks of Woodstock jail as the greatest school where he learned to study and understand the value of the only weapon by which labor can ever come to its own,—"The Ballot."

He loves to tell the stories of his childhood experiences and the experiences of his early manhood as Town Clerk and as a member of the Indiana Legislature one term, his five years' experience in Hulman's Wholesale Grocery House, of his joy in firing a locomotive on the Vandalia Railroad, and of his grief because his aged mother could not sleep when he started out with the engine, fearing something might befall him, and how, to make her happy, he quit the job.

I find him very often, even in these days of pressing work, reading all alone to his old father, who is eighty-three years of age and almost blind. It is good to see this man, who is known in more countries and to more human beings than any other living man, surrendering himself completely to his friends when they call upon him. Three weeks ago he and his comrade wife, Katherine Debs (he calls her "Kate"), came to spend the evening with my family. We had many neighbors with us and the precise hour agreed upon "Gene" came down the street on his bicycle and went to the kitchen and without assistance prepared the supper. You, comrades, who have seen this man of heart and soul poised like a panther when he steps upon the platform and hurls the words that scorch and flash like fire, should have seen the gleam of domestic pleasure and joyous comradeship when he stood in the long apron and enthusiastically cooked a good supper in the kitchen of the "Old Red House" on Sixth Street, where so many "Soapbox Travelers and Apostles of Truth" have found shelter and food and repaired their raiment. And then after supper, until after midnight, we saw his soul aflame upon his face as he recited the wrongs of labor in Colorado and told of the heroism of the outraged comrades and workers in accursed Telluride.

Again, he loves best, I am sure, to go out into the country. We often go together. The last time we drove ten miles under the trees along the Wabash and when his quick eye saw a Kentucky cardinal in the woods, he stopped the horse and sat listening to the clear falling notes of this sweet whistler, and when we heard a mocking bird, like a child, he clasped his hands together and was lost as long as the song lasted in worshipful adoration of the wondrous music that stirred the still atmosphere into responsive vibration. After our dinner at a farmhouse we sat on a fallen "naked sycamore" on the "Banks of the Wabash," and there I saw deeper into the soul of this great comrade and brother. The universality of his vision was revealed and he poured forth, as though inspired, an analysis of world conditions, a forecast of things certain to occur, that made almost the waters in the river stop, listen and applaud. He described with great particularity the Chicago Republican convention (it was before it occurred, sometime in early May), its certainty to be a dull, apathetic, heartless proceeding, and the St. Louis convention marking the disintegration of a great political party,—Bryan's dying struggle to save the Democracy and the utter impossibility of preventing the coming together of capitalists, powers and influences, the effect upon the minds of the workers, the revelation of the true position of Capital vs. Labor and the tremendous and resistless growth of the Socialist movement. If he had had ten thousand workers before him, he could not have uttered more polished sentences, more words of deep significance, more prophetic epigrams than I heard alone, sitting on the fallen sycamore. But such things are not lost; he has uttered as great things to men who seemed as trees, but some day these same men will move as though a tornadic wind was upon them and then they will remember when and where they heard the first great words that inspired them.

It was near six o'clock when we came home and the toil-stained workers were going in all directions to their cottages, huts, hovels, boat-houses and tents. I shall never forget the look of compassionate understanding that came into his face as he reiterated some of the things he had so eloquently uttered in their behalf to the Wabash sycamore that afternoon, but now his words find open ears and go clear and welcome to hungry hearts. The words of this great comrade are finding lodgment and bearing fruitage, and the time of emancipation is not far off.

You comrades do not mistake the significance of events.

I know a million men and women are alive in America today, and millions more will soon be ready to help create the Co-operative Commonwealth, where men and women, great in soul and mind and strong in bodies and sure in life, shall be industrially free and realize the beneficence and uplifting power of Industrial Democracy. In that day we can know more of and better understand "Debs at Home," for now he is tireless and literally a wandering agitator, an apostle of truth, an awakener of the dead in spirit.

What would humanity be without such men, produced from their longings and aspirations? When you see him, give him the best love of your heart; inspire and encourage him for yet better efforts in your behalf. His life is of yours, ye toilers; his heart, his brain, his body, his soul are aflame with truth in your cause. Go the journey with him for your own sake. He is bone and marrow, flesh and blood of and for you. You will not soon see his like again. There are everywhere now, in all countries of the world, other great comrades, but nature will not soon conspire again to produce another Debs.

STEPHEN MARION REYNOLDS.

Terre Haute, Indiana, July 28, 1908.

WRITINGS

MARGUERITE MARIE DEBS

Where Daisy Sleeps

To Mother!
Sweetest to us of all the earth.
We called her "Daisy."

Terre Haute, Ind., May, 1906

The grass grows green
Where Daisy sleeps;
The Mulberry tree its vigil
    keeps
Where Daisy sleeps.

The wind blows soft
Where daisy sleeps;
The modest, blue-eyed violet
    peeps
Where Daisy sleeps.

The birds sing sweet
Where Daisy sleeps;
The mournful willow bends
    and weeps
Where Daisy sleeps.

The sun shines bright
Where Daisy sleeps;
Each changing season sows
    and reaps
Where Daisy sleeps.

The flowers bloom fair
Where Daisy sleeps;
The evening shadow softly
    creeps
Where Daisy sleeps.

Our hearts beat true
Where Daisy sleeps;
And Love its watch forever
    keeps
Where Daisy sleeps.

How I Became a Socialist

New York Comrade, April, 1902

As I have some doubt about the readers of "The Comrade" having any curiosity as to "how I became a Socialist" it may be in order to say that the subject is the editor's, not my own; and that what is here offered is at his bidding—my only concern being that he shall not have cause to wish that I had remained what I was instead of becoming a Socialist.

On the evening of February 27, 1875, the local lodge of the Brotherhood of Locomotive Firemen was organized at Terre Haute, Ind., by Joshua A. Leach, then grand master, and I was admitted as a charter member and at once chosen secretary. "Old Josh Leach," as he was affectionately called, a typical locomotive fireman of his day, was the founder of the brotherhood, and I was instantly attracted by his rugged honesty, simple manner and homely speech. How well I remember feeling his large, rough hand on my shoulder, the kindly eye of an elder brother searching my own as he gently said, "My boy, you're a little young, but I believe you're in earnest and will make your mark in the brotherhood." Of course, I assured him that I would do my best. What he really thought at the time flattered my boyish vanity not a little when I heard of it. He was attending a meeting at St. Louis some months later, and in the course of his remarks said: "I put a tow-headed boy in the brotherhood at Terre Haute not long ago, and some day he will be at the head of it."

Twenty-seven years, to a day, have played their pranks with "Old Josh" and the rest of us. When last we met, not long ago, and I pressed his good, right hand, I observed that he was crowned with the frost that never melts; and as I think of him now:

> "Remembrance wakes, with all her busy train,
> Swells at my breast and turns the past to pain."

My first step was thus taken in organized labor and a new influence fired my ambition and changed the whole current of my career. I was filled with enthusiasm and my blood fairly leaped in my veins. Day and night I worked for the brotherhood. To see its watchfires glow and observe the increase of its sturdy members were the sunshine and shower of my life. To attend the "meeting" was my supreme joy, and for ten years I was not once absent when the faithful assembled.

At the convention held in Buffalo in 1878 I was chosen associate editor of the magazine, and in 1880 I became grand secretary and treasurer. With all the fire of youth I entered upon the crusade which seemed to fairly glitter with possibilities. For eighteen hours at a stretch I was glued to my desk reeling off the answers to my many correspondents. Day and night were one. Sleep was time wasted and often, when all oblivious of her presence in the still small hours my mother's hand turned off the light, I went to bed under protest. Oh, what days! And what quenchless zeal and consuming vanity! All the firemen everywhere—and they were all the world—were straining:

> "To catch the beat
> On my tramping feet."

My grip was always packed; and I was darting in all directions. To tramp through a railroad yard in the rain, snow or sleet half the night, or till daybreak, to be ordered out of the roundhouse for being an "agitator," or put off a train, sometimes passenger, more often freight, while attempting to deadhead over the division, were all in the program, and served to whet the appetite to conquer. One night in midwinter at Elmira, N. Y., a conductor on the Erie kindly dropped me off in a snowbank, and as I clambered to the top I ran into the arms of a policeman, who heard my story and on the spot became my friend.

I rode on the engines over mountain and plain, slept in the

cabooses and bunks, and was fed from their pails by the swarthy stokers who still nestle close to my heart, and will until it is cold and still.

Through all these years I was nourished at Fountain Proletaire. I drank deeply of its waters and every particle of my tissue became saturated with the spirit of the working class. I had fired an engine and been stung by the exposure and hardship of the rail. I was with the boys in their weary watches, at the broken engine's side and often helped to bear their bruised and bleeding bodies back to wife and child again. How could I but feel the burden of their wrongs? How the seed of agitation fail to take deep root in my heart?

And so I was spurred on in the work of organizing, not the firemen merely, but the brakemen, switchmen, telegraphers, shopmen, track-hands, all of them in fact, and as I had now become known as an organizer, the calls came from all sides and there are but few trades I have not helped to organize and less still in whose strikes I have not at some time had a hand.

In 1894 the American Railway Union was organized and a braver body of men never fought the battle of the working class.

Up to this time I had heard but little of Socialism, knew practically nothing about the movement, and what little I did know was not calculated to impress me in its favor. I was bent on thorough and complete organization of the railroad men and ultimately the whole working class, and all my time and energy were given to that end. My supreme conviction was that if they were only organized in every branch of the service and all acted together in concert they could redress their wrongs and regulate the conditions of their employment. The stockholders of the corporation acted as one, why not the men? It was such a plain proposition—simply to follow the example set before their eyes by their masters—surely they could not fail to see it, act as one, and solve the problem.

It is useless to say that I had yet to learn the workings of the capitalist system, the resources of its masters and the weakness of its slaves. Indeed, no shadow of a "system" fell athwart my pathway; no thought of ending wage-misery marred my plans. I was too deeply absorbed in perfecting wage-servitude and making it a "thing of beauty and a joy forever."

It all seems very strange to me now, taking a backward look, that my vision was so focalized on a single objective point that I utterly failed to see what now appears as clear as the noonday sun—so clear that I marvel that any workingman, however dull, uncomprehending, can resist it.

But perhaps it was better so. I was to be baptized in Socialism in the roar of conflict and I thank the gods for reserving to this fitful occasion the fiat, "Let there be light!"—the light that streams in steady radiance upon the broadway to the Socialist republic.

The skirmish lines of the A. R. U. were well advanced. A series of small battles were fought and won without the loss of a man. A number of concessions were made by the corporations rather than risk an encounter. Then came the fight on the Great Northern, short, sharp, and decisive. The victory was complete—the only railroad strike of magnitude ever won by an organization in America.

Next followed the final shock—the Pullman strike—and the American Railway Union again won, clear and complete. The combined corporations were paralyzed and helpless. At this juncture there were delivered, from wholly unexpected quarters, a swift succession of blows that blinded me for an instant and then opened wide my eyes—and in the gleam of every bayonet and the flash of every rifle *the class struggle was revealed*. This was my first practical lesson in Socialism, though wholly unaware that it was called by that name.

An army of detectives, thugs and murderers were equipped with badge and beer and bludgeon and turned loose; old hulks of cars were fired; the alarm bells tolled; the people were terrified; the most startling rumors were set afloat; the press volleyed and thundered, and over all the wires sped the news that Chicago's white throat was in the clutch of a red mob; injunctions flew thick and fast, arrests followed, and our office and headquarters, the heart of the strike, was sacked, torn out and nailed up by the "lawful" authorities of the federal government; and when in company with my loyal comrades I found myself in Cook county jail at Chicago with the whole press screaming conspiracy, treason and murder, and by some fateful coincidence I was given the cell occupied just previous to his execution by the assassin of Mayor Carter Harrison, Sr., overlooking the spot, a few feet distant, where the anarchists were hanged a few years before, I had another exceedingly practical and impressive lesson in Socialism.

Acting upon the advice of friends we sought to employ John Harlan, son of the Supreme Justice, to assist in our defense—a defense memorable to me chiefly because of the skill and fidelity of our lawyers, among whom were the brilliant Clarence Darrow and the venerable Judge Lyman Trumbull, author of the thirteenth amendment to the constitution, abolishing slavery in the United States.

Mr. Harlan wanted to think of the matter over night; and the next morning gravely informed us that he could not afford to be identified with the case, "for," said he, "you will be tried upon the same theory as were the anarchists, with probably the same result." That day, I remember, the jailer, by way of consolation, I suppose, showed us the blood-stained rope used at the last execution and explained in minutest detail, as he exhibited the gruesome relic, just how the monstrous crime of lawful murder is committed.

But the tempest gradually subsided and with it the bloodthirstiness of the press and "public sentiment." We were not sentenced to the gallows, nor even to the penitentiary—though put on trial for conspiracy—for reasons that will make another story.

The Chicago jail sentences were followed by six months at Woodstock and it was here that Socialism gradually laid hold of me in its own irresistible fashion. Books and pamphlets and letters from socialists came by every mail and I began to read and think and dissect the anatomy of the system in which workingmen, however organized, could be shattered and battered and splintered at a single stroke. The writings of Bellamy and Blatchford early appealed to me. The "Co-operative Commonwealth" of Gronlund also impressed me, but the writings of Kautsky were so clear and conclusive that I readily grasped, not merely his argument, but also caught the spirit of his socialist utterance—and I thank him and all who helped me out of darkness into light.

It was at this time, when the first glimmerings of Socialism were beginning to penetrate, that Victor L. Berger—and I have loved him ever since—came to Woodstock, as if a providential instrument, and delivered the first impassioned message of Socialism I had ever heard—the very first to set the "wires humming in my system." As a souvenir of that visit there is in my library a volume of "Capital," by Karl Marx, inscribed with the compliments of Victor L. Berger, which I cherish as a token of priceless value.

The American Railway Union was defeated but not conquered—overwhelmed but not destroyed. It lives and pulsates in the Socialist movement, and its defeat but blazed the way to economic freedom and hastened the dawn of human brotherhood.

Outlook for Socialism in the United States

International Socialist Review, September, 1900

The sun of the passing century is setting upon scenes of extraordinary activity in almost every part of our capitalistic old planet. Wars and rumors of wars are of universal prevalence. In the Philippines our soldiers are civilizing and Christianizing the natives in the latest and most approved styles of the art, and at prices ($13 per month) which commend the blessing to the prayerful consideration of the lowly and oppressed everywhere.

In South Africa the British legions are overwhelming the Boers with volleys of benedictions inspired by the same beautiful philanthropy in the name of the meek and lowly Nazarene; while in China the heathen hordes, fanned into frenzy by the sordid spirit of modern commercial conquest, are presenting to the world a carnival of crime almost equaling the "refined" exhibitions of the world's "civilized" nations.

And through all the flame and furore of the fray can be heard the savage snarlings of the Christian "dogs of war" as they fiercely glare about them, and with jealous fury threaten to fly at one another's throats to settle the question of supremacy and the spoil and plunder of conquest.

The picture, lurid as a chamber of horrors, becomes complete in its gruesome ghastliness when robed ministers of Christ solemnly declare that it is all for the glory of God and the advancement of Christian civilization.

This, then, is the closing scene of the century as the curtain slowly descends upon the blood-stained stage—the central figure, the pious Wilhelm, Germany's sceptered savage, issuing his imperial "spare none" decree in the sang froid of an Apache chief—a fitting climax to the rapacious regime of the capitalist system.

Cheerless indeed would be the contemplation of such sanguinary scenes were the light of Socialism not breaking upon mankind. The skies of the East are even now aglow with the dawn; its coming is heralded by the dispelling of shadows, of darkness and gloom. From the first tremulous scintillation that gilds the horizon to the sublime march to meridian splendor the light increases till in mighty flood it pours upon the world.

From out of the midnight of superstition, ignorance and slavery the disenthralling, emancipating sun is rising. I am not gifted with prophetic vision, and yet I see the shadows vanishing. I behold near and far prostrate men lifting their bowed forms from the dust. I see thrones in the grasp of decay; despots relaxing their hold upon scepters, and shackles falling, not only from the limbs, but from the souls of men.

It is therefore with pleasure that I respond to the invitation of the editor of the International Socialist Review to present my views upon the "Outlook for Socialism in the United States." Socialists generally will agree that the past year has been marked with a propaganda of unprecedented activity and that the sentiment of the American people in respect to Socialism has undergone a most remarkable change. It would be difficult to imagine a more ignorant, bitter and unreasoning prejudice than that of the American people against Socialism during the early years of its introduction by the propagandists from the other side.

I never think of these despised and persecuted "foreign invaders" without a feeling of profound obligation, akin to reverence, for their noble work in laying the foundations deep and strong, under the most trying conditions, of the American movement. The ignorant mass, wholly incapable of grasping their splendid teachings or appreciating their lofty motives, reviled against them. The press inoculated the public sentiment with intolerance and malice which not infrequently found expression through the policeman's club when a few of the pioneers gathered to engraft the class-conscious doctrine upon their inhospitable "free-born" American fellow citizens.

Socialism was cunningly associated with "anarchy and bloodshed," and denounced as a "foul foreign importation" to pollute the fair, free soil of America, and every outrage to which the early agitators were subjected won the plaudits of the people. But they persevered in their task; they could not be silenced or suppressed. Slowly they increased in number and gradually the movement began to take root and spread over the country. The industrial conditions consequent upon the development of capitalist production were now making themselves felt and Socialism became a fixed and increasing factor in the economic and political affairs of the nation.

The same difficulties which other countries had experienced in the process of party organization have attended the development of the movement here, but these differences, which relate mainly to tactics and methods of propaganda, are bound to disappear as the friction of the jarring factions smoothens out the rough edges and adjusts them to a concrete body—a powerful section in the great international army of militant Socialism.

In the general elections of 1898 upwards of 91,000 votes were cast for the Socialist candidates in the United States, an increase in this "off year" of almost two hundred per cent over the general elections of two years previous, the presidential year of 1896. Since the congressional elections of 1898, and more particularly since the municipal and state elections following, which resulted in such signal victories in Massachusetts, two members of the legislature and a mayor, the first in America, being elected by decided majorities—since then Socialism has made rapid strides in all directions and the old politicians no longer reckon it as a negative quantity in making their forecasts and calculating their pluralities and majorities.

The subject has passed entirely beyond the domain of sneer and ridicule and now commands serious treatment. Of course, Socialism is violently denounced by the capitalist press and by all the brood of subsidized contributors to magazine literature, but this only confirms the view that the advance of Socialism is very properly recognized by the capitalist class as the one cloud upon the horizon which portends an end to the system in which they have waxed fat, insolent and despotic through the exploitation of their countless wage-working slaves.

In school and college and church, in clubs and public halls everywhere, Socialism is the central theme of discussion, and its advocates, inspired by its noble principles, are to be found here, there and in all places ready to give or accept challenge to battle. In the cities the corner meetings are popular and effective. But rarely is such a gathering now molested by the "authorities," and then only where they have just been inaugurated. They are too numerously attended by serious, intelligent and self-reliant men and women to invite interference.

Agitation is followed by organization, and the increase of branches, sections and clubs goes forward with extraordinary activity in every part of the land.

In New England the agitation has resulted in quite a general organization among the states, with Massachusetts in the lead; and the indications are that, with the vigorous prosecution of the campaign already inaugurated, a tremendous increase in the vote will be polled in the approaching national elections. New York and Pennsylvania will show surprising socialist returns, while Ohio, Michigan, Indiana, Illinois, Missouri and Kentucky will all round up with a large vote. Wisconsin has already a great vote to her credit and will increase it largely this year. In the west and northwest, Kansas, Iowa and Minnesota will forge to the front, and so also will Nebraska, the Dakotas, Montana, Oregon, Washington, Idaho and Colorado. California is expected to show an immense increase, and the returns from there will not disappoint the most sanguine. In the southwest, Texas is making a stirring campaign, and several papers, heretofore Populist, will support our candidates and swell the socialist vote, which will be an eye-opener when announced.

On the whole, the situation could scarcely be more favorable and the final returns will more than justify our sanguine expectations.

It must not be overlooked, however, when calculations are made, that this is a presidential year and that the general results will not be so favorable as if the elections were in an "off year." Both the Republican and Democratic parties will, as usual, strain every nerve to whip the "voting kings" into line and every conceivable influence will be exerted to that end. These vast machines operate with marvelous precision and the wheels are already in motion. Corruption funds, national, state and municipal, will flow out like lava tides; promises will be as plentiful as autumn leaves; from ten thousand platforms the Columbian orator will agitate the atmosphere, while brass bands, torchlight processions, glittering uniforms and free whisky, dispensed by the "ward-heeler," will lend their combined influence to steer the "patriots" to the capitalist chute that empties into the ballot box.

The campaign this year will be unusually spectacular. The Republican party "points with pride" to the "prosperity" of the country, the beneficent results of the "gold standard" and the "war record" of the administration. The Democratic party declares that "imperialism" is the "paramount" issue, and that the country is certain to go to the "demnition bow-wows" if Democratic officeholders are not elected instead of the Republicans. The Democratic slogan is "The Republic vs. the Empire," accompanied in a very minor key by 16 to 1 and "direct legislation where practical."

Both these capitalist parties are fiercely opposed to trusts, though what they propose to do with them is not of sufficient importance to require even a hint in their platforms.

Needless is it for me to say to the thinking workingman that he has no choice between these two capitalist parties, that they are both pledged to the same system and that whether the one or the other succeeds, he will still remain the wage-working slave he is today.

What but meaningless phrases are "imperialism," "expanpansion," "free silver," "gold standard," etc., to the wage-worker? The large capitalists represented by Mr. McKinley and the small capitalists represented by Mr. Bryan are interested in these "issues," but they do not concern the working class.

What the workingmen of the country are profoundly interested in is the private ownership of the means of production and distribution, the enslaving and degrading wage-system in which they toil for a pittance at the pleasure of their masters and are bludgeoned, jailed or shot when they protest—this is the central, controlling, vital issue of the hour, and neither of the old party platforms has a word or even a hint about it.

As a rule, large capitalists are Republicans and small capitalists are Democrats, but workingmen must remember that they are all capitalists, and that the many small ones, like the fewer large ones, are all politically supporting their class interests, and this is always and everywhere the capitalist class.

Whether the means of production—that is to say, the land, mines, factories, machinery, etc.—are owned by a few large Republican capitalists, who organize a trust, or whether they be owned by a lot of small Democratic capitalists, who are opposed to the trust, is all the same to the working class. Let the capitalists, large and small, fight this out among themselves.

The working class must get rid of the whole brood of masters and exploiters, and put themselves in possession and control of the means of production, that they may have steady employment without consulting a capitalist employer, large or small, and that they may get the wealth their labor produces, all of it, and enjoy with their families the fruits of their industry in comfortable and happy homes, abundant and wholesome food, proper clothing and all other things necessary to "life, liberty and the pursuit of happiness." It is therefore a question not of "reform," the mask of fraud, but of revolution. The capitalist system must be overthrown, class-rule abolished and wage-slavery supplanted by coöperative industry.

We hear it frequently urged that the Democratic party is the "poor man's party," "the friend of labor." There is but one way to relieve poverty and to free labor, and that is by making common property of the tools of labor.

Is the Democratic party, which we are assured has "strong socialistic tendencies," in favor of collective ownership of the means of production? Is it opposed to the wage-system, from which flows in a ceaseless stream the poverty, misery and wretchedness of the children of toil? If the Democratic party is the "friend of labor" any more than the Republican party, why is its platform dumb in the presence of Cœur d'Alene? It knows the truth about these shocking outrages—crimes upon workingmen, their wives and children, which would blacken the pages of Siberia—why does it not speak out?

What has the Democratic party to say about the "property

and educational qualifications" in North Carolina and Louisiana, and the proposed general disfranchisement of the negro race in the southern states?

The differences between the Republican and Democratic parties involve no issue, no principle in which the working class have any interest, and whether the spoils be distributed by Hanna and Platt, or by Croker and Tammany Hall is all the same to them.

Between these parties socialists have no choice, no preference. They are one in their opposition to Socialism, that is to say, the emancipation of the working class from wage-slavery, and every workingman who has intelligence enough to understand the interest of his class and the nature of the struggle in which it is involved, will once and for all time sever his relations with them both; and recognizing the class-struggle which is being waged between producing workers and non-producing capitalists, cast his lot with the class-conscious, revolutionary Socialist party, which is pledged to abolish the capitalist system, class-rule and wage-slavery—a party which does not compromise or fuse, but, preserving inviolate the principles which quickened it into life and now give it vitality and force, moves forward with dauntless determination to the goal of economic freedom.

The political trend is steadily toward Socialism. The old parties are held together only by the cohesive power of spoils, and in spite of this they are steadily disintegrating. Again and again they have been tried with the same results, and thousands upon thousands, awake to their duplicity, are deserting them and turning toward Socialism as the only refuge and security. Republicans, Democrats, Populists, Prohibitionists, Single Taxers are having their eyes opened to the true nature of the struggle and they are beginning to

> "Come as the winds come, when
> Forests are rended;
> Come as the waves come, when
> Navies are stranded."

For a time the Populist party had a mission, but it is practically ended. The Democratic party has "fused" it out of existence. The "middle-of-the-road" element will be sorely disappointed when the votes are counted, and they will probably never figure in another national campaign. Not many of them will go back to the old parties. Many of them have already come to Socialism, and the rest are sure to follow.

There is no longer any room for a Populist party, and progressive Populists realize it, and hence the "strongholds" of Populism are becoming the "hot-beds" of Socialism.

It is simply a question of capitalism or socialism, of despotism or democracy, and they who are not wholly with us are wholly against us.

Another source of strength to Socialism, steadily increasing, is the trades-union movement. The spread of Socialist doctrine among the labor organizations of the country during the past year exceeds the most extravagant estimates. No one has had better opportunities than the writer to note the transition to Socialism among trades-unionists, and the approaching election will abundantly verify it.

Promising, indeed, is the outlook for Socialism in the United States. The very contemplation of the prospect is a well-spring of inspiration.

Oh, that all the working class could and would use their eyes and see; their ears and hear; their brains and think. How soon this earth could be transformed and by the alchemy of social order made to blossom with beauty and joy.

No sane man can be satisfied with the present system. If a poor man is happy, said Victor Hugo, "he is the pick-pocket of happiness. Only the rich and noble are happy by right. The rich man is he who, being young, has the rights of old age; being old, the lucky chances of youth; vicious, the respect of good people; a coward, the command of the stout-hearted; doing nothing, the fruits of labor." * * *

With pride and joy we watch each advancing step of our comrades in Socialism in all other lands. Our hearts are with them in their varying fortunes as the battle proceeds, and we applaud each telling blow delivered and cheer each victory achieved.

The wire has just brought the tidings of Liebknecht's death. The hearts of American Socialists will be touched and shocked by the calamity. The brave old warrior succumbed at last,

DEBS, HIS FATHER AND BROTHER (See Page 58)

but not until he heard the tramp of International Socialism, for which he labored with all his loving, loyal heart; not until he saw the thrones of Europe, one by one, begin to totter, not until he had achieved a glorious immortality.

The American Movement

The twentieth century, according to the prophecy of Victor Hugo, is to be the century of humanity.

In all the procession of centuries gone, not one was for humanity. From the very first tyranny has flourished, freedom has failed; the few have ruled, the many have served; the parasite has worn the purple of power, while honest industry has lived in poverty and died in despair.

But the eternal years, the centuries yet to come, are for humanity and out of the misery of the past will rise the civilization of the future.

The nineteenth century evolved the liberating and humanizing movement; the twentieth century will witness its culmination in the crash of despotism and the rise of world-wide democracy, freedom and brotherhood.

It was while in exile, in 1864, that Hugo wrote:

"The transformation of the crowd into the people—profound task! It is to this labor that the men called Socialists have devoted themselves during the last forty years. The author of this book, however insignificant he may be, is one of the oldest in this labor. If he claims his place among these philosophers, it is because it is a place of persecution. A certain hatred of Socialism, very blind, but very general, has raged for fifteen or sixteen years, and is still raging most bitterly among the influential classes. Let it not be forgotten that true Socialism has for its end the elevation of the masses to the civic dignity, and that, therefore, the principal care is for moral and intellectual cultivation."

If, as we are quite ready to believe, the twentieth century realizes the prophecy of the French poet and "bursts full-blossomed on the thorny stem of time," as the century of humanity, it will be the denouement of the socialist agitation that began in the preceding century—the fruition of the international socialist movement.

In the closing years of the last century, following in the wake of the French revolution, the tendencies in Europe were unmistakably toward what has since developed into modern socialism. Of course the early stages were nebulous and vague, and the trend was not yet strongly marked or clearly disclosed.

But as the inventive genius of man asserted itself in the industrial world; as the use of steam as motive power expanded and machinery was introduced and its application to industry became more general, with its inevitable effects upon artisans, laborers and small tradesmen, the movement was accelerated in varying forms, chiefly utopian, until many years afterward, toward the middle of the nineteenth century, when it was crystallized by the genius of Marx, Engels, Lassalle and others, who caught the revolutionary current, clarified it and sent it circling around the globe on its mission of freedom and fraternity.

The earliest traces of socialism in the United States had their origin in the stream of immigration that flowed from the old world to the new and bore upon its bosom the germs of discontent warmed into life in the effete feudalism of European civilization.

We shall not here undertake to chronicle the many attempts, covering more than half a century, or until about 1840, to spread socialism or semi-socialistic doctrine among the American people and thus turn the tide of labor agitation in that direction. The times were fruitful of industrial and social unrest and the many schemes and plans that were proposed, utopian, impractical, impossible though they undoubtedly were, were at the same time the signs and symptoms of social gestation, the fore-runners of the mighty change that was laying hold of governments and institutions and destined to revolutionize them all and level the human race upward to the plane of an all-embracing civilization.

Almost eighty years ago Robert Owen, dreamer, enthusiast and humanitarian, came from England to America, to make the new continent blossom with utopian splendor. His series of experiments in communism, doomed to disappointment and failure, are an interesting study in the early years of the

American movement; and although in the light of our present knowledge of industrial evolution his undertaking may seem visionary and foolish to some, he rendered invaluable service in clearing away the brush and dispelling the fog; and the history of Socialism cannot be written without his name.

Decidedly less utopian and more practical and promising were the developments in the forties when what is known as Fourierism played its interesting and historic role in America.

Many of the most intellectual men and women of the day were attracted to the movement.

The most ardent enthusiasm seized the devotees and they set to work with hand and heart to convert the American wilderness into the promised land of milk and honey.

Of course the dominant strain was emotional and sympathetic, but there was nevertheless a solid sub-stratum of scientific soundness in the undertaking, as is proved conclusively by the writings of the men who so heartily gave it support.

Brook Farm, a beautiful reminiscence, tinged with disappointment, was founded near Boston in 1841. Among the many illustrious names associated with Brook Farm the following have peculiar interest after sixty years: George Ripley, Ralph Waldo Emerson, Horace Greeley, James Russell Lowell, John Greenleaf Whittier, William Cullen Bryant, Albert Brisbane, Ellery Channing, James Freeman Clarke, Theodore Parker, A. Bronson Alcott, John Thomas Codman, Henry D. Thoreau, Nathaniel Hawthorne, George Bancroft, Charles A. Dana and George William Curtis.

The Brook Farm Association, organized by "intellectuals" who had no knowledge of the laws of economic determinism or of the historic evolution of society, was ideal in conception and breathed the air of equality and brotherhood.

The association declared its object to be "a radical and universal reform, rather than to redress any particular wrong. * * *"

In the "preliminary statement" the members announced that the work they had undertaken was not a "mere resolution, but a necessary step in the progress which no one can be blind enough to think has yet reached its limit."

They said, furthermore: "We believe that humanity, trained

by these long centuries of suffering and struggle, led on by so many saints and heroes and sages, is at length prepared to enter into that universal order toward which it has perpetually moved."

"Thus * * * we declare that the imperative duty of this time and this country, nay, more, that its only salvation and the salvation of civilized countries, lies in the reorganization of society according to the unchanging laws of human nature and of universal harmony."

These passages are indicative of a clear perception for that time and would require but little remodeling to adapt them for incorporation into a modern scientific socialist platform.

The closing paragraph, which follows, is worthy to be preserved in socialist literature. It voices in lofty strain the conviction of the Brook Farmers in the ultimate realization of their hope for something like a co-operative commonwealth.

They say: "And whatever may be the result of any special efforts, we can never doubt that the object we have in view shall be finally attained; that human life shall yet be developed, not in discord and misery, but in harmony and joy, and that the perfected earth shall at last bear on her bosom a race of men worthy of the name."

This was written in January, 1844, and the whole document bears evidence of socialistic thought and tendencies.

Ralph Waldo Emerson wrote: "And truly, I honor the generous ideas of the socialists, the magnificence of their theories, and the enthusiasm with which they have been urged."

Albert Brisbane, Parke Godwin and Horace Greeley, the latter unique and in some respects the most clear-sighted and practical of them all, were commanding figures in that day.

All of them had human blood in their veins—all had democratic instincts and perceived more or less clearly the drift of the time, the tendency toward collective society, industrial freedom and social justice.

In the meantime Marx and his coadjutors were clearing the murky atmosphere of the old world. They were dissecting the prevailing mode of production and capitalist society in general and in their researches discovered the fundamental law of social development in the "materialistic conception of history," the scientific basis of socialist thought and activity throughout the world.

From this time forward the working class movement had a scientific foundation, the scattered and contentious factions were gradually united and harmonized, and socialism became a distinct and recognized factor in the industrial and political destiny of the race.

Following the example and taking inspiration from the pioneers of the old world, and re-enforced by the socialists who crossed the water and at once began the proselyting inherent in the revolutionary spirit, the Americans took heart; they entered upon their labors with renewed zeal, scattered the seed of socialist philosophy and it struck root in American soil.

Albert Brisbane was one of the commanding figures in inspiring and directing the American movement. He was a pronounced socialist and as early as 1840 set forth his views in a volume entitled "Social Destiny of Man: or Association and Reorganization of Industry."

In this work Brisbane made a strong plea and cogent argument in favor of co-operative industry and "an equitable distribution of profits to each individual."

Going to Europe in 1848, Brisbane for the first time met Karl Marx at Cologne, of whom he afterward wrote as follows: "I found there Karl Marx, the leader of the popular movement. The writings of Marx on Labor and Capital and the Social theories he then elaborated have had more influence on the great Socialistic movement of Europe than that of any other man. He it was who laid the foundation of that modern collectivism which at present bids fair to become the leading Socialist doctrine of Europe. He was then just rising into prominence; a man of some thirty years, short, solidly built, with a fine face and bushy black hair. His expression was that of great energy, and behind his self-contained reserve of manner were visible the fire and passion of a great soul.
*　　*　　*　　*　　*　　*　　*"

"Briefly stated, as represented by the collectivism of today, his doctrine demands the abolition of individual ownership of the natural wealth of the world—the soil, the mines, the inventions and creations of industry which are the means of production, as well as of the machinery of the world. This wealth, furnished by nature or created by the genius of humanity, is to be made collective property, held by the state (collectively) for the equal advantage of the whole body of the people. Governments are to represent the collective intelligence of the nation; to manage, direct and supervise all general operations and relations of an industrial character. * * *"

Brisbane traveled extensively in Europe, met the men of note in the principal countries, and studied the industrial and social conditions with a view to propagating the collectivist movement in the United States. On his return, filled with the spirit of enthusiasm, he vigorously entered upon his work of agitation and is fairly entitled to the credit of having rendered great service in the pioneer work of starting the Socialist movement in America.

Without desire to disparage any of the men of that time by invidious comparison, the immense personality and rustic simplicity, coupled with the keen perception, rugged honesty and intense earnestness of Horace Greeley, command special admiration.

The power of Greeley's influence in the early history of the Socialist movement in America, when hate and persecution were aroused by the mere mention of it, has never yet been fairly recognized. He has been called "our later Franklin" and deserves the title.

Parton, the biographer of Greeley, said: "The subject of Greeley's oratory is one alone; it is ever the same; the object of his public life is single. It is the *'Emancipation of Labor,'* its emancipation from ignorance, vice, servitude, insecurity, poverty. This is his chosen, *only* theme, whether he speaks from the platform or writes for the *Tribune.*"

Horace Greeley was in the true sense a *Labor Leader.* He was the first president of Typographical Union No. 6 of New York City and took advanced ground on every question that affected the working class.

There was nothing conservative about the views of Greeley on the labor question. He was, above all else, radical and progressive, that is to say, revolutionary, and the labor leaders of today could with credit to themselves and benefit to their organizations study his character and writings and follow his example.

The upheaval in Europe in 1848 forced many of the radicals and Socialists into exile; and the general tide that set in toward the western world bore many of these restless spirits to our shores; and no sooner were they landed before they began to sow the revolutionary seed and organize the propaganda they had been compelled to abandon on the other side.

The German Socialists who came over were the very men needed here at that time. They were trained and disciplined in the "old guard"; they had the rugged bearing and fearlessness of army veterans and they knew no such word as discouragement or failure.

Among these sturdy agitators William Weitling bore a conspicuous part in preparing the way for organization and for action along political lines.

From this time the propaganda became more active and also clearer and more definite in character.

The movement was gradually evolving from the haze of communism that clung to it through all its early years and was beginning to take form as an independent political organization with the central object of conquering the powers of government as a means of emancipating the working class from wage-slavery.

Labor unions, turner bunds and singing societies were organized all through the fifties, all tending in the same direction, and though not all pronounced, having substantially the same end in view.

In this brief sketch we have not the space to record in detail the many attempts that were made to organize a national working class political movement in the United States. This must be the work of the historian and fortunately for the reader and student he has recently appeared. The first authentic volume upon the subject is the "History of Socialism in the United States," by Morris Hillquit, a book of over three hundred and fifty pages, written in excellent style and treating ably and exhaustively the various stages of the development from its inception to the large and growing movement of our day.

The little volume entitled "A Brief History of Socialism in America," by Frederic Heath, editor of the *Social Democratic Herald,* a valuable collection of historical data to which has been added much original matter, both interesting and instructive, is also well worthy of perusal.

Professor Richard T. Ely, in his "Labor Movement in America," discussing the "Beginnings of Modern Socialism," says in reference to the period we are now considering: "The Socialism of today may be said to date from the European revolutions of 1848, all of which soon terminated disastrously for the people as opposed to their rulers. Many German refugees sought our shores, and some of them were ardent Socialists and Communists, who endeavored to propagate their ideas. Wilhelm Weitling, a tailor, born in Magdeburg in 1808, was prominent among these" * * * and "became one of the first to scatter those seeds of economic radicalism which have brought forth such large increase in the social democracy of our own times." * * *

"The first large society to adopt and propagate Socialism in America was composed of the German Gymnastic Unions (Turnvereine). The Socialistic Turverein of New York drew up a constitution for an association, to be composed of the various local gymnastic unions, and published it in 1850. A preliminary gathering of a few delegates was held in New York in the Shakespeare Hotel, then the headquarters of the 'progressive' elements among the Germans. It was finally decided to call a meeting of delegates, to be held in Philadelphia, on October 5th of the same year, to effect a permanent organization. Several Turnvereine acted on the suggestion, and among others, delegates were present from New York, Boston and Baltimore. The first name adopted was 'Associated Gymnastic Unions of North America,' which was, however, changed the following year to 'Socialist Gymnastic Union.'

Through the sixties and seventies the agitation steadily increased, local organizations were formed in various parts of the country, but they were chiefly for the passing day and after serving their temporary purpose, disappeared.

The American Civil War and the emancipation of the negro

race which followed, resulting in millions of "free" negroes being thrown upon the "labor market," had its effect in developing capitalist production.

The years following the war marked an era of extraordinary industrial and commercial activity. Inventive genius was taxed to provide machinery and the power necessary to operate it in factory, mill and mine. Manufacturing developed at an enormous rate. The railroads were penetrating the great west and the population spread over the vast domain.

Then came the symptoms of congestion, the glutted markets and the clogging of productive machinery.

The "good times" had come to a sudden end; factories and workshops closed down; railroads reduced wages and discharged thousands.

The country swarmed with unemployed workingmen; everybody was ominously discussing the "panic" and the "hard times."

Discontent was brewing and strikes were threatened by the idle workers.

The railroad strikes and many others broke out in the financial crisis of 1873.

It was a period of financial bankruptcy, industrial stagnation and general gloom.

The sheriff's hammer was heard everywhere beating the dolorous funeral marches of departed prosperity.

It was during this panic that the "tramp" era was inaugurated in the United States and the tramp became a recognized factor in our social life.

The trades-union movement had organized rapidly during the years of industrial prosperity. Many of the trades had formed national organizations and when the crash came, the strikes followed in rapid order.

In July, 1877, the railroad strikes, supported by the railroad brotherhoods, notably the Brotherhood of Locomotive Engineers and Brotherhood of Locomotive Firemen, waged with intense severity and resulting in widespread rioting, bloodshed and destruction of property, spread over a vast area of the country and threatened the direst consequences if the grievances of the strikers were not adjusted.

This was among the first strikes in which the writer had an active part and many incidents and scenes are remembered which would make an interesting chapter of proletarian history.

The stories of these strikes were written by Allan Pinkerton, the detective, in a curious volume entitled "Strikers, Communists, Tramps and Detectives." The volume has the portrait of the late P. M. Arthur, grand chief of the Brotherhood of Locomotive Engineers, who was then regarded as a radical labor agitator, as the frontispiece. It also contains a complete expose of the brotherhood, illustrated with diagrams and including its ceremony of initiation, signs, passwords and all of its secret inner workings.

The strikes spread rapidly east and west and were followed by rioting and violence in most of the railroad centers. The Pittsburg riots were the most disastrous in the loss of life and destruction of property. In his account of it, colored to suit the capitalistic interests he represented, Allan Pinkerton, describing the charge of the militia upon the mob, says:

"Suddenly a little puff of smoke shot out from a second story window, followed by a ringing report and a quick cry from a soldier who had been struck, but not dangerously wounded."

"Back along the column came the officers, exhorting the men to be patient and not return the fire.

"The speed of the troops increased. The energy of the mob redoubled. The pistol-shot from the window seemed almost a signal, for instantly afterwards, from along the crowd's front, several more shots were fired, and but a few minutes more had elapsed until from behind every lamp-post, over every hydrant head, and from out every door and window, shot the flame, shot the smoke, the flame and the bullets.

"Soldiers fell; and now their comrades returned the fire, while, as in every other instance, the disorganized, howling mob received far the worst punishment. Some of the wounded soldiers would escape with their lives through the devices, and at the personal risk, of humane people along the street who gave them help and shelter. Others, not so fortunate, were heartlessly murdered when too helpless for defense." * * *

"At one point where a good deal of killing had been done the previous day, and where a building at the corner of the streets not only was completely riddled with bullets, but bore evidence of the earnest efforts in behalf of religion by the Young Men's Christian Association in the shape of a poster upon which was placarded the startling warning: 'PREPARE TO MEET THY GOD."

The strikes were finally crushed out and the leaders driven out and blacklisted.

It was in this struggle that the powers of the federal courts were first invoked to break a railroad strike. The strike leaders and committees were arrested by order of the federal judges, sitting at Indianapolis, Ind., and committed to jail upon various trumped up charges.

The late President Benjamin Harrison had the exclusive distinction of having served the railway corporations in the dual capacity of lawyer and soldier. He prosecuted the strikers in the federal courts, securing prison sentences for them, and he also organized and commanded a company of soldiers during the strike, and made speeches denouncing the strikers.

Ten years later he was elevated to the presidency of the United States.

The loss of the strike was a staggering blow to organized labor, and many unions passed out of existence. Upon the railroads the mere suspicion of belonging to a union was sufficient ground for instant discharge.

In time, however, the ban was removed, the corporations feeling themselves the masters of the situation, and with returning financial and industrial activity, the work of organization was resumed with greater energy and determination than ever before.

In the events that followed swiftly during these years it will be noted that the United States had become entirely Europeanized in respect to the suppression of exploited and discontented workingmen.

It is scarcely necessary to observe in this connection that capitalism is the same everywhere, that like causes produce like results.

Wherever capitalism appears, in pursuit of its mission of

exploitation, there will Socialism, fertilized by misery, watered by tears, and vitalized by agitation be also found, unfurling its class-struggle banner and proclaiming its mission of emancipation.

During all of these years of strikes and strife, of occasional victory and frequent defeat for labor, the Socialist agitation was kept up as far as conditions and means would allow. Under the most unfavorable circumstances the comrades did what they could, held their ground and patiently waited for a more favorable turn in the situation.

Following the Paris Commune in 1871, and its tragic ending, many French radicals came to our shores and gave new spirit to the movement. Referring to these Professor Ely in his "Labor Movement in America," says:

"In 1871 a new impulse was received from the French refugees who came to America after the suppression of the uprising of the commune in Paris, and brought with them a spirit of violence, but a more important event in this early period was the order of the congress of the International held in the Hague in 1872, which transferred to New York the 'General Council' of the association. Modern Socialism had then undoubtedly begun to exist in America. The first proclamation of the Council from their new headquarters was an appeal to the workingmen 'to emancipate labor and eradicate all international and national strife.'"

"In the spring of 1872 'an imposing demonstration' in favor of eight hours took place in New York City. The paper before me estimates the number of those taking part in the procession through the principal streets at twenty thousand, and among the other societies were the various New York sections of the International Workingmen's Association, bearing a banner with their motto, 'Workingmen of all Countries, Unite!' The following year witnessed the disasters in the industrial and commercial world * * *; and the distress consequent thereupon was an important aid to their propaganda. The 'Exceptional Law' passed against Socialists, by the German Parliament in 1878, drove many Socialists from Germany to this country, and these have strengthened the cause of American Socialism through membership in trades-unions and in the Socialistic Labor Party."

"There have been several changes among the Socialists in party organization and name since 1873, and national conventions or congresses have met from time to time. Their dates and places of meeting have been Philadelphia, 1874; Pittsburg, 1876; Newark, 1877; Allegheny City, 1880; Baltimore and Pittsburg, 1883, and Cincinnati, 1885. The name Socialistic Labor Party was adopted in 1877 at the Newark convention. In 1883 the split between the moderates and extremists had become definite, and the latter held their congress in Pittsburg and the former in Baltimore."

In 1876 the Workingmen's Party was organized and in 1877, at the convention held at Newark, it became the Socialistic Labor Party. The course of the party was marked by bitter internal dissension. While the membership was largely made up of radicals they were elementally inharmonious and at cross purposes.

The common point of union was hostility to the prevailing regime; beyond that the trouble began, for the anarchists and communists were still in the same movement with the Socialists, having yet to be differentiated in the subsequent industrial and social development.

The Socialists were intent upon building up a working class party for independent political action; the anarchists repudiated the ballot and advocated the overthrow of capitalist rule by any means, including force.

August Spies, who was afterward executed for his alleged complicity in the Haymarket riots, was at this time a prominent member of the party. He used anarchism and socialism as synonymous terms. He said:

"Anarchism, or Socialism, means the reorganization of society upon scientific principles and the abolition of causes which produce vice and crime."

George Engel, who shared the same cruel fate, said:

"Anarchism and Socialism are as much alike, in my opinion, as one egg is to another. They differ only in their tactics. The anarchists have abandoned the way of liberating humanity which Socialists would take to accomplish this. I say: Believe no more in the ballot, and use all other means at your command."

These differences in tactics alluded to by Engel not only created violent dissensions in the party, but resulted in the withdrawal of the anarchists into groups of their own, followed later by the execution and imprisonment of their leaders because of their alleged participation in the Haymarket riots.

But with all the difficulties that confronted it on every hand and the fierce factional contention within its own ranks, the Socialist Labor Party, composed of thoughtful, intelligent men, aggressive and progressive, of rugged honesty and thrilled with the revolutionary spirit and the aspiration for freedom, became from its inception a decided factor in the labor movement. It first appeared upon the scene when the country was seething with discontent, the result of the prolonged period of financial and industrial depression that began in 1873 and like a scourge spread rapidly over the country, leaving desolation and gloom in its wake. To the working class it was an ordeal of fire, but the suffering and sacrifice were not in vain. Economic necessity determined the course of events and the workers, some of them at least, had their eyes opened to the cause of their misery and were thus impelled to action looking to the abolition of the existing industrial disorder, based upon wage-slavery, rather than giving themselves wholly, as they had hitherto done, to the fruitless task, as it now appeared, of ameliorating its effects and consequences. It was these men, led by the foreign radicals, who had long before been scourged by the capitalist masters in their own lands, who rallied to the revolutionary standard of the new working class party.

That such a party was born to a tempestuous career was, of course, a foregone conclusion. Its early trials and struggles tested the dauntless spirit of the comrades who engaged in them and constitute a thrilling chapter—which one day will be adequately understood and appreciated—in the labor movement of the United States.

The busy, ignorant world about this revolutionary nucleus knew little or nothing about it; had no conception of its significance and looked upon its adherents as foolish fanatics whose antics were harmless and whose designs would dissolve like bubbles on the surface of a stream.

Looking backward it is not difficult to see what importance

THE LIBRARY, DEBS' HOME (See Page 59)

attaches to this beginning of the political organization of the working class, as a class, for the distinct purpose of conquering the public powers and emancipating the toilers from the inhumanity of wage-slavery.

Discussing this period and the work covered by it, Morris Hillquit, in his "History of Socialism in the United States," says:

"The Socialist Labor Party was the dominant factor in the Socialist movement of this country for more than twenty years, and its variegated career forms the most intricate and interesting part of the history of American Socialism."

"At the first glance it appears a series of incoherent events, ill-considered political experiments, sudden changes of policy, incongruous alliances, internal and external strife, and a succession of unaccountable ups and downs, with no perceptible progress or gain."

"But the confusion is only apparent. On closer analysis we find a logical thread running all through the seemingly devious course of the party, and a good reason for every one of its seemingly planless moves."

"The difficulties which beset the path of the Socialist Labor Party were extraordinary. As one of the first Socialist parties organized in this country on a national scale, it had to cope with the usual adversities which attend every radical movement at the outset of its career—weakness and diffidence in its own ranks, hostility and ridicule from the outside."

These were stirring times. The trade-union movement was entering upon a period of unprecedented activity. The Knights of Labor were in the ascendant and other labor unions were multiplying and rapidly increasing their membership. Everywhere the voice of the agitator was heard. In March, 1885, was inaugurated the strike of the Knights of Labor on the Gould Southwest Railway system, to be followed by the greater strike on the same system in 1886, which spread rapidly over the states of Missouri, Illinois, Arkansas, Kansas and Texas, and threatened to involve the railway traffic of all the western and southwestern states. It was one of the most notable labor strikes and brought the Knights of Labor conspicuously before the whole country. The Knights were finally beaten, although the fight was so stubbornly contested and the public was so thoroughly aroused that Congress was prevailed upon to investigate the trouble and the committee issued a detailed report in two parts, containing about eleven hundred pages.

On May 1 of the same year the general strikes for the eight hour work day broke out in various parts of the country, involving several hundred thousand organized workers, most of whom met with disappointment and failure.

The agitation carried on during this time for the shorter work day, known as the eight hour movement, culminated on May 4, 1886, in the Haymarket riots at Chicago, and the outrageous execution of the anarchists on November 11 of the following year, a foul blot on our capitalistic civilization that will remain to damn it forever.

The murderous assaults upon peaceable meetings and the brutal clubbing of orderly workingmen by the police of Chicago at the behest of their political superiors, the tools of the capitalist class, goaded the leaders almost to desperation and led to the Haymarket massacre, a fiendish plot to silence the agitation and crush the movement for an eight hour work day which was spreading over the country; and, it must be confessed, it served for a time at least the malign purpose of the pretended supporters of "law and order." But as certain as retributive justice pursues her course, the dragon's teeth sown by the capitalist hand in the Haymarket tragedy, taking root in the blood of innocent workingmen, will yet spring from the pregnant soil of freedom to avenge the crimes of plutocratic tyranny and misrule.

In 1884 Laurence Gronlund published his "Co-Operative Commonwealth," and he was doubtless right when he claimed, six years later, that this work had contributed its full share to the spread of Socialism. Gronlund said that as late as 1880 he could count all the native American Socialists on the fingers of one hand. When the patient labors, the bitter poverty and shocking privations of this pioneer Socialist are taken into account, his untimely and almost tragic death seems to have been, after all, a blessed balm to his weary soul. He gave his life to civilize the world and was rewarded with suffering and death.

Four years after Gronlund's "Co-Operative Commonwealth" appeared, in 1888, Edward Bellamy published his "Looking Backward," and it had a most wonderful effect upon the people. He struck a responsive popular chord and his name was upon every tongue. The editions ran into the hundreds of thousands and the people were profoundly stirred by what was called the vision of a poetic dreamer. Although not an exposition of scientific socialism, Bellamy's social romance, "Looking Backward," with its sequel, "Equality," were valuable and timely contributions to the literature of Socialism and not only aroused the people but started many on the road to the revolutionary movement. The quick and wide response to the author's plea for a social readjustment evinced not only the discontent of the people, but their eager readiness to grasp at anything that might give promise of escape from the poverty, the insecurity, the daily horrors of the existing order. Thousands were moved to study the question by the books of Bellamy and thus became Socialists and found their way into the Socialist movement.

In February, 1888, the strike occurred on the Burlington system, involving all its engineers and firemen and some of its brakemen and switchmen. P. M. Arthur, then grand chief of the Brotherhood of Locomotive Engineers, was threatened with federal court proceedings on account of a boycott which had been placed upon the C., B. & Q. cars and was so effective that it looked as if a complete tie-up of traffic would result from it. The boycott was raised and the strike began to wane. But the contest continued almost a year and it cost the brotherhoods fully two million dollars. At last, however, the strikers were exhausted and compelled to yield to total defeat.

Thus was it proved by the loss of another great railroad strike—not one of which was ever won by the brotherhoods—that when the supreme test of strength comes the railway unions are always crushed by the railway corporations.

The defeat of this and other strikes, together with the fact that most railway employes were ineligible to the then existing brotherhoods, led to the organization of the American Railway Union in 1893, which embraced all the employes in the railway service. The new union grew rapidly. Soon after it was organized it engaged in and won several minor strikes. In April,

1894, the strike on the Great Northern, involving all the employes of the entire system, was fought, and resulted in a complete victory for the union in less than three weeks. A short time later another strike was threatened owing to disagreement growing out of the construction of the agreement. For the second time the A. R. U. came out victorious. At this time thousands were pouring into the union all over the country. Then followed the Pullman strike, in the latter part of June.

The Pullman company, backed by the combined railway corporations, represented by the General Managers' Association, resolved to crush the union. They not only failed, but the union paralyzed their traffic and defeated them all. Seeing that the union was triumphant they changed their tactics. They had the United States marshal of Illinois swear in an army of deputies, ostensibly to protect property, but in fact to incite tumult. In his official report to the council of Chicago the Chief of Police said that these "deputies" consisted of thieves, thugs and ex-convicts, the worst element that had ever been turned loose on any city. As soon as the deputies began to operate, as directed by their leaders, and under cover of night, trouble began, and this is what the corporations wanted. Peace and order were fatal to them as turbulence and violence were fatal to the union. They understood this perfectly. Hence the deputies and disorder. Immediately these thugs began to perform, the capitalist papers and Associated Press flashed broadcast the falsehood that the strikers were on the warpath and threatened destruction to every living thing. The falsehood caught on like magic. Far and wide the cry went up: "Down with the A. R. U.! Down with anarchy!" The tide turned. The triumphant union and defeated corporations changed places. With practically the whole population aroused against the A. R. U. every outrage upon it was not only possible, but perpetrated with mad zeal in the name of patriotism. The A. R. U. had no press, no way of getting its side before the people, and thousands of the very workers in whose behalf it was fighting and had staked everything, turned upon it and joined in the flood of angry denunciation that was launched upon it.

Injunctions by the hundred were issued and served by all

the courts between the Ohio and the Pacific. A half dozen burly ruffians, by order of the federal authorities—precisely whom could never be learned—backed up a cart at the union headquarters, forced their way into the offices, sacked them, taking records, books, private papers and unopened letters, without warrant of any description, nailing up the headquarters and hauling the booty to the federal building.

How is this for a specimen of "law and order" the capitalist class and their brood of hirelings so ceaselessly harp about?

In violation of law and precedent and in defiance of the protest of the governor of Illinois, the mayor of Chicago and an overwhelming majority of the people, Grover Cleveland, then President of the United States, forced the federal troops into the state for the sole purpose of aiding the corporations to crush the union and defeat the strike, and when history shall be truthfully written, this crime will make the name of Cleveland the synonym of infamy forever.

Thousands of falsehoods were coined and circulated by the capitalist press, shifting the blame of lawlessness and crime from the instigators to innocent men; the leaders were arrested without charges and jailed without trial, headquarters were broken up, a special grand jury was sworn in expressly to indict, a notorious capitalist union-hater being made foreman, and a hundred other flagrant violations of the law and outrages upon justice were committed in the name of law to defeat justice and enthrone corporate rapacity.

The venality of capitalist government never made so bold an exhibition of itself. It was scandalous beyond expression and shocking to the last degree. Every department of the federal government was freely placed at the service of the railroad corporations and Republican and Democratic officials vied with each other in cheerful and servile obedience to their masters.

When the government and its capitalist lackeys had completed their service as corporation scavengers, General Miles, the military satrap, like a vulture stuffed with carrion, pompously exclaimed at a plutocratic banquet in honor of his gallant services:

"*I have broken the backbone of this strike.*"

Such sublime heroism in such a holy cause, Grover Cleveland, Nelson Miles, et al., will not be forgotten nor remain unrewarded.

The *Coming Nation*, started at Greensburg, Ind., by J. A. Wayland, in 1893, was the first popular propaganda paper to be published in the interest of Socialism in this country. It reached a large circulation and the proceeds were used in founding and developing the Ruskin Co-operative colony in Tennessee. Later Mr. Wayland began the publication of the *Appeal to Reason*, and now it numbers its subscribers by the hundreds of thousands. It is not saying too much for the *Appeal* that it has been a great factor in preparing the American soil for the seed of Socialism. Its enormous editions have been and are being spread broadcast and copies may be found in the remotest recesses and the most inaccessible regions. The propaganda thus organized by Mr. Wayland, for which he has peculiar genius, and carried forward and enlarged constantly with the aid of a corps of able comrades, has been and is a source of incalculable strength in promoting education among the workers and building up the general movement.

The periodical and weekly press, so necessary to any political movement, is now developing rapidly and there is every reason to believe that within the next few years there will be a formidable array of reviews, magazines, illustrated journals and daily and weekly papers to represent the movement and do battle for its supremacy.

The last convention of the American Railway Union was the first convention of the Social Democracy of America, and this was held at Chicago in June, 1897, the delegates voting to change the railway union into a working class political party.

The *Railway Times*, the official paper of the union, became the *Social Democrat* and later the *Social Democratic Herald*, and is now published at Milwaukee in the interest of the Socialist party.

The Social Democracy, the evolution of unionism crushed by the weight of despotic power, was the logical extension and expansion of the American Railway Union, and the direct outgrowth of the great industrial uprising known as the Pullman strike and the brutal tyranny and relentless persecution that followed it.

The General Managers' Association pursued the American Railway Union with fiendish ferocity, determined to stamp out the last spark of its life, and as a result, when the few surviving delegates met in national convention in the year named, the last they ever held as a railway labor union, the American Railway Union, loved and respected by labor, and feared and hated by capital, was metamorphosed into the Social Democracy.

At the national convention which followed a year later, in June, 1898, a split occurred, one wing adhering to the colonization scheme, making that the chief end of their movement, while the latter abandoned the colonization feature and struck out for political action as a working class party. The latter was known as the Social Democratic Party and progressed rapidly from the start, while the former soon exhausted its resources and passed out of existence.

The Socialist Labor Party, in which internal dissension had been brewing for some time, divided into separate factions in July, 1899, the anti-administration faction uniting with the Social Democratic Party in the following year, giving the united party the name of the Socialist Party, the name it bears today.

In the brief summary of the development of the American movement much has had to be omitted for the want of space. To sketch in outline merely, with the hope of stimulating to further reading and study of the history and literature of the Socialist movement has been the purpose of this brief treatise.

Scarcely, however, can reference be omitted to the helpful influence of the popular pen of Robert Blatchford, the author of "Merrie England" and other works, and one of the most simple, attractive and convincing writers on Socialism in all the world. Hundreds of thousands of copies of "Merrie England" have been sold and given away and the demand still continues. The work of Mr. Blatchford is specially adapted to beginners. He has the rare faculty of making himself interesting to the workingman and working woman, addressing himself to them in their own simple language and illustrating his argument in the same simple and convincing fashion. Robert Blatchford and his writings have contributed materially to the spread of Socialism in this country and are justly entitled to the grateful acknowledgment of the American movement.

Reference to Karl Marx, Ferdinand Lassalle, Frederick Engels, William Liebknecht and August Bebel, the titans of revolutionary socialism, and their contemporaries and successors, need not be made in these brief pages, nor to the Socialist classics which are so well known and may be read in all languages.

The immortal shibboleth of Marx: "Workingmen of all countries, unite! You have nothing to lose but your chains—you have a world to gain," is the rallying cry of the class struggle, the inspiration of the working class, and is heard echoing and re-echoing around the world.

The Socialist vote in the United States shows a steady and, all things considered, satisfactory progress of the movement.

In the national election of 1892 the Socialist vote was 21,164.

In 1896 the vote was 36,274.

In 1900 the Socialist Party cast 87,814 votes and the Socialist Labor Party 39,739 votes, a total of 127,553 votes.

Since the election of 1900 there has been greater activity in organizing and a more widespread propaganda than ever before. In the elections of the past it can scarcely be claimed that the Socialist movement was represented by a national party. It entered these contests with but few states organized and with no resources worth mentioning to sustain it during the campaign.

It is far different today.

The Socialist party is organized in almost every state and territory in the American Union. Its members are filled with enthusiasm and working with an energy born of the throb and thrill of revolution. The party has a press supporting it that extends from sea to sea, and is as vigilant and tireless in its labors as it is steadfast and true to the party principles.

The Socialist party stands upon a sound platform, embodying the principles of International Socialism, clearly and eloquently expressed, and proclaims its mission of conquest on the basis of the class struggle. Its tactics are in harmony with its principles, and both are absolutely uncompromising.

Viewed today from any intelligent standpoint the outlook of the Socialist movement is full of promise to the workers of coming freedom.

It is the break of dawn upon the horizon of human destiny and it has no limitations but the walls of the universe.

What party strife or factional turmoil may yet ensue we neither know nor care. We only know that the principles of Socialism are necessary to the emancipation of the working class and to the true happiness of all classes and that its historic mission is that of a conquering movement. We know that day by day, nourished by the misery and vitalized by the aspirations of the working class, the area of its activity widens, it grows in strength and increases its mental and moral grasp, and when the final hour of capitalism and wage slavery strikes, the Socialist movement, the greatest in all history—great enough to embrace the human race—will crown the class struggles of the centuries with victory and proclaim FREEDOM TO ALL MANKIND.

Unionism and Socialism

The labor question, as it is called, has come to be recognized as the foremost of our time. In some form it thrusts itself into every human relation, and directly or indirectly has a part in every controversy.

A thousand "solutions" of the labor question find their way into print, but the question not only remains unsolved, but steadily assumes greater and graver proportions. The nostrums have no effect other than to prove their own inefficacy.

There has always been a labor question since man first exploited man in the struggle for existence, but not until its true meaning was revealed in the development of modern industry did it command serious thought or intelligent consideration, and only then came any adequate conception of its importance to the race.

Man has always sought the mastery of his fellow-man. To enslave his fellow in some form and to live out of his labor has been the mainspring of human action.

To escape submission, not in freedom, but in mastery over others, has been the controlling desire, and this has filled the world with slavery and crime.

In all the ages of the past, human society has been organized and maintained upon the basis of the exploitation and degradation of those who toil. And so it is today.

The chief end of government has been and is to keep the victims of oppression and injustice in subjection.

The men and women who toil and produce have been and are at the mercy of those who wax fat and scornful upon the fruit of their labor.

The labor question was born of the first pang of protest that died unvoiced in the breast of unrequited toil.

The labor movement of modern times is the product of past ages. It has come down to us for the impetus of our day, in pursuit of its world-wide mission of emancipation.

Unionism, as applied to labor in the modern sense, is the fruit and flower of the last century.

In the United States, as in other countries, the trade union dates from the beginning of industrial society.

During the colonial period of our history, when agriculture was the principal pursuit, when the shop was small and work was done by hand with simple tools, and the worker could virtually employ himself, there was no unionism among the workers.

When machinery was applied to industry, and mill and factory took the place of the country blacksmith shop; when the workers were divorced from their tools and recruited in the mills; when they were obliged to compete against each other for employment; when they found themselves in the labor market with but a low bid or none at all upon their labor power; when they began to realize that as toolless workingmen they were at the mercy of the tool-owning masters, the necessity for union among them took root, and as industry developed, the trade union movement followed in its wake and became a factor in the struggle of the workers against the aggressions of their employers.

In his search for the beginnings of trade unionism in our country, Prof. Richard T. Ely, in his "Labor Movement in America," says: "I find no traces of anything like a modern trades union in the colonial period of American history, and it is evident, on reflection, that there was little need, if any, of organization on the part of labor at that time." * * *

"Such manufacturing as was found consisted largely in the production of values-in-use. Clothing, for example, was spun and woven, and then converted into garments in the household for its various members. The artisans comprised chiefly the carpenter, the blacksmith and the shoemaker; many of whom worked in their own little shops with no employes, while the number of subordinates in any one shop was almost invariably small, and it would probably have been difficult to find a journeyman who did not expect in a few years, to become an independent producer."

This was the general condition from the labor standpoint at the close of the eighteenth century. But with the dawn of the new century and the application of machinery and the spread of industry that followed came the beginning of the change. The workers gradually organized into unions and began to take active measures to increase their wages and otherwise improve their condition. Referring to this early period in the rise of unionism, the same author records the incident of one of the first strikes as follows: "Something very like a modern strike occurred in the year 1802. The sailors in New York received $10 a month, but wished an increase of $4 a month, and endeavored to enforce their demands by quitting work. It is said that they marched about the city, accompanied by a band, and compelled seamen, employed at the old wages, to leave their ships and join them. But the iniquitous combination and conspiracy laws, which viewed concerted action of laborers as a crime, were then in force in all modern lands, and 'the constables were soon in pursuit, arrested the leader, lodged him in jail, and so ended the earliest of labor strikes.'"

This sounds as if it had been the occurrence of yesterday, instead of more than a hundred years ago. The combination and conspiracy laws have been repealed, but the labor leader fares no better now than when these laws were still on the statute books. The writ of injunction is now made to serve the purpose of the master class, and there is no possible situation in which it cannot be made to apply and as swiftly and surely strike the vital point and paralyze the opposition to the master's rule.

We need not at this time trace the growth of the trade union from its small and local beginnings to its present national and international proportions; from the little group of hand-workers in the service of an individual employer to the armies of organized and federated workers in allied industries controlled by vast corporations, syndicates and trusts. The fact stands forth in bold relief that the union was born of necessity and that it has grown strong with the development of industry and the increasing economic dependence of the workers.

A century ago a boy served his apprenticeship and became the master of his trade. The few simple tools with which work was then done were generally owned by the man who used them; he could provide himself with the small quantity of raw material he required, and freely follow his chosen pursuit and enjoy the fruit of his labor. But as everything had to be produced by the work of his hands, production was a slow process, meagre of results, and the worker found it necessary to devote from twelve to fifteen hours to his daily task to earn a sufficient amount to support himself and family.

It required most of the time and energy of the average worker to produce enough to satisfy the physical wants of himself and those dependent upon his labor.

There was little leisure for mental improvement, for recreation or social intercourse. The best that can be said for the workingman of this period is that he enjoyed political freedom, controlled in large measure his own employment, by virtue of his owning the tools of his trade, appropriated to his own use the product of his labor and lived his quiet, uneventful round to the end of his days.

This was a new country, with boundless stretches of virgin soil. There was ample room and opportunity, air and sunlight, for all.

There was no millionaire in the United States; nor was there a tramp. These types are the products of the same system. The former is produced at the expense of the latter, and both at the expense of the working class. They appeared at the same time in the industrial development and they will disappear together with the abolition of the system that brought them into existence.

The application of machinery to productive industry was followed by tremendous and far-reaching changes in the whole structure of society. First among these was the change in the status of the worker, who, from an independent mechanic or small producer, was reduced to the level of a dependent wage-worker. The machine had leaped, as it were, into the arena of industrial activity, and had left little or no room for the application of the worker's skill or the use of his individual tools.

The economic dependence of the working class became more and more rigidly fixed—and at the same time a new era dawned for the human race.

The more or less isolated individual artisans were converted into groups of associated workers and marshalled for the impending social revolution.

It was at this time that the trades-union movement began to take definite form. Unorganized, the workers were not only in open competition with each other for the sale of their labor power in the labor market, but their wages could be reduced, and their hours of labor lengthened at will, and they were left practically at the mercy of their employers.

It is interesting to note the spirit evinced by the pioneers of unionism, the causes that impelled them and the reasons they assigned for banding themselves together in defense of their common interests. In this connection we again quote from Professor Ely's "Labor Movement in America," as follows:

"The next event to attract our attention in New York is an address delivered before 'The General Trades Unions of the City of New York,' at Chatham street chapel, on December 2, 1833, by Eli Moore, president of the union. This General Trades Union, as its name indicates, was a combination of subordinate unions 'of the various trades and arts in New York City and its vicinity,' and is the earliest example in the United States, so far as I know, of those Central Labor Unions which attempt to unite all the workingmen in one locality in one body, and which have now become so common among us. The address of Mr. Moore is characterized by a more modern tone than is found in most productions of the labor leaders of that period. The object of these unions is stated to be 'to guard against the encroachments of aristocracy, to preserve our natural and political rights, to elevate our moral and intellectual condition, to promote our pecuniary interests, to narrow the line of distinction between the journeyman and employer, to establish the honor and safety of our respective vocations upon a more secure and permanent basis, and to alleviate the distress of those suffering from want of employment.'"

This is a remarkably clear statement of the objects of unionism in that early period, and indicates to what extent workingmen had even then been compelled to recognize their craft interests and unite and act together in defense thereof.

So far, and for many years later, the efforts of trades-unions were confined to defensive tactics, and to the amelioration of objectionable conditions. The wage-system had yet to develop its most offensive features and awaken the workers to the necessity of putting an end to it as the only means of achieving their freedom; and it was this that finally forced the extension of organized activity from the economic to the political field of labor unionism.

As the use of machinery became more general and competition became more intense; as capital was centralized and industry organized to obtain better results, the workers realized their dependence more and more, and unionism grew apace. One trade after another fell into line and raised the banner of economic solidarity. Then followed strikes and lockouts and other devices incident to that form of warfare. Sometimes the unionists gained an advantage, but more often they suffered defeat, lost courage and abandoned the union, only to return to the scene of disaster with renewed determination to fight the battle over again and again until victory should at last perch upon the union banner.

Oh, how many there were, whose names are forgotten, who suffered untold agonies to lay the foundation of the labor movement, of whose real mission they had but the vaguest conception!

These pioneers of progress paved the way for us, and deserve far more at our hands than we have in our power to do for them. We may at best rescue their nameless memory from the darkness of oblivion, and this we undertake to do with the liveliest sense of obligation for the service they rendered, and the sacrifices they made in the early and trying stages of the struggle to improve the condition and advance the welfare of their fellow-toilers.

The writer has met and known some of these untitled agitators of the earlier day, whose hearts were set on organizing their class, or at least, their branch of it, and who had the courage to undertake the task and accept all the bitter consequences it imposed.

The union men of today have little or no conception of what the pioneer unionists had to contend with when they first started forth on their mission of organization. The organizer of the present time has to face difficulties enough, it is true,

MR. DEBS AND HIS LITTLE GIRARD COMRADES (See Page 243)

but as a rule the road has at least been broken for his approaching footsteps; the union has already been organized and a committee meets him at the station and escorts him to the hotel.

Far different was it with the pioneer who left home without "scrip in his purse," whose chief stock consisted in his ability to "screw his courage to the sticking point" and whom privation and hardship only consecrated more completely to his self-appointed martyrdom.

Starting out, more than likely, after having been discharged for organizing a local union of his craft, or for serving on a committee, or interceding for a fellow, or "talking back" to the boss, or any other of the numerous acts which mark the conduct of the manly worker, distinguishing him from his weak and fawning brother, and bringing upon him the reprobation of his master—starting out to organize his fellow-workers, that they might fare better than fell to his lot, he faced the world without a friend to bid him welcome, or cheer him onward. Having no money for railroad fare he must beat his way, but such a slight inconvenience does not deter him an instant. Reaching his destination he brushes up as well as his scanty toilet will allow and then proceeds with due caution to look up "the boys," careful to elude the vigilance of the boss, who has no earthly use for a worthless labor agitator.

We shall not attempt to follow our pioneer through all his tortuous windings, nor have we space to more than hint at the story of his cruel persecution and pathetic end.

Our pioneer, leaving home, in many an instance, never saw wife and child again. Repulsed by the very men he was hungering to serve, penniless, deserted, neglected and alone, he became "the poor wanderer of a stormy day," and ended his career a nameless outcast. Whatever his frailties and faults, they were virtues all, for they marked the generous heart, the sympathetic soul who loves his brother and accepts for himself the bitter portion of suffering and shame that he may serve his fellowman.

The labor agitator of the early day held no office, had no title, drew no salary, saw no footlights, heard no applause, never saw his name in print, and fills an unknown grave.

The labor movement is his monument, and though his name is not inscribed upon it, his soul is in it, and with it marches on forever.

From the small beginnings of a century ago the trades-union movement, keeping pace with the industrial development, has become a tremendous power in the land.

The close of the Civil War was followed by a new era of industrial and commercial activity, and trades-unions sprang up on every hand. Local organizations of the same craft multiplied and were united in national bodies, and these were in time bound together in national and international federation.

The swift and vast concentration of capital and the unprecedented industrial activity which marked the close of the nineteenth century were followed by the most extraordinary growth in the number and variety of trades-unions in the history of the movement; yet this expansion, remarkable as it was, has not only been equalled, but excelled, in the first years of the new century, the tide of unionism sweeping over the whole country, and rising steadily higher, notwithstanding the efforts put forth from a hundred sources controlled by the ruling class to restrain its march, impair its utility or stamp it out of existence.

The history of the last thirty years of trades-unionism is filled with stirring incident and supplies abundant material for a good-sized volume. Organizations have risen and fallen, battles have been fought with varying results, every device known to the ingenuity of the ruling class has been employed to check the movement, but through it all the trend has been steadily toward a more perfect organization and a more comprehensive grasp of its mighty mission. The strikes and boycots and lockouts which occurred with startling frequency during this period, some of them accompanied by riots and other forms of violence, tell their own tragic story of the class struggle which is shaking the foundations of society, and will end only with the complete overthrow of the wage-system and the freedom of the working class from every form of slavery.

No strike has even been lost, and there can be no defeat for the labor movement.

However disastrous the day of battle has been, it has been worth its price, and only the scars remain to bear testimony that the movement is invincible and that no mortal wound can be inflicted upon it.

What has the union done for the worker? Far more than these brief pages will allow us to place on record.

The union has from its inception taught, however imperfectly, the fundamental need of solidarity; it has inspired hope in the breast of the defeated and despairing worker, joining his hand with the hand of his fellow-worker and bidding them lift their bowed bodies from the earth and look above and beyond the tribulations of the hour to the shining heights of future achievement.

The union has fought the battles of the worker upon a thousand fields, and though defeated often, rallied and charged again and again to wrest from the enemy the laurels of victory.

The union was first to trace in outline the lesson above all others the workingman needs to learn, and that is the collective interest and welfare of his class, in which his own is indissolubly bound, and that no vital or permanent change of conditions is possible that does not embrace his class as a whole.

The union has been a moral stimulus as well as a material aid to the worker; it has appealed to him to develop his faculties and to think for himself; to cultivate self-reliance and learn to depend upon himself; to have pride of character and make some effort to improve himself; to sympathize with and support his fellow-workers and make their cause his own.

Although these things have as yet been only vaguely and imperfectly accomplished, yet they started in and have grown with the union, and to this extent the union has promoted the class-conscious solidarity of the working-class.

It is true that the trades-union movement has in some essential respects proved a disappointment, but it may not on this account be repudiated as a failure. The worst that can in truth be said of it is that it has not kept up with the procession of events, that it lacks the progressive spirit so necessary to its higher development and larger usefulness, but there are reasons for this and they suggest themselves to the most casual student of the movement.

When workingmen first began to organize unions every effort was made by the employing class to stamp out the incipient "rebellion." This was kept up for years, but in spite of all that could be done to extinguish the fires of revolt, the smouldering embers broke forth again and again, each time with increased intensity and vigor; and when at last it became apparent to the shrewder and more far-seeing members of the capitalist family that the union movement had come to stay, they forthwith changed their tactics, discarding their frowns and masking their features with the most artful smiles as they extended their greeting and pronounced their blessing upon this latest and greatest benefaction to the human race.

In fewer words, seeing that they could not head it off, they decided to take it by the hand and guide it into harmless channels.

This is precisely the policy pursued, first and last, by the late Marcus A. Hanna, and it will not be denied that he had the entire confidence of the capitalist class and that they clearly recognized his keen perception, astute diplomacy and sagacious leadership in dealing with the union movement.

Mr. Hanna denominated the national leaders of the trades-unions as his "lieutenants;" had the "Civic Federation" organized and himself elected president, that he and his lieutenants might meet upon equal ground and as often as necessary; he slapped them familiarly on the back, had his picture taken with them and cracked jokes with them; and all the time he was doing this he was the beau ideal of Wall street, the ruling voice in the capitalist councils, and all the trusts, syndicates and combines, all the magnates, barons, lords and plutocrats in one voice proclaimed him the ruler of rulers, the political prophet of their class, the corner stone and central pillar in the capitalist temple.

Mr. Hanna did not live to see his plan of "benevolent feudalism" consummated, nor to be elected President of the United States, as his Wall street admirers and trades-union friends intended, but he did live long enough to see the gathering clouds of the social revolution on the political horizon; and to prevent the trades-union movement from becoming a factor in it, he taxed the resources of his fertile brain and bended all the energies of his indomitable will. Clearer sighted than all others of his class, he was promptly crowned their leader. He saw what was coming and prepared to meet and defeat it, or at least put off the crisis to a later day.

The trades-union movement must remain a "pure and simple" organization. It must not be subject to the laws of evolution; it must be securely anchored to its conservative, time-honored policy, hold fast to its good name and preserve inviolate all the traditions of the past. Finally, it must eschew politics as utterly destructive of trades-union ends, and above all, beware of and guard against the contamination of socialism, whose breath is disruption and whose touch is death.

That was the position of Senator Hanna; it is that of the smaller lights who are serving as his successors. It is this position that is taken by the press, the pulpit and the politician; it is this position that is reflected in the trades-union movement itself, and voiced by its officials, who are at once the leaders of labor and the lieutenants of capital, and who, in their dual role, find it more and more difficult to harmonize the conflicting interests of the class of whom they are the leaders and the class of whom they are the lieutenants.

It is not claimed for a moment that these leaders are corrupt in the sense that they would betray their trust for a consideration. Such charges and intimations are frequently made, but so far as we know they are baseless and unjust in almost every instance; and it is our opinion that an accusation of such gravity is never justified, whatever the circumstances, unless the proof can be furnished to support the charge and convict the offender.

But the criticism to which these leaders are properly subject is that they fear to offend the capitalist class, well knowing that the influence of this class is potential in the labor union, and that if the labor lieutenant fails of obedience and respect to his superior capitalist officers, he can soon be made to feel their displeasure, and unless he relents, his popularity wanes and he finds himself a leader without an office.

The late Peter M. Arthur, of the Brotherhood of Locomotive Engineers, was a conspicuous example of this kind of leadership. There was frequently the most violent opposition to him, but his standing with the railway corporations secured him in his position, and it was simply impossible to dislodge him. Had he been radical instead of conservative, had he stood wholly on the side of the engineers instead of cultivating the good offices of the managers and placating the corporations, he would have been deposed years ago and pronounced a miserable failure as a labor leader.

The capitalist press has much to do with shaping the course of a labor leader; he shrinks from its cruel attacks and he yields, sometimes unconsciously, to its blandishments and honeyed phrases, and in spite of himself becomes a servile trimmer and cowardly time-server.

The trades-union movement of the present day has enemies within and without, and upon all sides, some attacking it openly and others insidiously, but all bent either upon destroying it or reducing it to unresisting impotency.

The enemies of unionism, while differing in method, are united solidly upon one point, and that is in the effort to misrepresent and discredit the men who, scorning and defying the capitalist exploiters and their minions, point steadily the straight and uncompromising course the movement must take if it is to accomplish its allotted task and safely reach its destined port.

These men, though frequently regarded as the enemies, are the true friends of trades-unionism and in good time are certain to be vindicated.

The more or less open enemies have inaugurated some interesting innovations during the past few years. The private armies the corporations used some years ago, such as Pinkerton mercenaries, coal and iron police, deputy marshals, etc., have been relegated to second place as out of date, or they are wholly out of commission. It has been found after repeated experiments that the courts are far more deadly to trades-unions, and that they operate noiselessly and with unerring precision.

The rapid fire injunction is a great improvement on the

gatling gun. Nothing can get beyond its range and it never misses fire.

The capitalists are in entire control of the injunction artillery, and all the judicial gunner has to do is to touch it off at their command.

Step by step the writ of injunction has invaded the domain of trades-unionism, limiting its jurisdiction, curtailing its powers, sapping its strength and undermining its foundations, and this has been done by the courts in the name of the institutions they were designed to safeguard, but have shamelessly betrayed at the behest of the barons of capitalism.

Injunctions have been issued restraining the trades-unions and their members from striking, from boycotting, from voting funds to strikes, from levying assessments to support their members, from walking on the public highway, from asking non-union men not to take their places, from meeting to oppose wage reductions, from expelling a spy from membership, from holding conversation with those who had taken or were about to take their jobs, from congregating in public places, from holding meetings, from doing anything and everything, directly, indirectly or any other way, to interfere with the employing class in their unalienable right to operate their plants as their own interests may dictate, and to run things generally to suit themselves.

The courts have found it in line with judicial procedure to strike every weapon from labor's economic hand and leave it defenseless at the mercy of its exploiter; and now that the courts have gone to the last extremity in this nefarious plot of subjugation, labor, at last, is waking up to the fact that it has not been using its political arm in the struggle at all; that the ballot which it can wield is strong enough not only to disarm the enemy, but to drive that enemy entirely from the field.

The courts, so notoriously in control of capital, and so shamelessly perverted to its base and sordid purposes is, therefore, exercising a wholesome effect upon trades-unionism by compelling the members to note the class character of our capitalist government and driving them to the inevitable conclusion that the labor question is also a political question and that the working class must organize their political power that they may wrest the government from capitalist control and put an end to class rule forever.

Trades-unionists for the most part learn slowly, but they learn surely, and fresh object lessons are prepared for them every day.

They have seen a Democratic President of the United States send the federal troops into a sovereign state of the Union in violation of the constitution, and in defiance of the protest of the governor and the people, to crush a body of peaceable workingmen at the behest of a combination of railroads bent on destroying their union and reducing them to vassalage.

They have seen a Republican President refuse to interpose his executive authority when militarism, in the name of the capitalist class, seized another sovereign state by the throat and strangled its civil administration to death while it committed the most dastardly crimes upon defenseless workingmen in the annals of capitalist brutality and military despotism.

They have seen a composite Republican-Democratic congress, the legislative tool of the exploiting class, pass a military bill which makes every citizen a soldier and the President a military dictator.

They have seen this same congress, session after session, making false promises to deluded labor committees; pretending to be the friends of workingmen and anxious to be of service to them, while at the same time in league with the capitalist lobby and pledged to defeat every measure that would afford even the slightest promise of relief to the working class. The anti-injunction bill and the eight hour measure, pigeon-holed and rejected again and again in the face of repeated promises that they should pass, tell their own story of duplicity and treachery to labor of the highest legislative body in the land.

They have seen Republican governors and Democratic governors order out the militia repeatedly to shoot down workingmen at the command of their capitalist masters.

They have seen these same governors construct military

prisons and "bull pens," seize unoffending workingmen without warrant of law and thrust them into these vile quarters for no other reason than to break up their unions and leave them helpless at the feet of corporate rapacity.

They have seen the supreme court of the nation turn labor out without a hearing, while the corporation lawyers, who compose this august body, and who hold their commissions in virtue of the "well done" of their capitalist retainers, solemnly descant upon the immaculate purity of our judicial institutions.

They have seen state legislatures, both Republican and Democratic, with never an exception, controlled bodily by the capitalist class and turn the committees of labor unions empty-handed from their doors.

They have seen state supreme courts declare as unconstitutional the last vestige of law upon the statute books that could by any possibility be construed as affording any shelter or relief to the labor union or its members.

They have seen these and many other things and will doubtless see many more before their eyes are opened as a class; but we are thankful for them all, painful though they be to us in having to bear witness to the suffering of our benighted brethren.

In this way only can they be made to see, to think, to act, and every wrong they suffer brings them nearer to their liberation.

The "pure and simple" trade-union of the past does not answer the requirements of today, and they who insist that it does are blind to the changes going on about them, and out of harmony with the progressive forces of the age.

The attempt to preserve the "autonomy" of each trade and segregate it within its own independent jurisdiction, while the lines which once separated them are being obliterated, and the trades are being interwoven and interlocked in the process of industrial evolution, is as futile as to declare and attempt to enforce the independence of the waves of the sea.

A modern industrial plant has a hundred trades and parts of trades represented in its working force. To have these workers parcelled out to a hundred unions is to divide and not to organize them, to give them over to factions and petty leadership and leave them an easy prey to the machinations of the enemy. The dominant craft should control the plant or, rather, the union, and it should embrace the entire working force. This is the industrial plan, the modern method applied to modern conditions, and it will in time prevail.

The trade autonomy can be expressed within the general union, so far as that is necessary or desirable, and there need be no conflict on account of it.

The attempt of each trade to maintain its own independence separately and apart from others results in increasing jurisdictional entanglements, fruitful of dissension, strife and ultimate disruption.

The work of organizing has little, if any, permanent value unless the work of education, the right kind of education, goes hand in hand with it.

There is no cohesiveness in ignorance.

The members of a trade-union should be taught the true import, the whole object of the labor movement and understand its entire program.

They should know that the labor movement means more, infinitely more, than a paltry increase in wages and the strike necessary to secure it; that while it engages to do all that possibly can be done to better the working conditions of its members, its higher object is to overthrow the capitalist system of private ownership of the tools of labor, abolish wage-slavery and achieve the freedom of the whole working class and, in fact, of all mankind.

Karl Marx recognized the necessity of the trade union when he said, * * * "the general tendency of capitalist production is not to raise, but to sink the average standard of wages or to push the value of labor more or less to its minimum limit. Such being the tendency of things in this system, is this saying that the working class ought to renounce their resistance against the encroachments of capital, and abandon their attempts at making the best of the occasional chances for their temporary improvement? If they did, they would be degraded to one level mass of broken wretches past salvation. * * * By cowardly giving way in their every-day conflict with capital, they would certainly disqualify themselves for the initiating of any larger movement."

Marx also set forth the limitations of the trade-union and indicated the true course it should pursue as follows:

"At the same time, and quite apart from the general servitude involved in the wage system, the working class ought not to exaggerate to themselves the ultimate working of these every-day struggles. They ought not to forget that they are fighting with effects, but not with the causes of those effects; that they are retarding the downward movement, but not changing its direction; that they are applying palliatives, not curing the malady. They ought, therefore, not to be exclusively absorbed in these unavoidable guerilla fights incessantly springing up from the never-ceasing encroachments of capital or changes of the market. They ought to understand that, with all the miseries it imposes upon them, the present system simultaneously engenders the material conditions and the social forms necessary for an economic reconstruction of society. Instead of the conservative motto, 'A fair day's wages for a fair day's work!' they ought to inscribe on their banner the revolutionary watchword, 'Abolition of the wage system.' * * * * * *

"Trades unions work well as centers of resistance against the encroachments of capital. They fail partially from an injudicious use of their power. They fail generally from limiting themselves to a guerilla war against the effects of the existing system, instead of simultaneously trying to change it, instead of using their organized forces as a lever for the final emancipation of the working class, that is to say, the ultimate abolition of the wage system."

In an address to the Knights of St. Crispin, in April, 1872, Wendell Phillips, the eloquent orator and passionate hater of slavery in every form, said:

"I hail the Labor movement for the reason that it is my only hope for democracy."

Wendell Phillips was right; he spoke with prophetic insight. He knew that the labor movement alone could democratize society and give freedom to the race.

In the same address he uttered these words, which every trade-unionist should know by heart:

"Unless there is a power in your movement, industrially and politically, the last knell of democratic liberty in this Union is struck."

The orator then proceeded to emphasize the urgent need of developing the political power of the movement; and it is just this that the trade-unionist should be made to clearly understand.

The cry, "no politics in the union," "dragging the union into politics," or "making the union the tail of some political kite," is born of ignorance or dishonesty, or a combination of both. It is echoed by every ward-heeling politician in the country. The plain purpose is to deceive and mislead the workers.

It is not the welfare of the union that these capitalist henchmen are so much concerned about, but the fear that the working class, as a class, organized into a party of their own, will go into politics, for well they know that when that day dawns their occupation will be gone.

And this is why they employ their time in setting the union against the political party of the working class, the only union labor party there ever was or ever will be, and warning the members against the evil designs of the socialists.

The important thing to impress upon the mind of the trade-unionist is that it is his duty to cultivate the habit of doing his own thinking.

The moment he realizes this he is beyond the power of the scheming politician, the emissary of the exploiter, in or out of the labor movement.

The trades-union is not and can not become a political machine, nor can it be used for political purposes. They who insist upon working class political action not only have no intention to convert the trades-union into a political party, but they would oppose any such attempt on the part of others.

The trades-union is an economic organization with distinct economic functions and as such is a part, a necessary part, but a part only of the Labor Movement; it has its own sphere of activity, its own program and is its own master within its economic limitations.

But the labor movement has also its political side and the trades-unionist must be educated to realize its importance and to understand that the political side of the movement must be *unionized* as well as the economic side; and that he is not in fact a union man at all who, although a member of the union on the economic side, is a non-unionist on the political side; and while striking for, votes against the working class.

The trades-union expresses the economic power and the Socialist party expresses the political power of the Labor movement.

The fully developed labor-unionist uses both his economic and political power in the interest of his class. He understands that the struggle between labor and capital is a *class* struggle; that the working class are in a great majority, but divided, some in trades-unions and some out of them, some in one political party and some in another; that because they are divided they are helpless and must submit to being robbed of what their labor produces, and treated with contempt; that they must unite their class in the trades-union on the one hand and in the Socialist party on the other hand; that industrially and politically they must act together as a class against the capitalist class and that this struggle is a class struggle, and that any workingman who deserts his union in a strike and goes to the other side is a scab, and any workingman who deserts his party on election day and goes over to the enemy is a betrayer of his class and an enemy of his fellowman.

Both sides are organized in this class struggle, the capitalists, however, far more thoroughly than the workers. In the first place the capitalists are, comparatively, few in number, while the workers number many millions. Next, the capitalists are men of financial means and resources, and can buy the best brains and command the highest order of ability the market affords. Then again, they own the earth, and the mills and mines and locomotives and ships and stores and the jobs that are attached to them, and this not only gives them tremendous advantage in the struggle, but makes them for the time the absolute masters of the situation.

The workers, on the other hand, are poor as a rule, and ignorant as a class, *but they are in an overwhelming majority.* In a word, they have the power, but are not conscious of it. This then is the supreme demand; to make them conscious of the power of their class, or class-conscious workingmen.

The working class alone does the world's work, has created its capital, produced its wealth, constructed its mills and factories, dug its canals, made its roadbeds, laid its rails and operates its trains, spanned the rivers with bridges and tunnelled the mountains, delved for the precious stones that glitter upon the bosom of vulgar idleness and reared the majestic palaces that shelter insolent parasites.

The working class alone—and by the working class I mean all useful workers, all who by the labor of their hands or the effort of their brains, or both in alliance, as they ought universally to be, increase the knowledge and add to the wealth of society—the working class alone is essential to society and therefore the only class that can survive in the world-wide struggle for freedom.

We have said that both classes, the capitalist class and the working class are organized for the class struggle, but the organization, especially that of the workers, is far from complete; indeed, it would be nearer exact to say that it has but just fairly begun.

On the economic field of the class struggle the capitalists have their Manufacturers' Association, Citizens' Alliance, Corporations' Auxiliary, and—we must add—Civic Federation, while on the political field they have the Republican party and the Democratic party, the former for large capitalists and the latter for small capitalists, but both of them for capitalists and both against the workers.

Standing face to face with the above named economic and political forces of the capitalists the workingmen have on the economic field their trades-unions, and on the political field their working class Socialist party.

In the class struggle the workers must unite and fight together as one on both economic and political fields.

The Socialist party is to the workingman politically what the trades-union is to him industrially; the former is the party of his class, while the latter is the union of his trade.

The difference between them is that while the trades-union is confined to the trade, the Socialist party embraces the entire working class, and while the union is limited to bettering conditions under the wage system, the party is organized to conquer the political power of the nation, wipe out the wage system and make the workers themselves the masters of the earth.

In this program, the trades-union and the Socialist party, the economic and political wings of the labor movement, should not only not be in conflict, but act together in perfect harmony in every struggle whether it be on the one field or the other, in the strike or at the ballot box. The main thing is that in every such struggle the workers shall be united, shall in fact be unionists and no more be guilty of scabbing on their party than on their union, no more think of voting a capitalist ticket on election day and turning the working class over to capitalist robbery and misrule than they would think of voting in the union to turn it over to the capitalists and have it run in the interest of the capitalist class.

To do its part in the class struggle the trades-union need no more go into politics than the Socialist party need go into the trades. Each has its place and its functions.

The union deals with trade problems and the party deals with politics.

The union is educating the workers in the management of industrial activities and fitting them for co-operative control and democratic regulation of their trades,—the party is recruiting and training and drilling the political army that is to conquer the capitalist forces on the political battlefield; and having control of the machinery of government, use it to transfer the industries from the capitalists to the workers, from the parasites to the people.

In his excellent paper on "The Social Opportunity," published in a recent issue of the International Socialist Review, Dr. George D. Herron, discussing trades-unions and their relation to the Socialist party, and the labor movement in general, clearly sees the trend of the development and arrives at conclusions that are sound and commend themselves to the thoughtful consideration of all trades-unionists and Socialists. Says Dr. Herron:

"On the one side, it is the trade-unionist who is on the firing line of the class struggle. He it is who blocked the wheels of the capitalist machine; he it is who has prevented the unchecked development of capitalist increase; he it is who has prevented the whole labor body of the world from being kept forever at the point of mere hunger wages; he it is who has taught the workers of the world the lesson of solidarity, and delivered them from that wretched and unthinking competition with each other which kept them at the mercy of capitalism; he it is who has prepared the way for the co-operative commonwealth. On the other hand, trade unionism is by no means the solution of the workers' problem, nor is it the goal of the labor struggle. It is merely a capitalist line of defense within the capitalist system. Its existence and its struggles are necessitated only by the existence and predatory nature of capitalism. * * *

* * * "Organized labor has an instinct that far outreaches its intelligence, and that far outreaches the intelligence of the preaching and teaching class,—the instinct that the workers of the world are bound up together in one common destiny; that their battle for the future is one; and that there is no possible safety or extrication for any worker unless all the workers of the world are extricated and saved from capitalism together. * * *

* * * "Until the workers shall become a clearly defined socialist movement, standing for and moving toward the unqualified co-operative commonwealth, while at the same time understanding and proclaiming their immediate interests, they will only play into the hands of their exploiters, and be led by their betrayers.

"It is the Socialist who must point this out in the right way. He is not to do this by seeking to commit trade-union bodies to the principles of Socialism. Resolution or commitments of this sort accomplish little good. Nor is he to do it by taking a servile attitude toward organized labor, nor by meddling with the details or the machinery of the trade-unions. Not by trying to commit Socialism to trade-unionism, nor trade-unionism to Socialism, will the Socialist end be accomplished. It is better to leave the trade-unions do their distinctive work, as the workers' defense against the encroachments of capitalism, as the economic development of the worker against the economic development of the capitalist, giving unqualified support and sympathy to the struggles of the organized worker to sustain himself in his economic sphere. But let the Socialist also build up the character and harmony and strength of the socialist movement as a political force, that it shall command the respect and confidence of the worker, irrespective of his trade or his union obligations. It is urgent that we so keep in mind the difference between the two developments that neither shall cripple the other. The Socialist movement, as a political development of the workers for their economic emancipation, is one thing; the trade-union development, as an economic defense of the workers within the capitalist system, is another thing. Let us not interfere with the internal affairs of the trade-unions, or seek to have them become distinctively political bodies in themselves, any more than we would seek to make a distinctive political body in itself of a church, or a public school, or a lawyer's office. But let us attend to the harmonious and commanding development of the Socialist political movement as the channel and power by which labor is to come to its emancipation and its commonwealth."

We have quoted thus at length to make clear the position of the writer who has given close study to the question and in the paper above quoted has done much to light the way to sound tactics and sane procedure.

It is of vital importance to the trades-union that its members be class-conscious, that they understand the class struggle and their duty as union men on the political field, so that in every move that is made they will have the goal in view, and while taking advantage of every opportunity to secure concessions and enlarge their economic advantage, they will at the same time unite at the ballot box, not only to back up the economic struggle of the trades-union, but to finally wrest the government from capitalist control and establish the working class republic.

SOCIALISM.

There are those who sneeringly class Socialism among the "ism" that appear and disappear as passing fads, and pretend to dismiss it with an impatient wave of the hand. There is just enough in this great world movement to them to excite their ridicule and provoke their contempt. At least they would have us think so and if we take them at their word their ignorance does not rise to the level of our contempt, but entitles them to our pity.

To the workingman in particular it is important to know what Socialism is and what it means.

Let us endeavor to make it so clear to him that he will readily grasp it and the moment he does he becomes a Socialist.

It is our conviction that no workingman can clearly understand what Socialism means without becoming and remaining a Socialist. It is simply impossible for him to be anything else and the only reason that all workingmen are not Socialists is that they do not know what it means.

They have heard of Socialism—and they have heard of anarchy and of other things all mixed together—and without going to any trouble about it they conclude that it is all the same thing and a good thing to let alone.

Why? Because the capitalist editor has said so; the politician has sworn to it and the preacher has said amen to it, and surely that ought to settle it.

But it doesn't. It settles but one thing and that is that the capitalist is opposed to Socialism and that the editor and politician and preacher are but the voices of the capitalist. There are some exceptions, but not enough to affect the rule.

Socialism is first of all a political movement of the working class, clearly defined and uncompromising, which aims at the overthrow of the prevailing capitalist system by securing control of the national government and by the exercise of the public powers, supplanting the existing capitalist class government with Socialist administration—that is to say, changing a republic in name into a republic in fact.

Socialism also means a coming phase of civilization, next in order to the present one, in which the collective people will own and operate the sources and means of wealth production, in which all will have equal right to work and all will co-operate together in producing wealth and all will enjoy all the fruit of their collective labor.

In the present system of society, called the capitalist system, since it is controlled by and supported in the interest of the capitalist class, we have two general classes of people; first, capitalists, and second, workers. The capitalists are few, the workers are many; the capitalists are called capitalists because they own the productive capital of the country, the lands, mines, quarries, oil and gas wells, mills, factories, shops, stores, warehouses, refineries, tanneries, elevators, docks, wharves, railroads, street cars, steamships, smelters, blast furnaces, brick and stone yards, stock pens, packing houses, telegraph wires and poles, pipe lines, and all other sources, means and tools of production, distribution and exchange. The capitalist class who own and control these things also own and control, of course, the millions of jobs that are attached to and inseparable from them.

It goes without saying that the owner of the job is the master of the fellow who depends upon the job.

Now why does the workingman depend upon the capitalist for a job? Simply because the capitalist owns the tools with which work is done, and without these the workingman is almost as helpless as if he had no arms.

Before the tool became a machine, the worker who used it also owned it; if one was lost or destroyed he got another, The tool was small; it was for individual use and what the workingman produced with it was his own. He did not have to beg some one else to allow him to use his tools—he had his own.

But a century has passed since then, and in the order of progress that simple tool has become a mammoth machine.

The old hand tool was used by a single worker—and owned by him who used it.

The machine requires a thousand or ten thousand workers to operate it, but they do not own it, and what they produce with it does not go to them, but to the capitalist who does own it.

The workers who use the machine are the slaves of the capitalist who owns it.

They can only work by his permission.

The capitalist is a capitalist solely for profit—without profit he would not be in business an instant. That is his first and only consideration.

In the capitalist system profit is prior to and more important than the life or liberty of the workingman.

The capitalist's profit first, last and always. He owns the tools and only allows the worker to use them on condition that he can extract a satisfactory profit from his labor. If he cannot do this the tools are not allowed to be used—he locks them up and waits.

The capitalist does no work himself; that is, no useful or necessary work. He spends his time watching other parasites in the capitalist game of "dog eat dog," or in idleness or dissipation. The workers who use his tools give him all the wealth they produce and he allows them a sufficient wage to keep them in working order.

The wage is to the worker what oil is to the machine.

The machine cannot run without lubricant and the worker cannot work and reproduce himself without being fed, clothed and housed; this is his lubricant and the amount he requires to keep him in running order regulates his wage.

Karl Marx, in his "Wage, Labor and Capital," makes these points clear in his own terse and masterly style. We quote as follows:

"The free laborer sells himself, and that by fractions. From day to day he sells by auction, eight, ten, twelve, fifteen hours of his life to the highest bidder—to the owner of the raw material, the instruments of work and the means of life; that is, to the employer. The laborer himself belongs neither to an owner nor to the soil; but eight, ten, twelve, fifteen hours of his daily life belong to the man who buys them. The laborer leaves the employer to whom he has hired himself whenever he pleases; and the employer discharges him whenever he thinks fit; either as soon as he ceases to make a profit out of him or fails to get as high a profit as he requires. But the laborer whose only source of earning is the sale of his labor power cannot leave *the whole class of its purchasers,* that is the capitalist class, without renouncing his own existence. He does not belong to this or that particular employer, but he does belong to the *capitalist class;* and more than that: it is his business to find an employer; that is, among this capitalist class it is his business to discover *his own particular purchaser."*

Coming to the matter of wages and how they are determined, Marx continues:

"Wages are the price of a certain commodity, labor-power. Wages are thus determined by the same law which regulates the price of any other commodity.

"Thereupon the question arises, how is the price of a commodity determined?

"By means of competition between buyers and sellers and the relations between supply and demand—offer and desire.

" * * * Now the same general laws which universally regulate the price of commodities, regulate, of course, *wages, the price of labor.*

"Wages will rise and fall in accordance with the proportion between demand and supply; that is, in accordance with the conditions of the competition between capitalists as buyers and laborers as sellers of labor. The fluctuations of wages correspond in general with the fluctuation in the price of commodities. *Within these fluctuations the price of labor is regulated by its cost of production; that is, by the duration of labor which is required in order to produce this commodity, labor power.*

"*Now what is the cost of production of labor power?*

"*It is the cost required for the production of a laborer and for his maintenance as a laborer.*

" * * * *The price of his labor is therefore determined by the price of the bare necessaries of his existence."*

This is the capitalist system in its effect upon the working class. They have no tools, but must work to live. They throng the labor market, especially when times are hard and work is scarce, and eagerly, anxiously look for some one willing to use their labor power and bid them in at the market price.

To speak of liberty in such a system is a mockery; to surrender is a crime.

The workers of the nation and the world must be aroused.

In the capitalist system "night has drawn her sable curtain down and pinned it with a star," and the great majority grope in darkness. The pin must be removed from the curtain, even thought it be a star.

But the darkness, after all, is but imaginary. The sun is marching to meridian glory and the world is flooded with light.

Charlotte Perkins Stetson, the inspired evangel of the coming civilization, says:

> "We close our eyes and call it night,
> And grope and fall in seas of light,
> Would we but understand!"

Not for a moment do we despair of the future. The greatest educational propaganda ever known is spreading over the earth.

The working class will both see and understand. They have the inherent power of self-development. They are but just beginning to come into consciousness of their power, and with the first glimmerings of this consciousness the capitalist system is doomed. It may hold on for a time, for even a long time, but its doom is sealed.

Even now the coming consciousness of this world-wide working class power is shaking the foundations of all governments and all civilizations.

The capitalist system has had its day and, like other systems that have gone before, it must pass away when it has fulfilled its mission and made room for another system more in harmony with the forces of progress and with the onward march of civilization.

The centralization of capital, the concentration of industry and the co-operation of workingmen mark the beginning of the end. Competition is no longer "the life of trade." Only they are clamoring for "competition" who have been worsted in the struggle and would like to have another deal.

The small class who won out in the game of competition and own the trusts want no more of it. They know what it it, and have had enough. Mr. John D. Rockefeller needs no competition to give life to his trade, and his pious son does not expatiate upon the beauties of competition in his class at Sunday school.

No successful capitalist wants competition—for himself—he only wants it for the working class, so that he can buy his labor power at the lowest competitive price in the labor market.

The simple truth is, that competition in industrial life belongs to the past, and is practically outgrown. The time is approaching when it will be no longer possible.

The improvement and enlargement of machinery, and the ever-increasing scale of production compel the concentration of capital and this makes inevitable the concentration and co-operation of the workers.

The capitalists—the successful ones, of course,—co-operate on the one side; the workers—who are lucky enough to get the jobs—on the other side.

One side gets the profit, grow rich, live in palaces, ride in yachts, gamble at Monte Carlo, drink champagne, choose judges, buy editors, hire preachers, corrupt politics, build universities, endow libraries, patronize churches, get the gout, preach morals and bequeath the earth to their lineal descendants.

The other side do the work, early and late, in heat and cold; they sweat and groan and bleed and die—the steel billets they make are their corpses. They build the mills and all the machinery; they man the plant and the thing of stone and steel begins to throb. They live far away in the outskirts, in cottages, just this side of the hovels, where gaunt famine walks with despair and "Les Miserables" leer and mock at civilization. When the mills shut down, they are out of work and out of food and out of home; and when old age begins to steal away their vigor and the step is no longer agile, nor the sinew strong, nor the hand cunning; when the frame begins to bend and quiver and the eye to grow dim, and they are no longer fit as labor power to make profit for their masters, they are pushed aside into the human drift that empties into the gulf of despair and death.

The system, once adapted to human needs, has outlived its usefulness and is now an unmitigated curse. It stands in the way of progress and checks the advance of civilization.

If by its fruit we know the tree, so by the same token do we know our social system. Its corrupt fruit betrays its foul and unclean nature and condemns it to death.

The swarms of vagrants, tramps, outcasts, paupers, thieves, gamblers, pickpockets, suicides, confidence men, fallen women, consumptives, idiots, dwarfed children; the disease, poverty, insanity and crime rampant in every land under the sway of capitalism rise up and cry out against it, and hush to silence all the pleas of its *mercenaries* and strike the knell of its doom.

The ancient and middle-age civilizations had their rise, they ruled and fell, and that of our own day must follow them.

Evolution is the order of nature, and society, like the units that compose it, is subject to its inexorable law.

The day of individual effort, of small tools, free competition, hand labor, long hours and meagre results is gone never to return. The civilization reared upon this old foundation is crumbling.

The economic basis of society is being transformed.

The working class are being knit together in the bonds of co-operation, they are becoming conscious of their interests as a class, and marshalling the workers for the class struggle and collective ownership.

With the triumph of the workers the mode of production and distribution will be completely revolutionized.

Private ownership and production for profit will be supplanted by social ownership and production for use.

The economic interests of the workers will be mutual. They will work together in harmony instead of being arrayed against each other in competitive warfare.

The collective workers will own the machinery of production, and there will be work for all and all will receive their socially due share of the product of their co-operative labor.

It is for this great work that the workers and their sympathizers must organize and educate and agitate.

The Socialist movement is of the working class itself; it is from the injustice perpetrated upon, and the misery suffered by this class that the movement sprang, and it is to this class it makes its appeal. It is the voice of awakened labor arousing itself to action.

As we look abroad and see things as they are, the capitalists intrenched and fortified and the workers impoverished, ignorant and in bondage, we are apt to be overawed by the magnitude of the task that lies before the Socialist movement, but as we become grounded in the Socialist philosophy, as we understand the process of economic determinism and grasp the principles of industrial and social evolution the magnitude of the undertaking, far from daunting the Socialist spirit, appeals to each comrade to enlist in the struggle because of the very greatness of the conflict and the immeasurable good that lies beyond it, and as he girds himself and touches elbows with his comrades his own latent resources are developed and his blood thrills with new life as he feels himself rising to the majesty of a man.

Now he has found his true place, and though he be reviled against and ostracized, traduced and denounced, though he be reduced to rags, and tormented with hunger pangs, he will bear it all and more, for he is battling for a principle, he has been consecrated to a cause and he cannot turn back.

To reach the workers that are still in darkness and to open their eyes, that is the task, and to this we must give ourselves with all the strength we have, with patience that never fails and an abiding faith in the ultimate victory.

The moment a worker sees himself in his true light he severs his relations with the capitalist parties, for he realizes at once that he no more belongs there than Rockefeller belongs in the Socialist party.

What is the actual status of the workingman in the capitalist society of today?

Is he in any true sense a citizen?

Has he any basis for the claim that he is a free man?

First of all, he cannot work unless some capitalist finds it to his interest to employ him.

Why not? Because he has no tools and man cannot work without them.

Why has he no tools? Because tools in these days are, as a rule, great machines and very costly, and in the capitalist system are the private property of the capitalists.

This being true, the workingman, before he can do a tap of work, before he can earn a dime to feed himself, his wife or his child, must first consult the tool-owning capitalist; or, rather, his labor-buying superintendent. Very meekly, therefore, and not without fear in his heart and trembling in his knees, he enters the office and offers his labor power in exchange for a wage that represents but a part, usually a small part, of what his labor produces.

His offer may be accepted or rejected.

Not infrequently the "boss" has been annoyed by so many job-hunters that he has become irritable, and gruffly turns the applicant away.

But admitting that he finds employment, during working hours he is virtually the property of his master.

The bell or the whistle claims him on the stroke of the hour. He is subject to the master's shop regulations and these, of course, are established solely to conserve his master's interests. He works, first of all, for his master, who extracts the surplus value from his labor, but for which he would not be allowed to work at all. He has little or no voice in determining any of the conditions of his employment.

Suddenly, without warning, the shop closes down, or he is discharged and his wage, small at best, is cut off. He has to live, the rent must be paid, the wife and children must have clothing and food, fuel must be provided, and yet he has no job, no wages and no prospect of getting any.

Is a worker in that position free?

Is he a citizen?

A man?

No! He is simply a wage-slave, a job-holder, while it lasts, here today and gone tomorrow.

For the great body of wage-workers there is no escape; they cannot rise above the level of their class. The few who do are the exceptions that prove the rule.

And yet there are those who have the effrontery to warn these wage-slaves that if they turn to Socialism they will lose all incentive to work, and their individuality will fade away.

Incentive and individuality forsooth! Where are they now?

Translated into plain terms, this warning means that a slave who is robbed of all he produces, except enough to keep him in producing condition, as in the present system, has great incentive to work and is highly individualized, but if he breaks his fetters and frees himself and becomes his own master and gets all his labor produces, as he will in Socialism, then all incentive to work vanishes, and his individuality, so used to chains and dungeons, unable to stand the air of freedom, withers away and is lost forever.

The capitalists and their emissaries who resort to such crude attempts at deception and imposture betray the low estimate they place on the intelligence of their wage-workers and also show that they fully understand to what depths of ignorance and credulity these slaves have sunk in the wage-system.

In the light of existing conditions there can be no reform that will be of any great or permanent benefit to the working class.

The present system of private ownership must be abolished and the workers themselves made the owners of the tools with which they work, and to accomplish this they must organize their class for political action and this work is already well under way in the Socialist party, which is composed of the working class and stands for the working class on a revolutionary platform, which declares in favor of the collective ownership of the means of production and the democratic management of industry in the interest of the whole people.

What intelligent workingman can hold out against the irresistible claim the Socialist movement has upon him? What reason has he to give? What excuse can he offer?

None! Not one!

The only worker who has an excuse to keep out of the socialist movement is the unfortunate fellow who is ignorant and does not know better. He does not know what Socialism is. That is his misfortune. But that is not all, nor the worst of all. He thinks he knows what it is.

In his ignorance he has taken the word of another for it,

whose interest it is to keep him in darkness. So he continues to march with the Republican party or shout with the Democratic party, and he no more knows why he is a Republican or Democrat than he knows why he is not a Socialist.

It is impossible for a workingman to contemplate the situation and the outlook and have any intelligent conception of the trend and meaning of things without becoming a Socialist.

Consider for a moment the beastly debasement to which womanhood is subjected in capitalist society. She is simply the property of man to be governed by him as may suit his convenience. She does not vote, she has no voice and must bear silent witness to her legally ordained inferiority.

She has to compete with man in the factories and workshops and stores, and her inferiority is taken advantage of to make her work at still lower wages than the male slave gets who works at her side.

As an economic dependent, she is compelled to sacrifice the innate refinement, the inherent purity and nobility of her sex, and for a pallet of straw she marries the man she does not love.

The debauching effect of the capitalist system upon womanhood is accurately registered in the divorce court and the house of shame.

In Socialism, woman would stand forth the equal of man— all the avenues would be open to her and she would naturally find her fitting place and rise from the low plane of menial servility to the dignity of ideal womanhood.

Breathing the air of economic freedom, amply able to provide for herself in Socialist society, we may be certain that the cruel injustice that is now perpetrated upon her sex and the degradation that results from it will disappear forever.

Consider again the barren prospect of the average boy who faces the world today. If he is the son of a workingman his father is able to do but little in the way of giving him a start.

He does not get to college, nor even to the high school, but has to be satisfied with what he can get in the lower grades, for as soon as he has physical growth enough to work he must find something to do, so that he may help support the family.

His father has no influence and can get no preferred employment for him at the expense of some other boy, so he thankfully accepts any kind of service that he may be allowed to perform.

How hard it is to find a place for that boy of yours!

What shall we do with Johnnie? and Nellie? is the question of the anxious mother long before they are ripe for the labor market.

"The child is weak, you know," continues the nervous, loving little mother, "and can't do hard work; and I feel dreadfully worried about him."

What a picture! Yet so common that the multitude do not see it. This mother, numbered by thousands many times over, instinctively understands the capitalist system, feels its cruelty and dreads its approaching horrors which cast their shadows upon her tender, loving heart.

Nothing can be sadder than to see a mother take the boy she bore by the hand and start to town with him to peddle him off as merchandise to some one who has use for a child-slave.

To know just how that feels one must have had precisely that experience.

The mother looks down so fondly and caressingly upon her boy; and he looks up into her eyes so timidly and appealingly as she explains his good points to the business man or factory boss, who in turn inspects the lad and interrogates him to verify his mother's claims, and finally informs them that they may call again the following week, but that he does not think he can use the boy.

Well, what finally becomes of the boy? He is now grown, his mother's worry is long since ended, as the grass grows green where she sleeps—and he, the boy? Why, he's a factory hand—a *hand*, mind you, and he gets a dollar and a quarter a day when the factory is running.

That is all he will ever get.

He is an industrial life prisoner—no pardoning power for him in the capitalist system.

No sweet home, no beautiful wife, no happy children, no books, no flowers, no pictures, no comrades, no love, no joy for him.

Just a hand! A human factory hand!

Think of a hand with a soul in it!

In the capitalist system the soul has no business. It cannot produce profit by any process of capitalist calculation.

The working hand is what is needed for the capitalist's tool and so the human must be reduced to a hand.

No head, no heart, no soul—simply a hand.

A thousand hands to one brain—the hands of workingmen, the brain of a capitalist.

A thousand dumb animals, in human form—a thousand slaves in the fetters of ignorance, their heads having run to hands—all these owned and worked and fleeced by one stock-dealing, profit-mongering capitalist.

This is capitalism!

And this system is supported alternately by the Republican party and the Democratic party.

These two capitalist parties relieve each other in support of the capitalist system, while the capitalist system relieves the working class of what they produce.

A thousand hands to one head is the abnormal development of the capitalist system.

A thousand workingmen turned into hands to develop and gorge and decorate one capitalist paunch!

This brutal order of things must be overthrown. The human race was not born to degeneracy.

A thousand heads have grown for every thousand pairs of hands; a thousand hearts throb in testimony of the unity of heads and hands; and a thousand souls, though crushed and mangled, burn in protest and are pledged to redeem a thousand men.

Heads and hands, hearts and souls, are the heritage of all.

Full opportunity for full development is the unalienable right of all.

He who denies it is a tyrant; he who does not demand it is a coward; he who is indifferent to it is a slave; he who does not desire it is dead.

The earth for all the people! That is the demand.

The machinery of production and distribution for all the people! That is the demand.

The collective ownership and control of industry and its democratic management in the interest of all the people! That is the demand.

The elimination of rent, interest and profit and the production of wealth to satisfy the wants of all the people! That is the demand.

Co-operative industry in which all shall work together in harmony as the basis of a new social order, a higher civilization, a real republic! That is the demand.

The end of class struggles and class rule, of master and slave, of ignorance and vice, of poverty and shame, of cruelty and crime—the birth of freedom, the dawn of brotherhood, the beginning of MAN! That is the demand.

This is Socialism!

Reply to John Mitchell

The fifteenth annual convention of the United Mine Workers of America met at Indianapolis, Ind., January 18 and continued in session to and including January 27, 1904.

The regular convention was followed by a special session (from March 5 to March 7 inclusive,), made necessary by the failure of the regular convention to effect a satisfactory renewal of the interstate agreement with the operators, which expired March 31, 1904.

For a time a strike seemed imminent, there being intense opposition to the wage-reduction which the operators declared to be their ultimatum.

The convention rejected the ultimatum of the operators, but the matter was finally referred to the local unions, and the latter, yielding to the importunities of the national officers, voted to accept the terms of the operators, and the threatened strike was averted.

A few days later Eugene V. Debs wrote the following letter in reference to the matter which appeared in the *Social Democratic Herald* of Milwaukee, Wis., in its issue of April 9, 1904:

MR. DEBS.

Terre Haute, Ind., March 31, 1904.
To the S. D. Herald:

Now that the threatened coal strike has ended in a tame surrender, and a two years' scale at a reduction of wages has been virtually forced upon the miners by a coalition of their leaders with the operators, a certain small and obscure press dispatch—a mere word to the wise, yet sufficient at the time—takes on immense interest in its prophetic significance.

The delegates to the late Indianapolis convention of miners whom I had occasion to address, will no doubt remember my words, and those who were angered because I told them in plain terms what has since come true almost to the letter, will perhaps be willing to forgive me.

But to the dispatch. Here it is just as it was sent out by the Associated Press from Pittsburg under date of March 6 and just as it appeared in the morning dailies of the same date:

"Pittsburg, Pa., March 6.—The Post tomorrow will say:

"There was by no means a hopeless spirit among the returning coal operators from the Indianapolis convention with the miners which closed Saturday with a disagreement.

"From the best of authority the Post was informed yesterday that the break in the negotiations between the two interests is not a permanent one and that by March 21, another meeting of joint sub-committees will be held quietly. The whole matter will again be discussed among them and a solution to the present difficulty sought. It was further said that there was every reason for believing that the ultimate end of the whole matter would be the acceptance of the lower rate by the miners, or the 85 cents a ton base for pick mining, for the next two years."

Here we have it that the operators knew in advance that there would be no strike and that the miners would accept the reduction, and this they knew notwithstanding the fact that the convention, by a solid vote of the states, had refused to accept the reduction and virtually declared for a strike.

Let us examine the situation a moment. The joint convention of miners and operators adjourned sine die March 5. No agreement had been reached. All negotiations were ended. A strike, so the papers declared, was inevitable. Only a miracle could prevent it.

The miners and operators returned to their homes. Preparations began for war. It was at this juncture that the above dispatch went out from Pittsburg. It was doubtless intended as a "tip" to the capitalists and stock gamblers of the country, and was issued immediately upon the return of the Pennsylvania operators from the Indianapolis convention.

Pittsburg, be it remembered, is the home of President Robbins of the Pittsburg Coal Co. and floor leader and spokesman of the operators in all joint conventions with the miners. It is quite evident, therefore, that "the best of authority" quoted in the above dispatch was none other than Robbins and it is equally evident that he knew what he was talking about, for his prediction of surrender, made in face of the fact that the national convention had virtually declared for war, was fulfilled to the letter.

The question is, did Robbins, chief of the operators, have an understanding with Mitchell, president of the miners? It must be admitted that it looks that way. Proof may be lacking, but the circumstances combine to make that conclusion almost inevitable.

When the miners first met in convention President Mitchell and the other leaders were quite aggressive. They were going to sweep all opposition before them and get what they wanted, for they had an organization that could and would carry the day.

A set of demands, including increased wages, was at once formulated and the performance began. Mitchell, taking the floor for the miners, proved by the facts and figures that they were asking only what was reasonable, that the financial reports of the coal companies showed large increase in profits over the preceding years, that the operators could well afford to make the concessions and that they, the miners, were "terribly in earnest" and that the United Mine Workers of America would under no possible circumstances "take a backward step."

As the fight progressed the leaders of the miners made one concession after another until they had finally surrendered everything. But the operators were not satisfied. They had come with love in their hearts and a made-to-order, warranted-to-fit reduction of wages in their grips, just because they were all in the same economic class and their interests were therefore identical, and to prove it they permitted their own leaders to scale down the bulging wages of the opulent coal diggers.

But the delegates, having given up everything, balked at last. Even Mitchell's "masterful effort" in behalf of the operators fell flat.

The reduction would not go down.

The convention voted to fight and the delegates went home to prepare for hostilities.

Now read the dispatch again in the light of what followed.

As soon as the convention adjourned, the leaders of the miners began to work upon the rank and file, very many of whom are so pitifully ignorant that they look upon a union official as a Chinaman does upon his Joss.

President Mitchell, from being "terribly in earnest" in behalf of the miners, became the special pleader of the operators.

Oh, what a transformation!

Mitchell, the labor leader, and Robbins, the labor exploiter, pooling issues and joining hands to force down the wages of the mine slaves!

Oh, what a spectacle!

With all possible haste the national and state leaders made their rounds among the faithful. The "dangerous" locals and districts were all visited and mass meetings held to save the operators.

The slaves had instinctively rebelled against the wage cut, and the rebellion must be put down by their own leaders if they expected the plaudits of the capitalist exploiters and the "well done" of the pulpit, press and "public."

Alternate pleas, warnings and threats were turned on until the fires were put out and the day was saved for the operators.

Only a little while ago Gompers warned the capitalists that reduction of wages would not be tolerated and solemnly enjoined his followers to resist them to the last.

Mitchell, Shaffer and other lieutenants of Gompers are the active allies of the capitalists in enforcing reductions.

Watch the developments!

To conclude: The United Mine Workers of America has been struck by lightning. EUGENE V. DEBS.

This letter was answered by Mr. John Mitchell and his colleagues in a communication which appeared in the same paper on May 21, 1904, as follows:

MR. MITCHELL AND HIS COLLEAGUES.

Indianapolis, Ind., May 7, 1904.
Editor Social-Democratic Herald:

In your issue of April 9 you publish an article over the signature of Eugene V. Debs containing a mass of misstatements with the apparent purpose of making your readers believe that the officials of the United Mine Workers of America, and particularly President Mitchell, have betrayed the trust reposed in them by their constituents by using their official position for the benefit of the employers instead of for the welfare of the employes.

Mr. Debs' knowledge of mining affairs is limited, by virtue of his lack of time and opportunity for personal investigation, and must of necessity be general and superficial. He has not sufficient knowledge of the mining industry to be a competent critic of our trade politics, and yet, if he had confined himself to a criticism of those policies, they might have passed unchallenged, so far as we are concerned. But when, without investigation of the facts, he takes an Associated Press dispatch, distorts it to suit his own purpose and jumbles it up with a number of other things that never existed except in his own diseased imagination, in order to prove that the officials of the United Mine Workers are dishonest, we believe that justice to ourselves and the organization we represent demands that his statements shall be refuted and his purpose laid bare.

Men of experience in the labor movement usually pass by, unheeded, the insinuations circulated by the paid agents of capital for the purpose of destroying their influence and weakening the power of resistance of their organization, but, when those insinuations are uttered and circulated by a man who for years has leaned upon the sympathies of the wage workers as the crucified martyr of a lost cause, the halo of glory he has painted about himself cannot shield him from the contempt of honest men. What is this wonderful press dispatch around which Mr. Debs' imagination has built such a magnificent net work? We reproduce it from his own article:

"Pittsburg, Pa., March 6, 1904.

"There was by no means a hopeless spirit among the returning coal operators from the Indianapolis convention which the miners closed Saturday with a disagreement.

"From the best authority the Post was informed yesterday that the break in the negotiations between the two interests is not a permanent one and that by March 21, another meeting of joint sub-committees will be held quietly. The whole matter will again be discussed among them and a solution to the present difficulty sought. It was further said that there was every reason for believing that the ultimate end of the whole matter would be the acceptance of the lower rate by the miners, or the 85 cents a ton base for pick mining for the next two years."

"Here," says Mr. Debs, "we have it that the operators knew in advance that there would be no strike." That statement is false. The dispatch does not assert that the operators knew there would be no strike and nothing but a warped mind could so construe it. The United Mine Workers' convention on March 7 passed a resolution submitting the acceptance or rejection of the ultimatum of the operators to a referendum vote of the members affected. The vote was taken on the afternoon of March 15. It was sent by the local tellers in sealed envelopes to national headquarters, and these envelopes were not opened until the national tellers opened them on March 17. It would have been impossible for the Pittsburg correspondent, Frank Robbins, John Mitchell, or even the versatile and prophetic Mr. Debs to have known on March 6 what the result of that vote would be.

That is misstatement No. 1 refuted.

In a subsequent interview in the Terre Haute *Sunday Tribune* Mr. Debs dares anyone to put his finger on a single word that is not true or deny a single allegation. There is scarcely a truthful statement in the entire article. Let us be specific. The joint convention of Miners and Operators adjourned sine die March 5. No agreement had been reached, but negotiations were not broken off as asserted by Mr. Debs. When it became apparent that the operators would not move from their final proposition of five and fifty-five one hundredths per cent reduction, and the miners must either accept that proposition or strike, the sub-scale committee, composed of two delegates from each of the four states represented, selected by the representatives from those states, and eight operators selected in a similar manner, publicly withdrew from the conference for a few minutes and held a consultation. As the miners had not yet decided upon their line of policy and might not be able to do so for some time, it was decided that the scale committee should re-convene on March 21 at which time the operators would be notified whether the miners had decided to strike or not. Consequently negotiations were continued.

That is misstatement No. 2 refuted.

Mr. Debs says, "The miners and operators returned to their homes. Preparations began for war. It was at this juncture that the above dispatch went out from Pittsburg."

The dispatch was sent out from Pittsburg March 6. The miners' convention did not adjourn until March 7 and the delegates could not have been at home preparing for war at the time alleged.

That is misstatement No. 3 refuted.

Again Mr. Debs says, "Pittsburg, be it remembered, is the home of President Robbins of the Pittsburg Coal Co. and the floor leader and spokesman of the operators in all the joint conventions with the miners. It is quite evident, therefore, that 'the best authority,' quoted in the above dispatch, was none other than Mr. Robbins." When the joint convention adjourned on March 5 the miners immediately went into convention to outline their policy. It did not finish its work until the afternoon of March 7. A delegation of operators remained in Indianapolis awaiting the result. Frank Robbins was one of that delegation. He did not leave Indianapolis until the evening of March 7 and could not, therefore, have been the returning coal operator quoted in the dispatch.

That is misstatement No. 4 refuted.

We quote further from Mr. Debs, "The national convention had (on March 5) virtually declared for war," and further on he says: "The convention voted to fight and the delegates went home to prepare for hostilities." It had done nothing of the kind. Mr. Debs knows as well as any man that the declaring of a strike does not always mean success to the strikers. His experience in 1894 is conclusive proof of that fact. A repetition of the strike of 1894 would have been as disastrous to the United Mine Workers of America as that strike was to the American Railway Union. Many of the delegates believed that it would be better for the miners to accept the reduction offered than to take the chances of war, especially when the employers had selected the battle ground, but they were bound by instructions and could not violate them. When the officials were approached by these delegates they advised them to obey their instructions. To meet this situation the convention on March 5 selected a committee composed of two members from each district to formulate plans to meet the crisis. The committee reported on March 7 and recommended that the ultimatum of the operators be submitted to the miners affected for their acceptance or rejection, the vote to be taken between the hours of one and six P. M. of March 15, and the mines to be idle that afternoon in order to give every member an opportunity to vote who desired to. The officials supported that proposition and it was agreed to by the convention. It will thus be seen that there was no virtual declaration of war on March 5 and that the convention had not voted to fight.

That is misstatement No. 5 refuted.

These are the alleged truths upon which Mr. Debs builds his flimsy insinuations and attempt to destroy the reputation of honest men. We have refuted them. Every delegate who attended the convention knows our statements are true. There was no secrecy about these actions. If Mr. Debs had wanted to know the truth, a simple investigation would have revealed it to him. It is very evident that he was not seeking for the truth. The innuendoes used by Mr. Debs clearly prove this assertion. Here are some of them:

"The question is, did Robbins, chief of the operators, have an understanding with Mitchell, president of the miners?"

"But the delegates, having given up everything, balked at last. Even Mitchell's 'masterful effort' in behalf of the operators fell flat."

"As soon as the convention adjourned the leaders of the miners began to work upon the rank and file, many of whom are so pitifully ignorant that they look upon a union official as a Chinaman does upon his Joss."

"Mitchell, the labor leader, and Robbins, the labor exploiter, pooling issues and joining hands to force down the wages of the mine slaves. Oh, what a transformation!"

There is some more along the same line, but that is the gist of it. Neither Mr. Debs nor any other person ever heard Mr.

Mitchell make a "masterful" or any other kind of an effort in behalf of the operators. Every effort he has ever made has been in behalf of the wage workers. The miners have something substantial to show for these efforts in directing their organization. Even after the reduction they have accepted has been taken off they have over seventy per cent higher wages than they had in 1897, from two to four hours per day less labor, improved conditions in the mines, and the privilege of expressing their opinion on all social, political and religious questions without fear of discharge. We doubt very much if Mr. Debs with all his organizing ability, dynamic energy, prophetic vision and brilliant oratory can show results for his labor equivalent to these for the present generation of men. If higher wages, shorter hours, healthier and safer conditions of employment and greater freedom of speech is the result of "pooling issues with Robbins, the labor exploiter," it would seem to be a very profitable pool for the wage workers. But Debs knows that no such pool exists. He knows, or at least ought to know, that these results have been obtained through a strong organization intelligently directed. If we were disposed to use the same methods as Mr. Debs we could with perfect propriety assert that "Proof may be lacking but the circumstances combine to make the conclusion almost inevitable" that he is being paid by the operators to destroy the United Mine Workers in order that the operators may dominate the miners as they did prior to 1897. We would not be mean enough to even insinuate such a thing. Debs asserts that many of the miners are so "pitifully ignorant that they look upon a union official as a Chinaman does upon his Joss." He knew that statement was wrong when he made it. There are degrees of intelligence amongst miners as there is amongst all classes of people. Taken as a whole their intelligence will compare favorably with any class of our citizens, rich or poor. They are men that cannot be led about by the whims of anybody. Any proposition presented to them for consideration must appeal to their intelligence before they will support it, and they do not hesitate to take issue with a union official whenever in their judgment the union official is wrong. Some of them undoubtedly love and respect their officials, but not one can be found who looks upon them as a deity or as a Chinaman looks upon his Joss.

The entire expression is an insult to men who are the equals of Mr. Debs physically, morally and intellectually. He speaks about the prophecy made in his speech at Indianapolis during the Mine Workers' convention. What was that prophecy? He asserted that we had reached the crest of the wave of so-called industrial activity, that the turn of the tide was downward, and no matter how strong our organization might be, we would be compelled to accept reductions in our wages. This prophecy was made while negotiations were pending with the operators and they were still insisting upon a reduction of fifteen per cent. If Mr. Mitchell had made a public utterance of that kind at the time Mr. Debs made it, the miners would have been compelled to accept a fifteen per cent reduction instead of a five and one-half per cent. The public can judge for itself who is the person that betrayed his trust, whether it was Mr. Debs, who announced that the miners must accept a reduction when the operators were clamoring for fifteen per cent off, or Mr. Mitchell, who fought the issue until the last possible penny had been obtained. Mr. Debs apparently assumes that as a friend of the miners it was his duty to inform them of the perfidy of their officials. What a wonderful friendship his must be. The position of Mr. Mitchell and his associates was expressed in the miners' convention of March 5 and was carried by the afternoon papers of that date. The dispatch which he quotes was published in the morning papers of March 6. On March 7 the mine workers' convention decided to submit the acceptance or rejection of the proposition to the miners themselves, and instructed the national officials to send a copy of their recommendation to every local union. If Mr. Debs was the friend of the miners that he pretends to be, and if he had any proof of dishonesty on the part of the officials, or of collusion between them and the operators to reduce the wages of the miners, he should have furnished them the evidence of it before the vote was taken. Mr. Debs had no such proof and we know that it did not exist.

When the bituminous miners of Indiana in convention at Terre Haute, knowing the facts, passed a resolution condemning the action of Mr. Debs, he immediately began to whine. In the interview published in the Terre Haute *Sunday Tribune,* above referred to, he asserts that "Labor may always be relied upon to crucify its friends." What a woeful wail coming from the lips of a man who started the cry of "crucify them" against Mr. Mitchell and his associates.

Much more might be said in reply to the falsities contained in his article, but enough has been told. Whether he is alone in this attack or is merely carrying out a preconcerted plan to destroy the trade union movement we do not know. He may succeed in injuring us personally, but the trade union movement is based upon eternal principles of evolutionary development and he can no more destroy it or divert it from the fulfillment of its destiny than he can destroy the waters of the Mississippi with a stone or change its channel with a Chinese chopstick.

JOHN MITCHELL.
T. L. LEWIS.
W. B. WILSON.

This was followed by the reply of Mr. Debs in the issue of the *Social Democratic Herald* of June 4 and republished in the issue of June 25, as follows:

MR. DEBS.

Terre Haute, Ind., May 28, 1904.

To the S. D. Herald:

The brief article I had in the *Herald* of April 9 in reference to the wage reduction forced upon the coal miners by the mine owners, assisted by the national officers of the United Mine Workers, has not been ignored as Mr. Mitchell said it would be when it was first brought to his attention. It required Mr. Mitchell to summon the aid of his colleagues, six weeks of time and several columns of space to point out the "misstatements," and so hopeless did they find the task that they had to confess failure in vulgar resort to personal detraction.

The alleged reply consists wholly of words. From first to last it is a quibble over minor points. Every material fact is evaded; every irrelevant detail is brought out and made to do duty in the circular procession.

The essential truth of my statement has not and will not be denied. It cannot be answered by personal abuse, nor extinguished by a deluge of meaningless words.

Suppose I were foolish enough to pose as a "martyr," what has that to do with the case? Does it alter the fact that Mr. Mitchell, Mr. Wilson and Mr. Lewis used all the power of their official positions to help the operators reduce the wages of the miners, and this after Mr. Mitchell had proved conclusively that the reduction was "unwarranted" and after he had declared he would never consent to it?

Never mind about the "diseased imagination," the "crucified martyr," and the particular hour of adjournment. Is the above statement true or is it false?

Mr. Mitchell virtually admits it and his explanation places him in the attitude of a general on a field of battle, first assuring his soldiers that their cause is just and that they must face the enemy like men, and then, on the eve of the fight, turning about and saying to the same soldiers who had so lustily cheered him: "I have been in conference with the general on the other side and he has convinced me that we are taking desperate chances of being whipped, and so I advise that you accept the terms of the enemy and retreat from the field without a fight."

As to the personal insinuations which are supposed to serve where argument fails, I regret as much as Mr. Mitchell seems to enjoy the meagerness of my service to the working class, but little as that service may amount to, I have the satisfaction of knowing that it is not of a quality to inspire the capitalist press to convince me that I am the greatest labor leader on earth.

And little as I may claim, as compared with Mr. Mitchell, there is yet enough to include an almost fatal sunstroke, sustained on a public highway, the only place allowed me under a federal injunction, while rallying a body of coal miners to unite in the fight for an increase of wages and join the United Mine Workers of America.

Mr. Mitchell claims that I accused him of dishonesty. I deny it. No such charge was made by me. I am concerned with acts and facts and not with motives. Mr. Mitchell's honesty is not in question. Let that be conceded. Results remain the same.

Now what are the questions in controversy?

First—In my article of April 9 I incorporated a press dispatch sent out by the Pittsburg *Post* on March 6, saying that it, the *Post*, had it upon the "best authority" that there would be no strike, that the miners would accept the reduction, and that a two years' contract would be signed.

The dispatch was sent out after the convention of miners at Indianapolis had turned down the ultimatum of the operators, and a strike seemed so imminent that the press uniformly declared that "only a miracle could prevent it."

The prediction made in the dispatch came true to the letter. There was no strike, the reduction was accepted and the contract was made for two years.

The dispatch was undoubtedly sent out on the "best authority." It was true prophecy. Now, the question is, Who is the "best authority" as to whether the miners will strike or not? Did the *Post* speak upon such authority? The outcome verifies it. Again, did the *Post* have such authority, or did it lie? The *Post* is friendly to Mr. Mitchell; will he say it lied? Will he have the *Post* name its "best authority"?

I inferred that the *Post's* "best authority" was Mr. F. L. Robbins, leader of the mine owners, who lives in Pittsburg, where the *Post* is published, and I then asked, "Did Robbins, leader of the operators, have an understanding with Mitchell, president of the miners," and I answered, "It must be admitted that it looks that way."

This is the point that excites the wrath of the union officials. I now repeat it. To me it looks that way. I cannot avoid that conclusion.

The only error I made was in the date of adjournment. The convention adjourned March 7, not the 5th. Upon this point I stand corrected, but it is wholly immaterial. The convention refused the ultimatum of the operators on the 5th, the press reports saying "the vote was cast in the face of the opposition of President Mitchell and the other national officers." Next day the *Post* sent out its prophetic dispatch. That is the point at issue, the action of the convention and the *Post's* prophetic announcement next day. The date of adjournment does not alter the fact in the smallest degree.

"But," says Mr. Mitchell, "Mr. Robbins had not returned to Pittsburg and therefore could not have given the *Post* the information—that disposes of the 'misstatement.'" Not quite. The *Post* had a representative at Indianapolis and there are telegraph wires between there and Pittsburg.

When I said that in my opinion there was an "understanding" between Robbins and Mitchell I simply meant what I said. The men are on friendly personal terms. There is nothing wrong about that. When "they shook hands in the presence of the delegates and engaged in earnest conversation and were loudly applauded by the convention" there was no objection to that.

But the miners voted down the operators in spite of Mitchell's protest. That is a fact, is it not?

And when the operators were voted down Mitchell and the national officers of the union appealed to the referendum.

Would they have resorted to the referendum if the delegates had voted to accept instead of rejecting the reduction?

The national officers also had themselves authorized by the delegates to "explain the situation" to the local unions in sending out the vote, and this "explanation" took every form that could be devised to whip the rank and file into submission to the operators.

As an instance of this "explanation" the speech of Mr. Lewis at Linton was a shining success. He was given full credit by the capitalist press for having turned defeat into victory and carrying the day for the reduction and against the strike.

But to complete the evidence. When the operators were turned down by the miners' convention and a strike seemed inevitable, the Pittsburg *Post* coolly declared that it had it upon the "best authority" that there would be no strike, that the miners would give in; and then it went on to state precisely what the basis of final settlement would be and that the contract would be signed for two years. Less than two weeks later all these things came to pass to the very letter.

Now this "best authority" was doubtless Robbins speaking

through the "returning operators" mentioned in the dispatch, who knew that the matter would go to the local unions, and had the assurance that Mitchell and the national officers would use all their influence in favor of the reduction and that with the national officers on their side the referendum vote would defeat the strike and enforce the reduction.

In other words, the operators felt certain that the union officials could and would swing the vote of the organization and the prophecy that was fulfilled was made accordingly.

But even if Mr. Mitchell gave the operators no single word of assurance, his actions and utterances were sufficient and the fact remains unchanged. They knew his position and counted on his influence, and he did not disappoint them.

Notwithstanding this more than 67,000 members of his organization, representing its highest intelligence, voted against the reduction, rejecting his advice and impeaching his leadership, and I happen to know that a large proportion of them heartily approve and are ready to stand by every statement contained in my article.

Here are a few lines just received from a member of the Miners' Union: "I want to thank you for telling the truth about the settlement. The operators beat us with the help of our own officers. Six months ago a man would have been mobbed if he had said a word about Mitchell in this neighborhood. Now you can hear him condemned everywhere. You have more friends among the miners here today than John Mitchell."

The four alleged "misstatements" Mr. Mitchell claims to have disposed of in his attempted denial are in fact one and the same, and hinge upon the simple error in the date of adjournment, which, as I have shown, is utterly inconsequential and has no bearing whatever upon the material facts of the statement which stand as wholly unimpeached as when they were first written down.

To sum up, here is substantially what I stated: That Mr. Mitchell led the miners in their conference with the operators; that he said: "This year the demands of the miners referring to the absolute run of mine basis and the present wage scale must be met or the mines will cease to produce coal," that he demanded a uniform wage for all inside and outside labor and a 7-cent differential; that he advised his followers to stand firm; that he declared he would never yield; that the United Mine Workers would take no backward step; that the reduction proposed by the operators was unwarranted and would not be accepted; that last year's earnings of the Pittsburg Coal Co. were $20,000,000, showing a large increase in profits; that he and the miners were "terribly in earnest," etc., etc.

I have the reports before me and the proof that this was his attitude and these his utterances is simply overwhelming.

What next? Why, a few days later, we hear him saying to his followers: "Your national officers want you to accept this cut."

What do you think of it, Mr. Mitchell?

Would it be possible for an enemy to place you in a more unfavorable light than you are placed by your own official words and acts?

You said all these things and did not mean them. You yielded one point and then another, after declaring you would not yield; finally when you had surrendered all your demands you declared that you would insist upon the old scale, and that you *would not recede* from it. But you *did recede* from it. You not only yielded everything you originally demanded but you agreed to a reduction. Not only this, but *you did all in your official power to enforce that reduction*.

Are these facts or are they falsehoods, and if they are facts they accord perfectly with your capitalistic philosophy that "there is no necessary conflict between capital and labor." It is only necessary for labor to have leaders with the civic federation label upon them and peacefully submit to slavery and degradation.

What right has Mr. Mitchell to talk about the capitalist press as the "paid agents of capital"? Is it not the capitalist press that has poured out its fulsome eulogy upon Mr. Mitchell and heralded him as the greatest leader of labor in all history?

It is my right, Mr. Mitchell, to arraign that press as the enemy of labor, but not your right, for you are a prime favorite with that press and the class who own that press, and when you denounce it you are guilty of ingratitude to the power that largely made you what you are.

Is it a sure sign that I am trying to destroy the Miners' Union because I am opposed to the reduction of the miners' wages? Is this the best specimen of pure and simple labor union logic these gentlemen have to offer?

What I am really trying to destroy is the mine owners' influence in the Mine Workers' Union. To that I plead guilty and there I draw the line. The operators know it and hate me accordingly. The mine workers, most of them, do not, as yet, know it and they share the hatred of their masters. But I can wait.

It is true that the district convention of miners, held here, denounced me; it is also true that I said in reference to such action that "labor may generally be relied upon to crucify its friends." This Mr. Mitchell is pleased to call a "whine." These words were used to characterize the action of the men who said, "We have got to denounce Debs to set ourselves right with the operators." They understood me and this is sufficient. And mark me, Mr. Mitchell, and don't forget it, that body of miners, or their successors, will rescind those resolutions, and when they are finally directed where they properly belong you may have less occasion than you fancy you now have, even with the operators on your side, for self-congratulation.

In the meantime I have no resentment but entire sympathy for those who denounced me. They acted for their masters and simply emphasized their own wage slavery.

Mine Owner Robbins was wise when he said to the miners' delegates: "The union between the operators and miners has been a partnership for several years that I have been proud of."

There is a whole volume in that paragraph.

And there is another in the utterance of Vice President T. L. Lewis of the United Mine Workers when the strike seemed certain: "If Senator Hanna had lived there would have been no strike. His influence would have been powerful enough to force the operators to listen to reason."

What a commentary upon the United Mine Workers and its leaders!

Operator Robbins and labor leader Mitchell and his colleagues, Governor Peabody and President Gompers, David Parry and Sherman Bell all belong to the same capitalist political party that supports the same capitalist administration that assassinates eight-hour and anti-injunction bills and treats labor like a galley slave.

To me it seems not only like sarcasm but positively tragic to hear Mr. Mitchell and his colleagues boast of the "great benefits" that have come to the miners and the "substantial" things they are now enjoying in face of the fact that thousands of them are totally idle, that those employed in the coal fields of Indiana today do not average above two days of work a week, that they are in debt, housed in shacks and eke out a miserable existence as the coal digging victims of wage slavery.

These miners get 85 cents for digging a ton of coal for which the people in that immediate vicinity pay $3.50. The operators, of course, get rich; the miners, of course, stay poor. Truly, an ideal arrangement.

Small wonder that the "interstate movement" perfectly suits the operators, that the United Mine Workers under the leadership of Mitchell, Wilson and Lewis is so satisfactory to them that they agree to collect its dues by deducting them from the wages of the miners, without which the union would go to pieces; and this is one of the reasons why Mr. Mitchell did not dare to break with Mr. Robbins, and why Mr. Mitchell helped Mr. Robbins to force the wage reduction upon the miners.

Mr. Mitchell has profound regard for the good will of the capitalist and great consideration for his feelings, interests and general importance, so great that he issues a proclamation to the miners of the country calling upon them to refrain from work while a capitalist is being buried, with not the remotest thought of showing such extreme respect to the memory of the dead when instead of a rich capitalist it is only a hundred and eighty poor coal diggers, stark and mutilated, blown up in a mine through the criminal negligence of the capitalist owners for whom they were digging up profits.

Mr. Mitchell sees "no necessary conflict between labor and capital." Then why the United Mine Workers? What excuse has it to exist? Its whole record is one of conflict, honorable conflict, waged under difficulties and involving hunger, rags and death, and every page of it tells in harrowing phrase of the necessary conflict between the capitalist and the wage worker, the exploiter and his victim, the master and his slave.

If there is no "necessary" conflict, why any at all? Why do not the operators raise wages instead of lowering them? What have the miners been striking for all these years? Is it not because they have had to fight tooth and nail for every particle they have ever received? Has all this been unnecessary? Does Mr. Mitchell draw salary as president of the Mine Workers to continue this "unnecessary" conflict, or to put an end to it by letting the operators control his union and advising the miners to thankfully accept what the operators see fit to allow them?

It is doubtless because he sees no "necessary" conflict between capital and labor that Mr. Mitchell is a Republican in politics. He also claims to be a friend of President Roosevelt —and so is Sherman Bell.

Mr. Mitchell's friend Roosevelt hasn't the power as chief executive and commander-in-chief of the nation to prevent the snuffing out of a state constitution, the brutal banishment of Mother Jones, the burial alive of that real labor leader, C. H. Moyer, and the murder and mobbing of miners in Colorado by the military criminals in authority.

Grover Cleveland served the capitalists by invading the state of Illinois and Theodore Roosevelt serves them just as loyally by keeping out of Colorado.

President Roosevelt may be your friend, Mr. Mitchell, but he is not the friend of the exploited class you are supposed to stand for. He is not my friend, nor do he and I belong to the same party, or stand for the same principles.

Mr. Mitchell says "there is no necessary conflict between capital and labor." I say there is no possible peace between them. Every hour of truce is at the price of slavery. This is Mr. Mitchell's fundamental error. From this all others spring and he has yet to face their consequences.

Personally, I have not the slightest feeling about the matter. There was a time when I admired and applauded Mitchell's leadership. I thought I saw the coming of a man.

But alas! Little by little I have seen him succumb to the blandishments of the plutocrats. He is today their beau ideal as a labor leader.

The man was never born who can honestly serve both capitalist and wage worker, both master and slave.

Time will tell!

There is a mass of evidence and other matter I have had to omit. Space will not allow its use and I have already exceeded proper bounds. I have a proposition:

Messrs. Mitchell, Wilson and Lewis allude to themselves as "men who are the equals of Mr. Debs physically, morally and intellectually." Good! Now, then, I want the truth and shall assume that these gentlemen want the same. There is not space in a paper for full discussion of this question, nor is such discussion satisfactory or final. I aver that the essential facts set forth in my article in the *Herald* of April 9 are true and can be maintained by overwhelming proof. Mr. Mitchell says there is scarcely a truthful statement in the entire article. He also says "there is no necessary conflict between capital and labor." I challenge Mr. Mitchell to meet me upon these issues before the members of his own organization, the miners of Illinois, his own state, and of Spring Valley, the city in which he lives. Mr. Mitchell may have both Mr. Wilson and Mr. Lewis to help him.

Let the case be presented to the miners whose union I am charged with attempting to destroy and let them render the verdict. EUGENE V. DEBS.

Supplementary to the above the following and final letter of Mr. Debs appeared in the same paper July 2, 1904:

MR. DEBS.

Terre Haute, Ind., June 24, 1904.
To the S. D. Herald:

Some time ago I said that John Mitchell, president of the United Mine Workers, and Francis L. Robbins, president of the Pittsburg Coal Company, understood each other perfectly in reference to the settlement of the threatened coal strike which reduced the miners' wages; and that Mr. Robbins and the operators had the assistance of Mr. Mitchell in enforcing the reduction and were able to predict it with accuracy long before it was finally agreed to by the rank and file of the miners. Mr. Mitchell denied this over his signature and Mr. Robbins, according to the Pittsburg *Labor World,* said it was a "contemptible lie."

The Pittsburg *Dispatch* of June 7 has an extended account of an incident that may not be corroborative but it is certainly significant, and, like the proverbial straw, shows which way the wind blows.

Mr. Mitchell has gone to Europe and it is not my purpose to attack him in his absence but simply to put this incident on record for future reference.

The article in question is headed with a five-column cut of an elaborate banquet scene, the guests consisting of mine owners, mine workers and capitalist politicians. At the table of honor are Mr. Mitchell and Mr. Robbins, with Patrick Dolan, district president, between them as the central figure and toastmaster of the evening.

Mr. Dolan's boast is that he has never read a book on economics and he proves it daily in his works. In a recent action for libel brought against a local paper by a couple of organizers for the Socialist Labor Party, Mr. Dolan testified for the defendant. In answer to a question he said that Socialism and anarchy were one and the same thing. Asked how that was he said: "They are both against the flag." If the rearmost straggler in the rank and file were as far advanced as Mr. Dolan, his leader, the darkness would be complete and the cause of labor all but hopeless.

Such a leader is conclusive evidence that there are vast stretches between his followers and daylight.

What Mr. Dolan does not know about labor makes him hate Socialism and fits him to preside at a banquet where workers are used as dummies to renew allegiance to the reign of their masters.

The *Dispatch* article has the following double-column headlines:

"MINERS START A BOOM FOR COMBINE LEADER" —"F. L. ROBBINS APPROVED FOR UNITED STATES SENATOR AT DINNER IN HONOR OF LABOR OFFICIALS"—"THEIR GRACEFUL COMPLIMENT."

The account in part follows:

"In the presence of the recipient of the honor, coal operators and organized coal miners of western Pennsylvania formally proposed Francis L. Robbins, president of the Pittsburg Coal Company, for the United States senate at a banquet last night at the Henry Hotel. The banquet was in honor of John Mitchell, president of the United Mine Workers, and District Secretary William Dodds to wish the two godspeed on a European tour they are about to make in the interest of their organization. Even Mitchell joined in the tribute to Robbins, which was taken up by others."

"Although hailed as the next senator from Pennsylvania, Mr. Robbins confined his remarks to an eulogy of Mitchell and Dodds."

* * * * * * *

"Mitchell and Dodds were presented with diamond mementoes of the esteem of the operators and miners."

"Secretary Dodds started the Robbins movement. Dodds is secretary of a district of 37,000 organized miners. He formally proposed Mr. Robbins for United States senator. The coal president was cheered for several minutes. He said he attended the banquet to do honor to two friends."

"The presence of operators and miners," said Mr. Robbins, "defines the proper relation between capital and labor, employer and employed. One thing has led up to the present state of affairs: *Miners recognize that conservative men must be placed at the head of their organization.*" * * *

"If the future shows a change it will be because labor does not continue to put conservative men at the head of their organization."

"THE ONLY MENACE TO ORGANIZED LABOR NOW IS SOCIALISM, AND SOCIALISM MUST BE RELEGATED TO THE REAR."

"Mr. Mitchell then spoke and among other things is reported as saying that:

"He believes harmonious relations between organized capital and organized labor can be obtained without labor surrendering any of its rights or capitalism surrendering its rights."

The foregoing appeals strongly for comment, especially the statement of Mr. Robbins, coal baron and labor leader, that Socialism is a menace to organized labor, but I will only say that Mr. Robbins knows quite well that Socialism is a menace only to the class suggested by his name and that this prompts him to assail it while he places diamond decorations upon the "conservative" leaders of his coal-digging wage-slaves.

The fact that Mr. John Mitchell, labor leader, sees nothing wrong in accepting a diamond badge from the rich and designing exploiters of his poor and pilfered followers; that he evidently has not the least conception of what such a testimonial really symbolizes, may serve sufficiently in mitigation to shield him from merited contempt and condemnation.

EUGENE V. DEBS.

The editions of the *Herald* containing the letters were speedily exhausted, and as there seemed to be an increasing interest in the controversy it was finally concluded to publish the correspondence in pamphlet form to supply the great demand.

CELL OCCUPIED BY DEBS IN WOODSTOCK JAIL

The Federal Government and the Chicago Strike

Reply to the article on "The Government in the Chicago Strike of 1894" in McClure's Magazine, July, 1904, by Grover Cleveland, ex-President of the U. S.

Written for and rejected by McClure's Magazine. Published by Appeal to Reason, August 27, 1904.

In the July issue of *McClure's Magazine* ex-President Grover Cleveland has an article on "The Government in the Chicago Strike of 1894." That there may be no mistake about the meaning of "government" in this connection it should be understood that Mr. Cleveland has reference to the Federal government, of which he was the executive head at the time of the strike in question, and not to the State government of Illinois, or the municipal government of Chicago, both of which were overridden and set at defiance by the executive authority, enforced by the military power of the Federal government under the administration of Mr. Cleveland.

CLEVELAND VINDICATES HIMSELF.

The ex-President's article not only triumphantly vindicates his administration but congratulates its author upon the eminent service he rendered the republic in a critical hour when a labor strike jarred its foundations and threatened its overthrow.

It may be sheer coincidence that Mr. Cleveland's eulogy upon his patriotic administration and upon himself as its central and commanding figure appears on the eve of a national convention composed largely of his disciples, who are urging his fourth nomination for the presidency for the very reasons set forth in the article on the Chicago strike.

However this may be, it is certain that of his own knowledge ex-President Cleveland knows nothing of the strike he discusses; that the evidence upon which he acted officially and upon which he now bases his conclusion was *ex parte*, obtained wholly from the railroad interests and those who represented or were controlled by these interests, and it is not strange, therefore, that he falls into a series of errors beginning with the cause of the disturbance and running all through his account of it, as may be proved beyond doubt by reference to the "Report on the Chicago Strike" by the "United States Strike Commission" of his own appointment.

WHAT WAS THE CHICAGO STRIKE?

Simply one of the many battles that have been fought and are yet to be fought in the economic war between capital and labor. Pittsburg, Homestead, Buffalo, Latimer, Pana, Cœur d'Alene, Cripple Creek and Telluride recall a few of the battles fought in this country in the world-wide struggle for industrial emancipation.

When the strike at Chicago occurred did President Cleveland make a personal examination? No.

Did he grant both sides a hearing? He did not.

In his fourteen-page magazine article what workingman, or what representative of labor, does he cite in support of his statements or his official acts? Not one.

I aver that he received every particle of his information from the capitalist side, that he was prompted to act by the capitalist side, that his official course was determined wholly, absolutely, by and in the interest of the capitalist side, and that no more thought or consideration was given to the other side—the hundreds of thousands of workingmen whose lives and whose wives and babes were at stake—than if they had been so many swine or sheep that had balked on their way to the shambles.

THE OBJECT OF FEDERAL INTERFERENCE.

From the Federal judge who sat on the bench as the protege of the late George M. Pullman, to whose influence he was indebted for his appointment—as he was to the railroad companies for the annual passes he had in his pocket—down

WRITINGS.   183

to the last thug sworn in by the railroads and paid by the railroads (p. 340 report of Strike Commission) to serve the railroads as United States deputy marshal, the one object of the Federal Court and its officers was, not the enforcement of law and preservation of order, but the breaking up of the strike in the interest of the railroad corporations, and it was because of this fact that John P. Altgeld, Governor of Illinois, and John P. Hopkins, Mayor of Chicago, were not in harmony with President Cleveland's administration and protested against the Federal troops being used in their state and city for such a malign purpose.

This is the fact and I shall prove it beyond doubt before this article is concluded.

CLEVELAND OMITS REFERENCE TO JUDGE WOODS.

The late Judge William A. Woods figured as one of the principal judges in the Chicago affair, issuing the injunctions, citing the strikers to appear before him and sentencing them to jail without trial, but President Cleveland discreetly omits all reference to him; and although he introduces copies of many documents, his article does not include copies of the telegrams that passed between Judge Woods from his home at Indianapolis and the railroad managers at Chicago before he left home to hold court in the latter city.

Judge Woods had the distinction of convicting the writer and his colleagues without a trial and of releasing William W. Dudley of "Blocks of Five" memory in spite of a trial.

Judge Woods is dead and I do not attack the dead. I have to mention his name, and this of itself is sufficient.

PULLMAN'S CONTEMPT OF COURT.

During the strike the late George M. Pullman was summoned to appear before the Federal Court to give testimony. He at once had his private car attached to an eastbound train and left the city, treating the court with sovereign contempt. On his return, accompanied by Robert Todd Lincoln, his attorney, he had a tete-a-tete with the court, "in chambers," and that ended the matter. He was not required to testify, nor to appear in open court. The striker upon whom there fell even the suspicion of a shadow of contempt was sentenced and jailed with alacrity. Not one was spared, not one invited to a "heart-to-heart" with his honor, "in chambers."

A CHALLENGE TO CLEVELAND.

In reviewing the article of ex-President Cleveland I wish to adduce the proof of my exceptions and denials, as well as the evidence to support my affirmations, but I realize that in the limited space of a single issue it is impossible to do this in complete and satisfactory manner; and as the case is important enough to be revived, after a lapse of ten years, by Mr. Cleveland, and as the side of labor has never yet reached the people, I am prompted to suggest a fair and full hearing of both sides on the public rostrum or in a series of articles, and I shall be happy to meet Mr. Cleveland or any one he may designate in such oral or written discussion, and if I fail to relieve the great body of railroad men who composed the American Railway Union of the criminal stigma which Mr. Cleveland has sought to fasten upon them, or if I cannot produce satisfactory evidence that the crimes charged were instigated by the other side—the side in whose interest President Cleveland brought to bear all the powers of the Federal government—I will agree to publicly beg forgiveness of the railroads, apologize to the ex-President and cease my agitation forever.

THE CAUSE OF THE PULLMAN STRIKE.

It is easy for Mr. Cleveland and others who were on the side of the railroads to introduce copies of documents, reports, etc., for the simple reason that the Federal Court at Chicago compelled the telegraph companies to deliver up copies of all our telegrams and copies of the proceedings of the convention and other meetings of the American Railway Union, including secret sessions, but the Federal Court did not call upon the railroads to produce the telegrams that passed among themselves, nor between their counsel and the Federal authorities, nor the printed proceedings of the General Managers' Association for public inspection and as a basis for criminal prosecution.

HAD THE STRIKE WON.

Nevertheless, there is available proof sufficient to make it clear to the unprejudiced mind, to the honest man who seeks the truth, that the United States government, under the administration of President Grover Cleveland, was at the beck and call of the railroad corporations, acting as one through the "General Managers' Association," and that these corporations, with the Federal Courts and troops to back them up, had swarms of mercenaries sworn in as deputy marshals to incite violence as a pretext for taking possession of the headquarters of the American Railway Union by armed force, throwing its leaders into prison without trial and breaking down the union that was victorious, maligning, brow-beating and persecuting its peaceable and law-abiding members and putting the railroad corporations in supreme control of the situation.

That was the part of President Cleveland in the Chicago strike, and for this achievement the railroad combine and the trusts in general remember him with profound gratitude, and are not only willing but anxious that he shall be President of the United States forevermore.

A PRECEDENT FOR FUTURE ACTION.

In the closing paragraph of his article Mr. Cleveland compliments his administration upon having cleared the way "which shall hereafter guide our nation safely and surely in the exercise of its functions which represent the people's trust." The word "people's" is not only superfluous but mischievous and fatal to the truth. Omit that and the ex-President's statement will not be challenged.

CLEVELAND'S FIRST MOVE.

How did President Cleveland begin operations in the Chicago strike. Among the first things he did, as he himself tells us, was to appoint Edwin Walker as special counsel for the government.

Who was Edwin Walker?

"An able and prominent attorney," says Mr. Cleveland.

Is that all?

Not quite. At the time President Cleveland and his Attorney-General, Richard Olney, designated Edwin Walker, upon recommendation of the railroads, as special counsel to the government, for which alleged service he was paid a fee that amounted to a fortune, *the said Edwin Walker was*

CORRIDOR IN WOODSTOCK JAIL WHERE DEBS EXERCISED

WRITINGS. 187

already the counsel for the Chicago, Milwaukee & St. Paul Railway.

Turning for a moment to "Who's Who In America," we find:

"Walker, Edwin, lawyer, * * * removed to Chicago in 1865; has represented several railroads as general solicitor since 1860. Illinois counsel for C., M. & St. P. R. R. since 1870; also partner in firm of W. P. Rend & Co., coal miners and shippers. Was counsel for the railway companies and special counsel for the United States in the lawsuits growing out of the great railroad strike of 1894."

THE SIGNIFICANCE OF THE APPOINTMENT.

Here is the situation: There is a conflict between the General Managers' Association, representing the railroads, and the American Railway Union, representing the employes. Perfect quiet and order prevail, as I shall show, but the railroads are beaten to a standstill, utterly helpless, cannot even move a mail car, simply because their employes have quit their service and left the premises in a body. Note also that the employes were willing to haul the mail trains and all other trains, refusing only to handle Pullman cars until the Pullman Company should consent to arbitrate its disagreement with its striking and starving employes. But the railroad officials determined that if the Pullman cars were not handled the mail cars should not move.

This is how and why the mails were obstructed and this was the pretext for Federal interference. In a word, President Cleveland, obedient to the railroads, took sides with them and supported them in their conflict with their employes with all the powers of the Federal government.

STRIKE COMMISSION REPORT VS. CLEVELAND.

To bear out these facts it is not necessary to go outside of the official report of the Strike Commission, which anyone may verify at his pleasure. The only reason I do not incorporate the voluminous evidence is that the space at my command must be economized for other purposes.

It is thus made clear that President Cleveland and his

Cabinet placed the government at the service of the railroads.

Edwin Walker, their own attorney, made the agent of the government and put in supreme command of the railroad and government forces! What an unholy alliance! And what a spectacle and object lesson!

Upon Walker's representations Cleveland acted; upon Walker's demand, the Federal soldiers marched into Chicago; upon Walker's command, the great government of the United States obeyed with all the subserviency of a trained lackey.

SUPPOSE CLEVELAND HAD APPOINTED DARROW?

Suppose that President Cleveland had appointed Clarence S. Darrow, attorney for the American Railway Union, instead of Edwin Walker, attorney of the General Managers' Association, as special counsel for the government!

And suppose that Darrow had ordered the offices of the General Managers' Association sacked, the books, papers and correspondence, including the unopened private letters of the absent officers, packed up and carted away and the offices put under the guard of Federal ruffians, in flagrant violation of the Constitution of the United States, as was done by order of Walker with the offices of the American Railway Union!

And suppose, moreover, that the American Railway Union, backed up by Darrow, agent of the United States government, had sworn in an army of "thugs, thieves and ex-convicts" (see official report of Michael Brennan, superintendent of Chicago police to the Council of Chicago) to serve the American Railway Union as deputy United States marshals and "conservators of peace and order!"

And suppose, finally, that the expected trouble had followed, would anyone in possession of his senses believe that these things had been done to protect life and property and preserve law and order?

That is substantially the case that President Cleveland is trying to make for himself and his administration out of their participation in the Chicago strike.

THE REAL LAWBREAKER THE RAILROADS.

The implication that runs through Mr. Cleveland's entire article is that the railway corporations were paragons of peace and patriotism, law and order, while the railway employes were a criminal, desperate and bloodthirsty mob which had to be suppressed by the strong arm of the government.

No wonder the ex-President is so dear to the iron heart of the railroad trust and every other trust that uses the government and its officers and soldiers to further its own sordid ends.

Let us consider for a moment these simple questions:

Who are the more law-abiding, the predatory railroad corporations or the hard-worked railroad employes?

What railroad corporation in the United States lives up to the law of the land? Not one.

What body of railroad employes violates it? Not one.

THE BRAZEN DEFIANCE OF LAW BY THE RAILROADS.

The railroad corporations are notorious for their brazen defiance of every law that is designed to curb their powers or restrain their rapacity.

The railroad corporations have their lobby at Washington and at every State capital; they bribe legislators, corrupt courts, debauch politics and commit countless other legal and moral crimes against the commonwealth.

The railway employes are a body of honest, useful, self-sacrificing, peace-loving men, who never have been, and never will be, guilty of the crimes committed by their corporate masters.

And yet President Cleveland serves the corporate masters and exalts and glorifies the act while he attempts to absolve the criminals and fasten the insufferable stigma upon honest men.

Nothing further is required to demonstrate beyond all cavil the capitalist class character of our present government.

THE STRIKE COMMISSION'S REPORT.

Now for a few facts about the strike. It began May 11, 1894, and was perfectly peaceable and orderly until the army of "thugs, thieves and ex-convicts," as Superintendent of Police Brennan called them in his official report to the Council of Chicago, were sworn in as deputies by the United States marshal at the command of Edwin Walker, attorney of the

General Managers' Association and special counsel to the government. Let us quote the report of the Strike Commission, consisting of Carroll D. Wright, Commissioner of Labor, who served ex-officio; John D. Kernan, of New York, and N. E. Worthington, of Illinois, two lawyers, appointed by President Cleveland.

Let it be noted that the railway employes, that is to say, labor, the working class, had no representative on this Commission.

From the report they issued we quote as follows:

A. R. U. LEADERS ADVISE AGAINST STRIKE.

"It is undoubtedly true that the officers and directors of the American Railway Union did not want a strike at Pullman and advised against it. * * * (P. xxvii.) (Yet the people were told over and over and still believe that Debs ordered the strike.)

RAILROADS SET THE EXAMPLE.

"It should be noted that until the railroads set the example a general union of railroad employes was never attempted." (P. xxxi.)

"The refusal of the General Managers' Association to recognize and deal with such a combination of labor as the American Railway Union seems arrogant and absurd when we consider its standing before the law, its assumptions, and its past and obviously contemplated future action." (P. xxxi.)

"* * * the rents (at Pullman) are from 20 to 25 per cent higher than rents in Chicago or surrounding towns for similar accommodations." (P. xxxv.)

STRIKE COMMISSION CONTRADICTS CLEVELAND.

"The strike occurred on May 11, and from that time until the soldiers went to Pullman, about July 4, 300 strikers were placed about the company's property, professedly to guard it from destruction or interference. This guarding of property in strikes is, as a rule, a mere pretense. Too often the real object of guards is to prevent newcomers from taking the strikers' places, by persuasion, often to be followed, if ineffectual, by intimidation and violence. The Pullman Company claims this was the real object of these guards. *These strikers at Pullman are entitled to be believed to the contrary in this matter, because of their conduct and forbearance after May 11. It is in evidence, and uncontradicted, that no violence or destruction of property by strikers or sympathizers took place at Pullman, and that until July 3* (when the Federal troops came upon the scene) *no extraordinary protection was had from the police and military against even anticipated disorder."* (P. xxxviii.)

This paragraph from the report of Mr. Cleveland's own Commission is sufficient answer to Mr. Cleveland's article. It is conclusive, crushing, overwhelming.

DEPUTIES STARTED THE TROUBLE.

There was no trouble at Pullman, nor at Chicago, nor elsewhere, until the railroad-United States deputy marshals were sworn in, followed by the Federal troops.

Governor Altgeld, patriot and statesman, knew it and protested against the troops.

Mayor John P. Hopkins knew it and declared that he was fully competent to preserve the peace of the city.

SUPERINTENDENT OF POLICE CALLED THEM "THUGS."

Michael Brennan, superintendent of the Chicago police, knew it and denounced the deputy marshals Edwin Arnold's hirelings, the General Managers' Association's incendiaries and sluggers, as "thugs, thieves and ex-convicts."

These were the "gentlemen" President Cleveland's government pressed into service upon requisition of the railroads to preserve order and protect life and property, and this is what the ex-President calls "the power of the National government to protect itself in the exercise of its functions."

As to just what these "functions" are when Grover Cleveland is President, the railroad corporations understand to a nicety and agree to by acclamation.

PROFOUND PEACE RESTORED.

The only trouble, when the "deputies" were sworn in, followed by the soldiers, was that there was no trouble. That is the secret of subsequent proceedings. The railroads were paralyzed. Profound peace reigned. The people demanded of the railroads that they operate their trains. They could not do it. Not a man would serve them. They were completely defeated and the banners of organized labor floated triumphant in the breeze.

Beaten at every point, their schemes all frustrated, outgeneraled in tactics and strategy, the corporations played their trump card by an appeal to the Federal judiciary and the Federal administration. To this appeal the response came quick as lightning from a storm cloud.

PEACE FATAL TO MANAGERS' ASSOCIATION.

Peace and order were fatal to the railroad corporations. Violence was as necessary to them as peace was to the employes. They realized that victory could only be snatched from labor by an appeal to violence in the name of peace.

First, deputy marshals. The very day they were appointed the trouble began. The files of every Chicago paper prove it. The report of the Strike Commission does the same.

That was what they were hired for and their character is sufficient evidence of their guilt.

Second, fires (but no Pullman palace cars were lighted) and riots (but no strikers were implicated).

Third, the capitalist-owned newspapers and Associated Press flashed the news over all the wires that the people were at the mercy of a mob and that the strikers were burning and sacking the city.

Fourth, the people (especially those at a distance who knew nothing except what they saw in the papers) united in the frenzied cry: "Down with anarchy! Down with the A. R. U.! Death to the strikers!"

DISTURBANCES STARTED BY DEPUTY MARSHALS.

The first trouble instigated by the deputy marshals was the signal for the Federal Court injunctions, and they came like a succession of lightning flashes.

Next, the general offices of the American Railway Union were sacked and put under guard and communication destroyed. (Later Judge Grosscup rebuked the Federal satraps

WRITINGS. 193

who committed this outrageous crime, but he did not pretend to bring them to justice.)

Next, the leaders of the strike were arrested, not for crime, but for alleged violation of an injunction.

Next, they were brought into court, denied trial by jury, pronounced guilty by the same judge who had issued the injunction, and sent to jail for from three to six months.

THE CONCLUDING WORDS NOT YET WRITTEN.

The Supreme Court of the United States, consisting wholly of trained and successful corporation lawyers, affirmed the proceeding and President Cleveland says that they have "written the concluding words of this history."

Did the Supreme Court of the United States write the "concluding words" in the history of chattel slavery when it handed down Chief Justice Taney's decision that black men had "no rights that the white man was bound to respect?"

These "concluding words" will but hasten the overthrow of wage slavery as the "concluding words" of the same Supreme Court in 1857 hastened the overthrow of chattel slavery.

The railroad corporations would rather have destroyed their property and seen Chicago perish than see the American Railway Union triumphant in as noble a cause as ever prompted sympathetic, manly men to action in this world.

PEACE OVERTURES TURNED DOWN.

The late Mayor Pingree of Detroit came to Chicago with telegrams from the mayors of over fifty of the largest cities urging that there should be arbitration. (P. xxxix, Report of Strike Commission.) He was turned down without ceremony, and afterwards declared that the railroads were the only criminals and that they were responsible for all the consequences.

June 22, four days before the strike against the railroads, or, rather, the boycott of Pullman cars, took effect, there was a joint meeting of the railroad and Pullman officials. (P. xlii, Report of Strike Commission.) At this meeting it was resolved to defeat the strikers, wipe out the American Railway Union, and, to use their exact words, "that we act unitedly to that end."

DEBS' RELEASE FROM WOODSTOCK JAIL

This was the only joint meeting of the kind that had ever been held between the officials of the railroad companies and the Pullman company. They mutually determined to stand together to defeat the strike and destroy the union.

Now, to show what regard these gentlemen have for courts and law and morals, this incident will suffice:

RAILWAY OFFICIALS PERJURE THEMSELVES.

When the officers of the American Railway Union were indicted by a special and packed grand jury and placed on trial for conspiracy, the general managers of the railroads were put on the witness stand to testify as to what action had been taken at the joint railroad and Pullman meeting described, and each and every one of them perjured himself by swearing that he had no recollection of what had taken place at that meeting. Sitting within a few feet of them I saw their faces turn scarlet under the cross-examination, knowing that they were testifying falsely; that the court knew it, and that every one present knew it; but they stuck to their agreement and uniformly failed to remember that they had resolved to stand together, the railroads agreeing to back the Pullman company in defeating their famishing employes, and the Pullman company pledging itself to stand by the railroads in destroying the American Railway Union.

That is what their own record shows they resolved to do, and a little later they concluded to forget all about it, and to this they swore in a Federal Court of law.

I have copies of the court records, including the testimony, to prove this, and the files of all the Chicago dailies of that time contain the same testimony.

These are the gentlemen who have so much to say about law and order—the vaunted guardians of morals and good citizenship.

When A. B. Stickney, president of the Chicago Great Western, who had been victimized by them, told them to their faces that there was not an honest official among them and that he would not trust one of them out of his sight, they did not attempt any defense, for they knew that their accuser was on the inside and in position to make good his assertions.

THE DEPUTIES AS VIEWED BY THE COMMISSION.

I must now introduce a little evidence from the report of the Strike Commission bearing upon the United States deputy marshals who were sworn in by the railroads "to protect life and property and preserve the peace":

Page 356: Superintendent Brennan, of the Chicago police, testifies before the Commission that he has a number of deputy marshals in the county jail *arrested while serving the railroads as United States deputy marshals for highway robbery.*

NEWSPAPER REPORTERS' EVIDENCE.

Page 370: Ray Stannard Baker, then a reporter for the Chicago *Record,* now on the staff of *McClure's Magazine,* testified as follows in answer to the question as to what he knew of the character of the deputy marshals: "From my experience with them it was very bad. I saw more cases of drunkenness, I believe, among the United States deputy marshals than I did among the strikers."

Pages 366 and 367: Malcomb McDowell, reporter for the Chicago *Record,* testified: "The United States deputy marshals and the special deputy sheriffs were sworn in by the hundreds about the 3d and 4th of July, and prior to that, too, and everybody who saw them knew they were not the class of men who ought to be made deputy marshals or deputy sheriffs." * * * "In regard to most of the deputy marshals they seemed to be hunting trouble all the time." * * * "At one time a serious row nearly resulted because some of the deputy marshals standing on the railroad track jeered at the women that passed and insulted them." * * * "I saw more deputy marshals drunk than I saw strikers drunk."

These were Edwin Walker's justly celebrated guardians of the peace.

Page 370: Harold I. Cleveland, reporter for the Chicago *Herald,* testified: "I was on the tracks of the Western Indiana fourteen days." * * * "I saw in that time a couple of hundred deputy marshals. I think they were a very low, contemptible set of men."

HIRED AND PAID BY THE RAILROADS.

Now follows what the Strike Commissioners themselves have to say about the deputy marshals, and their words are specially commended to the thoughtful consideration of their chief, President Cleveland: "United States deputy marshals, to the number of 3,600, were selected by and appointed at request of the General Managers' Association, and of its railroads. They were armed and paid by the railroads, and acted in the double capacity of railroad employes and United States officers. While operating the railroads they assumed and exercised unrestricted United States authority when so ordered by their employers, or whenever they regarded it as necessary. They were not under the direct control of any government official while exercising authority. This is placing officers of the government under control of a combination of railroads. It is a bad precedent, that might well lead to serious consequences."

THE GOVERNMENT SERVES THE CORPORATIONS.

Here we have it, upon the authority of President Cleveland's own Commission, that the United States government under his administration furnished the railroad corporations with government officers in the form of deputy marshals to take the places of striking employes, operate the trains and serve in that dual capacity in any way that might be required to crush out the strike. This is perhaps more credit than the ex-President expected to receive. His own Commission charges him, in effect, with serving the railroads as strike-breaker by furnishing government employes to take the places of striking railroad men and arming them with pistols and clubs and with all the authority of government officials.

Page after page bears testimony of the disreputable character of the deputy marshals sworn in to the number of several thousand and turned loose like armed bullies to "preserve the peace."

The report of the Strike Commission contains 681 pages. I have a mass of other testimony, but for the purpose of this article have confined myself to the report of Mr. Cleveland's own Commission.

HOW THE STRIKERS WERE DEFEATED.

Hundreds of pages of evidence are given by impartial witnesses to establish the guilt of the railroad corporations, to prove that the leaders of the strike counselled peace and order; that the strikers themselves were law-abiding and used their influence to prevent disorder; that there was no trouble until the murderous deputy marshals were sprung upon the community, and that these instigated trouble to pave the way for injunctions and soldiers and change of public sentiment, thereby defeating the strike.

CONFIRMED BY CLEVELAND.

President Cleveland, unwittingly, confirms this fact. On page 232 of his article he quotes approvingly the letter written to Edwin Walker, special counsel of the government and regular counsel of the railroads, by Attorney-General Richard Olney, as follows: "It has seemed to me that if the rights of the United States (Railroads?) were vigorously asserted in Chicago, the origin and center of the demonstration, the result would be to make it a failure everywhere else, and to prevent its spread over the entire country."

That is the point, precisely the point, and Mr. Cleveland admits it. It is not the "obstruction of the mails," nor disorder, nor the violation of law, that arouses Mr. Cleveland's government and prompts it to "vigorous" assertion of its powers, but the "demonstration," that is, the strike against the railroads; and to put this down, not to move the mails or restore order—a mere pretext which was fully exposed by Governor Altgeld—was the prime cause of Federal interference, and to "make it a failure everywhere" all constitutional restraints were battered down, and as a strike-breaker President Cleveland won imperishable renown.

STRIKE LEADERS EXONERATED BY THE COMMISSION.

Particular attention is invited to the following, which appears on page xlv:

"There is no evidence before the Commission that the officers of the American Railway Union at any time participated in or advised intimidation, violence or destruction of property.

They knew and fully appreciated that as soon as mobs ruled the organized forces of society would crush the mobs and all responsible for them in the remotest degree, and that this means defeat."

And yet they all served prison sentences. Will President Cleveland please explain why? And why they were refused a trial?

IN WHOSE INTERESTS WERE CRIMES COMMITTED?

Read the above paragraph from the report of the Strike Commission and then answer these questions:

To whose interest was it to have riots and fires, lawlessness and crime?

To whose advantage was it to have disreputable "deputies" do these things?

Why were only freight cars, largely hospital wrecks, set on fire?

Why have the railroads not yet recovered damages from Cook county, Illinois, for failing to protect their property? Why are they so modest and patient with their suits?

The riots and incendiarism turned defeat into victory for the railroads. They could have won in no other way. They had everything to gain and the strikers everything to lose.

The violence was instigated in spite of the strikers, and the report of the Commission proves that they made every effort in their power to preserve the peace.

When a crime is committed in the dark the person who is supposed to be benefitted by it is sought out as the probable culprit, but we are not required to rely upon presumption in this case, for the testimony against the railroads is too clear and complete and convincing to admit of doubt.

IMPRISONED WITHOUT TRIAL.

If the crimes committed during the Chicago strike were chargeable to the strikers, why were they not prosecuted? If not, why were they sentenced to prison?

The fact that they were flung into prison without evidence and without trial, and the fact that the Supreme Court affirmed the outrage, seemed to afford Mr. Cleveland special satisfac-

DEBS' FIRST GREETING BY THE COMMITTEE

tion, and he accepts what he calls the "concluding words" of the court as his own final vindication.

JUDGE TRUMBULL'S OPINION.

The late Senator and Judge Lyman Trumbull, for many years United States Senator, chairman of the Senate Committee on Judiciary, Supreme Judge of Illinois, author of the thirteenth amendment to the Constitution of the United States, personal friend of Abraham Lincoln, and, above all, an honest man, wrote: "The doctrine announced by the Supreme Court in the Debs case places every citizen at the mercy of any prejudiced or malicious Federal judge who may think proper to imprison him."

President Cleveland doubtless understands the import of these ominous words. Let the people, the working people, whom the ex-President regards merely as a mob to be suppressed when they peaceably protest against injustice—let them contemplate these words at their leisure.

When the strike was at its height and the railroads were defeated at every turn, the Federal Court hastily impaneled a special grand jury to indict the strikers. The foreman of this jury was chosen specially because he was a violent union hater, and he afterward betrayed his own capitalist colleagues in a matter they had entrusted to his integrity.

The jury was impaneled, not to investigate, but to indict.

A *Tribune* reporter, who refused to verify a false interview before the jury, and thereby perjure himself to incriminate the writer, was discharged. The Chicago *Times* published the particulars.

An indictment was speedily returned. "To the penitentiary," was the cry of the railroads and their henchmen. A trial jury was impaneled. Not a juror was accepted who was of the same political party as the defendants. Every possible effort was made to rush the strike leaders to the State prison.

THE FAILURE OF THE PROSECUTION.

After all the evidence of the prosecution had been presented they realized that they had miserably failed. Not one particle of incriminating testimony could the railroads produce with all the sleuth hounds they had at their command.

Next came our turn. The General Managers were dumbfounded when they were, one after the other, put on the stand. Eighty-six witnesses were in court to testify as to the riots and fires. Assistant Chief Palmer and other members of the Fire Department were on hand to testify that when they were trying to extinguish the flames in the railroad yards they caught men in the act of cutting the hose and that these men wore the badges of deputy marshals. Other witnesses were policemen who were ready to testify that they had caught these same deputies instigating violence and acts of incendiarism.

THE JURY DUMBFOUNDED.

The jury had been packed to convict. When our evidence began to come in their eyes fairly bulged with astonishment. There was a perfect transformation scene. The jurors realized that they had been steeped in prejudice and grossly deceived.

The General Managers testified that they did not remember what had taken place at the joint General Managers' and Pullman meeting. Their printed proceedings were called for. They looked appealingly to Edwin Walker. The terror that overspread their features can never be forgotten by those who witnessed it. Their own printed proceedings would expose their mendacity and convict them of conspiracy and crime. Something must be done, and done quickly. Court adjourned for lunch. When it reconvened Judge Grosscup gravely announced that a juror had been suddenly taken ill and that the trial could not proceed.

THE "ILLNESS" OF A JUROR.

The next day and the next the same announcement was repeated. We offered to proceed in any of the several ways provided in such exigencies. The prosecution objected. The cry "To the penitentiary" had subsided. "To let go" was now the order of the railroads. Not another session of court must be held, for their printed proceedings, the private property in the strong box of each member, and full of matter that would convict them, would have to be produced. All the proceedings of the American Railway Union had been produced in evidence by order of the court and the court could not refuse to command the railroad officials to produce the proceedings of their association. These proceedings were brought in at the closing session of the trial, but by order of the court the defendants were forbidden to look into them, and Edwin Walker, the government counsel, watched them with the faithful eye of a trusted guardian.

We were not allowed to examine the proceedings of the General Managers' Association, notwithstanding our proceedings, telegrams, letters and other private communications had been brought into court by order of the judge, inspected by Edwin Walker and others, and printed in the court records for public inspection.

It was at this point that the court adjourned and the juror was taken "ill."

Ten years have elapsed. He is still "ill," and we are still waiting for the court to reconvene and the trial to proceed.

GOVERNMENT REFUSED TO GO ON WITH THE CASE.

Every proposition to continue the case was fiercely resisted by Edwin Walker, special counsel of the government and general counsel of the railroads.

Clarence S. Darrow objected to Mr. Walker's appearing in that dual capacity, representing at the same time the government and the railroads—the supposed justice of the one and the vengeful spirit of the other—but Judge Grosscup overruled the objection.

The trial was postponed again and again, the interest in it gradually subsiding, and many months afterward, when it was almost forgotten, the case was quietly stricken from the docket.

JURORS GREET DEFENDANTS.

When the remaining eleven jurors were discharged by the court, Edwin Walker extended his hand to them, but they rushed by him and surrounded the writer and his co-defendants, grasping their hands and assuring them, each and every one of them, that they were convinced of their innocence and only regretted that they had been prevented from returning their verdict accordingly. The details appear in the Chicago papers of that time.

At the very time we were being tried for conspiracy we were serving a sentence in prison for contempt, the program being that six months in jail should be followed by as many years in penitentiary.

For a jury to pronounce us innocent in substantially the same case for which we were already serving a sentence would mean not only our complete vindication, but the exposure of the Federal Court that had, at the behest of the railroads, sentenced us to prison without a trial.

And so the trial was abruptly terminated on account of the alleged illness of a juror and they could find no other to take his place.

These are the facts and I have all the documentary evidence in detail, and only lack of space prevents me from making the exhibits in this article.

If President Cleveland or the Railroad Managers doubt it I stand ready to meet them face to face in discussion of the issue upon any platform in America.

THE GREATEST INDUSTRIAL BATTLE IN HISTORY.

The Chicago strike was in many respects the grandest industrial battle in history, and I am prouder of my small share in it than of any other act of my life.

Men, women and children were on the verge of starvation at the "model city" of Pullman. They had produced the fabulous wealth of the Pullman corporation, but they, poor souls, were compelled to suffer the torment of hunger pangs in the very midst of the abundance their labor had created.

A hundred and fifty thousand railroad employes, their fellow members in the American Railway Union, sympathized with them, shared their earnings with them, and after trying in every peaceable way they could conceive of to touch the flint heart of the Pullman company—every overture being rejected, every suggestion denied, every proposition spurned with contempt—they determined not to pollute their hands and dishonor their manhood by handling Pullman cars and contributing to the suffering and sorrow of their brethren and their wives and babes. And rather than do this they laid down their tools in a body, sacrificed their situations and submitted to persecution, exile and the blacklist; to idleness, poverty, crusts and rags, and I shall love and honor these moral heroes to my latest breath.

There was more of human sympathy, or the essence of brotherhood, of the spirit of real Christianity in this act than in all the hollow pretenses and heartless prayers of those disciples of mammon who cried out against it, and this act will shine forth in increasing splendor long after the dollar worshipers have mingled with the dust of oblivion.

Had the carpenter of Nazareth been in Chicago at the time He would have been on the side of the poor, the heavy-laden and sore at heart, and He would have denounced their oppressors and been sent to prison for contempt of court under President Cleveland's administration.

President Cleveland says that we were put down because we had acted in violation of the Sherman Anti-Trust law of 1890. Will he kindly state what other trusts were proceeded against and what capitalists were sentenced to prison during his administration?

A TRIBUTE TO ALTGELD.

He waited ten years to cast his aspersions upon the honor of John P. Altgeld, and if that patriotic statesman had not fallen in the service of the people, if he were still here to defend his official acts, it is not probable that the ex-President would have ventured to assail him.

Reluctantly, indeed, do I close without the space to incorporate his burning messages to President Cleveland and at least some extracts from his masterly speech on "Government by Injunction."

His memory requires no defense, but if it did I could speak better for him than for myself. He never truckled to corporate wealth; he did not compromise with his conscience; he was steadfast in his devotion to truth and in his fidelity to right, and he sought with all his strength to serve the people and the people will gratefully remember him as one of the true men, one of the great souls of his sordid age.

The Chicago strike is not yet settled, and its "concluding pages" are YET TO BE WRITTEN.

You Railroad Men

Written for Appeal to Reason, February 3, 1906

FOREWORD

At the time this remarkable paper was written and published in the *Appeal to Reason*, two years ago, "fool dinner pail" prosperity flourished like a green bay tree.

One there was who, wanting an audience for his voice of warning, yet sounded with his pen a loud alarm. Debs had in the beginning of his life's labors allowed the railroad companies to coin his brawn and his brain in their service, but had since devoted himself, with an earnestness sublime, to the study of the condition of wage workers in general and railroad employes in particular. From his hard experience and many years of study he was in position to know, and he did know. Whatever else has been said, no detractor has questioned his honesty and the fine fiber of his magnificent manhood.

Yet, his warning went unheeded. The so-called "labor press," as well as the capitalist papers, decried him as an alarmist and a mischief-maker.

How swiftly and how accurately has his forecast been verified! We see the system he has arraigned trembling and crashing, we hear the hunger tread of the unemployed, and the tragedy he foretold is in the "rat-tat-tat" on a million kitchen doors.

Industry is confounded and labor is confused. By the statement of the railroad companies themselves a half million railroad workers alone are out of employment.

Choked into despair, it is to be hoped that Debs' mighty appeal to them, which is here republished, will now be read and assimilated by railroad men and the way of Socialism learned.

BRUCE ROGERS.

Girard, Kansas, March, 1908.

This appeal is made particularly to railway employes, among whom I began my career as a wage-worker, with whom I spent twenty-seven consecutive years—the complete span of my young manhood—as co-employe, labor organizer and union official, and for whom I shall have an affectionate regard of peculiar tenderness that will end only with my days.

The very relation I bear them inspires me with the liveliest sense of obligation to that great body of brave and brawny men whose hands, as hard as their hearts are soft, first grasped my own in welcome as a recruit to the army of toil; whose honest faces, beaming with approval, first warmed my heart and stirred my blood, and whose applause, the first I ever knew, fired my boyhood years with high resolves. In every dark and trying hour these comrades of my early years stood staunch and true and pushed me on and raised me up that others might see my face and know my name, while they remained unnoticed, unapplauded, the soldiers of obscurity, the rank and file, the lower class, the common herd, who made and move this world and who should be, and yet will be, its ruling aristocracy.

I believe it can be said with truth, as I am sure it can without vanity, that I personally know, and am personally known to, more railroad employes than any other man in the country; and with equal truth, I believe, that the great majority who know me—better than this, the whole body of them, with but few exceptions—feel kindly toward me, and may be claimed my personal friends.

In all my travels—and I have been moving almost continually these twelve years past, over all the railways of the continent, especially since the railway corporations forcibly divorced me from their employes—in all my travels I have never made a trip, nor ever expect to, without feeling many times the touch of kindness, oft in stealth, of my old comrades of railroad days.

It is not, therefore, because of any lessening of our mutual regard that I am no longer in active touch with them, but because of the stern decree of fate which commanded me to go where they might not yet follow for a while, but where they will be found in good time, united with their class, and battling manfully for freedom.

I could yet be the "grand" officer of a railway brotherhood, have a comfortable office, a large salary, plenty of friends, including railway and public officials, and read my praises as an "ideal labor leader" in capitalist newspapers, but my convictions would not allow it, and so I had to resign, and having no choice about it, I am entitled to no credit for quitting a "good" position and plunging recklessly into "a career of folly, failure and disgrace."

It was not easy to resign, and I had to insist upon it in a way that hurt me as much as it did the loyal brothers from whom I had to tear myself apart; and it has been the first and almost the only case of voluntary resignation from a similar organization.

I had been with the Brotherhood of locomotive firemen almost from its birth; had organized the Brotherhood of Railroad Brakemen, now the Brotherhood of Railway Trainmen; had helped to organize the Switchmen's Mutual Aid Association, the Brotherhood of Railway Carmen, the Order of Railway Telegraphers, and other labor unions, and was now to organize, with half a dozen others, the American Railway Union, to embrace all railway workers, so that the engine wiper and section man might come in for their share of consideration as well as the engineer and conductor.

There is where I broke with the railway officials. They were perfectly willing that we should have a firemen's union, but they were not willing for us to have a union that would unite all employes in the service in the equal interest of all.

This much by way of introduction. Now a word as to the purpose of this writing. I have something to say to the railway employes of America. It may not be considered as amounting to much, but I think it of importance enough to ask the railway workers to follow me through with patience, and think over what I have to say at their own leisure.

You railroad men are told that I am too radical, that I am dangerous, that as a "leader" I am a failure, and a good many other things, but the time will come when you will know that from first to last I was true to you, and because of that very fact the corporations you work for warn you against me; and you will furthermore know that, for the opposite reason, most of your present leaders are not true to your best interests. They are "popular" with the public, and your railway officials sing their praises on every occasion and tell you over and again how wise and good these "leaders" are and how lucky you are and how proud you should be to command their valuable services.

Time will tell and I can wait. I am not courting your flattery nor evading your blame. I am seeking no office; aspiring to no honors; have no personal ax to grind. But I have something to say to you and shall look straight into your eyes while saying it. I shall speak the truth—as I see it—no more and no less, in kindness and without malice or resentment.

I should tell you what I think you ought to know though all of you turned against me and despised me.

I am not wiser than you, but have had more experience with capitalists and more chance to study their system of fleecing and fooling labor than most of you. I am not better than you —not so good, in fact—for there is no better man on earth than an honest workingman. So I shall not preach to you, nor moralize you, nor even venture to advise you, but I shall put a few facts before you that may temporarily disturb your digestion, but if you will stick to them and assimilate them you will feel yourself growing stronger and you will thank me for having changed your mental bill of fare.

Taken in the aggregate, there is no division of the working class more clannish and provincial, more isolated from other divisions of labor's countless army, than railway employes, the workers engaged, directly and indirectly, in steam railway transportation. Nor is there a group or department in the entire working class that, outside of its own sphere of industrial activity, is more ignorant of the true essentials of the labor question or more oblivious of the class struggle and the fundamental principles and objects of the labor movement.

To verify this statement it is not necessary to refer to the unorganized, unskilled and poorly-paid employes; on the contrary, let a dozen engineers and the same number of conductors, picked at random, be put upon the stand and catechized from a primer on economics and see what percentage of them can give even a definition of the term. They know how to run engines and trains and, as a rule, that is practically the limit of their knowledge. That is all the corporations want them to know, and, from their point of view, all they are fit to know.

It is true that they read journals published by their unions in which a five-column account is given of a reception to some "noble grand chief," and as many columns more about babies born and brothers buried, but which may be searched in vain for a line of revolutionary economics to nourish their brain, open the eyes, give cheer to the heart or aspiration to the soul of a corporation slave.

The several unions of railway employes, considered in any militant sense, are not labor unions at all. Warren S. Stone, grand chief of the Brotherhood of Locomotive Engineers, worthy successor of the late P. M. Arthur, is on record as having pledged his word to a well known railway manager that the Brotherhood of Locomotive Engineers should never go out on strike while he was its executive head. The same grand chief is on record as threatening John J. Hannahan, grand master of the Brotherhood of Locomotive Firemen, with keeping his engineers at work on the Northern Pacific system, virtually scabbing on the firemen, if the latter went out on strike.

If the Brotherhood of Locomotive Engineers was a bona fide labor union instead of the fossilized tool of railway corporations its grand chief would be peremptorily impeached for treason to the working class.

The *Civic Federation Review* loves to print the portrait of Mr. Stone and idealize him as a "leader of labor" worthy to sit at the feast with, and at the feet of, August Belmont, Andrew Carnegie, Archbishop Ireland and other millionaire labor exploiters who regard workingmen as sheep to be sheared and skinned and slaughtered, and asses to be harnessed and worked and whipped, and, from that point of view, the engineers and the rest of the railway unions are to be congratulated upon their astute leadership.

It is not that Mr. Stone is personally dishonest and corrupt; he may be, and I think he is, perfectly conscientious in what he says and does, and the same is doubtless true of the grand officers of the other railway unions, but that is not the question.

If workingmen are betrayed and defeated and made to suffer, it makes little difference if their misfortunes are due to dishonest, or ignorant and incompetent, leadership.

The question is not, Are these leaders honest? Let that be conceded. The question is, Are they true to the working class? If their official attitude does not square with the working class as a whole, then they are not in line with the true interests of their own union and are not *in fact* the friends, but the enemies of labor; not serving, but betraying those who trust and follow them.

In saying this and making the further statement that the existing railway brotherhoods are of far more actual benefit to the railway corporations than they are to the employes who support them, and that in some essential respects they are a positive detriment to their members in teaching them to venerate a "grand" officer, subjecting themselves, bound and gagged, to his "official sanction," and in keeping them in economic ignorance—in saying these things, it is possible that Grand Chief Stone of the Engineers, and other "grand" officials will take issue; and here let me say that nothing would please me better than the chance to meet Mr. Stone before his engineers, or any other grand official before his followers, at any time, or in any public place, to prove every assertion herein made, and more, too; and I shall not object if the grand officers invite their friends, the railway officials, to occupy their accustomed seats on the platform, but I will not guarantee that the menu will be as agreeable to their corporation palates as that served at a recent Chicago banquet of the Order of Railway Conductors, or at the average brotherhood convention.

Now to another branch of the question: According to the report of the interstate commerce commission there were, for the year ended June 30, 1904, a total of 1,206,121 employes on the railways of the United States, as against 1,017,653 in 1900, an increase in four years of 278,468. How many thousands of unemployed there are, ready to take jobs when they are offered, in event of a strike, or otherwise, the reports do not say. Since 1904 there has been great increase in railroad activities and it is probable that the total has since reached 1,400,000. In 1894 the number was 779,608. That was during the last period of "hard times." In the ten years since, from 1894 to 1904, from "panic" to "prosperity," the number of railway employes has been almost doubled, the actual increase being 620,392, an average of over 60,000 a year. Fully five hundred thousand (500,000) new railroad men have been made in that time, and they have swelled the brotherhoods to unprecedented limits.

Now keep your eye "peeled" for the signal for the return trip from "prosperity" to "panic."

That is not a matter of guess, but of arithmetic.

It may not come next month nor next year, but it will come, and the longer it is coming the longer will be the backward trip.

Railway employes, as a rule, do not know why there are alternating periods of "panic" and 'prosperity"; panic that paralyzes, but prosperity that does not prosper, except for the plutocrats. The reason they do not know is that they are ignorant of working class economics, which are not discussed by their leaders, nor in their journals, and this accounts for the further fact that nearly all of them vote these sufferings upon themselves, as non-political labor unionists uniformly do, while their unions, vaccinated by the corporation doctor against politics, become parties to "grand balls," such as the Brotherhood of Locomotive Firemen has given in Chicago, and the "grand banquet" held by the Order of Railway Conductors in the same city, where the "grand march" is led by the capitalist mayor and a "grand" officer, and "grand" officials of the railroads beam approvingly, while "grand" corporation politicians disport themselves in huge diamonds and swallow-tails and "grand" speeches are spouted about the "brotherhood of capital and labor," the choicest lobster on the bill; the whole "green goods" affair being concocted by a tool of the corporations who belongs to the union and who, as a smooth politician, is on the pay roll at the city hall, or the state house, or capitol. Such nauseating exhibitions—planned by sycophants and patronized by plutocrats—are given to hoodwink the common herd and keep it forever in the capitalist corrals of wage slavery.

Political conspiracy is the term to apply to these doings of the henchmen of capital, masquerading in the garb of labor, who are so fearful that their dupes may wake up and go into politics.

But to return for a moment. Keep your eye open for that signal! When Wall Street says the word you'll see the signal, but it will not prevent you and your little union from going into the ditch. The signal and the slump will come together.

Several hundred thousand of you will be left high and dry; no jobs, but plenty of time to tramp and think. What next? Sweeping reductions of wages. Next—Strikes? Probably. And then? Defeat and disaster!

That's the history of all the "panics" of the last thirty years. They have all been ushered in with widespread railroad strikes, and when the crash has come the brotherhoods have burst like bubbles and been crushed like egg-shells, utterly powerless to give their members the least particle of protection. This is what has uniformly come to the unions that waste their time at such child's play as "exemplification of secret work" and studying signs and passwords, as if every corporation did not have its union reporter to inform it of every move worth knowing.

And so it will be again. Mark it! Make a note of it! Ask your grand officer about it and make a note of his answer. Don't allow him to dodge by calling me a calamity howler. He will help you after the lightning has struck your job by certifying that you are entitled to another, but you will have to hunt it alone, and in the meantime the "brotherhood of capital and labor" will have suspended and cannot save your wife from eviction, nor your children from starvation.

Think it out; don't let go till you do! Don't take my word; rely on yourself! I can't help you railway slaves. You only can help yourselves. No one else can. If you don't even know that you are slaves in the existing capitalist system, the gods have mercy on you, for your blindness is complete; your condition is pitiable and there is no hope for you but death.

The most pathetic object to me is a corporation slave with a dazzling diamond or a constellation of brass buttons to decorate his deformity and hide the hollows in his gray matter. He swells like a toad as he talks about the good wages "we" are paying; he is a part of the corporation, as a pimple is a part of the plutocrat. He has hinges in his knees. He fawns like a spaniel at the feet of an official, but snarls like a cur at the car inspector or track man. He believes in the "brotherhood of capital and labor"; he is "conservative"; is opposed to politics in the union or the journal; talks about his masters as "our superiors"; is proud of his pusillanimity; does with alacrity what he is ordered to do and asks no questions; is a scab at heart, if not in fact; has no trace of manhood, no self-respect, no honor—craven-hearted and stony-souled—and when he dies Judas Iscariot will have another recruit for his army of the damned.

In his address to the joint committee of the several brotherhoods of railway employes that called at the White House on November 14, 1905, to plead in behalf of the railway corporations, President Roosevelt, among other things, said: "I would be false to your interests if I failed to do justice to the capitalist as much as to the wage-worker."

The president was much impressed by the delegation and the delegation by him. The president was really addressing his own brethren, for, like themselves, he was a brotherhood man, and had the grip, sign and pass-words, all up to date; and they were all agreed that no injustice must be done the poor capitalists. The latter themselves were not in evidence. Their president and their brotherhoods would see that no harm came to them.

In his message to the banquet of the Order of Railway Conductors, given at Chicago on December 31, 1905, in behalf of the railroad corporations, and presided over by Major (?) B. B. Ray, paymaster, U. S. A., in recognition of his faithful services in lining up railway employes in support of the corporation ticket on election day, and as smooth a politician as ever came down the avenue—in his communication to this corporation auxiliary, regretting his inability to mingle with the railway presidents and managers who were in attendance to point around at the conductors as evidence that the working class in general, and the railway slaves in particular, were opposed to rate legislation—in his telegram of regret Vice-President Fairbanks, once himself a railroad attorney and now a magnate, said:

"The Order of Railway Conductors * * * recognizes in full degree the right of both employer and employe and understands full well that in a large sense the interests of one are the interests of the other, and that the interests of neither can be disregarded without harm to both."

Precisely! "Our interests are one," exclaimed the fox, after devouring the goose. "Same here," answered the hawk, with the feathers of the dove still clinging to his beak. "I'm with you," chipped in the shark; and "I congratulate you upon your wise political economy" was the amen of the lion as the lamb's tail disappeared down the red lane.

Toastmaster Ray, the mortgaged major of the railroads, read another telegram of regret from President "Jim" Hill, of the Great Northern, and then President Delano, of the Wabash, was introduced and proceeded to orate on "Opposition to Railroad Rate Legislation." The dummies are reported to have nodded in hearty approval every time he looked at them. President Delano might have stayed at home and used a string to operate his puppets.

Upon this important point of "identity of interests," between lion and mutton, President Roosevelt, Vice-President Fairbanks and all the railroad presidents, corporations and brotherhoods are a unit.

The railroads furnish the lion and the brotherhoods the mutton.

It is upon this false basis, this vicious assumption, this fundamental lie, that the railroad brotherhoods are organized, and in that capacity they are of incalculable value to the railroads, the very bulwarks of their defense, and the sure means of keeping the great body of railway employes in economic ignorance, and, therefore, unorganized, divided and helpless.

Such unionism means organized strength for the railroads and organized weakness for the employes. And the latter foot the bill. No wonder their grand officers get annual passes and their delegates free trains. The stupid employes pay for them all an hundredfold.

And to what base purpose the railroad magnates put these brotherhoods to still further intrench their power and perpetuate their reign of robbery!

At this very moment they are using them as political pokers to stir up the fire of public sentiment against rate legislation. And the poor dupes that pay the dues don't even know that their unions are in politics, corporation politics, the dirtiest of all politics.

On their own account the unions are forbidden to have anything to do with politics—that would fracture their delicate diaphragm—but when the corporations need them as political tools—ah, that's different; that's what they are for!

Cannot you hoodwinked railway slaves begin to see something?

In all the history of organized labor, from the earliest times to the present day, no body of union workingmen ever served in a more humiliating and debasing role than that in which the railway unions appear at this very hour before the American people and the world.

It is a spectacle for the gods, and future generations will marvel that such an exhibition of servility was possible in the twentieth century.

Union workingmen, rallying round the robbers of the working class, and defending them against their own people!

It is true that there is nothing in rate legislation for the workingman, but the incident loses none of its significance on that account.

The free use of the brotherhoods by and for the corporations, at election time, when the legislature meets, when congress is in session, whenever and wherever required—that is the point.

How smoothly this emergency appliance works!

The corporations sniff danger: they send for their officials—the officials for the "grand chiefs" of the brotherhoods—the "grand chiefs" for their decoy ducks, and presto! a joint committee—and it is a "joint" committee—serves notice on the president and the country that the million and more railway employes want no interference with the divine right of the railroad robbers to hold up the people.

Then another set of political tools of the same robbers take their cue and bound to their feet in the capitalist congress and in a serio-comic burst of paid-for passion, exclaim: "Don't you see, gentlemen, that organized labor, the horny-handed nobility of the land, the muscle and sinew, the very backbone of the nation, recognizes this measure as a menace to its "full dinner pail" and interposes its righteous indignation! Gentlemen, we dare not make such an assault upon the dignity, the sacred rights, aye, the very life of honest toil!"

That settles it! The trick is done. The Goulds, Vanderbilts and Harrimans are on top, their slaves at the bottom, and their "identity of interests" is once more triumphantly vindicated.

I purpose now to deal briefly with that ghastly lie itself.

In what way, Mr. Railroad Slave, is your interest identical with that of "Jim" Hill, your master?

He owns the railway system that you workingmen built and now operate.

He pulls every dollar of profit out of it for himself he can, and leaves you not one dollar more than he must.

If you don't suit him, he discharges you, and you then have to pull up stakes and hunt another master. He gets the lion's share, you get what's left; and in the aggregate that is fixed by what is required to fill your dinner pail, cover you with overalls and maintain a habitation where you can raise more wage-slaves to take your place when you are worn out and go to the scrap heap.

The "Jim" Hills live out of your labor—out of your ignorance—for if you were not densely stupid you would not be their dumb-driven cattle.

Now they and their politicians and preachers and "labor leaders" tell you how bright and smart you are to flatter your ignorance, and keep you from opening your eyes to your slavish condition, and above all, to the wage-system, which lies at the bottom of your poverty and degradation.

Your interests as wage-slaves are not only *not* identical with, but are directly opposed to, the interests of the "Jim" Hills and the railroad corporations, and I challenge any of your "grand chiefs" to deny it in my presence on any public platform.

You have got to get rid of the capitalist leeches that suck your hearts' blood through the quill of "identity of interests."

They are in the capitalist class; you are in the working class. They gouge out profits; what's left you get for wages. They perform no useful work; you deform your bodies with slavery. They are millionaires; you are paupers. They have everything; you do everything. They live in palaces; you in shanties. They have abundance of leisure and mountains of money; you have neither. Finally, they are few; *you are legions!*

Poor, dumb giant, you could in a breath extinguish your pigmy exploiter, were you only conscious of your overmastering power!

The workers made and operate all the railroads; the capitalists had and have nothing to do with either. They pocket the proceeds on a basis of watered stock and other "stock," in the form of employes, and then issue fraudulent reports to show on what a small margin of profit they are actually doing business.

In this connection it should be said that the railroads pad their "operating expenses" outrageously to deceive their employes and the general public, and their reports can be shown to be full of duplicity and fraud. They are not required to itemize their "operating expenses" in their reports to the interstate commerce commission; this they only do in the reports of the directors to the stockholders, and an examination of these will disclose the swindle and show how much reliance can be placed in the public reports of private grafters.

Mr. Railway Slave, to resume our interview, you are not in the same class with the "Jim" Hills of the railroads. You don't visit their homes; nor they at yours. You don't ride in their private cars and yachts and automobiles. Your wives don't wear the same kind of clothes and jewelry and move in the same circle with theirs. You don't join them in their luxuriant travels to Europe when they are received by the crowned heads and other parasites and given a private audience by the pope. You stay at home and sweat and suffer to foot all the bills; they do all the rest.

To sum up: They are in the capitalist class; you in the working class. They are masters; you slaves. They fleece and pluck; you furnish the wool and feathers.

That is the basis of the class struggle.

Upon that basis you have got to organize and fight before you can move an inch toward freedom.

You have got to unite in the same labor union and in the same political party and *strike and vote together,* and the hour you do that, the world is yours.

The railroads will oppose this; they want to keep you divided and at their mercy. Your grand officers will oppose it; they want to keep you divided and continue to draw their salaries.

When you have a little time figure out the amount annually paid to the grand officers of the railway unions in salaries and expenses, and you will be amazed; you will also understand why railroad employes will never get together as long as their grand officers can prevent it.

By the way, why do you persist in calling your officers "Grand Chiefs" and "Grand Masters"? Are they "grand" because you are petty?

The working class, the rank and file, are *grander* than all the labor leaders, good and bad, that ever lived.

A "Master" implies slaves. It is bad enough to be slaves without glorying in it. A "Master" is bad enough; a "Grand Master" is the limit, especially if the title is voluntarily conferred by the slaves.

There was a time when I did not realize this and many other things I now do. The difference is that I have learned to think and can now see these things as they are.

The capitalist class! The working class! The class struggle! These are the supreme economic and political facts of this day and the precise terms that express them.

These are the grim realities in the existing capitalist system, and the sooner you drop your brotherhood toys and deal with the labor question, to which most of you are strangers, the better will it be for you.

What is the labor question?

It is the question of the working class organizing to overthrow the capitalist class, emancipating itself from wage slavery and making itself the ruling class of the world.

Can this be done?

Anything can be done by the working class.

Labor has but to awaken to its own power. Then the earth and all its fullness will be for labor. Now the exploiters of labor have it; and they must be put out of that business and into useful service.

First of all, you railroad workers, you million and almost a half of slaves, must wake up; realize that you are a part of the working class and that the whole working class must unite, close up the ranks and present a solid front, every day in the year, election day especially included.

As individual wage-slaves you are helpless and your condition hopeless. As a *class,* you are the greatest power between the earth and the stars. As a *class,* your chains turn to spider-webs and in your presence capitalists shrivel up and blow away.

The individual wage-slave must recognize the power of class unity and do all he can to bring it about.

That is what is called *class-consciousness,* in the light of which may be seen the *class struggle* in startling vividness.

The class-conscious worker recognizes the necessity of organization, economic and political, and of using every weapon at his command—the strike, the boycott, the ballot and every other—to achieve his emancipation.

He, therefore, joins the union of his *class* and the party of his *class* and gives his time and energy to the work of educating and lining up his *class* for the struggle of his *class* for emancipation.

You railroad men may think you are doing this now, but you are not. You are wasting most of your time and money for that which will bring no returns.

Let me tell you a few things the railroad corporations and your leaders, between whom there is an "identity of interests," are having you do to occupy your time and keep you chained to the kennels of your masters.

First—They have you divided into petty groups, each trying to be *it,* and not one having any real power for working class good.

Second—They have you quarreling about jurisdiction and about an "open door," and the corporations smile serenely while you play with these toys.

Your jurisdiction squabbles never will be settled, but grow worse. At places the B. L. E. and B. L. F. are at swords' points, and the O. R. C. and B. R. T. are ready to fly at each others' throats; and so intense is the petty craft jealousy that they are ready to scab on one another.

And if they ever go out on strike, particularly the B. L. E., their own former members, victimized by them, will rise up to smite them.

The other day I met a man who had an official position that paid him $5,000.00 a year. Said he to me: "I will quit this job for but one thing, and that will be to take an engine when the B. L. E. go out on strike." He used to be a member.

There are any number of men scattered over the country—most of them its own former members—waiting for the B. L. E. to strike, and the day is not distant when that union will reap the harvest it has sown.

Third—You are kept apart from other workers, for it would be dangerous if you affiliated with them and got an idea above the round-house or caboose or cab you work in. Besides, you might get class-conscious and that would endanger your slavery.

Fourth—You spend hours in the lodge room, "riding the goat," getting the secret work "down fine," giving "passwords" and "signs," and unpacking job-lots of "secret work" that any railroad official in the country can have any day he wants it.

These are but bibs and rattles for mental babies, and the more time you amuse yourselves with them the less danger there is of your thinking about anything that will break your chains and set you free.

These are a few of the things; I have not space for more. The hundreds of columns of stale stuff rehashed for years in your journals that might be called goose gossip would, perhaps, be excusable in the official organ of some feeble-minded asylum, but it is woefully out of place in a working class publication.

Now let me say a few more things—and space will allow only a few of the many that might be put down—that you may think about at your leisure.

The Brotherhood of Locomotive Engineers is forty-two years old and has never won a strike of any consequence in all its career.

It is called a success because the corporations make some concessions to it so as to use it as a battering ram against other employes in the service; and this is substantially true of all the "brotherhoods."

Then, again, the brotherhoods are used against each other.

The union switchmen on the Denver and Rio Grande, at Pittsburg and other places; the engineers on the C., B. & Q.; the telegraph operators on the A. & P., M., K. & T., Great

Northern and Northern Pacific; and the machinists on the Santa Fe are but a few of the long list of victims of the "dog-eat-dog" unionism, a quarter of a century behind the times.

But the grand officers of the several unions attend one another's conventions and join in solemn chorus in telling the delegates of each other's union what wise grand officers they have, how kind the corporations are to them, and how proud they ought to be of their noble brotherhoods.

In the next few years locomotive engineers will become motormen and firemen will disappear. It is safe to say that in another twenty years locomotive firemen will be practically of the past. They can then cling to their last straw—their insurance policy—and that is the main thing that holds them together today. But for that they would soon cave in, and that is true of them all. They are then, primarily, coffin clubs and not labor unions. They care for the sick and bury the dead—a good thing, incidentally, for the corporations. To get the full benefits, it is necessary to be maimed or killed.

It is well to bury the dead, but the living are infinitely more important.

One effective blow to break the chains of wage slavery is better than a century of attention to dead bodies.

Class-consciousness is better than corpse-consciousness.

A good deal more that should be said must be omitted for the want of time and space.

It is my hope that the facts here presented may lead the railroad workers to study the real labor question. A few of them only know what Socialism is, and they are Socialists. The rest are opposed to it because the little they know about it is not true.

No honest workingman understands Socialism without embracing it.

The railroad workers, if they want their eyes opened, must read class struggle literature.

The Appeal to Reason, with a circulation of over three hundred thousand copies, can be obtained for a trifle—fifty cents for a whole year—and if they can't afford that, they can send ten cents for a trial subscription.

They cannot afford to remain in ignorance of the class struggle, or of what Socialism really means.

A mighty social revolution is impending—it is shaking the earth from center to circumference, and only the dead may be deaf to its rumblings.

Revolutionary education and organization is the vital need of the working class.

Let every railroad employe who is alive enough to want to know how the working class can emancipate the working class and walk the earth free, and enjoy all its manifold blessings, subscribe for a revolutionary paper and read it for a year; and he will then find himself with the rest of us, in class-conscious array, in the struggle for freedom.

The Appeal to Reason, already suggested, will make an excellent beginning. There is a long list of other papers and magazines that can be read with profit.

Drop a card to J. Mahlon Barnes, National Secretary Socialist party, 180 E. Washington street, Chicago, asking him to send you printed matter in regard to this working class party, and also to send you a list of Socialist papers and magazines, and a catalog of working class books and pamphlets.

Great is the privilege we enjoy in being permitted to take part in this mighty historic struggle.

The base and cowardly will sneer and sneak to the rear, but the brave and true, though hell itself gape, will do battle with all the blood in their veins, and write their names in living letters on the shining scroll of LABOR's EMANCIPATION.

The Growth of Socialism

Written for Success Magazine

The article being reduced and some vital passages omitted, on account of space limitations, it was reproduced in its complete form in the Appeal to Reason, March 17, 1906.

Not many of those schooled in old-party politics have any adequate conception of the true import of the labor movement. They read of it in the papers, discuss it in their clubs, criticise labor unions, condemn walking delegates, and finally conclude that organized labor is a thing to be tolerated so long, only, as it keeps within "proper bounds," but to be put down summarily the moment its members, like the remnants of Indian tribes on the western plains, venture beyond the limits of their reservations. They utterly fail or refuse to see the connection between labor and politics, and are, therefore, woefully ignorant of the political significance of the labor movement of the present day.

It is true that in all the centuries of the past labor has been "put down" when it has sought some modicum of its own, or when it has even yearned for some slight amelioration of its wretched condition, as witness the merciless massacre of the half-famished and despairing subjects of the Russian czar, a few months ago, for daring to hope that their humble petition for a few paltry concessions might be received and considered by his mailed and heartless majesty.

It is likewise true, that, in the present day, and in the United States, all the powers of government stand ready to "put down" the working class whenever it may be deemed necessary in the interest of its industrial masters.

All great strikes prove that the government is under the control of corporate capital and that the army of office-holders is as subservient to the capitalist masters as is the army of wage-workers that depends upon them for employment.

But, true as these things are, it is not true that labor is

ignorant of them, nor is it true that such conditions will continue forever.

The labor movement has advanced with rapid strides, during the last few years, and is, today, the most formidable factor in quickening the social conscience and in regenerating the human race. It is not the millions that are enrolled as members of labor unions that give power and promise to this world movement, but the thousands, rather, that are not trade-unionists merely, but working class unionists as well; that is to say, working men and women who recognize the identity of the industrial and political interests of the whole working class; or, in other words, are conscious of their class interests and are bending all the powers of their minds and bodies, spurred by the zeal that springs from comradeship in a common cause, to effect the economic and political solidarity of the whole mass of labor, irrespective of race, creed or sex.

These class-conscious workers—these Socialists—realize the fact that the labor question, in its full and vital sense, is also a political question, and that the working class must be taught to extend the principle of unionism to the political field, and there organize on the basis of their economic class interests; and, although they are engaged in a herculean task, the forces of industrial evolution and social progress are back of them, and all the powers of reaction cannot prevail against them.

The labor movement has had to fight its way, inch by inch, from its inception to its present position, and to this very fact is due the revolutionary spirit, indomitable will, and unconquerable fiber it has developed, and which alone fit it for its mighty historic mission.

In the beginning the workers organized in their respective trades simply to improve working conditions. They had no thought of united political action. The employing class at once combined to defeat every attempt at organization on the part of its employes; but, notwithstanding this opposition, the trade union, which had become an economic necessity, grew steadily until at last the employers were compelled to recognize and deal with it. Being unable to destroy it, they next proceeded to control its operations by confining it to its narrowest possible limitations, thus reducing it to inefficiency—from a menace to a convenience.

The late Marcus A. Hanna crushed the trade union with an iron boot in the beginning of his career as a capitalist. In his maturer years he became its patron saint. He did not change in spirit, but in wisdom. What is true of Mr. Hanna is true of the principal members of the Civic Federation, that economic peace congress conceived by far-sighted capitalists, sanctified by plutocratic prelates, and presided over by a gentleman who, but a few months ago, engaged James Farley and his army of five thousand professional strike-breakers to defeat the demands and destroy the unions of his New York subway employes.

A new unionism has struggled into existence, and the coming year will witness some tremendous changes. The old forms cramp and fetter the new forces. As these new forces develop, the old forms must yield and finally give way to transformation.

The old unionism, under the inspiration of a Civic Federation banquet, exclaims jubilantly: "The interests of labor and capital are identical. Hallelujah!"

To this stimulating sentiment the whole body of exploiting capitalists give hearty assent; all its politicians, parsons, and writers join in enthusiastic approval; and woe be to the few clear, calm, and candid protestants who deny it. Their very loyalty becomes treason, and the working class they seek to serve is warned against them, while the false leaders are loaded with fulsome adulation.

But, nevertheless, the clear voice of the awakened and dauntless few cannot be silenced. The new unionism is being heard. In trumpet tones it rings out its revolutionary shibboleth to all the workers of the earth: Our interests are identical—let us combine, industrially and politically, assert our united power, achieve our freedom, enjoy the fruit of our labor, rid society of parasitism, abolish poverty, and civilize the world!

The old unionism, living in the dead past, still affirms that the interests of labor and capital are identical.

The new unionism, vitalized and clarified by the living present, exclaims: We know better; capitalists and wage-workers have antagonistic economic interests; capitalists buy and workers sell labor power, the one as cheaply and the other as dearly as possible; they are locked in a life-and-death class-struggle; there can be no identity of interests between masters and slaves—between exploiters and exploited—and there can be no peace until the working class is triumphant in this struggle and the wage system is forever wiped from the earth.

The months immediately before us will witness a mighty mustering of the working class, on the basis of the class struggle, and the day is not far distant when they will be united in one vast economic organization in which all the trades will be represented, "separate as the waves, yet one as the sea," and one great political party that stands uncompromisingly for the working class and its program of human emancipation.

In the late national election, for the first time, the hand of the working class was clearly seen.

The Socialist party is distinctively the party, and its vote is distinctively the vote, of the working class.

More than four hundred thousand of these votes were counted; probably twice as many were cast. This was but the beginning. From now on there is "a new Richmond in the field."

There is but one issue from the standpoint of labor, and that is: Labor versus Capital. Upon that basis the political alignment of the future will have to be made. There is no escape from it.

For the present the ignorance of the workers stands in the way of their economic and political solidarity, but this can and will be overcome. In the meantime, the small capitalists and the middle class are being ground to atoms in the mill of competition. Thousands are being driven from the field entirely, beaten in the struggle, bankrupt and hopeless, to be swallowed up in the surging sea of wage-slavery; while thousands of others cling to the outer edge, straining every nerve to stem the torrent that threatens to sweep them into the abyss, their condition so precarious that they anticipate the inevitable and make common issue with the wage-workers in the struggle to overthrow the capitalist system and reconstruct society upon a new foundation of co-operative industry and the social ownership of the means of life.

Of all the silly sayings of the self-satisfied of the present day, the oft-repeated falsehood that there are "no classes" in this country takes the lead, and is often made to serve as the prelude to the preposterous warning that periodically peals from rich and sumptuous club banquets, at which the president and other patriots are guests, that "it is treason to array class against class in the United States."

If there are no classes, how can they be arrayed against each other?

The fact is that precisely the same classes and conditions that exist in the monarchies of the old world have also developed in our capitalist republic. The working class sections, including the tenements and slums of New York and London, are strikingly similar; and the wealth-owning class of the United States represents as distinct an aristocracy as England can boast, while the laboring elements of both countries are distinctively in the "lower class" by themselves and practically on the same degraded level.

Deny it as may the retainers of the rich, the classes already exist; they are here, and no amount of sophistication can remove them, nor the chasm that divides them. The rare and exceptional wage-worker who escapes from wage-slavery simply proves the rule and emphasizes the doom of his class in capitalist society.

The existing classes and the struggle going on between them are not due to the mischievous influence of labor agitators, as certain politicians and priests, the emissaries of the "rich and respectable," would have it appear.

The long swell of the wave but expresses the agitation of the deep.

The agitator is the product of unrest—his is the voice of the social deep; and, though he may be reviled as a demagogue who preys upon the ignorance of his fellows, the unrest continues and the agitation increases until the cause of it is removed and justice is done.

Classes and class rule and their attendant progress and poverty, money and misery, turmoil and strife, are inherent in the capitalist system. Why? Simply because one set of men owns the tools with which wealth is produced, while another set uses them, and there is an irrepressible conflict over the division of the product.

The capitalist owns the tools he does not use; the worker uses the tools he does not own.

The principal tools of production and distribution in the United States—mammoth machines, complex social instruments, made and used co-operatively by millions of workingmen, their very lives, their wives and babes being dependent upon them—are the private property of a few hundred capitalists, and are operated purely to make profits for these capitalists, regardless of the poverty and wretchedness that ensue to the masses.

In virtue of the individual ownership of the social instruments of production, one capitalist may exploit the labor of a million workingmen and become a billionaire, while the million workers struggle through life in penury and want, to a bleak and barren old age, to find rest at last in the pauper asylum, the morgue and the potter's field.

This vast and resourceful country should be free from the scourge of poverty and the blight of ignorance; but it never will be until the private ownership of the means of sustaining life is abolished and society is organized on the basis of social ownership of the social means of wealth production and the inalienable right of all to work and to produce freely to satisfy their physical needs and material wants. It is for this great organic change, this world-wide social revolution, that the Socialists of all countries are organizing, that it may be intelligently guided, and come, if possible, in peace and order when the people and conditions have been prepared for it.

The present order of society is developing all the symptoms of degeneracy and dissolution. Only the individualist self-seekers and their mercenaries—they who believe in making the animal struggle for existence perpetual, in climbing to the top over the corpses of their fellows—only they are satisfied, or would appear to be, and expatiate upon our marvelous prosperity, and the incomparable glory of our "free institutions."

The man who can look upon New York or Chicago, today,

and utter such sentiments should blush for his perverted sense of justice, to say nothing of his total lack of humanity.

Many thousands of men, women and children suffer for food and shiver in the cold in these typical capitalist cities, while the beef trust is crammed to bursting and the cotton kings of the South burn cotton to keep up prices.

Has the world ever heard of such monstrous iniquity—such unspeakable crime? In the name of all that has heart in it not yet turned to adamant, has human life any value, even that of the lowest grade of merchandise? And is it not high time to call a halt to the ravages of capitalism and give a little thought and consideration to humanity?

Let us briefly note some of the crying evils which infest the class-ruled society of the present day. First of all, millions are poverty-stricken, the result, mainly, of no work or low wages. The great book of Robert Hunter, on "Poverty," recently published, abounds in facts, supported by incontrovertible proofs, which silence all doubt upon this point.

In New York City, alone, fifty thousand children, when they go to school at all, go without sufficient and proper food, and one corpse in every ten is dumped into the potter's field.

New York and Chicago are filled with unemployed and suffering, and in the country at large ten millions are in want. In the shoemaking industry, fifty-one per cent of the laborers receive less than three hundred dollars per year. In cotton spinning, the wages of thousands average from two hundred and twenty dollars to four hundred and sixty dollars per year. During the last year tens of thousand of coal miners were allowed to work but from one to three days per week. Fall River capitalists reduce wages three times in rapid succession, and lock out and starve their employes for six months, declaring that they cannot afford to pay the high prices for cotton, while the planters of the South burn up the cotton to keep up prices rather than clothe the naked whose labor produced it.

The state of Colorado seethes with military brutality and reeks with political corruption because the mine owners are practically proprietors of the state and propose to do as they please with their own; and they who have the temerity to protest are branded outlaws and bull-penned, deported, or shot dead in their tracks.

The United States senate is dominated by the special representatives of the trusts and corporations, and several of its members are under indictment for playing the game of their masters in their own personal interests. Think of Senator Chauncey M. Depew reforming the abuses of the railroads, or Thomas C. Platt stopping the extortion of the express companies, in the interest of the people!

The Pennsylvania Railroad company dictated the recent election of the United States senator from Pennsylvania, and the most flagitious political debauchery attended the election of many others, such proceedings being regarded as so entirely in consonance with our capitalist-owned republic as to excite little more than passing notice.

Only a short time ago the late John H. Reagan, the venerable ex-senator of Texas, in discussing the federal courts, said that he expected no improvement in them "as long as railroad lawyers are allowed to go on the bench to interpret legislation affecting the management of the railroads." As long as the railroads are privately owned they will have their judges on the bench, and the government, that is to say, the capitalist politicians, will do their bidding.

Judge Reagan closed his sweeping arraignment of the courts as follows: "I have seen such gross perversions of the law by the courts that I have lost confidence in them and regret that I cannot feel the respect for them that I once felt."

These are ominous words and from a source that gives them the weight of high authority.

Census figures recently published show that "every fifth child between the ages of ten and fifteen in the United States is a breadwinner. One out of every three of these children workers is a girl. There are one million seven hundred and fifty thousand one hundred and seventy-eight children employed, an increase of thirty-three and one-third per cent in ten years."

The land frauds, postal steals, and Indian graft all cry out in condemnation of private ownership of capital, the source and inspiration of all the political corruption that, like a pestilence, blights the land.

Charles F. Kelly, speaker of the house of delegates, at St. Louis, the convicted boodler, in making his confession, described in a few graphic words the methods and motives of office-holders and politicians in the grab-all regime of profitocracy. Said he: "Our combine was not along party lines. Both democrats and republicans belonged to it. My experience has been that boodlers line up according to their own interests, and not under party standards. In the majority of the wards of St. Louis both the democratic party and the republican usually nominate men to go to the house of delegates for the money they can get out of it. Each party man votes for his own fellows, and either one that gets in serves those who rob the city of franchises."

Be it noted that the corrupters of courts, the bribers of legislators, and the debauchers of public morals are all capitalists in high standing, the gentry whose subservient and hypocritical underlings are forever preaching about "law and order" to the working class.

In the face of these frightful eruptions on the body-politic, President Roosevelt coolly informs us that we are passing through a period of "noteworthy prosperity," and that "we must raise still higher our standard of commercial ethics, and we must insist more and more upon those fundamental principles of our country—equality before the law and obedience to the law. *In no other way can the advance of Socialism, whether evolutionary or revolutionary, be checked.*"

The words "still higher" seem like sarcasm when applied to our so-called "standard of commercial ethics," that is mired in profit-mongering and can never rise above the sordid level of brutal self-interest in the declining stages of the competitive system.

The commercial pirates who rob the nation of its franchises and organize monopolies to exploit the people are not in the business of raising the standards of ethics, commercial or otherwise. The only ethics they know is to "get there"; the end always justifying the means.

Just at present President Roosevelt, typical capitalist executive that he is, is after the railroads—so we are told. His organs assure us that he proposes to bring these great corporations to their knees, and make them obey the law and stop robbing the people. And yet President Roosevelt has had one of these criminal offenders in his own cabinet.

It is known of all men that Paul Morton, late secretary of the navy, is a self-confessed lawbreaker, who would now be serving a prison sentence if the law in his case had been enforced.

Then, again, can President Roosevelt consistently crack the whip above the heads of these corporations after sharing in the special privileges they enjoy at the expense of the people? In making his political campaigns, and on other occasions since he has become a commanding figure in national politics, the railroad corporations have provided Mr. Roosevelt with the most luxurious special trains, sumptuously furnished and abundantly stocked, *free of charge.* The thousands of dollars of expense thus incurred by the railroad corporations could not have been without some consideration, and, whatever that may be, it is not calculated to inspire self-respecting and candid men who think for themselves with faith in the sincerity of the president when he vaults into the arena to do battle against the railroads as the champion of the people.

It is not to reform the evils of the day but to abolish the social system that produces them that the Socialist party is organized. It is the party not of reform but of revolution, knowing that the capitalist system has had its day and that a new social order, based upon a new system of industry, must soon supplant the fast decaying one we now have.

Every social system changes ceaselessly, and, ultimately, having fulfilled its mission, passes away.

Capitalism is the connecting link between feudalism and Socialism.

The industrial forces are now making for Socialism, preparing the way for it, and sooner or later it is sure to come.

On the one hand the capitalist class are combining their resources, centralizing their capital, co-operating instead of competing, organizing industry, and eliminating competition. This is the new and better way. It is good as far as it goes. It is the limited application of the economic principles of Socialism.

On the other hand, the working class are organizing. They

are beginning to spell solidarity and to pronounce Socialism. They are yearning for emancipation from the galling yoke of wage-slavery, and with all the power of their minds, all the strength of their bodies and all the passion of their souls they are crusading against the ignorance of their fellow-workers and the prejudice of the people.

Steadily the number of class-conscious toilers is increasing, and higher and higher rises the tide that is to sweep away the barriers to progress and civilization.

Let others talk about the tariff and finance—the enlightened workers demand the ownership of the tools of industry and they are building up the Socialist party as a means of getting them.

The working class alone made the tools; the working class alone can use them, and the working class must, therefore, own them.

This is the revolutionary demand of the Socialist movement. The propaganda is one of education and is perfectly orderly and peaceable. The workers must be taught to unite and vote together *as a class* in support of the Socialist party, the party that represents them as a class, and when they do this the government will pass into their hands and capitalism will fall to rise no more; private ownership will give way to social ownership, and production for profit to production for use; the wage-system will disappear, and with it the ignorance and poverty, misery and crime that wage-slavery breeds; the working class will stand forth triumphant and free, and a new era will dawn in human progress and in the civilization of mankind.

An Ideal Labor Press

The Metal Worker, May, 1904

The prime consideration in the present industrial system is profit. All other things are secondary. Profit is the life blood of capital—the vital current of the capitalist system, and when it shall cease to flow the system will be dead.

The capitalist is the owner of the worker's tools. Before the latter can work he must have access to the capitalist's toolhouse and permission to use the master's tools. What he produces with these tools belongs to the master, to whom he must sell his labor power at the market price. The owner of the tools is therefore master of the man.

Only when the capitalist can exact a satisfactory profit from his labor power is the worker given a job, or allowed to work at all.

Profit first; labor, life, love, liberty—all these must take second place.

In such a system labor is in chains, and the standard of living, if such it may be called, is corner-stoned in crusts and rags.

Under such conditions ideas and ideals are not prolific among the sons and daughters of toil.

Slavery does not excite lofty aspirations nor inspire noble ideals.

The tendency is to sodden irresolution and brutish inertia.

But this very tendency nourishes the germ of resistance that ripens into the spirit of revolt.

The labor movement is the child of slavery—the offspring of oppression—in revolt against the misery and suffering that gave it birth.

Its splendid growth is the marvel of our time, the forerunner of freedom, the hope of mankind.

Ten thousand times has the labor movement stumbled and

fallen and bruised itself, and risen again; been seized by the throat and choked and clubbed into insensibility; enjoined by courts, assaulted by thugs, charged by the militia, shot down by regulars, traduced by the press, frowned upon by public opinion, deceived by politicians, threatened by priests, repudiated by renegades, preyed upon by grafters, infested by spies, deserted by cowards, betrayed by traitors, bled by leeches, and sold out by leaders, but, notwithstanding all this, and all these, it is today the most vital and potential power this planet has ever known, and its historic mission of emancipating the workers of the world from the thraldom of the ages is as certain of ultimate realization as the setting of the sun.

The most vital thing about this world movement is its educational propaganda—its capacity and power to shed light in the brain of the working class, arouse them from their torpor, develop their faculties for thinking, teach them their economic class interests, effect their solidarity, and imbue them with the spirit of the impending social revolution.

In this propaganda the life-breath of the movement, the press, is paramount to all other agencies and influences, and the progress of the press is a sure index of the progress of the movement.

Unfortunately, the workers lack intelligent appreciation of the importance of the press; they also lack judgment and discrimination in dealing with the subject, and utterly neglect some good papers, and permit them to perish, while others that are anything but helpful or beneficial to the cause they are supposed to represent are liberally patronized and flourish in the ignorance and stupidity which support them.

The material prosperity of a labor paper of today is no guarantee of its moral or intellectual value. Indeed, some of the most worthless labor publications have the finest mechanical appearance, and are supported by the largest circulations.

Such a press is not only not a help to labor but a millstone about its neck, that only the awakening intelligence of the working class can remove.

How thoroughly alive the capitalists are to the power of the press! And how assiduously they develop and support it that it may in turn buttress their class interests!

The press is one of their most valuable assets, and, as an investment, pays the highest dividends.

When there is trouble between capital and labor the press volleys and thunders against labor and its unions and leaders and all other things that dare to breathe against the sacred rights of capital. In such a contest labor is dumb, speechless; it has no press that reaches the public, and must submit to the vilest calumny, the most outrageous misrepresentation.

The lesson has been taught in all the languages of labor and written in the blood of its countless martyred victims.

Labor must have a press as formidable as the great movement of the working class requires, to worthily represent its dignity and fearlessly and uncompromisingly advocate its principles.

Every member of a trade union should feel himself obligated to do his full share in the important work of building up the press of the labor movement; he should at least support the paper of his union, and one or more of the papers of his party, and, above all, he should read them and school himself in the art of intelligent criticism, and let the editor hear from him when he has a criticism to offer or a suggestion to make.

The expense of supporting the labor press is but a trifle to the individual member—less than the daily outlay for other trifles that are of no benefit, and can easily be dispensed with.

The editor of a labor paper is of far more importance to the union and the movement than the president or any other officer of the union. He ought to be chosen with special reference to his knowledge upon the labor question and his fitness to advocate and defend the economic interests of the class he represents.

The vast amount of capitalist advertising some labor publications carry certifies unerringly to the worthlessness of their literary contents. Capitalists do not, as a rule, advertise in labor papers that are loyal to working class interests. It is only on condition that the advertising colors and controls the editorial that the capitalist generously allows his patronage to go to the labor paper.

The workingman who wants to read a labor paper with the true ring, one that ably, honestly and fearlessly speaks for the working class, will find it safe to steer clear of those that are loaded with capitalist advertising and make his selection from those that are nearly or quite boycotted by the class that live and thrive upon the slavery and degradation of the working class.

The labor press of today is not ideal, but it is improving steadily, and the time will come when the ideal labor press will be realized; when the labor movement will command editors, writers, journalists, artists of the first class; when hundreds of papers, including dailies in the large cities, will gather the news and discuss it from the labor standpoint; when illustrated magazines and periodicals will illuminate the literature of labor and all will combine to realize our ideal labor press and blaze the way to victory.

*Childhood

Appeal to Reason

What sweet emotions the recollections of childhood inspires, and how priceless its treasured memories in our advancing and declining years!

Laughing eyes and curly hair, little brown hands and bare feet, innocent and care-free, trusting and loving, tender and pure, what an elevating and satisfying influence these little gods have upon our maturer years!

Childhood! What a holy theme! Flowers they are, with souls in them, and if on this earth man has a sacred charge, a holy obligation, it is to these tender buds and blossoms of humanity.

Yet how many of them are prematurely plucked, fade and die and are trampled in the mire. Many millions of them have been snatched from the cradle and stolen from their play to be fed to the forces that turn a workingman's blood into a capitalist's gold, and many millions of others have been crushed and perverted into filth for the slums and food for the potter's field.

Childhood is at the parting of the ways which lead to success or failure, honor or disgrace, life or death. Society is, or ought to be, profoundly concerned in the nature of the environment that is to mold the character and determine the career of its children, and any remissness in such duty is rebuked by the most painful of penalties, and these are inflicted with increasing severity upon the people of the United States.

Childhood is the most precious charge of the family and the community, but our capitalist civilization sacrifices it ruthlessly to gratify its brutal lust for pelf and power, and the march of its conquest is stained with the blood of infants and paved with the puny bones of children.

What shall the harvest be?

---

* Illustration page 125.

The millions of children crushed and slain in the conquest of capitalism have not died in vain. From their little martyr graves all over this fair land their avenging images are springing up, as it were, against the system that murdered them and pronouncing upon it, in the name of God and humanity, the condemnation of death.

The Crimson Standard

Appeal to Reason

A vast amount of ignorant prejudice prevails against the red flag. It is easily accounted for. The ruling class the wide world over hates it, and its sycophants, therefore, must decry it.

Strange that the red flag should produce the same effect upon a tyrant that it does upon a bull.

The bull is enraged at the very sight of the red flag, his huge frame quivers, his eyes become balls of fire, and he paws the dirt and snorts with fury.

The reason of this peculiar effect of a bit of red coloring upon the bovine species we are not particularly interested in at this moment, but why does it happen to excite the same rage in the czar, the emperor and the king; the autocrat, the aristocrat and the plutocrat?

Ah, that is simple enough.

The red flag, since time immemorial, has symbolized the discontent of the downtrodden, the revolt of the rabble.

That is its sinister significance to the tyrant and the reason of his mingled fear and frenzy when the "red rag," as he characterizes it, insults his vision.

It is not that he is opposed to red as a color, or even as an emblem, for he has it in his own flags and banners, and it never inflames his passion when it is blended with other colors; but red alone, unmixed and unadulterated, the pure red that symbolizes the common blood of the human family, the equality of mankind, the brotherhood of the race, is repulsive and abhorrent to him because it is at once an impeachment of his title, a denial of his superiority and a menace to his power.

Precisely for the reason that the plutocrat raves at the red flag the proletaire should revere it.

To the plutocrat it is a peril; to the proletaire a promise.

The red flag is an omen of ill, a sign of terror to every tyrant, every robber and every vampire that sucks the life of labor and mocks at its misery.

It is an emblem of hope, a bow of promise to all the oppressed and downtrodden of the earth.

The red flag is the only race flag; it is the flag of revolt against robbery; the flag of the working class, the flag of hope and high resolve—the flag of Universal Freedom.

Roosevelt's Labor Letters

Appeal to Reason, May 18, 1907

The letter of President Roosevelt to the Moyer and Haywood conference of New York is in strange contrast with the one previously addressed by him to the Chicago conference on the same subject. The two letters are so entirely dissimilar in spirit and temper that they seem to have been written by different persons. In the first the President bristles with defiance, in the last he is the pink of politeness.

The first letter utterly failed of its purpose. Organized labor did not lie down and be still at the command of the President. On the contrary, it growled more fiercely than before; in fact, showed its teeth to the President, who has become so used to exhibiting his own. And lo—what a change! The President receives a labor committee, talks over matters for an hour and then addresses a letter to the conference through the chairman, beginning "My Dear Mr. Henry," explaining that he is ready to perform his duty if only the conference will point it out to him, and putting the whole blame on "Debs and the Socialists," whom he charges with using "treasonable and murderous language," but not a word of explanation does he vouchsafe in regard to his denunciation of Moyer and Haywood, the real, and in fact the only, point at issue.

Again has the President vindicated his reputation as one of the smoothest of politicians and one of the most artful and designing of demagogues.

We hope the lesson here taught as to what workingmen can accomplish by the power of united effort is not lost upon the working class. The first letter of the President was an insult to labor, and had labor submitted, the President's contempt for it would have been intensified by its cravenness.

The second letter was a virtual apology and nothing less than the firm attitude of labor extorted it.

The President's position, however, is not less enviable than before. Since he seeks escape from castigation for his outrageous attack upon Moyer and Haywood upon the ground that Debs had used "treasonable and murderous language" and that it was his duty as President to denounce it, a few questions will be in order and when the President has answered these we have a few more to which answers are also desired.

Did the President ever hear of one Sherman Bell?

Is it not a fact that said Sherman Bell is a personal friend of the President and that in a letter written in the President's own hand he commends said Sherman Bell in the most exalted terms?

Has the President ever heard of the expression, "To hell with habeas corpus; we'll give 'em postmortems," commended as "patriotic" by the capitalist press at the time it was made?

Does not the President know that it was his highly esteemed personal friend, Sherman Bell, who coined this phrase?

Is it "treasonable and murderous"?

Did the President condemn it?

Will he do so now?

Would he have done so if it had been Debs instead of Bell?

Why does he "conceive it to be his duty" to condemn Debs and not Bell?

Because Bell stands for capital and Debs for labor?

Has Debs ever said anything that, with reference to treason and murder, can be compared to this expression of his boon companion, Sherman Bell?

Will the President please answer?

Again, has the President ever heard of one Lieut. T. E. McClelland?

And of the expression, "To hell with the constitution," made by said McClelland?

Is this treasonable language?

Did the President condemn it?

Or, is it patriotic language when used in defense of capital and treasonable only when used in defense of labor?

Does the President know one Adjutant General Bulkeley Wells, the "officer of the law" who forcibly seized Moyer, Haywood and Pettibone and "special-trained" them to Idaho?

WRITINGS. 249

Does he know that his labor commissioner, Carroll D. Wright, condemns said Bulkeley Wells as a "mob leader" in his official report of the Colorado troubles?

Does the President approve mobs?

And consort with mob leaders?

While denouncing mobs?

Has he denounced Bulkeley Wells?

Will he do so?

Is the President aware that the Mine and Smelter Trust, behind the prosecution of Moyer, Haywood and Pettibone, bought the legislature of Colorado outright, thereby defeating an eight-hour measure which a popular majority of more than 46,000 votes had commanded said legislature to enact into law?

And that those mine and smelter owners are among his personal friends?

Is there any treason in this?

Has the President condemned it?

Dare he do so?

Is this his idea of "exact justice"?

A "square deal"?

Again, is kidnapping according to "law and order"?

If the kidnapped are workingmen?

And charged by their kidnappers with being murderers?

And by the President "undesirable citizens"?

Would the President have taken the same view of workingmen had kidnapped capitalists instead of capitalists kidnapping workingmen?

If it had been Ryan, Root, and Paul Morton, instead of Moyer, Haywood and Pettibone?

Will the President kindly answer?

Has the President ever heard the expression, "They shall never leave Idaho alive?"

Is this "murderous" language?

Except when used by "officers of the law"?

Has the President condemned it?

Does he approve it?

Has the President heard of one W. E. Borah, senator-elect, indicted for theft?

Visiting at the White House and coming out "smiling and confident"?

Is he innocent and desirable in spite of his indictment and Haywood guilty and undesirable in spite of the lawful presumption to the contrary?

Has the President ever heard of one Theodore Roosevelt?

Charged by the New York *Tribune* and other leading capitalist papers in 1896 with threatening to lead an armed force to Washington to prevent the inauguration of a lawfully-elected President of the United States?

Is there any "treason" or "murder" in this?

Does the President remember one John P. Altgeld?

And one Theodore Roosevelt who in the same year of 1896 said that said Altgeld and one Debs should be lined up against a dead wall and shot?

Which said Roosevelt never denied until four years later, when he became candidate for Vice President?

Is this the "temperate" language of a perfectly "desirable" citizen?

Does the President remember one Governor Roosevelt, of New York, who ordered his militia to Croton Dam to shoot some of the workingmen who elected him for venturing to ask the enforcement of the eight-hour law of that state?

And to protect the contractors who were violating the law?

Is this more of the President's "exact justice to all"?

Will the President kindly explain what he regards as inexact justice?

Or exact injustice?

Or injustice of any kind?

Or if his "exact justice to all" is not buncombe served in stilted style?

Can the President say or do any wrong?

Would he admit it if he did?

Has he ever done so?

When the President rebuked the labor unions for attempting to "influence the course of justice" did he not know it was violent kidnapping they were protesting against?

That they were seeking to influence the course, not of justice, but of injustice?

Resisting, not law, but mob violence cloaked as law?

At the time the President administered this rebuke had he

not himself read his letter condemning Moyer and Haywood to members of the supreme court when their case was pending in said court?

Was this not an attempt to "influence the course of justice"? Will the President publicly rebuke it?

When Moyer, Haywood and Pettibone, three workingmen, rugged as Patrick Henry, honest as Abraham Lincoln and brave as John Brown, were brutally kidnapped and told that they would be killed by the outlaws who kidnapped them; when two conspiring governors were the instigators of the kidnapping and all legal rights denied; when the special train lay in wait to rush them to their doom while their wives listened in vain all night long for their returning footsteps; when all law was cloven down, all justice denied, all decency defied and all humanity trampled beneath the brutal hoofs of might, a monstrous crime was committed, not against Moyer, Haywood and Pettibone merely, but against the working class, against the human race, and, by the eternal, that crime, even by the grace of Theodore Roosevelt, shall not go unwhipped by justice.

"Undesirable citizens" they are to the Christless perverts who exploit labor to degeneracy and mock its misery; turn the cradle into a coffin and call it philanthropy, and debauch the nation's politics and morals in the name of civilization.

"Undesirable citizens" though they are, these are the loyal leaders of the men who have toiled in the mines and who have been subjected to every conceivable outrage; "who have had their homes broken into and who have been beaten, bound, robbed, insulted and imprisoned"; who have been chained to posts in the public highway, deported from their families under penalty of death, and bullpenned while their wives and daughters were outraged. In the light of all these crimes perpetrated upon these men in violation of every law by brutal mobs, led by the President's own personal friends, as the official reports of his own labor commissioner will show, without a word of protest from him, it requires sublime audacity, to put it mildly, for the President to affirm that he stands for "exact justice to all" and that he "conceives it to be his duty" to denounce "treasonable and murderous" language.

If the miners of Colorado had been less patient than beasts

of burden they would have risen in revolt against the outrages perpetrated upon them by their heartless corporate masters.

Were a mob of workingmen to seize Theodore Roosevelt and chain him to a post on a public street in Washington in broad daylight, as a mob of his capitalist friends seized and chained a workingman in Colorado, or throw him into a foul bullpen, without cause or provocation, prod him with bayonets and outrage his defenseless family while he was a prisoner, as was done in scores of well-authenticated cases in both Colorado and Idaho, would he then be in the mood to listen complacently to hypocritical homilies upon the "temperate" use of language, the sanctity of "law and order" and the beauty of "exact justice to all"?

And if he heard of some man who had sufficient decency to denounce the outrages he and his family had suffered, would he then "conceive it to be his duty," as he tells us, to condemn the language of such a man as "treasonable and murderous" and the man himself as "inciting bloodshed," and therefore an "undesirable citizen"?

Labor Omnia Vincit

Written for Labor Day Souvenir, Central Labor Union, Boston, Mass., September, 1895

I would hail the day upon which it could be truthfully said, "Labor conquers everything," with inexpressible gratification. Such a day would stand first in Labor's Millennium, that prophesied era when Christ shall begin his reign on the earth to continue a thousand years.

The old Latin fathers did a large business in manufacturing maxims, and the one I have selected for a caption of this article has been required to play shibboleth since, like "a thing of beauty and a joy forever," it came forth from its ancient laboratory.

It is one of those happy expressions which embodies quite as much fancy as fact.

The time has arrived for thoughtful men identified with labor—by which I mean the laboring classes—to inquire, what does labor conquer? or what has it conquered in all the ages? or what is it now conquering?

If by the term conquer is meant that labor, and only labor, removes obstacles to physical progress—levels down mountains or tunnels them—builds railroads and spans rivers and chasms with bridges—hews down the forests—digs canals, transforms deserts into gardens of fruitfulness—plows and sows and reaps, delves in the mines for coal and all the precious metals—if it is meant that labor builds all the forges and factories, and all the railroads that girdle the world and all the ships that cleave the waves, and mans them, builds all the cities and every monument in all lands—I say if such things are meant when we vauntingly exclaim, "labor conquers everything," no one will controvert the declaration—no one will demur—with one acclaim the averments will stand confessed.

But with all these grand achievements to the credit of labor, how stands labor itself? Having subdued every obstacle to physical progress, what is its condition? The answer is humiliating beyond the power of exaggeration and the aphorism, *"Labor Omnia Vincit,"* becomes the most conspicuous delusion that ever had a votary since time began.

It will be well for labor on Labor day to concentrate its vision on the United States of America. The field is sufficiently broad and there are enough object lessons in full view to engage the attention of the most critical, and it will be strange indeed if the inquiry is not made. What has labor conquered up to date in the United States? The inquiry is fruitful of thought. What is the testimony of the labor press of the country, corroborated by statistics which defy contradiction? It is this, that the land is cursed with wage slavery—with the condition that labor, which, according to the proverb, "conquers everything," is itself conquered and lies prostrate and manacled beneath the iron hoofs of a despotism as cruel as ever cursed the world.

To hew and dig, to build and repair, to toil and starve, is not conquering in any proper sense of the term. Conquerors are not clothed in rags. Conquerors do not starve. The homes of conquerors are not huts, dark and dismal, where wives and children moan like the night winds and sob like the rain. Conquerors are not clubbed as if they were thieves, shot down as if they were vagabond dogs, nor imprisoned as if they were felons, by the decrees of despots. No! Conquerors rule—their word is law. Labor is not in the condition of a conqueror in the United States.

Go to the coal mines, go to the New England factories, go to Homestead and Pullman, go to the sweat shops and railroad shops, go to any place in all of the broad land where anvils ring, where shuttles fly, where toilers earn their bread in the sweat of their faces, and exclaim, *"Labor Omnia Vincit,"* and you will be laughed to scorn.

Why is it that labor does not conquer anything? Why does it not assert its mighty power? Why does it not rule in congress, in legislatures and in courts? I answer because it is factionized, because it will not unify, because, for some inscrutable reason, it prefers division, weakness and slavery, rather than unity, strength and victory.

Will it always be thus unmindful of its power and prerogatives? I do not think so. Will it always tamely submit to degradation? I protest that it will not. Labor has the ballot. It has redeeming power. I write from behind prison bars, the victim of a petty tyrant. My crime was that I sought to rescue Pullman slaves from the grasp of a monster of greed and rapacity.

I think a day is coming when *"Labor Omnia Vincit"* will change conditions. I hear the slogan of the clans of organized labor. It cheers me. I believe with the poet that

> A Labor Day is coming when our starry flag shall wave,
> Above a land where famine no longer digs a grave,
> Where money is not master, nor the workingman a slave—
> For the right is marching on.

EUGENE V. DEBS.

McHenry County Jail, Woodstock, Ill., August 5, 1895.

Open Letter to President Roosevelt

Toledo Socialist, April 21, 1906

Dear Mr. President:

The address delivered by you yesterday at the cornerstone ceremony at Washington has been carefully read and among other things I observe the following:

"We can no more and no less afford to condone evil in a man of capital than evil in a man of no capital. The wealthy man who exults because there is a failure of justice in the effort to bring some trust magnate to an account for his misdeeds is as bad, and no worse than, the so-called labor leader who clamorously strives to excite a foul class feeling on behalf of some other labor leader who is implicated in murder."

Obviously you have reference in this paragraph to the leaders of labor in Colorado who were recently seized without warrant of law, forcibly taken from the state of which they are citizens, and incarcerated in the penitentiary of another state in which only convicted criminals are confined. I know of no other labor leaders to whom these remarks could apply, and it seems equally plain that I am one of the "so-called" leaders, if not the particular one, who is "striving to excite a foul class feeling in their behalf."

Permit me to ask you, Mr. President, how you know that these men are implicated in murder? Have they been tried and found guilty by due process of law?

Since when, Mr. President, are men charged with crime presumed and pronounced guilty until they are found innocent?

It is true that you do not name these men, but convict them by innuendo. Is this fair? Is it just? A square deal? Is it not, in fact, Mr. President, cowardly to take such an advantage of your high office to pronounce the guilt of three of your fellow citizens, who have as yet not been tried and against whom nothing has been proved?

These men, Mr. President, are workingmen; do you know of any capitalists who have ever been treated in the same way?

Suppose a lot of thugs were to seize a number of capitalists at the hour of midnight, put them in irons, hustle them aboard a special train, rush them into another state and throw them into the penitentiary. Would you take the same view of the case, coolly pronounce their guilt and proceed to deliver your homily upon good citizenship, the "square deal," and law and order?

If instead of Moyer, Haywood and Pettibone it had been Depew, Platt and Paul Morton—that is to say, if instead of innocent workingmen they had been criminal capitalists—would you have treated them in precisely the same manner?

You have told us over and over again, Mr. President, that rich and poor should be treated alike; that all are entitled to the equal protection of the law. That is what you say in substance in the paragraph above quoted. You have repeated this so often that it has become a stale platitude. You have also repeatedly stated that profession without practice is dishonest and hypocritical.

Very well, Mr. President, we will take you at your word; we will judge you by your acts.

I shall not now address myself to you as a "so-called" labor leader, but as your fellow-citizen of the United States.

You, Mr. President, are the chief executive of the nation. You are the conservator of the constitution of the United States and you have publicly sworn to support it.

Three citizens have been forcibly seized and deported from the state of their residence into another state in flagrant violation of the constitution of the United States. These men now languish in prison cells.

Let me repeat the charge, Mr. President, without detail. Three citizens of the republic have been deprived of the protection vouchsafed to them under the constitution of the United States. This fact is known of all men; denied by none, not even their accusers. There is not a shadow of doubt about it. It is a clear-cut case. All the country knows it. You, Mr. President, know it. Now, then what are you going to do about it?

Will you make your acts square with your words; your practice with your profession?

It is up to you, Mr. President! You are reputed to have great moral courage and you certainly have great power. Under the constitution, the one that has been violated, the one you have sworn to support, you have the power to redress the wrong that has been done. Will you do it?

All that I am asking is that you shall perform your sworn duty; you are not expected to do more, and you cannot do less without violating your oath of office and betraying your official trust.

If you do not believe, Mr. President, that the constitution has been violated, or, if you have the least doubt about it, please call upon me to prove it.

I am not now handling a "muck-rake"; not looking down, but up; up to you and awaiting your answer.

You are perhaps aware, Mr. President, that some of us are accused of advocating violence. It is not true. As a matter of fact we are resisting violence. In your address yesterday you quoted the commandment, "Thou shalt not steal!" Let me quote another, "Thou shalt not kill." This is precisely what we are trying to prevent, not lawful punishment, but cold-blooded murder.

In treating with Moyer, Haywood and Pettibone, our comrades, every law and all decency have been trampled under foot. The state in which these men have been stripped of their legal rights and treated as felons is notoriously in control of corporations whose absolute sway has been questioned by these leaders of the working class; and this, and this alone, constitutes their crime, and for this they have been marked for corporate vengeance.

These men, Mr. President, are our comrades, our brothers, and we propose to stand by them and see that justice is done them.

A fair trial will free and vindicate them as certain as the sun shines.

Knowing them as we do to be men of pure character, of

absolute integrity and all other things of good report among men, we know that they are wholly incapable of committing the crime with which they have been charged.

It is not pretended that they were in the same state at the time the crime was committed. Not a shadow of crime rests upon them other than the alleged confession of a self-confessed criminal.

These are facts, Mr. President, and in view of these facts we would be craven indeed if we allowed our brothers to be made the victims of such an infamous conspiracy without doing all in our power to save them.

Every step thus far taken against these men has been in violation of law, and the purpose of the whole proceeding is so apparent that any man with eyes can see it.

In this connection, Mr. President, when the question of law and order is raised, I beg of you to remember that we are dealing with corporations that have usurped the powers of state governments; that defy the legally expressed will of the people, as in Colorado, where a majority of forty-six thousand votes was overridden and treated with contempt; corporations whose crime-inciting shibboleths are: "To hell with the constitution"; "To hell with habeas corpus."

These corporations rule the states and we have had evidence enough to know how they treat law when it interferes with their predatory program.

We are not in favor of violence, but seeking to avoid it. The facts prove it.

We are not objecting to a fair trial, but to a packed jury and a corporation court and the consummation of a criminal conspiracy.

"Thou shalt not kill!" This applies to capitalists as well as workingmen.

If Moyer, Haywood and Pettibone were capitalists instead of workingmen we should still do our utmost to see that they were given a "square deal."

Murder in any form is abhorrent, but most terribly so when committed under the forms and in the names of law and justice.

Wendell Phillips said that John Brown would have had twice

as good a right to hang Governor Wise as Governor Wise had to hang John Brown.

All we are asking and insisting upon is that our accused brothers shall have the protection of the law, a fair hearing and just verdict, and upon that issue we are prepared to go before the American people.

Respectfully yours,
EUGENE V. DEBS.

December 2, 1859

Appeal to Reason, November 23, 1907

[This] is the immortal date upon which John Brown was led to [execut]ion. Louisa M. Alcott on that day christened him "Saint [John t]he Just." On that same day Longfellow wrote: "This [is] a great day in our history; the date of a new revolution, [a]s much needed as the old one. Even now, as I write, [they a]re leading Old John Brown to execution in Virginia for [attemp]ting to rescue slaves! This is sowing the wind to reap [the wh]irlwind, which will come soon."

[How] prophetic these words!

[Wit]hin a month the mutterings of the storm were heard in [the lan]d, and within a few months it broke forth in all its fury. [Dec]ember 2, 1859, had spoken!

[John] Brown was the spirit incarnate of the Revolution, and [his ex]ecution changed the destiny of the universe.

[The] hated agitator is now the sainted savior, and his name [ranks] highest among the immortals.

The Martyred Apostles of Labor

The New Time, February, 1898

The century now closing is luminous with great achievements. In every department of human endeavor marvelous progress has been made. By the magic of the machine which sprang from the inventive genius of man, wealth has been created in fabulous abundance. But, alas, this wealth, instead of blessing the race, has been the means of enslaving it. The few have come in possession of all, and the many have been reduced to the extremity of living by permission.

A few have had the courage to protest. To silence these so that the dead-level of slavery could be maintained has been the demand and command of capital-blown power. Press and pulpit responded with alacrity. All the forces of society were directed against these pioneers of industrial liberty, these brave defenders of oppressed humanity—and against them the crime of the century has been committed.

Albert R. Parsons, August Spies, George Engel, Adolph Fischer, Louis Lingg, Samuel Fielden, Michael Schwab and Oscar Neebe paid the cruel penalty in prison cell and on the gallows.

They were the first martyrs in the cause of industrial freedom, and one of the supreme duties of our civilization, if indeed we may boast of having been redeemed from savagery, is to rescue their names from calumny and do justice to their memory.

The crime with which these men were charged was never proven against them. The trial which resulted in their conviction was not only a disgrace to all judicial procedure but a foul, black, indelible and damning stigma upon the nation.

It was a trial organized and conducted to convict—a conspiracy to murder innocent men, and hence had not one redeeming feature.

It was a plot, satanic in all its conception, to wreak vengeance upon defenseless men, who, not being found guilty of the crime charged in the indictment, were found guilty of exercising the inalienable right of free speech in the interest of the toiling and groaning masses, and thus they became the first martyrs to a cause which, fertilized by their blood, has grown in strength and sweep and influence from the day they yielded up their lives and liberty in its defense.

As the years go by and the history of that infamous trial is read and considered by men of thought, who are capable of wrenching themselves from the grasp of prejudice and giving reason its rightful supremacy, the stronger the conviction becomes that the present generation of workingmen should erect an enduring memorial to the men who had the courage to denounce and oppose wage-slavery and seek for methods of emancipation.

The vision of the judicially murdered men was prescient. They saw the dark and hideous shadow of coming events. They spoke words of warning, not too soon, not too emphatic, not too trumpettoned—for even in 1886, when the Haymarket meetings were held, the capitalistic grasp was upon the throats of workingmen and its fetters were upon their limbs.

There was even then idleness, poverty, squalor, the rattling of skeleton bones, the sunken eye, the pallor, the living death of famine, the crushing and the grinding of the relentless mills of the plutocracy, which more rapidly than the mills of the gods grind their victims to dust.

The men who went to their death upon the verdict of a jury, I have said, were judicially murdered—not only because the jury was packed for the express purpose of finding them guilty, not only because the crime for which they suffered was never proven against them, not only because the judge before whom they were arraigned was unjust and bloodthirsty, but because they had declared in the exercise of free speech that men who subjected their fellowmen to conditions often worse than death were unfit to live.

In all lands and in all ages where the victims of injustice have bowed their bodies to the earth, bearing grievous burdens laid upon them by cruel taskmasters, and have lifted their eyes starward in the hope of finding some orb whose light inspired hope, ten million times the anathema has been uttered and will be uttered until a day shall dawn upon the world when the emancipation of those who toil is achieved by the brave, self-sacrificing few who, like the Chicago martyrs, have the courage of crusaders and the spirit of iconoclasts and dare champion the cause of the oppressed and demand in the name of an avenging God and of an outraged Humanity that infernalism shall be eliminated from our civilization.

And as the struggle for justice proceeds and the battlefields are covered with the slain, as Mother Earth drinks their blood, the stones are given tongues with which to denounce man's inhumanity to man—aye, to women and children, whose moanings from hovel and sweatshop, garret and cellar, arraign our civilization, our religion and our judiciary—whose wailings and lamentations, hushing to silence every sound the Creator designed to make the world a paradise of harmonies, transform it into an inferno where the demons of greed plot and scheme to consign their victims to lower depths of degradation and despair.

The men who were judicially murdered in Chicago in 1887, in the name of the great State of Illinois, were the avant couriers of a better day. They were called anarchists, but at their trial it was not proven that they had committed any crime or violated any law. They had protested against unjust laws and their brutal administration. They stood between oppressor and oppressed, and they dared, in a free (?) country, to exercise the divine right of free speech; and the records of their trial, as if written with an "iron pen and lead in the rock forever," proclaim the truth of the declaration.

I would rescue their names from slander. The slanderers of the dead are the oppressors of the living. I would, if I could, restore them to their rightful positions as evangelists, the proclaimers of good news to their fellowmen—crusaders, to rescue the sacred shrines of justice from the profanations of the capitalistic defilers who have made them more repulsive than Augean stables. Aye, I would take them, if I could, from peaceful slumber in their martyr graves—I would place joint to joint in their dislocated necks—I would make the halter the symbol of redemption—I would restore the flesh to their skeleton bones—their eyes should again flash defiance to the enemies of humanity, and their tongues, again, more eloquent than all the heroes of oratory, should speak the truth to a gainsaying world. Alas, this cannot be done—but something can be done. The stigma fixed upon their names by an outrageous trial can be forever obliterated and their fame be made to shine with resplendent glory on the pages of history.

Until the time shall come, as come it will, when the parks of Chicago shall be adorned with their statues, and with holy acclaim, men, women and children, pointing to these monuments as testimonials of gratitude, shall honor the men who dared to be true to humanity and paid the penalty of their heroism with their lives, the preliminary work of setting forth their virtues devolves upon those who are capable of gratitude to men who suffered death that they might live.

They were the men who, like Al-Hassen, the minstrel of the king, went forth to find themes of mirth and joy with which to gladden the ears of his master, but returned disappointed, and, instead of themes to awaken the gladness and joyous echoes, found scenes which dried all the fountains of joy. Touching his golden harp, Al-Hassen sang to the king as Parsons, Spies, Engel, Fielden, Fischer, Lingg, Schwab and Neebe proclaimed to the people:

> "O king, at thy
> Command I went into the world of men;
> I sought full earnestly the thing which I
> Might weave into the gay and lightsome song.
> I found it, king; 'twas there. Had I the art
> To look but on the fair outside, I nothing
> Else had found. That art not mine, I saw what
> Lay beneath. And seeing thus I could not sing;
> For there, in dens more vile than wolf or jackal
> Ever sought, were herded, stifling, foul, the
> Writhing, crawling masses of mankind. Man!
> Ground down beneath oppression's iron heel,
> Till God in him was crushed and driven back,
> And only that which with the brute he shares
> Finds room to upward grow."

Such pictures of horror our martyrs saw in Chicago, as others have seen them in all the great centers of population in the country. But, like the noble minstrel, they proceeded to recite their discoveries and with him moaned:

> "And in this world
> I saw how womanhood's fair flower had
> Never space its petals to unfold. How
> Childhood's tender bud was crushed and trampled
> Down in mire and filth too evil, foul, for beasts
> To be partakers in. For gold I saw
> The virgin sold, and motherhood was made
> A mock and scorn.
>
> I saw the fruit of labor
> Torn away from him who toiled, to further
> Swell the bursting coffers of the rich, while
> Babes and mothers pined and died of want.
> I saw dishonor and injustice thrive. I saw
> The wicked, ignorant, greedy, and unclean,
> By means of bribes and baseness, raised to seats
> Of power, from whence with lashes pitiless
> And keen, they scourged the hungry, naked throng
> Whom first they robbed and then enslaved."

Such were the scenes that the Chicago martyrs had witnessed and which may still be seen, and for reciting them and protesting against them they were judicially murdered.

It was not strange that the hearts of the martyrs "grew into one with the great moaning, throbbing heart" of the oppressed; not strange that the nerves of the martyrs grew "tense and quivering with the throes of mortal pain"; not strange that they should pity and plead and protest. The strange part of it is that in our high-noon of civilization a damnable judicial conspiracy should have been concocted to murder them under the forms of law.

That such is the truth of history, no honest man will attempt to deny; hence the demand, growing more pronounced every day, to snatch the names of these martyred evangelists of labor emancipation from dishonor and add them to the roll of the most illustrious dead of the nation.

Mother Jones

Appeal to Reason, November 23, 1907

"The 'Grand Old Woman' of the revolutionary movement" is the appropriate title given to Mother Jones by Walter Hurt. All who know her—and they are legion—will at once recognize the fitness of the title.

The career of this unique old agitator reads like romance. There is no other that can be compared to it. For fifteen years she has been at the forefront, and never once has she been known to flinch.

From the time of the Pullman strike in 1894, when she first came into prominence, she has been steadily in the public eye. With no desire to wear "distinction's worthless badge," utterly forgetful of self and scorning all selfish ambitions, this brave woman has fought the battles of the oppressed with a heroism more exalted than ever sustained a soldier upon the field of carnage.

Mother Jones is not one of the "summer soldiers" or "sunshine patriots." Her pulses burn with true patriotic fervor, and wherever the battle waxes hottest there she surely will be found upon the firing line.

For many weary months at a time she has lived amid the most desolate regions of West Virginia, organizing the half-starved miners, making her home in their wretched cabins, sharing her meagre substance with their families, nursing the sick and cheering the disconsolate—a true minister of mercy.

During the great strike in the anthracite coal district she marched at the head of the miners; was first to meet the sheriff and the soldiers, and last to leave the field of battle.

Again and again has this dauntless soul been driven out of some community by corporation hirelings, enjoined by courts, locked up in jail, prodded by the bayonets of soldiers, and threatened with assassination. But never once in all her self-surrendering life has she shown the white feather; never once given a single sign of weakness or discouragement. In the Colorado strikes Mother Jones was feared, as was no other, by the criminal corporations; feared by them as she was loved by the sturdy miners she led again and again in the face of overwhelming odds until, like Henry of Navarre, where her snow-white crown was seen, the despairing slaves took fresh courage and fought again with all their waning strength against the embattled foe.

Deported at the point of bayonets, she bore herself so true a warrior that she won even the admiration of the soldiers, whose order it was to escort her to the boundary lines and guard against her return.

No other soldier in the revolutionary cause has a better right to recognition in this edition than has Mother Jones.

Her very name expresses the Spirit of the Revolution.

Her striking personality embodies all its principles.

She has won her way into the hearts of the nation's toilers, and her name is revered at the altars of their humble firesides and will be lovingly remembered by their children and their children's children forever.

John Brown: History's Greatest Hero

Appeal to Reason, November 23, 1907

The most picturesque character, the bravest man and most self-sacrificing soul in American history, was hanged at Charlestown, Va., December 2, 1859.

On that day Thoreau said: "Some eighteen hundred years ago Christ was crucified. This morning, perchance, Captain Brown was hung. These are the two ends of a chain which is not without its links. He is not 'Old Brown' any longer; he is an Angel of Light. * * * I foresee the time when the painter will paint that scene, no longer going to Rome for a subject; the poet will sing it, the historian record it, and with the landing of the Pilgrims and the Declaration of Independence it will be the ornament of some future national gallery, when at least the present form of slavery shall be no more here. We shall then be at liberty to weep for Captain Brown."

Few people dared on that fateful day to breathe a sympathetic word for the grizzled old agitator. For years he had carried on his warfare against chattel slavery. He had only a handful of fanatical followers to support him. But to his mind his duty was clear, and that was enough. He would fight it out to the end, and if need be alone.

Old John Brown set an example of moral courage and of single-hearted devotion to an ideal for all men and for all ages.

With every drop of his honest blood he hated slavery, and in his early manhood he resolved to lay his life on Freedom's alter in wiping out that insufferable affliction. He never faltered. So God-like was his unconquerable soul that he dared to face the world alone.

How perfectly sublime!

He did not reckon the overwhelming numbers against him, nor the paltry few that were on his side. This grosser aspect of the issue found no lodgment in his mind or heart. He was right and Jehovah was with him. His was not to reckon consequences, but to strike the immortal blow and step from the gallows to the throne of God.

Not for earthly glory did John Brown wage his holy warfare; not for any recognition or reward the people had it in their power to bestow. His great heart was set upon a higher goal, animated by a loftier ambition. His grand soul was illumined by a sublimer ideal. A race of human beings, lowly and despised, were in chains, and this festering crime was eating out the heart of civilization.

In the presence of this awful plague logic was silent, reason dumb, pity dead.

The wrath of retributive justice, long asleep, awakened at last and hurled its lurid bolt. Old John Brown struck the blow and the storm broke. That hour chattel slavery was dead.

In the first frightful convulsion the slave power seized the grand old liberator by the throat, put him in irons and threw him into a dungeon to await execution.

Alas! it was too late. His work was done. All Virginia could do was to furnish the crown for his martyrdom.

Victor Hugo exclaimed in a burst of reverential passion: "John Brown is grander than George Washington!"

History may be searched in vain for an example of noble heroism and sublime self-sacrifice equal to that of Old John Brown.

From the beginning of his career to its close he had but one idea and one ideal, and that was to destroy chattel slavery; and in that cause he sealed his devotion with his noble blood. Realizing that his work was done, he passed serenely, almost with joy, from the scenes of men.

His calmness upon the gallows was awe-inspiring; his exaltation supreme.

Old John Brown is not dead. His soul still marches on, and each passing year weaves new garlands for his brow and adds fresh lustre to his deathless glory.

Who shall be the John Brown of Wage-Slavery?

Martin Irons, Martyr

December 9, 1900

It was in 1886 that Martin Irons, as chairman of the executive board of the Knights of Labor of the Gould southwest railway system, defied capitalist tyranny, and from that hour he was doomed. All the powers of capitalism combined to crush him, and when at last he succumbed to overwhelming odds, he was hounded from place to place until he was ragged and foot-sore and the pangs of hunger gnawed at his vitals.

For fourteen long years he fought single-handed the battle against persecution. He tramped far, and among strangers, under an assumed name, sought to earn enough to get bread. But he was tracked like a beast and driven from shelter. For this "poor wanderer of a stormy day" there was no pity. He had stood between his class and their oppressors—he was brave, and would not flinch; he was honest, and he would not sell; this was his crime, and he must die.

Martin Irons came to this country from Scotland a child. He was friendless, penniless, alone. At an early age he became a machinist. For years he worked at his trade. He had a clear head and a warm heart. He saw and felt the injustice suffered by his class. Three reductions in wages in rapid succession fired his blood. He resolved to resist. He appealed to his fellow-workers. When the great strike came, Martin Irons was its central figure. The men felt they could trust him. They were not mistaken.

When at the darkest hour Jay Gould sent word to Martin Irons that he wished to see him, the answer came, "I am in Kansas City." Gould did not have gold enough to buy Irons. This was the greatest crime of labor's honest leader. The press united in fiercest denunciation. Every lie that malignity could conceive was circulated. In the popular mind

Martin Irons was the blackest-hearted villain that ever went unhung. Pinkerton blood-hounds tracked him night and day.

But through it all this loyal, fearless, high-minded workingman stood steadfast.

The courts and soldiers responded to the command of their masters, the railroads; the strike was crushed and the workingmen were beaten.

Martin Irons had served, suffered for and honored his class. But he had lost. His class now turned against him and joined in the execration of the enemy. This pained him more than all else. But he bore even this without a murmur, and if ever a despairing sigh was wrung from him it was when he was alone.

And thus it has been all along the highway of the centuries, from Jesus Christ to Martin Irons.

Let it not be said that Irons was not crucified. For fourteen years he was nailed to the cross, and no martyr to humanity ever bore his crucifixion with finer fortitude.

He endured the taunts and jeers and all the bitter mockery of fate with patient heroism; and even when the poor dumb brutes whose wounds and bruises he would have swathed with his own heart-strings turned upon and rent him, pity sealed his lips and silent suffering wrought for him a martyr's crown.

Martin Irons was hated by all who were too base or ignorant to understand him. He died despised, yet shall he live beloved.

No president of the United States gave or tendered him a public office in testimony of his service to the working class. The kind of service he rendered was too honest to be respectable, too aggressive and uncompromising to be popular.

The blow he struck for his class will preserve his memory. In the great struggle for emancipation he nobly did his share, and the history of labor cannot be written without his name.

He was an agitator, and as such shared the common fate of all. Jesus Christ, Joan of Arc, Elijah Lovejoy, John Brown, Albert Parsons and many others set the same example and paid the same penalty.

For the reason that he was a despised agitator and shunned of men too mean and sordid to comprehend the lofty motive that inspired him, he will be remembered with tenderness and love long after the last of his detractors shall have mouldered in a forgotten grave.

It was in April, 1899, in Waco, Texas, that I last pressed this comrade's hand. He bore the traces of poverty and broken health, but his spirit was as intrepid as when he struck the shield of Hoxie thirteen years before; and when he spoke of Socialism he seemed transfigured, and all the smouldering fires within his soul blazed from his sunken eyes once more.

I was pained, but not surprised, when I read that he had "died penniless in an obscure Texas town." It is his glory and society's shame that he died that way.

His weary body has at last found rest, and the grandchildren of the men and women he struggled, suffered and died for will weave chaplets where he sleeps.

His epitaph might read: "For standing bravely in defense of the working class, he was put to death by slow torture."

Martin Irons was an honest, courageous, manly man. The world numbers one less since he has left it.

Brave comrade, love, and farewell.

Thomas McGrady

Appeal to Reason, December 14, 1907

It is a strange and pathetic coincidence that almost at the very moment I completed the introduction to the brochure of Thomas McGrady on "The Catholic Church and Socialism," now in press, the sad news came that he had passed away, and the painful duty now devolves upon me to write the word "finis" at the close of his work and add a few words of obitual eulogy.

It is not customary among Socialists to pronounce conventional and meaningless panegyrics upon departed comrades; nor to pay fulsome tribute to virtues they never possessed. Mere form and ceremony have had their day—and a long and gloomy day it has been—and can have no place among Socialists when a comrade living pays his last reverent regards to a comrade dead.

Thomas McGrady was born at Lexington, Ky., June 6, 1863. In 1887, at 24 years of age, he was ordained as a Catholic priest at the Cathedral of Galveston, Tex. His next pastorate was St. Patrick's church, Houston, followed by his transfer to St. Patrick's church, Dallas, Tex. In 1890 he returned to his Kentucky home, beginning his pastoral service there in Lexington, his native city. Later he went to St. Anthony's church, Bellevue, Ky., and it was here, in 1896, that he began his first serious study of economic, political and social questions. He was first attracted by Henry George's Single Tax, but abandoned that as inadequate after some Socialist literature fell into his hands, and he became convinced that nothing less than a social revolution, and the abolition of the capitalist competitive system would materially better the existing industrial and social condition of the people.

Father McGrady, who always had the lofty courage of his

convictions, now avowed himself a Socialist. He drank deep at the fountain of Socialist literature and mastered its classics. His library contained the works of the standard authors of all nations.

It was at this time that Father McGrady was at the very pinnacle of his priestly power and popularity. He was young, just past thirty, brilliant and scholarly. His magnetic personality was irresistible. Tall, fully six feet, splendidly proportioned, commanding, he was a magnificent specimen of physical manhood. He had a massive head, a full, fine face, florid complexion, clear features, and the bluest, kindliest and most expressive of eyes.

Widely and deeply read, cultured in the genuine sense, sociable and sympathetic, Father McGrady attracted friends by an irresistible charm, and held them by the same magic power.

He was an orator and a wit, a scholar and a humanitarian.

He had the exquisite fancy of a poet and could dally, according to mood, with a daisy or a star.

In his heroic and finely moulded physical proportions, his large and shapely head, clear complexion and expressive eyes, he resembled strongly Robert G. Ingersoll.

This resemblance was accentuated by the kindly and infectious humor, the brilliant flashes of wit, the terse and epigrammatic speech, and the keen and incisive satire of which both were master.

These two men, had they not been separated by the cruel and hateful prejudices inherent in capitalist society, and all its conventional institutions, would have been the boonest of friends and loved each other as brothers.

Father McGrady soon began to feel that his new convictions did not fit his old conventicle. Honesty and candor being his predominant characteristics, the truth that dawned upon his brain found ready expression from his eloquent lips. He took his congregation into his confidence and told them frankly that he was a Socialist. Thenceforward every discourse attested that fact. He was warned by the bishop, threatened by the archbishop, but his flock closed around him, a living, throbbing citadel. He ministered to them in their suffering, comforted them in their sorrow, solemnized their nuptial vows, baptized their babes, tenderly laid to rest their dead, and they truly loved him.

But the conviction that the orthodox pulpit and the forum of freedom were irreconcilable, and that as a priest he was in the fetters of theology, grew upon him, and in spite of the pleadings and protestings of his followers he resigned his pastorate and withdrew from the priesthood. The touching scene attending his farewell sermon has never been described, and never will be, in human speech. The congregation, seeming more like one great family, under Father McGrady's tender and affectionate ministrations, felt striken as if by an unspeakably sad personal bereavement, and sat in silence as they paid homage to their departing friend and pastor in sobs and tears.

The tremendous public reception given the modern Saul at Cincinnati, across the Ohio from his Kentucky home, is vividly remembered by thousands who struggled in the crush of common humanity to get within sound of his voice. He was now a full-fledged Social Revolutionist, and like his immortal prototype of many centuries ago, the common people heard him gladly.

The formal abdication of the priesthood by Father McGrady created a great sensation. The dignitaries of the church affected pious rejoicing. The recreant priest had long been a thorn in their complacent flesh. It was well that the holy church was purged of his pernicious influence.

Columns of reports appeared in the daily papers, and the features of the converted priest, with which these accounts were embellished, became familiar to hundreds of thousands. A Socialist priest was indeed an anomaly. Vast concourses of people were attracted by the mere mention of his name. When he was announced to speak, standing room was always at a premium.

McGrady was now at his best. The deep convictions he was now free to express flowered in his speech and his oratory, like the peals of a great organ and the chimes of sweet bells, moved and swayed the eager masses. Everywhere the eloquent exponent of Socialism and pleader for the oppressed was in demand. His fame preceded his footsteps. Auditoriums, theaters and public halls were taxed to their capacity. The eloquent Socialist evangelist was now one of the commanding figures of the American platform. He was doing, superbly doing, the grand work for which he had been fitted as if by special providence. From the Atlantic seaboard to the Pacific slope his resonant voice was heard and the multitude were stirred by his burning message of social regeneration.

It was in the midst of these oratorical triumphs that the first distinct shock of organized opposition was felt. The capitalist press as a unit, and as if by preconcerted action, cut him out of its columns. The sensation created by McGrady's leap from the Catholic pulpit to the Socialist platform had been fully exploited as far as its news value was concerned, and now the renegade priest, as his whilom paters in Christ, who profess to love their enemies, call him, must be relegated to oblivion by being totally ignored. The church he formerly served so faithfully now began to actively pursue him. Where he was announced to speak priests admonished the faithful, either openly from the pulpit or covertly through the confessional, not to stain their souls by venturing near the anti-Christ. But this form of opposition, however vexatious, trying and difficult to overcome, but aroused the latent spirit of the crusader and intensified his determination. In the fierce fires of persecution, fed and fanned by religious ignorance and fanaticism, he was tempered for the far greater work that spread out before him, rich and radiant as a field of promise.

"Unhappy man!" as Hugo wrote of Marshal Ney, who bared his breast to the leaden hail of English foe on the field of Waterloo, "Thou wast reserved for French bullets!"

Notwithstanding that McGrady was attracting vast audiences, including many who had never before heard the philosophy of Socialism expounded, the very ones most desired, and without whom progress is impossible; notwithstanding the door receipts almost uniformly recouped the treasury of the local Socialists by a substantial net balance, certain "leaders," whose narrow prejudices were inflamed by the new agitator's success and increasing popularity in the movement, began to turn upon him, and sting him with venomous inuendo or attack him openly through the Socialist press.

Paradoxical as it may seem, he was denied the right to serve the Socialist movement—by Socialists.

Among the first charges brought against him—not by capitalists; they were too wise, if not too decent, to utter such a palpable untruth, but by men calling themselves Socialists—was that he had joined the movement as a "grafter," and was making Socialist speeches for "the money there was in it."

A baser falsehood, a more atrocious slander was never uttered.

Had McGrady been a miserable grafter instead of a great white soul, he would have remained in the pulpit. His people worshipped him and his "superiors" held out the most glittering inducements if he would only abandon his wicked and abominable "economic heresies." The eloquence and power of the young priest were widely recognized in church circles. A brilliant future spread out before him. He could easily become the petted and pampered favorite of the fathers. But he spurned the life of ease and luxury at the price of his self-respect. The positions of eminence he might attain by stifling his convictions sank to degradation from his lofty point of view.

Turning his back upon the wealth and luxury of the capitalist class he cast his lot with the proletariat, the homeless and hungry, the ragged and distressed, and this he did, according to some Socialists, to "graft" on them, and the cry was raised, "The grafter must go!"

It was this that shocked his tender sensibilities, silenced his eloquent tongue, and broke his noble and generous heart.

Those Socialists who vilified him as a "sky pilot," and as a "grafter," who declared him to be "unsound," "unscientific," and who indulged in similar tirade and twaddle, ought now to be satisfied. Their ambition has been realized. They scourged the "fakir" from the platform with whips of asps into a premature grave and he will trouble them no more. May they find it in their consciences to forgive themselves.

There is a deep lesson in the melancholy and untimely death of Comrade Thomas McGrady. Let us hope that so much good may result from it that the cruel sacrifice may be softened by the atonement and serve the future as a noble and inspiring example.

While it is the duty of every member to guard the movement against the imposter, the chronic suspicion that a man who has risen above the mental plane of a scavenger is a "grafter" is a besetting sin, and has done incalculable harm to the movement. The increasing cry from the same source that only the proletariat is revolutionary and that "intellectuals" are middle class reactionaries is an insult to the movement, many of whose staunchest supporters are of the latter type. Moreover, it would imply by its sneering allusion to the "intellectuals" that the proletariat are a brainless rabble, reveling in their base degeneracy and scorning intellectual enlightenment.

Many a fine spirit who would have served the movement as an effective agitator and powerful advocate, stung to the quick by the keen lash in the hand of a "comrade," has dropped into silence and faded into obscurity.

Fortunately the influence of these self-appointed censors is waning. The movement is no longer a mere fanatical sect. It has outgrown that period in spite of its sentinels and doorkeepers.

Between watchful devotion, which guards against imposters and chronic heresy hunting, which places a premium upon dirt and stupidity, and imposes a penalty upon brains and self-respect, there is a difference wide as the sea. The former is a virtue which cannot be too highly commended, the latter a vice which cannot be too severely condemned.

Thomas McGrady was an absolutely honest man. Almost ten years of intimate and varied relations with him enables the writer to conscientiously pay him this tribute—to place this perennial flower where he sleeps.

No attempt is made to convert our deceased comrade into a saint. Could he speak he would not be shorn of his foibles. Like all great souls he had his faults—the faults that attested his humanity and brought into more perfect relief the many virtues which adorned his manly character and enriched his noble life.

Thomas McGrady found joy in social service and his perfect consecration to his social ideals was the crowning glory of his life and the bow of promise at his death.

Looking Backward

Appeal to Reason, November 23, 1907

Before me lies a copy of the Philadelphia *Evening Herald,* bearing date of June 21, 1877. On that day the "Mollie Maguires" were executed, six of them—Boyle, McGeghan, Munley, Roarity, Carroll and Duffy—at Pottsville; four of them—Campbell, Doyle, Kelly and Donahue—at Mauch Chunk, and one—Lanahan—at Wilkesbarre. They all protested their innocence and all died game. Not one of them betrayed the slightest evidence of fear or weakening. The issue of the *Herald* referred to contains a full account of the executions, with portraits of the hapless victims.

Not long ago in the jail at Pottsville I stood on the spot where the six "Mollies" met their doom, and I uncovered in memory of their martyrdom.

Not one of them was a murderer at heart. All were ignorant, rough and uncouth, born of poverty and buffeted by the merciless tides of fate and chance.

To resist the wrongs of which they and their fellow-workers were the victims and to protect themselves against the brutality of their bosses, according to their own crude notions, was the prime object of the organization of the "Mollie Maguires." Nothing could have been farther from their intention than murder or crime. It is true that their methods were drastic, but it must be remembered that their lot was hard and brutalizing; that they were the neglected children of poverty, the products of a wretched environment.

At the scenes of the execution the tragedy is today, thirty years later, still spoken of in whispers. A vague dread of reviving the fearful past seems to silence the tongue of the resident when the subject is introduced. But bit by bit the truth has slowly and painfully filtered through the dungeon doors of false history, and the world is beginning to understand the true inwardness of the "Mollie Maguire" organization and its real relation to the labor movement.

These unfortunate victims of the basest betrayal since the days of Judas had no possible means of defense or justification. The corporate press howled like fiends incarnate for their blood. They had dared to assert themselves against a powerful and piratical corporation, and this was sufficient warrant for their extermination. Spies, informers and assassins wormed their slimy way into their councils. Bloody crimes were instigated and committed; the innocent and ignorant "Mollies" walked into the traps set for them.

The powers of the law now fell upon them with crushing effect. Their organization was annihilated. No friendly voice pleaded in extenuation of the crimes charged upon the leaders.

The labor movement was in its infancy; it had no press and no standing; no influence and no power. There was but one side to the tragedy and that was, of course, the capitalist side. The poor, dumb victims, bound and gagged, had but to await their bloody fate. At the grates of their cells the hounds of hell snarled and growled with savage ferocity to lap their blood. No helping hand was extended, and scarce a whisper of kindness was ventured in their behalf.

June 21, 1877, the curtain fell upon the last mournful act in this tragedy of toil. The executioner did his bidding and the gallows-tree claimed its victims.

On that day history turned harlot and the fair face of truth was covered with the hideous mask of falsehood.

For thirty years the press of corporate power has been lying grossly and outrageously about the "Mollie Maguires" and their organization. But the truth will out at last, and the time is near when the history of the Pennsylvania tragedy, as now written, will be radically revised and the names of these martyrs rescued from the cruel calumny with which they have been loaded.

The "Mollie Maguire" episode was incidental to the organization of the working class; a link in the chain of the labor movement.

The men who perished upon the scaffold as felons were

labor leaders, the first martyrs to the class struggle in the United States.

It is profoundly significant that Franklin B. Gowen, president of the Philadelphia & Reading railway, and chief prosecutor and persecutor of the "Mollie Maguires," sought in suicide a refuge from the avenging Nemesis that pursued him.

In the year 1876 the Workinmen's party was organized, and in the following year, 1877, after the execution of the "Molly Maguires," it became the Socialistic Labor party.

This same year the great railroad strikes swept like a tidal wave from the eastern to the western states.

Eight years later, in 1885, the Knights of Labor came into national prominence, and the great strikes on the Gould Southwest system in that year and the year following were inaugurated.

On May 1, 1886, hundreds of thousands of workers in various parts of the country went on strike to enforce the eight-hour work day, the agitation incident to the movement culminating in the Haymarket tragedy of May 4.

On November 11 of the following year, 1887 (twenty years ago today), occurred the infamous execution of the anarchists at Chicago. This judicial massacre constitutes the blackest page in American history. When Parsons, Spies, Fischer and Engel were launched into eternity to "vindicate the majesty of the law," a crime was committed of such enormity, that even at this late day the sober senses reel in its awful contemplation.

These fellow-workers and their four comrades—Lingg, Fielden, Schwab and Neebe—the first of whom died by violence in his cell, and the last three of whom were sentenced to the penitentiary and subsequently pardoned by the immortal Altgeld—were martyrs to the labor movement in the noblest sense of that term. They had fearlessly espoused the cause of labor and consecrated themselves body and soul to the working class. They had the true revolutionary spirit, were animated by the loftiest motives, and were utterly void of selfish ambitions.

The sordid capitalism which preys upon the life-blood of labor, whose ethics are expressed in beastly gluttony and insatiable greed, and whose track of conquest is strewn with the bones of its countless victims, pounced upon these men with the cruel malignity of fiends and strangled them to death.

A more cruel and heartless crime, a more flagrant outrage of justice, was never committed. Twenty years have passed since these leaders of labor paid the penalty of their loyalty, and marvelous have been the changes in public sentiment since that day. They would not now be executed under the same circumstances. The workers today are too far advanced, too well organized and too conscious of their class interests and duties to submit to such a monstrous outrage.

The recent trial and acquittal of Wm. D. Haywood proves it. Had labor been no farther advanced than it was twenty years ago, Moyer, Haywood, Pettibone and Adams would long since have shared the fate of Parsons, Spies, Fischer and Engel.

Since that fateful period of two decades ago, events have pressed each other closely in the world of labor. Three months after the execution of the Haymarket victims the C., B. & Q. strike broke out in Chicago, and the issue was hotly contested for almost a year before the employes finally succumbed to defeat. From that time forward strikes, boycotts and lockouts were numerous, a long series of industrial battles marking the path of the class struggle and the progress of the labor movement.

Homestead, Buffalo, Chicago, Latimer, Virden, Pana, Leadville, Coeur d'Alene, Telluride and Cripple Creek followed in swift succession, each the scene of a bloody battle in the historic struggle for emancipation.

The battle of the American Railway Union with the allied railroad corporations in 1894 developed extraordinary activity on the part of our capitalist government. The strikers were completely victorious at every point when the government openly took sides with the railroads and employed all its vast repressive machinery to defeat the strike and crush out the union.

The lessons of this strike were among the most valuable ever learned by the working class, and many thousands date their class-consciousness from that memorable conflict.

The more recent strikes in Colorado, Utah and other western states, culminating in the kidnapping conspiracy of the mine owners and the bold attempt to repeat the Haymarket and "Mollie Maguire" massacres, are still fresh in the memory of the people, especially the rugged miners who, under the banner of the Western Federation, fought with all the energy and bravery of desperation against the plots and wiles of the organized mine owners, as unscrupulous and heartless an aggregation of exploiters as ever robbed and murdered their fellow-beings.

Looking backward over the last thirty years, the progress of the labor movement can be clearly traced, and its contemplation is fruitful of inexpressible satisfaction. Looking forward, the skies are bright and all the tongues of the future proclaim the glad tidings of the coming Emancipation.

Labor Day Greeting

Social Democratic Herald, September, 1904

The workingman is the only man in whose presence I take off my hat. As I salute him, I honor myself.

The workingman—and this is the day to write him in capital letters—has given me what I have, made me what I am, and will make me what I hope to be; and I thank him for all, and above all for giving me eyes to see, a heart to feel and a voice to speak for the workingman.

Like the rough hewn stone from which the noble statue is chiseled by the hand of man, the Toiler is the rough-hewn bulk from which the perfect Man is being chiseled by the hand of God.

All the workingmen of the earth are necessary to the whole Workingman—and he alone will survive of all the human race.

Labor Day is a good day to rest the hands and give the brain a chance—to think about what has been, and is, and is yet to be.

The way has been long and weary and full of pain, and many have fallen by the wayside, but the Unconquerable Army of Labor is still on the march and as it rests on its arms today and casts a look ahead, it beholds upon the horizon the first glowing rays of the Social Sunrise.

Courage, comrades! The struggle must be won, for Peace will only come when she comes hand in hand with Freedom.

The right is with the labor movement and the gods of battle are with the Working Class.

The Socialist Party and the Trade Union Movement must be one today in celebration of Labor Day and pledge each other their mutual fidelity and support in every battle, economic and political, until the field is won and the Workingman is free.

Forget not the past on Labor Day! Think of Homestead! Think of Latimer! Think of Buffalo! Think of Coeur d'Alene! Think of Croton Dam! Think of Chicago! Think of Virden! Think of Pana! Think of Leadville! Think of Cripple Creek! Think of Victor! Think of Telluride!

These are some of the bloody battles fought in the past in the war of the Workers for Industrial Freedom and Social Justice.

How many and how fierce and bloody shall be the battles of the future?

Comrades, this is the day for Workingmen to think of the Class Struggle and the Ballot—the day for Labor to clasp the hand of Labor and girdle the globe with the International Revolutionary Solidarity of the Working Class.

We are all one—all workers of all lands and climes. We know not color, nor creed, nor sex in the Labor Movement. We know only that our hearts throb with the same proletarian stroke, that we are keeping step with our class in the march to the goal and that the solidarity of Labor will vanquish slavery and Humanize the World.

Proclamation to American Railway Union

Issued upon his sentence being affirmed by the Supreme Court of the United States

TERRE HAUTE, IND., June 1, 1895.

Sirs and Brothers—A cruel wrong against our great order, perpetrated by Wm. A. Woods, United States Circuit Judge, has been approved by the United States Supreme Court, and from under its shadow I address this communication to you; but though prison walls frown upon myself and others whom you chose as officials, I assure you that neither despondency nor despair has taken the place of the courage which has characterized our order since the storms of persecution first began to beat upon us. Hope has not deserted us. Our faith in the future of our great order is as strong as when our banners waved triumphantly over the Great Northern from St. Paul to the coast. Our order is still the undaunted friend of the toiling masses and our battle-cry now, as ever, is the emancipation of labor from degrading, starving and enslaving conditions. We have not lost faith in the ultimate triumph of truth over perjury, of justice over wrong, however exalted may be the stations of those who perpetrate the outrages.

THE STORM AND THE BATTLE.

I need not remind you, comrades of the American Railway Union, that our order in the pursuit of the right was confronted with a storm of opposition such as never beat upon a labor organization in all time. Its brilliant victory on the Great Northern and its gallant championship of the unorganized employes of the Union Pacific had aroused the opposition of every railroad corporation in the land.

To crush the American Railway Union was the one tie that united them all in the bonds of vengeance; it solidified the enemies of labor into one great association, one organization which, by its fabulous wealth, enabled it to bring into action resources aggregating billions of money and every appliance that money could purchase. But in this supreme hour the American Railway Union, undaunted, put forth its efforts to rescue Pullman's famine-cursed wage slaves from the grasp of an employer as heartless as a stone, as remorseless as a savage and as unpitying as an incarnate fiend. The battle fought in the interest of starving men, women and children stands forth in the history of Labor's struggles as the great "Pullman Strike." It was a battle on the part of the American Railway Union fought for a cause as holy as ever aroused the courage of brave men; it was a battle in which upon one side were men thrice armed because their cause was just, but they fought against the combined power of corporations which by the use of money could debauch justice, and, by playing the part of incendiary, bring to their aid the military power of the government, and this solidified mass of venality, venom and vengeance constituted the foe against which the American Railway Union fought Labor's greatest battle for humanity.

REWARDS AND PENALTIES.

What has been your reward for your splendid courage and manifold sacrifices? Our enemies say they are summed up in the one word "defeat." They point to the battlefield and say: "Here is where the host of the American Railway Union went down before the confederated enemy of labor." They point to the spot where Miles' serried soldiery stood with drawn swords, tramping steeds and shotted guns to kill innocent men whose only crime was devotion to wretched men and women, the victims of Pullman's greed. They designate the places where the minions of a despotic judge, the thieves and thugs, taken from Chicago slums, transformed into deputy marshals and armed with clubs and pistols, went forth to murder indiscriminately and to arouse the vengeance of the people by incendiary fires, and they point to the General Managers' Association, the Nero of the occasion, whose pitiless enmity of labor would have glorified in widespread conflagration rather than permitted a strike in the interest of famishing men, women and children, to have succeeded; and such disasters, say the enemies of labor, are the rewards of the courage of the A. R. U. men, a courage as invincible as was ever displayed by Spartans, and which makes Pullman's Labor Thermopylæ to live in history as long as the right has a defender in the ranks of American workingmen.

Brothers of the American Railway Union, even in defeat our rewards are grand beyond expression, rewards which come only to brave men, the consciousness of noble deeds performed in the holy cause of labor's emancipation. Cowards, the fawning, sycophantic poltroons of power, never knew the thrills of joy that reward the heroes of battles fought in the interest of the oppressed.

"Once to ev'ry man and nation comes a moment to decide,
In the strife of Truth and Falsehood, for the good or evil side."

The American Railway Union did decide. It espoused the cause of justice. It furrowed the land deeper with its plows of Truth and Courage than had fallen to the lot of any other labor organization since time began, and the seeds of emancipation which it sowed broadcast are germinating and a new era is destined to dawn upon labor.

TRUTH IT IS THAT THE

"Sons of brutish Force and Darkness," who have "drenched the earth with blood," chuckle over their victories. They point to the blacklisted heroes of the American Railway Union, idle and poor, and count upon their surrender. Their hope is that our order will disband; that persecution, poverty and prison will do the work. These gory-handed enemies of our order expect to put out our lodge fires, silence our battle cries, disrobe ourselves of courage and manhood, permit them to place their ironshod hoofs on our neck and sink us to fathomless depths of degradation and make the American Railway Union the synonym of all things the most detestable.

CAN THEY DO IT?

In the presence of prison doors and prison bars and weary months of incarceration, I answer a thousand times, NO! In the grasp of despotic power, as infamous and as cruel as ever blackened the records of Russia, I treat with ineffable scorn the power that without trial sends me and my official associates of the American Railway Union to prison. I do not believe, nor will I believe, that my brothers, beloved of our great order, will throw their courage away and join the ranks of the enemy, while their comrades, the victims of worse than Russian vengeance, are suffering in prison.

IN RUSSIA,

the land of the autocrat, liberty is unknown. In that thrice damned country liberty and justice, free speech and free press and trial by jury are banished, and a trail of blood and tears from the palace of the despot to prison and to death, made by men and women whose only crime is a desire for freedom, tell their doom; and yet in Russia imprisonment, torture and death only increase the ranks of men and women who cry, "Give me liberty or give me death."

In Russia, the victim of autocratic displeasure is denied a trial by a jury of his peers. Wm. A. Woods carries out the Russian practice. In Russia the doomed man or woman is arraigned before the supreme despot or one of his numerous satraps. Truth, justice, mercy are forever exiled, hope disappears and only words of satanic cruelty are uttered. Age, sex, character, innocence, name and condition count for nothing. It is enough to know that the brave soul yearned for freedom, and the penalty of exile, imprisonment, torture or death is inflicted, and it has come to this at last in the United States of America, that the law of injunction is the will of a despot, and by the exercise of this Russian power American Railway Union officials go to prison and the hope is that by the exercising of this power the American Railway Union will be crushed.

STAND BY YOUR ORDER!

At this supreme juncture I call upon the members of the American Railway Union to stand by their order. In God's own good time we will make the despot's prison, where innocent men suffer, monumental. We will link them with the legends and lore of labor's struggles to be read by our children and our children's children when Bartholdi's goddess of liberty with her torch enlightening the world has succumbed to the ravages of time.

Count me o'er earth's chosen heroes—they were souls that stood alone.
(While the men they agonized for threw the contumelious stone)
Stood serene and down the future saw the golden beam incline
To the side of perfect justice, mastered by their faith divine,
By one man's plain truth to manhood and to God's supreme design.

Flea and Donkey

A flea nestled in the ear of a donkey. The flea bit off the tip of a pore and lunched at leisure. The donkey brayed and kicked. Moral: The interests of fleas and donkeys are identical. (See revised code civic federation.)

Without fleas donkeys would have no incentive to kick and bray and would soon completely lose their donkeyality.

Eye to Eye

President Mitchell, of the United Mine Workers, is reported as saying that if only the capitalist and workingman will look straight into each other's eyes and speak the truth, there will be no more strikes. The trouble is that, inasmuch as the capitalist is on the back of the workingman, they can't look into each other's eyes unless the capitalist dismounts or the workingman twists his spine, and he is already suffering from curvature of that sorely-strained member of his saddled, bridled, whipped and spurred organism.

The capitalist can hardly be expected to rein up and get down purely to see the color of the optics of his "mount."

Stopped the Blacklist

Wayland's Monthly, September, 1902

It was on a mixed train on one of the mountain roads in the western states. The conductor and both brakemen had already shown me their old A. R. U. cards, which they treasured with almost affectionate tenderness. The soiled, illegible scraps were souvenirs of the "war," and revived a whole freight train of stirring reminiscences. The three weather-beaten trainmen were strangers prior to '94; they were off of three separate roads, and from three different states.

Each of the brakemen had told the story of his persecution after the strike. The companies had declared that no A. R. U. striker should ever have another job on a railroad, and they were doing their level best to make good their brutal avowal. These two brakemen had to suffer long in the role of the "wandering Jew." Again and again they had secured jobs, under assumed names and otherwise, but as soon as they were found out they were dismissed with the highly edifying information that the company no longer needed their services.

They were on the railroad blacklist. Only they know what this means who have been there. Many times had these brakemen been hungry, many times ejected from trains, often footsore after a weary walk to the next division point. But they bore it all and made no complaint. Fortunately they were both single men and their privations were at least free from the harrowing thought that wife and child were being tortured by their merciless persecutors. They finally conquered the blacklist and were once more allowed to become the slaves of the railroads.

* * * * * * *

It was about noon when the conductor tapped me on the

shoulder and invited me into the baggage end of the car to have dinner with the crew. They had their own kitchen and cooking utensils and had managed to dish up a most appetizing bill of fare. I was first served with a steaming platter of "mulligan," a popular dish with the mountain men. Then followed cold meat, bread and butter and hot coffee, topped off with a quarter section of pie.

The pipes were next lighted and a lively exchange of reminiscence followed.

The conductor was obliged to leave us for a time and while he was gone the two brakemen told me how he had "stopped the blacklist." It is a short but immensely suggestive story. The conductor, like all brave men, was too modest to tell it himself. Here it is:

Bill, that was the conductor's name, was running a train on the S―――― railway when the strike of '94 came. He was also chairman of the local grievance committee. He lost out with the rest and took his medicine without a whimper. When he left home to look for a job his wife had the cheerful assurance that she and the two children would soon hear from him and that they would be united again at an early day.

Bill secured five jobs in straight succession. He was a first-class railroad man and could fill any kind of position. But as fast as he got a job he lost it. The black demon was at his heels. He had offended his former master and now he and his loving wife and innocent babes must die.

The last job Bill had held good for some days before he was spied out and discharged. He drew $15, but he did not send it to his wife, nor did he use it on himself. Bill had a grim determination written in every line of his swarthy face when he pocketed that $15 and his discharge, and started toward the city. He stopped short before a hardware store and his eyes scanned the display in the window. In less than five minutes he had entered, investigated and emerged again.

With rapid strides the blacklisted man hurried toward the railroad station.

* * * * * * *

We next see Bill on the streets of his old home. His friends, if any remained, would scarce have recognized him. Upon his wan features there was an ugly look that boded ill to someone, and in his hip pocket a load six-shooter was ready for action.

The superintendent turned deadly pale when Bill entered. He instinctively read his indictment in Bill's grim visage before a word was spoken.

"What can I do for you, Mr. ———?" tremblingly asked the pilloried official.

"Not a damned thing," replied Bill, in a strange, hoarse voice.

"You know what I'm here for," continued the victim of the blacklist, "and if you've got any prayers to offer before I make a lead mine of your carcass, you'd better begin at once."

While Bill spoke the superintendent looked into the murderous pistol pointed at him by the desperate man, and an instant later his office was turned into a prayer meeting. Such piteous pleas were rarely heard from such coward lips.

Bill's heart was touched; he would give the craven assassin another chance.

Withdrawing the weapon and shoving it into his pocket, Bill looked the official straight in the eye and in a steady voice said: "You have beaten me out of five jobs and you are responsible for my wife and babies being homeless and hungry. You know that there is not a scratch upon my record as an employe, nor a stain upon my character as a man. You have deliberately plotted to torture and kill an innocent woman and two babies who depend upon my labor, and by God, you deserve to die like the dog you are. But I'm going to give you another chance for your life—mark me, just one. I shall get another job, and I shall refer to you as to my service record. If I lose that job, G—— d—— your black heart, you'll do your blacklisting in hell, not here, for I'll send you there as sure as my name's Bill ———."

The superintendent drew a long breath of relief when Bill turned on his heels and left him alone. He did not doubt Bill's word. It is hardly necessary to say that the blacklist was ended. Bill got the job and holds it to this day. Not a man on the road is more respected than he, especially by the officials.

Bill did not appeal to the courts. He took no chances on a

brace game. His nerve and his six-shooter settled the case and there were no costs to pay.

Bill and his two brakemen are now Socialists. The three hours I spent with those three men rolling over the western mountains I shall remember always with interest and satisfaction.

Prince and Proletaire

Wilshire's Magazine

The two types represented in the above caption are brought into vivid contrast by the visit of Prince Henry to our democratic domain and the hysterical demonstrations that assail him as he is whirled from point to point in his royal carousal among the plebeians. According to reports the royalty of the old world has been totally eclipsed by the democracy of the new, and his deputy imperial majesty is fairly dazzled and bewildered by the fast and furious display in his honor. At the opera in New York he was surrounded by a palpitating wall of nude flesh, ablaze with diamonds—a scene of gorgeous, glittering splendor compared with which the courts of kings are dim as dirt.

And this is but an incident among a thousand in which our democratic (?) people of every rank and station, save Socialistic alone, abase themselves in vulgar fawning at the feet of tyranny. Shall the titled snob be blamed for holding all such flunkeys in contempt?

Who is this royal lion in the democratic den? A total stranger from an alien land. What has he done to command the reverence of a god? Ask yourself if you can answer. It is not then to the man—for he's unknown—but to the Prince that Uncle Sam gets down full length into the dust and spreads the Stars and Stripes for royal feet to tread upon.

What difference is there between the monarchy of William and the republic of Roosevelt? Could the Lick telescope discover it?

Bear in mind that here "we" are the people; "we" live in "the land of the free and the home of the brave"; "we" are all sovereigns; "we" have no classes; "we" scorn royal snobs; "we" love liberty and despise display; "we" hold "divine right to rule" in contempt; "we"—

The simple truth is we are like the rest—we have prince and pauper, power and poverty, money and misery in our capitalist republic, just as they have in their capitalist monarchy across the water.

Chauncey M. Depew has 150 pairs of creased trousers; many of his sovereign constituents have patches on their only pair of pants.

In our great eastern cities more than half the people live in tenements unfit for habitation, and thousands of babes, denied fresh air, die every year.

The sweating dens are packed with human vermin, but Henry, by the grace of God, will not behold the reeking ballast of the "ship of state."

A few rods from the Waldorf in New York and the Auditorium in Chicago, are the districts of the doomed and damned. The squares of squalor and miles of misery inspire in men, instead of "Hoch der Kaiser," the wish "to hear the nightingale sing new marseillaises" and revive the ominous notes of "La Carmagnole."

> "Thus fares the land, by luxury betray'd;
> In nature's simplest charms at first array'd,
> But verging to decline, its splendors rise,
> Its vistas strike, its palaces surprise;
> While, scourged by famine from the smiling land,
> The mournful toiler leads his humble band;
> And while he sinks, without one arm to save,
> The country blooms—a garden, and a grave."

Not long ago the millionaires and labor leaders had a feast in New York; they met as one, and declared that henceforth they were "one and inseparable, now and forever." President Roosevelt ratified the compact by dining the leaders at the White House. But where are labor's representatives to the Prince Henry banquets and receptions? Have they been lost in the shuffle? Can it be that they are not fit to meet a prince? Absurd! This is a Republic; labor here is royal and wears the imperial crown. So, at least, Mr. Hanna and other poor and oppressed capitalists tell us, and surely they should know the working kings who rule them.

But again, where are the representatives of labor at these

courtly social functions? Why is no American workingman allowed near the prince except as menial and spaniel, to guard his noble majesty and do slavish obeisance to his every whim?

Why is there no inch of room for labor in any house or hall, or park, or boat in all this vaunted Republic when a "prince" is guest?

Why are the working class excluded from such "public" functions as rigidly as if they wore the stripes of convicts?

Why must a prince be guarded?

On "great occasions," such as the presence of a royal guest, the streets and alleys are reserved for the working class, and in these thoroughfares the dead-lines of the common herd are guarded with policemen's clubs.

How melancholy to see shivering humans, packed together like cattle in a car, rend one another in mad strife to honor those who look upon them as unclean and hold them in supreme contempt!

The working class of the United States, with few exceptions, cheered and shouted for the prince as though he had been their lord and savior. He cares no more for them, this pampered prince, than if they were so many sheep or swine, for he believes that royal blood, by God's decree, flows through his veins and that common humans are but beasts of burden.

Not long ago Ben Tillett came from England as the representative of labor. All his life he worked to help the men of toil. In point of honest worth Ben Tillett far outweighs ten thousand blooded princes. Yet workingmen, except the few, ignored him, and the scant regard they showed him is to their disgrace.

The point I make is, that from the time the ship that brought the prince touched our shore until it left again no workingman was tolerated in any banquet or reception tendered him in the name of the American people. Office-holders and politicians spouted, while capitalists lined the tables and wined and dined themselves—all of which simply proves that there are no classes in the United States, and that Socialism has no business in a republic.

The envoys for the coronation of King Edward have been announced by President Roosevelt. There will be no horny-handed prince of labor there. Whitelaw Reid, known only for being the opposite of Horace Greeley, and as small as he was great, will be our knee-breeched, official flunkey at the crowning of the king.

Of course it would not be consistent for our president to drop a crumb of comfort to the Boers.

Let it not be understood that I have the slightest feeling against Henry of Prussia; it is the prince I have no use for. Personally, he may be a good fellow, and I am inclined to believe he is, and if he were in trouble and I had it in my power to help he would find in me a friend. The amputation of his title would relieve him of his royal affliction and elevate him to the dignity of a man.

This is a necessary part of the mission of Socialism, and the revolutionary movement is sweeping over the United States as well as Germany.

It means the end of princes, the end of paupers and the beginning of Man.

> "To ears attuned, the victor's shouts
> Are crossing o'er the sea;
> Resounding like Jove's thunder peals
> The working class are free."

Revolution

New York Worker, April 27, 1907

This is the first and only International Labor Day. It belongs to the working class and is dedicated to the Revolution.

Today the slaves of all the world are taking a fresh breath in the long and weary march; pausing a moment to clear their lungs and shout for joy; celebrating in festal fellowship their coming Freedom.

All hail the Labor Day of May!
The day of the proletarian protest;
The day of stern resolve;
The day of noble aspiration.
Raise high this day the blood-red Standard of the Revolution!
The banner of the Workingman;
The flag, the only flag, of Freedom.

Slavery, even the most abject—dumb and despairing as it may seem—has yet its inspiration. Crushed it may be, but extinguished never. Chain the slave as you will, O Masters, brutalize him as you may, yet in his soul, though dead, he yearns for freedom still.

The great discovery the modern slaves have made is that they themselves their freedom must achieve. This is the secret of their solidarity; the heart of their hope; the inspiration that nerves them all with sinews of steel.

They are still in bondage, but no longer cower;
No longer grovel in the dust,
But stand erect like men.
Conscious of their growing power the future holds out to them her outstretched hands.

As the slavery of the working class is international, so the movement for its emancipation.

The salutation of slave to slave this day is repeated in every human tongue as it goes ringing round the world.

The many millions are at last awakening. For countless ages they have suffered; drained to the dregs the bitter cup of misery and woe.

At last, at last the historic limitation has been reached, and soon a new sun will light the world.

Red is the life-tide of our common humanity and red our symbol of universal kinship.

Tyrants deny it; fear it; tremble with rage and terror when they behold it.

We reaffirm it and on this day pledge anew our fidelity—come life or death—to the blood-red Banner of the Revolution.

Socialist greetings this day to all our fellow-workers! To the god-like souls in Russia marching grimly, sublimely into the jaws of hell with the Song of the Revolution in their death-rattle; to the Orient, the Occident and all the Isles of the Sea!

VIVE LA REVOLUTION!

The most heroic word in all languages is REVOLUTION.

It thrills and vibrates; cheers and inspires. Tyrants and time-servers fear it, but the oppressed hail it with joy.

The throne trembles when this throbbing word is lisped, but to the hovel it is food for the famishing and hope for the victims of despair.

Let us glorify today the revolutions of the past and hail the Greater Revolution yet to come before Emancipation shall make all the days of the year May Days of peace and plenty for the sons and daughters of toil.

It was with Revolution as his theme that Mark Twain's soul drank deep from the fount of inspiration. His immortality will rest at last upon this royal tribute to the French Revolution:

"The ever memorable and blessed revolution, which swept a thousand years of villainy away in one swift tidal wave of blood—one: a settlement of that hoary debt in the proportion of half a drop of blood for each hogshead of it that had been pressed by slow tortures out of that people in the weary stretch of ten centuries of wrong and shame and misery the like of which was not to be mated but in hell. There were two Reigns of Terror, if we would but remember it and consider it: the one wrought murder in hot passion, the other in heartless cold blood; the one lasted mere months, the other lasted a thousand years; the one inflicted death on ten thousand persons, the other upon a hundred millions; but our shudders are all for the horrors of the minor Terror, so to speak; whereas, what is the horror of swift death by the axe compared with lifelong death from hunger, cold, insult, cruelty and heartbreak? What is swift death by lightning compared with death by slow fire at the stake? A city cemetery could contain the coffins filled by that brief Terror, which we have all been so diligently taught to shiver at and mourn over, but all France could hardly contain the coffins filled by that older and real Terror which none of us has been taught to see in its vastness or pity as it deserves."

Arouse, Ye Slaves!

Appeal to Reason, March 10, 1906

The latest and boldest stroke of the plutocracy, but for the blindness of the people, would have startled the nation.

Murder has been plotted and is about to be executed in the name and under the forms of law.

Men who will not yield to corruption and browbeating must be ambushed, spirited away and murdered.

That is the edict of the Mine Owners' Association of the western states and their Standard Oil backers and pals in Wall street, New York.

These gory-beaked vultures are to pluck out the heart of resistance to their tyranny and robbery, that labor may be left stark naked at their mercy.

Charles Moyer and Wm. D. Haywood, of the Western Federation of Miners, and their official colleagues—men, all of them, and every inch of them—are charged with the assassination of ex-Governor Frank Steunenberg, of Idaho, who simply reaped what he had sown, as a mere subterfuge to pounce upon them in secret, rush them out of the state by special train, under heavy guard, clap them into the penitentiary, convict them upon the purchased perjured testimony of villains, and strangle them to death with the hangman's noose.

It is a foul plot; a damnable conspiracy; a hellish outrage.

The governors of Idaho and Colorado say they have the proof to convict. They are brazen falsifiers and venal villains, the miserable tools of the mine owners who, themselves, if anybody, deserve the gibbet.

Moyer, Haywood and their comrades had no more to do with the assassination of Steunenberg than I had; the charge is a ghastly lie, a criminal calumny, and is only an excuse to murder men who are too rigidly honest to betray their trust and too courageous to succumb to threat and intimidation.

Labor leaders that cringe before the plutocracy and do its bidding are apotheosized; those that refuse must be foully murdered.

Personally and intimately do I know Moyer, Haywood, Pettibone, St. John and their official co-workers, and I will stake my life on their honor and integrity; and that is precisely the crime for which, according to the words of the slimy "sleuth" who "worked up the case" against them, "they shall never leave Idaho alive."

Well, by the gods, if they don't, the governors of Idaho and Colorado and their masters from Wall street, New York, to the Rocky Mountains had better prepare to follow them.

Nearly twenty years ago the capitalist tyrants put some innocent men to death for standing up for labor.

They are now going to try it again. Let them dare!

There have been twenty years of revolutionary education, agitation and organization since the Haymarket tragedy, and if an attempt is made to repeat it, there will be a revolution and I will do all in my power to precipitate it.

The crisis has come and we have got to meet it. Upon the issue involved the whole body of organized labor can unite and every enemy of plutocracy will join us. From the farms, the factories and stores will pour the workers to meet the red-handed destroyers of freedom, the murderers of innocent men and the arch-enemies of the people.

Moyer and Haywood are our comrades, staunch and true, and if we do not stand by them to the shedding of the last drop of blood in our veins, we are disgraced forever and deserve the fate of cringing cowards.

We are not responsible for the issue. It is not of our seeking. It has been forced upon us; and for the very reason that we deprecate violence and abhor bloodshed we cannot desert our comrades and allow them to be put to death. If they can be murdered without cause so can we, and so will we be dealt with at the pleasure of these tyrants.

They have driven us to the wall and now let us rally our forces and face them and fight.

If they attempt to murder Moyer, Haywood and their brothers, a million revolutionists, at least, will meet them with guns.

They have done their best and their worst to crush and enslave us. Their politicians have betrayed us, their courts have thrown us into jail without trial and their soldiers have shot our comrades dead in their tracks.

The worm turns at last, and so does the worker.

Let them dare to execute their devilish plot and every state in this Union will resound with the tramp of revolution.

Get ready, comrades, for action! No other course is left to the working class. Their courts are closed to us except to pronounce our doom. To enter their courts is simply to be mulcted of our meagre means and bound hand and foot; to have our eyes plucked out by the vultures that fatten upon our misery.

Capitalist courts never have done, and never will do, anything for the working class.

Whatever is done we must do ourselves, and if we stand up like men from the Atlantic to the Pacific and from Canada to the Gulf, we will strike terror to their cowardly hearts and they will be but too eager to relax their grip upon our throats and beat a swift retreat.

We will watch every move they make and in the meantime prepare for action.

A special revolutionary convention of the proletariat at Chicago, or some other central point, would be in order, and, if extreme measures are required, a general strike could be ordered and industry paralyzed as a preliminary to a general uprising.

If the plutocrats begin the program, we will end it.

Growth of the Injunction

Social Democratic Herald, May 6, 1905

In the month of December, 1893, something over eleven years ago, a federal injunction was issued that broke all the records up to that time and stirred up the whole country. This injunction was issued by James G. Jenkins, judge of the United States Circuit Court, and restrained the employes of the Northern Pacific railway from quitting the service of that company under penalty of being found guilty of contempt and sent to jail.

The facts in the case, which are recalled by a recently published interview with Judge Jenkins, who has retired from the bench, were as follows:

The Northern Pacific, robbed and wrecked by the knaves who had control of its affairs, applied to the federal court in the person of Judge Jenkins for a receivership, which was promptly granted. Following this order of the court and the appointment of the receivers, the latter petitioned the court for an order making sweeping reductions in the wages of employes, and fearing that a strike might follow, the receivers asked the court at the same time to issue an order restraining the employes from leaving the service of the company, and this was also promptly granted. It was this latter order that aroused the storm and it raged fiercely for some months. Indignation meetings were held by labor unions, notably in Chicago, where a mass meeting was called for the special purpose of denouncing Judge Jenkins and demanding his impeachment. Obedient to the indignation and clamor of organized labor, Congressman McGann, of Illinois, introduced a resolution in Congress looking to the investigation of the affair by the judiciary committee, but, of course, nothing came from it, and it was not long before the judicial crime, for such it was, was forgotten.

The strange thing about it was that the employes did not strike under such extreme provocation, and this was due to the fact that their leaders, the national officers of the unions, urged them not to do so, and united in a letter to the general manager accepting the order of the court and acquiescing in the situation. The writer, who was then organizing the American Railway Union, tried to have the employes resent the despotic decree of the court and quit in a body from end to end of the line, but other counsels prevailed and they remained at work. It would have been interesting to see the ten or twelve thousand employes quit as one and defy the outrageous order of the court, and then see Jenkins make good his order and send them to jail. The judicial bluff would have been called and not only would they not have gone to jail, but the court would have stood exposed and rebuked and the reduction in the wages would have been restored. I am still waiting for organized workingmen to take advantage of just such an opening when ten thousand or more workers shall all be simultaneously in contempt for the defiance of some outrageous federal injunction. It will have a most wholesome effect—infinitely better than the servile pleas of labor leaders and legislative committees in the humiliating role of mendicants, crawling in the dust at the feet of their supposed servants.

Had the army of Northern Pacific employes resented the outrage of Judge Jenkins in 1893 by quitting in defiance of his injunction—and they would have done it but for the national officers of their unions—an object lesson of inestimable value would have been taught the courts and their capitalist masters, and the rapid evolution of the labor injunction which had then fairly set in would have been checked for a time at least, and it is doubtful if it had ever developed its present unrestrained restraining power.

Judge Henry Clay Caldwell, who was also on the federal bench at the time the Jenkins injunction was issued, declared strongly in opposition to it, saying:

"If receivers should apply for leave to reduce the existing scale of wages, before acting on their petition I would require them to give notice of the application to the officers or representatives of the several labor organizations to be affected by the proposed change, of the time and place of hearing, and would also require them to grant such officers or representatives leave of absence and furnish them transportation to the place of hearing and subsistence while in attendance, and I would hear both sides in person, or by attorneys, if they wanted attorneys to appear for them. * * * If, after a full hearing and consideration, I found that it was necessary, equitable and just to reduce the scale of wages, I would give the employes ample time to determine whether they would accept the new scale. If they rejected it they would not be enjoined from quitting the service of the court either singly or in a body."

Judge Jenkins gave the employes no hearing, no notice, no consideration. He simply ordered their wages reduced and told them that if they quit work he would send them to jail. This is the order—and a beautiful order it is in a land of boasted freedom—that Judge Jenkins now says has been vindicated and that the precedent then established by him is now followed by all courts. He is right. The evolution of the injunction has indeed been swift and what was regarded as exceedingly novel and venturesome a decade ago is now securely incorporated in our established system of capitalistic jurisprudence.

The late Judge Dundy, of Omaha, notoriously the creature of the Union Pacific, issued the order reducing wages on that system when it was in the hands of receivers appointed by him, but Judge Caldwell, who was on the Circuit bench and had prior jurisdiction, took the case away from Dundy, had the employes come into court and be heard, and, after hearing all the evidence, revoked the order of Dundy, restored the wage reductions and administered a scathing rebuke to the receivers.

Judge Caldwell was appointed to the Federal bench by President Lincoln. They don't appoint that kind of judges any more.

Such eminent lights as Dundy, Jenkins, Ricks, Taft, Ross, Woods, Grosscup and Kohlsaat now illumine the Federal bar and all their names are immortally associated with the evolution of the injunction and the subjugation of labor by judicial prowess.

One of the first and most illustrious in this line is Judge Taft, who won his spurs in the Toledo, Ann Arbor & North Michigan case. He has been a prime favorite with the corporations ever since, is now in the cabinet, and is being groomed for the presidency. As a candidate for the white house he has the two essential qualifications—unswerving loyalty to capital and unmitigated contempt for labor—and this should and doubtless will secure his nomination and election by an overwhelming majority.

In his published interview, Judge Jenkins, discussing his Northern Pacific injunction, says:

"Within the last twelve years, by reason of popular discontent at legal restraint, the issuance of this writ has been designated opprobriously as 'government by injunction.' Well, it is in a true and proper sense 'government by injunction,' for it is a government by law. The remedy has long existed and will exist so long as government by law continues, so long as we have liberty regulated by law, and not irresponsible, uncontrolled license to exercise one's sweet will without regard to others' rights, which is anarchy, and no howling of the mob can ever abolish it until government by law is wrecked and 'chaos is come again.'"

Let me ask Judge Jenkins if he would be of the same opinion if at the time he cut the wages of the Northern Pacific employes and restrained them from quitting some other judge had issued an order reducing his salary as judge and restraining him from resigning under penalty of being sent to jail. That is the position precisely in which he placed the employes of the Northern Pacific, and it is this that he now calls "liberty regulated by law." If that is liberty it would be interesting to know what slavery is.

It has been about fifteen years since the court injunction began to figure in labor affairs. It was threatened in the C., B. & Q. railroad strike of 1888, but not resorted to. After the Homestead strike, in 1892, during which Pinkertonism reached its culmination and this brutal form of warfare upon labor by Carnegie and Frick excited the most intense indignation, the injunction came into general use. It proved a great thing for the corporations, just what they had been looking for. No longer was there any need for a private Pinkerton army. That was a clumsy contrivance compared to the noiseless, automatic, self-acting injunction. The Pinkertons were expensive, cumbersome, aroused hatred and sometimes missed fire. The injunction was free from all these objections. One shock from the judicial battery and labor was paralyzed and counted out.

Since first introduced in the struggle between labor and capital the injunction has developed from the flintlock to the rapid-fire. Judge Jenkins enjoys in his retirement the distinction of having contributed one of its chief improvements. His fame is secure and so is his infamy. He need not worry about vindication. He was as loyal a judge as ever bowed to Mammon, as faithful a tool as ever served his master, and as consummate a hypocrite as ever stabbed liberty in the name of law.

The injunction is playing its usual role in the teamsters' strike in Chicago. The Team Owners' Association of Chicago are incorporated in West Virginia and by this trick become an interstate association and nestled under the wing of the United States court. The Federal injunction to destroy the strike and rout the strikers has already been applied for and granted. This goes without saying. What are Judges Grosscup and Kohlsaat on the bench for? Certainly not for the health of the teamsters. They are there to do what they were appointed to do by the president of the exploiting capitalists elected by the exploited workers.

At this writing carloads of negroes are being shipped into Chicago to take the places of the striking teamsters, while injunctions, like swords suspended by threads, hang above their heads and ten thousand regular soldiers with shotted guns are on the edge of the city awaiting the command to sprinkle the streets with the blood of labor.

Oh, that all the workers of Chicago would back up the teamsters and garment workers by throwing down their tools and quitting work! Twenty-four hours of such a strike would bring the masters to their knees. But they have too many unions and too many leaders for this, and so they must fight it out to the bitter end.

In the meantime the evolution of the injunction is making

for Socialism. Nothing more clearly shows that the labor question is also a political question and that to conquer their exploiters the working class must build up the Socialist party and capture the powers of government.

What's the Matter with Chicago?

Chicago Socialist, October 25, 1902

For some days William E. Curtis, the far-famed correspondent of the Chicago *Record-Herald,* has been pressing the above inquiry upon representative people of all classes with a view to throwing all possible light upon that vexed subject.

The inquiry is in such general terms and takes such wide scope that anything like a comprehensive answer would fill a book without exhausting the subject, while a review of the "interviews" would embrace the whole gamut of absurdity and folly and produce a library of comedy and tragedy.

Not one of the replies I have seen has sufficient merit to be printed in a paper read by grown folks, and those that purport to come from leaders of labor and representatives of the working class take the prize in what would appear to be a competitive contest for progressive assininity.

The leader, so-called, who puts it upon record in a capitalist paper and gives the libel the widest circulation, that Chicago is alright, so far as the workers are concerned, that they have plenty and are prosperous and happy, is as fit to lead the working class as is a wolf to guide a flock of spring lambs.

It is from the wage worker's point of view that I shall attempt an answer to the question propounded by Mr. Curtis, and in dealing with the subject I shall be as candid as may be expected from a Socialist agitator.

The question is opportune at this season, when the "frost is on the pumpkin," and the ballot is soon to decide to what extent the people really know "What is the matter with Chicago."

First of all, Chicago is the product of modern capitalism, and, like all other great commercial centers, is unfit for human habitation. The Illinois Central Railroad Company selected the site upon which the city is built and this consisted of a vast miasmatic swamp far better suited to mosquito culture than for human beings. From the day the site was chosen by (and of course in the interest of all) said railway company, everything that entered into the building of the town and the development of the city was determined purely from profit considerations and without the remotest concern for the health and comfort of the human beings who were to live there, especially those who had to do all the labor and produce all the wealth.

As a rule hogs are only raised where they have good health and grow fat. Any old place will do to raise human beings.

At this very hour typhoid fever and diphtheria are epidemic in Chicago and the doctors agree that these ravages are due to the microbes and germs generated in the catchbasins and sewers which fester and exhale their foul and fetid breath upon the vast swarms of human beings caught and fettered there.

Thousands upon thousands of Chicago's population have been poisoned to death by the impure water and foul atmosphere of this undrainable swamp (notwithstanding the doctored mortuary tables by which it is proven to prospective investors that it is the healthiest city on earth) and thousands more will commit suicide in the same way, but to compensate for it all Chicago has the prize location for money-making, immense advantage for profitmongering—and what are human beings compared to money?

During recent years Chicago has expended millions to lift herself out of her native swamp, but the sewage floats back to report the dismal failure of the attempt, and every germ-laden breeze confirms the report.

That is one thing that is the matter with Chicago. It never was intended that human beings should live there. A thousand sites infinitely preferable for a city could have been found in close proximity, but they lacked the "Commercial" advantages which are of such commanding importance in the capitalist system.

And now they wonder "What is the Matter with Chicago!"
Look at some of her filthy streets in the heart of the city,

chronically torn up, the sunlight obscured, the air polluted, the water contaminated, every fountain and stream designed to bless the race poisoned at its source—and you need not wonder what ails Chicago, nor will you escape the conclusion that the case is chronic and that the present city will never recover from the fatal malady.

What is true of Chicago physically is emphasized in her social, moral and spiritual aspects, and this applies to every commercial metropolis in the civilized world.

From any rational point of view they are all dismal failures.

There is no reason under the sun, aside from the profit considerations of the capitalist system, why two million humans should be stacked up in layers and heaps until they jar the clouds, while millions of acres of virgin soil are totally uninhabited.

The very contemplation of the spectacle gives rise to serious doubt as to the sanity of the race.

Such a vast population in such a limited area cannot feed itself, has not room to move and cannot keep clean.

The deadly virus of capitalism is surging through all the veins of this young mistress of trade and the eruptions are found all over the body social and politic, and that's "What's the matter with Chicago."

Hundreds of the *Record-Herald's* quacks are prescribing their nostrums for the blotches and pustules which have broken out upon the surface, but few have sense enough to know and candor enough to admit that the virus must be expelled from the system—and these few are Socialists who are so notoriously visionary and impracticable that their opinions are not worthy of space in a great paper printed to conserve the truth and promote the welfare of society.

This model metropolis of the West has broken all the records for political corruption. Her old rival on the Mississippi, catching the inspiration doubtless, has been making some effort to crown herself with similar laurels, but for smooth political jobbery and fancy manipulation of the wires, Chicago is still far in the lead. In the "Windy City" ward politics has long been recognized as a fine art and the collection is unrivalled anywhere.

From the millions of dollars filched from the millions of humans by the corporate owners of the common utilities, the reeking corruption funds flow like lava tides, and to attempt to purify the turbid stream by the "reform measures" proposed from time to time by the Republican-Democratic party in its internal conflict for the spoils of office, is as utter a piece of folly as to try with beeswax to seal up Mount Pelee.

Chicago has plutocrats and paupers in the ratio of more than sixteen to one—boulevards for the exhibition of the rich and alleys for the convenience of the poor.

Chicago has also a grand army of the most skilled pickpockets, artistic confidence operators, accomplished foot-pads and adept cracksmen on earth. So well is this understood that on every breeze we hear the refrain:

> "When Reuben comes to town,
> He's sure to be done brown—"

And this lugubrious truth is treated as the richest of jokes, with utter unconsciousness of the moral degeneracy it reflects, the crime it glorifies and the indictment of capitalist society it returns in answer to the *Record-Herald's* query: "What's the matter with Chicago"?

Besides the array of "talent" above mentioned, fostered by competitive society everywhere, the marshy metropolis by the lake may boast of a vast and flourishing gambling industry, an illimitable and progressive "levee" district, sweatshops, slums, dives, bloated men, bedraggled women, ghastly caricatures of their former selves, babies cradled in rags and filth, aged children, than which nothing could be more melancholy—all these and a thousand more, the fruit of our present social anarchy, afflict Chicago; and worst of all, our wise social philosophers, schooled in the economics of capitalist universities, preach the comforting doctrine that all these are necessary evils and at best can but be restricted within certain bounds; and this hideous libel is made a cloak that theft may continue to masquerade as philanthropy.

It is at this point that Chicago particularly prides herself upon her "charities," hospitals and eleemosynary endowments, all breathing the sweet spirit of Christian philanthropy—utterly ignorant of the fact, designedly or otherwise, that these very institutions are manifestations of social disease and are monumental of the iniquity of the system that must rear such whited sepulchres to conceal its crimes.

I do not oppose the insane asylum—but I abhor and condemn the cut-throat system that robs man of his reason, drives him to insanity and makes the lunatic asylum an indispensable adjunct to every civilized community.

With the ten thousand "charities" that are proposed to poultice the sores and bruises of society, I have little patience.

Worst of all is the charity ball. Chicago indulges in these festering festivals on a grand scale.

Think of cavorting around in a dress suit because some poor wretch is hungry; and of indulging in a royal carousal to comfort some despairing woman on the brink of suicide; and finally, that in "fashionable society" the definition of this mixture of inanity and moral perversion is "charity."

Fleece your fellows! That is "business," and you are a captain of industry. Having "relieved" your victims of their pelts, dance and make merry to "relieve" their agony. This is "charity" and you are a philanthropist.

In summing up the moral assets of a great (?) city, the churches should not be overlooked. Chicago is a city of fine churches. All the denominations are copiously represented, and sermons in all languages and of all varieties are turned out in job lots and at retail to suit the market.

The churches are always numerous where vice is rampant. They seem to spring from the same soil and thrive in the same climate.

And yet the churches are supposed to wage relentless warfare upon evil. To just what extent they have checked its spread in the "Windy City" may be inferred from the probing of the press into the body social to ascertain "What is the Matter with Chicago."

The preachers are not wholly to blame, after all, for their moral and spiritual impotency. They are wage-workers, the same as coal miners, and are just as dependent upon the capitalist class. How can they be expected to antagonize the interests of their employers and hold their jobs? The unskilled preachers, the common laborers in the arid spots of the vineyard, are often wretchedly paid, and yet they remain unorganized and have never struck for better wages.

"What's the matter with Chicago"? Capitalism!

What's the cure? Socialism!

Regeneration will only come with depopulation—when Socialism has relieved the congestion and released the people and they spread out over the country and live close to the grass.

The *Record-Herald* has furnished the people of Chicago and Illinois with a campaign issue.

If you want to know more about "What is the matter with Chicago," read the Socialist papers and magazines; read the platform of the Socialist party; and if you do, you will cut loose from the Republican-Democratic party, the double-headed political monstrosity of the capitalist class, and you will cast your vote for the Socialist party and your lot with the International Socialist Movement, whose mission it is to uproot and overthrow the whole system of capitalist exploitation, and put an end to the poverty and misery it entails—and that's "What's the matter with Chicago."

SPEECHES

Liberty

Speech at Battery D, Chicago, on his release from Woodstock Jail, November 22, 1895.

Manifestly the spirit of '76 still survives. The fires of liberty and noble aspirations are not yet extinguished. I greet you tonight as lovers of liberty and as despisers of despotism. I comprehend the significance of this demonstration and appreciate the honor that makes it possible for me to be your guest on such an occasion. The vindication and glorification of American principles of government, as proclaimed to the world in the Declaration of Independence, is the high purpose of this convocation.

Speaking for myself personally, I am not certain whether this is an occasion for rejoicing or lamentation. I confess to a serious doubt as to whether this day marks my deliverance from bondage to freedom or my doom from freedom to bondage. Certain it is, in the light of recent judicial proceedings, that I stand in your presence stripped of my constitutional rights as a freeman and shorn of the most sacred prerogatives of American citizenship, and what is true of myself is true of every other citizen who has the temerity to protest against corporation rule or question the absolute sway of the money power. It is not law nor the administration of law of which I complain. It is the flagrant violation of the constitution, the total abrogation of law and the usurpation of judicial and despotic power, by virtue of which my colleagues and myself were committed to jail, against which I enter my solemn protest; and any honest analysis of the proceedings must sustain the haggard truth of the indictment.

In a letter recently written by the venerable Judge Trumbull that eminent jurist says: "The doctrine announced by the supreme court in the Debs case, carried to its logical conclusion, places every citizen at the mercy of any prejudiced or malicious federal judge who may think proper to imprison him." This is the deliberate conclusion of one of the purest, ablest and most distinguished judges the Republic has produced. The authority of Judge Trumbull upon this question will not be impeached by anyone whose opinions are not deformed or debauched.

At this juncture I deem it proper to voice my demands for a trial by a jury of my peers. At the instigation of the railroad corporations centering here in Chicago I was indicted for conspiracy and I insist upon being tried as to my innocence or guilt. It will be remembered that the trial last winter terminated very abruptly on account of a sick juror. It was currently reported at the time that this was merely a pretext to abandon the trial and thus defeat the vindication of a favorable verdict, which seemed inevitable, and which would have been in painfully embarrassing contrast with the sentence previously pronounced by Judge Woods in substantially the same case. Whether this be true or not, I do not know. I do know, however, that I have been denied a trial, and here and now I demand a hearing of my case. I am charged with conspiracy to commit a crime, and if guilty I should go to the penitentiary. All I ask is a fair trial and no favor. If the counsel for the government, alias the railroads, have been correctly quoted in the press, the case against me is "not to be pressed," as they "do not wish to appear in the light of persecuting the defendants." I repel with scorn their professed mercy. Simple justice is the demand. I am not disposed to shrink from the fullest responsibility for my acts. I have had time for meditation and reflection and I have no hesitancy in declaring that under the same circumstances I would pursue precisely the same policy. So far as my acts are concerned, I have neither apology nor regrets.

Dismissing this branch of the subject, permit me to assure you that I am not here to bemoan my lot. In my vocabulary there are no wails of despondency or despair. However gloomy the future may appear to others, I have an abiding faith in the ultimate triumph of the right. My heart responds to the sentiments of the poet who says:

> "Swing back today, O prison gate,
>   O winds, stream out the stripes and stars,
>   O men, once more in high debate
>   Denounce injunction rule and czars.
> By Freedom's travail pangs we swear
> That slavery's chains we will not wear.
>
> "Ring joyously, O prison bell,
>   O iron tongue, the truth proclaim;
>   O winds and lightnings, speed to tell
>   That ours is not a czar's domain.
> By all the oracles divine
> We pledge defense of Freedom's shrine.
>
> "O freemen true! O sons of sires!
>   O sons of men who dared to die!
>   O fan to life old Freedom's fires
>   And light with glory Freedom's sky.
> Then swear by God's eternal throne,
> America shall be Freedom's home.
>
> "O workingmen! O Labor's hosts!
>   O men of courage, heart and will;
>   O far and wide send Labor's toasts
>   Till every heart feels Freedom's thrill,
> And freemen's shouts like billows roar
> O'er all the land from shore to shore."

Liberty is not a word of modern coinage. Liberty and slavery are primal words, like good and evil, right and wrong; they are opposites and coexistent.

There has been no liberty in the world since the gift, like sunshine and rain, came down from heaven, for the maintenance of which man has not been required to fight, and man's complete degradation is secured only when subjugation and slavery have sapped him of the last spark of the noble attributes of his nature and reduced him to the unresisting inertness of a clod.

The theme tonight is personal liberty; or giving it its full height, depth and breadth, American liberty, something that Americans have been accustomed to eulogize since the foundation of the Republic, and multiplied thousands of them continue in the habit to this day because they do not recognize the truth that in the imprisonment of one man in defiance of all constitutional guarantees, the liberties of all are invaded and placed in peril. In saying this, I conjecture I have struck the keynote of alarm that has convoked this vast audience.

For the first time in the records of all the ages, the inalienable rights of man, "life, liberty and the pursuit of happiness," were proclaimed July 4, 1776.

It was then that crowns, sceptres, thrones and the divine right of kings to rule sunk together and man expanded to glorious liberty and sovereignty. It was then that the genius of Liberty, speaking to all men in the commanding voice of Eternal Truth, bade them assert their heaven-decreed prerogatives and emancipate themselves from bondage. It was a proclamation countersigned by the Infinite—and man stood forth the coronated sovereign of the world, free as the tides that flow, free as the winds that blow, and on that primal morning when creation was complete, the morning stars and the sons of God, in anthem chorus, sang the song of Liberty.

It may be a fancy, but within the limitless boundaries of the imagination I can conceive of no other theme more appropriate to weave into the harmonies of Freedom. The Creator had surveyed his work and pronounced it good, but nothing can be called good in human affairs with liberty eliminated. As well talk of air without nitrogen, or water without oxygen, as of goodness without liberty.

It does not matter that the Creator has sown with stars the fields of ether and decked the earth with countless beauties for man's enjoyment. It does not matter that air and ocean teem with the wonders of innumerable forms of life to challenge man's admiration and investigation. It does not matter that nature spreads forth all her scenes of beauty and gladness and pours forth the melodies of her myriad-tongued voices for man's delectation. If liberty is ostracised and exiled, man is a slave, and the world rolls in space and whirls around the sun a gilded prison, a doomed dungeon, and though painted in all the enchanting hues that infinite art could command, it must still stand forth a blotch amidst the shining spheres of the sidereal heavens, and those who cull from the vocabularies of nations, living or dead, their flashing phrases with which to apostrophize Liberty, are engaged in perpetuating the most stupendous delusion the ages have known. Strike down liberty, no matter by what subtle and infernal art the deed is done, the spinal cord of humanity is sundered and the world is paralyzed by the indescribable crime.

Strike the fetters from the slave, give him liberty and he becomes an inhabitant of a new world. He looks abroad and beholds life and joy in all things around him. His soul expands beyond all boundaries. Emancipated by the genius of Liberty, he aspires to communion with all that is noble and beautiful, feels himself allied to all the higher order of intelligences, and walks abroad, redeemed from animalism, ignorance and superstition, a new being throbbing with glorious life.

What pen or tongue from primeval man to the loftiest intellect of the present generation has been able to fittingly anathematize the more than satanic crime of stealing the jewel of liberty from the crown of manhood and reducing the victim of the burglary to slavery or to prison, to gratify those monsters of iniquity who for some inscrutable reason are given breath to contaminate the atmosphere and poison every fountain and stream designed to bless the world!

It may be questioned if such interrogatories are worth the time required to state them, and I turn from their consideration to the actualities of my theme. As Americans, we have boasted of our liberties and continue to boast of them. They were once the nation's glory, and, if some have vanished, it may be well to remember that a remnant still remains. Out of prison, beyond the limits of Russian injunctions, out of reach of a deputy marshal's club, above the throttling clutch of corporations and the enslaving power of plutocracy, out of range of the government's machine guns and knowing the location of judicial traps and deadfalls, Americans may still indulge in the exaltation of liberty, though pursued through every lane and avenue of life by the baying hounds of usurped and unconstitutional power, glad if when night lets down her sable curtains, they are out of prison, though still the wage-slaves of a plutocracy which, were it in the celestial city, would wreck every avenue leading up to the throne of the Infinite by stealing the gold with which they are paved, and debauch Heaven's supreme court to obtain a decision that the command "thou shalt not steal" is unconstitutional.

Liberty, be it known, is for those only who dare strike the blow to secure and retain the priceless boon. It has been written that the "love of liberty with life is given" and that life itself is an inferior gift; that with liberty exiled life is a continuous curse and that "an hour of liberty is worth an eternity of bondage." It would be an easy task to link together gilded periods extolling liberty until the mind, weary with delight, becomes oblivious of the fact that while dreaming of security, the blessings we magnified had, one by one, and little by little, disappeared, emphasizing the truth of the maxim that "eternal vigilance is the price of liberty."

Is it worth while to iterate that all men are created free and that slavery and bondage are in controvention of the Creator's decree and have their origin in man's depravity?

If liberty is a birthright which has been wrested from the weak by the strong, or has been placed in peril by those who were commissioned to guard it as Gheber priests watch the sacred fires they worship, what is to be done? Leaving all other nations, kindred and tongues out of the question, what is the duty of Americans? Above all, what is the duty of American workingmen whose liberties have been placed in peril? They are not hereditary bondsmen. Their fathers were free born—their sovereignty none denied and their children yet have the ballot. It has been called "a weapon that executes a free man's will as lighting does the will of God." It is a metaphor pregnant with life and truth. There is nothing in our government it can not remove or amend. It can make and unmake presidents and congresses and courts. It can abolish unjust laws and consign to eternal odium and oblivion unjust judges, strip from them their robes and gowns and send them forth unclean as lepers to bear the burden of merited obloquy as Cain with the mark of a murderer. It can sweep away trusts, syndicates, corporations, monopolies, and every other abnormal development of the money power designed to abridge the liberties of workingmen and enslave them by the degradation incident to poverty and enforced idleness, as cyclones scatter the leaves of the forest. The ballot can do all this and more. It can give our civilization its crowning glory—the co-operative commonwealth.

To the unified hosts of American workingmen fate has committed the charge of rescuing American liberties from the grasp of the vandal horde that have placed them in peril, by seizing the ballot and wielding it to regain the priceless heritage and to preserve and transmit it without scar or blemish to the generations yet to come.

> "Snatch from the ashes of their sires
> The embers of their former fires,
> And he who in the strife expires
> Will add to theirs a name of fear
> That Tyranny shall quake to hear."

Standing before you tonight re-clothed in theory at least with the prerogatives of a free man, in the midst of free men, what more natural, what more in consonance with the proprieties of the occasion, than to refer to the incarceration of myself and associate officials of the American Railway Union in the county jail at Woodstock?

I have no ambition to avail myself of this occasion to be sensational, or to thrust my fellow prisoners and myself into prominence. My theme expands to proportions which obscure the victims of judicial tyranny, and yet, regardless of reluctance, it so happens by the decree of circumstances, that personal references are unavoidable. To wish it otherwise would be to deplore the organization of the American Railway Union and every effort that great organization has made to extend a helping hand to oppressed, robbed, suffering and starving men, women and children, the victims of corporate greed and rapacity. It would be to bewail every lofty attribute of human nature, lament the existence of the golden rule and wish the world were a jungle, inhabited by beasts of prey, that the seas were peopled with sharks and devil-fish and that between the earth and the stars only vultures held winged sway.

The American Railway Union was born with a sympathetic

soul. Its ears were attuned to the melodies of mercy, to catch the whispered wailings of the oppressed. It had eyes to scan the fields of labor, a tongue to denounce the wrong, hands to grasp the oppressed and a will to lift them out of the sloughs of despondency to highlands of security and prosperity.

Here and now I challenge the records, and if in all the land the American Railway Union has an enemy, one or a

WOODSTOCK JAIL, IN WHICH DEBS WAS CONFINED

million, I challenge them all to stand up before the labor world and give a reason why they have maligned and persecuted the order. I am not here to assert the infallibility of the organization or its officials, or to claim exemption from error. But I am here to declare to every friend of American toilers, regardless of banner, name or craft, that if the American Railway Union has erred, it has been on the side of sympathy, mercy and humanity—zeal in a great cause, devotion to the spirit of brotherhood which knows no artificial boundaries, whose zones are mapped by lines of truth as vivid as lightning, and whose horizon is measured only by the eye of faith in man's redemption from slavery.

I hold it to have been inconceivable that an organization of workingmen, animated by such inspirations and aspirations, should have become the target for the shafts of judicial and governmental malice.

But the fact that such was the case brings into haggard prominence a condition of affairs that appeals to all thoughtful men in the ranks of organized labor and all patriotic citizens, regardless of vocation, who note the subtle invasions of the liberties of the American people by the courts, sustained by an administration that is equally dead to the guarantees of the constitution.

It is in no spirit of laudation that I aver here tonight that it has fallen to the lot of the American Railway Union to arouse workingmen to a sense of the perils that environ their liberties.

In the great Pullman strike the American Railway Union challenged the power of corporations in a way that had not previously been done, and the analyzation of this fact serves to expand it to proportions that the most conservative men of the nation regard with alarm.

It must be borne in mind that the American Railway Union did not challenge the government. It threw down no gauntlet to courts or armies—it simply resisted the invasion of the rights of workingmen by corporations. It challenged and defied the power of corporations. Thrice armed with a just cause, the organization believed that justice would win for labor a notable victory, and the records proclaim that its confidence was not misplaced.

The corporations, left to their own resources of money, mendacity and malice, of thugs and ex-convicts, leeches and lawyers, would have been overwhelmed with defeat and the banners of organized labor would have floated triumphant in the breeze.

This the corporations saw and believed—hence the crowning act of infamy in which the federal courts and the federal armies participated, and which culminated in the defeat of labor.

Had this been all, the simple defeat of a labor organization, however disrupted and despoiled, this grand convocation of the lovers of liberty would never have been heard of. The robbed, idle and blacklisted victims of defeat would have suffered in silence in their darkened homes amidst the sobbings and wailings of wives and children. It would have been the oft repeated old, old story, heard along the track of progress and poverty for three-quarters of a century in the United States, where brave men, loyal to law and duty, have struck to better their condition or to resist degradation, and have gone down in defeat. But the defeat of the American Railway Union involved questions of law, constitution and government which, all things considered, are without a parallel in court and governmental proceedings under the constitution of the Republic. And it is this judicial and administrative usurpation of power to override the rights of states and strike down the liberties of the people that has conferred upon the incidents connected with the Pullman strike such commanding importance as to attract the attention of men of the highest attainments in constitutional law and of statesmen who, like Jefferson, view with alarm the processes by which the Republic is being wrecked and a despotism reared upon its ruins.

I have said that in the great battle of labor fought in 1894 between the American Railway Union and the Corporations banded together under the name of the "General Managers' Association," victory would have perched upon the standards of labor if the battle had been left to these contending forces—and this statement, which has been verified and established beyond truthful contradiction, suggests the inquiry, what other resources had the corporations aside from their money and the strength which their federation conferred?

In replying to the question, I am far within the limits of accepted facts when I say the country stood amazed as the corporations put forth their latent powers to debauch such departments of the government as were required to defeat labor in the greatest struggle for the right that was ever chronicled in the United States.

Defeated at every point, their plans all frustrated, outgeneraled in tactics and strategy, while the hopes of labor were brightening and victory was in sight, the corporations, goaded to desperation, played their last card in the game of oppression by an appeal to the federal judiciary and to the federal administration. To this appeal the response came quick as lightning from a storm cloud. It was an exhibition of the debauching power of money which the country had never before beheld.

The people had long been familiar with such expressions as "money talks," "money rules," and they had seen the effects of its power in legislatures and in congress. They were conversant with Jay Gould's methods of gaining his legal victories by "buying a judge" in critical cases. They had tracked this money power, this behemoth beast of prey, into every corporate enterprise evolved by our modern civilization, as hunters track tigers in India jungles, but never before in the history of the country had they seen it grasp with paws and jaws the government of the United States and bend it to its will and make it a mere travesty of its pristine grandeur.

The people had seen this money power enter the church, touch the robed priest at the altar, blotch his soul, freeze his heart and make him a traitor to his consecrated vows and send him forth a Judas with a bag containing the price of his treason; or, if true to his conviction, ideas and ideals, to suffer the penalty of ostracism, to be blacklisted and to seek in vain for a sanctuary in which to expound Christ's doctrine of the brotherhood of man.

The people had seen this money power enter a university and grasp a professor and hurl him headlong into the street because every faculty of mind, redeemed by education and consecrated to truth, pointed out and illumined new pathways to the goal of human happiness and national glory.

The people had seen this money power practicing every art of duplicity, growing more arrogant and despotic as it robbed one and crushed another, building its fortifications of the bones of its victims, and its palaces out of the profits of its piracies, until purple and fine linen on the one side and rags upon the other side, defined conditions as mountain ranges and rivers define the boundaries of nations—palaces on the hills, with music and dancing and the luxuries of all climes, earth, air and sea-huts in the valley, dark and dismal, where the music is the dolorous "song of the shirt" and the luxuries rags and crusts.

These things had been seen by the people, but it was reserved for them in the progress of the Pullman strike to see this money power, by the fiat of corporations, grasp one by one the departments of the government and compel them to do its bidding as in old plantation days the master commanded the obedience of his chattel slaves.

The corporations first attacked the judicial department of the government, a department which, according to Thomas Jefferson, has menaced the integrity of the Republic from the beginning.

They did not attack the supreme bench. A chain is no stronger than its weakest link, and the corporations knew where that was and the amount of strain it would bear. How did they attack this weakling in the judicial chain?

I am aware that innuendoes, dark intimations of venality are not regarded as courageous forms of arraignment, and yet the judicial despotism which marked every step of the proceedings by which my official associates and myself were doomed to imprisonment, was marked by infamies, supported by falsehoods and perjuries as destitute of truth as are the Arctic regions of orange blossoms.

Two men quarrelled because one had killed the other's dog with an ax. The owner of the dog inquired, "when my dog attacked you, why did you not use some less deadly weapon?" The other replied, "why did not your dog come at me with the end that had no teeth in it?"

There is an adage which says, "fight the devil with fire." In this connection why may it not be intimated that a judge who pollutes his high office at the behest of the money power has the hinges of his knees lubricated with oil from the tank of the corporation that thrift may follow humiliating obedience to its commands?

If not this, I challenge the world to assign a reason why a judge, under the solemn obligation of an oath to obey the constitution, should in a temple dedicated to justice, stab the

Magna Charta of American liberty to death in the interest of corporations, that labor might be disrobed of its inalienable rights and those who advocated its claim to justice imprisoned as if they were felons?

You may subject such acts of despotism to the severest analysis, you may probe for the motive, you may dissect the brain and lay bare the quivering heart, and, when you have completed the task, you will find a tongue in every gash of your dissecting knife uttering the one word "pelf."

Once upon a time a corporation dog of good reputation was charged with killing sheep, though he had never been caught in the act. The corporation had always found him to be an obedient dog, willing to lick the hand of his master, and declared that he was a peaceable and law-abiding dog; but one day upon investigation the dog was found to have wool in his teeth and thenceforward, though the corporation stood manfully by him, he was believed to be a sheep-killing dog. The world has no means of knowing what methods corporations employ to obtain despotic decrees in their interest, but it is generally believed that if an examination could be made, there would be found wool in the teeth of the judge.

I do not profess to be a student of heredity, and yet I am persuaded that men inherit the peculiarities of the primal molecules from which they have been evolved. If the modern man, in spite of our civilizing influences, books, stage and rostrum, has more devil than divinity in his nature, where rests the blame?

Leaving the interrogatory unanswered, as it has been in all the past, it is only required to say that men with the ballot make a fatal mistake when they select mental and moral deformities and clothe them with despotic power. When such creatures are arrayed in the insignia of authority, right, justice and liberty are forever in peril.

What reasons exist today for rhetorical apostrophes to the constitution of the Republic? Those who are familiar by experience, or by reading, with the pathways of the storms on the ocean will recall recollections of ships with their sails rent and torn by the fury of the winds, rolling upon the yeasty billows and flying signals of distress. Clouds had for days obscured sun and stars and only the eye of omnipotence could tell whither the hulk was drifting—and today the constitution of our ship of state, the chart by which she had been steered for a century, has encountered a judicial tornado and only the gods of our fathers can tell whither she is drifting. True, Longfellow, inspired by the genius of hope, sang of the good old ship:

> "We know what master laid thy keel,
> What workmen wrought thy ribs of steel,
> Who made each mast and sail and rope,
> What anvils rang, what hammers beat,
> In what a forge and what a heat
> Were shaped the anchors of thy hope."

But the poet wrote before the chart by which the good old ship sailed had been mutilated and torn and flung aside as a thing of contempt; before Shiras "flopped" and before corporations knew the price of judges, legislators and public officials as certainly as Armour knows the price of pork and mutton.

Longfellow wrote before men with heads as small as chipmunks and pockets as big as balloons were elevated to public office, and before the corporation ruled in courts and legislative halls as the fabled bull ruled in a china shop.

No afflatus, however divine, no genius, though saturated with the inspiring waters of Hippocrene, could now write in a spirit of patriotic fire of the old constitution, nor ever again until the people by the all pervading power of the ballot have repaired the old chart, closed the rents and obscured the judicial dagger holes made for the accommodation of millionaires and corporations, through which they drive their four-in-hands as if they were Cumberland gaps.

Here, this evening, I am inclined to indulge in eulogistic phrase of Liberty because once more I am permitted to mingle with my fellow-citizens outside of prison locks and bars.

Shakespeare said:

> "Sweet are the uses of adversity,
> Which, like the toad, ugly and venomous,
> Wears yet a precious jewel in his head."

I know something of adversity, and with such philosophy as I could summon have extracted what little sweetness it contained. I know little of toads, except that of the genus judicial, and if they have a precious jewel in their heads or hearts it has not fallen to my lot to find it, though the corporations seem to have been more successful.

The immortal bard also wrote that

> "This our life, exempt from public haunt,
> Finds tongues in trees, books in running brooks,
> Sermons in stones, and good in everything."

If to be behind prison bars is to be "exempt from public haunt," then for the past six months I may claim such exemption, with all the rapture to be found in listening to the tongues of trees, to the charming lessons taught by the books of the running brooks and to the profound sermons of the stones. There is not a tree on the Woodstock prison campus, or near by, to whose tongued melodies or maledictions I have not in fancy listened when liberty, despotism or justice was the theme.

The bard of Avon, the one Shakespeare of all the ages, was up to high-water mark of divine inspiration when he said there were those who could find tongues in trees, and never since trees were planted in the garden of Eden has the tongue of a tree voiced a sentiment hostile to liberty.

Thus, when in prison and exempt from judicial persecution, the tongues of trees as well as the tongues of friends taught me that sweets could be extracted from adversity.

Nor was I less fortunate when I permitted my fancy to see a book in a running brook as it laughed and sang and danced its way to the sea, and find that on every page was written a diviner song to liberty and love and sympathy than was ever sung by human voice.

And as for the stones in Woodstock prison, they were forever preaching sermons and their themes were all things good and evil among men.

In prison my life was a busy one, and the time for meditation and to give the imagination free rein was when the daily task was over and night's sable curtains enveloped the world in darkness, relieved only by the sentinel stars and the earth's silver satellite "walking in lovely beauty to her midnight throne."

It was at such times that the "Reverend Stones" preached their sermons, sometimes rising in grandeur to the Sermon on the Mount.

It might be a question in the minds of some if this occasion warrants the indulgence of the fancy. It will be remembered that Aesop taught the world by fables and Christ by parables, but my recollection is that the old "stone preachers" were as epigrammatic as an unabridged dictionary.

I remember one old divine who, one night, selected for his text George M. Pullman, and said: "George is a bad egg—handle him with care. Should you crack his shell the odor would depopulate Chicago in an hour." All said "Amen" and the services closed. Another old sermonizer who said he had been preaching since man was a molecule, declared he had of late years studied corporations, and that they were warts on the nose of our national industries,—that they were vultures whose beaks and claws were tearing and mangling the vitals of labor and transforming workingmen's homes into caves. Another old stone said he knew more about strikes than Carroll D. Wright, and that he was present when the slaves built the pyramids; that God Himself had taught His lightning, thunderbolts, winds, waves and earthquakes to strike, and that strikes would proceed, with bullets or ballots, until workingmen, no longer deceived and cajoled by their enemies, would unify, proclaims their sovereignty and walk the earth free men.

O, yes, Shakespeare was right when he said there were sermons in stones. I recall one rugged-visaged old stone preacher who claimed to have been a pavement bowlder in a street of heaven before the gold standard was adopted, and who discussed courts. He said they had been antagonizing the decrees of heaven since the day when Lucifer was cast into the bottomless pit. Referring to our Supreme Court he said it was a nest of rodents forever gnawing at the stately pillars supporting the temple of our liberties. I recall how his eyes, as he lifted their stony lids, flashed indignation like orbs of fire, and how his stony lips quivered as he uttered his maledictions of judicial treason to constitutional liberty.

But occasionally some old bald-headed ashler, with a heart beating responsive to every human joy or sorrow, would preach a sermon on love or sympathy or some other noble trait that in spite of heredity still lived even in the heart of stones. One old divine, having read some of the plutocratic papers on the Pullman strike and their anathemas of sympathy, when one workingman's heart, throbbing responsive to the divine law of love, prompted him to aid his brother in distress, discussed sympathy. He said sympathy was one of the perennial flowers of the Celestial City, and that angels had transplanted it in Eden for the happiness of Adam and Eve, and that the winds had scattered the seed throughout the earth. He said there was no humanity, no elevating, refining, ennobling influences in operation where there was no sympathy. Sympathy, he said, warmed in every ray of the sun, freshened in every breeze that scattered over the earth the perfume of flowers and glowed with the divine scintillation of the stars in all the expanse of the heavens.

Referring to the men and women of other labor organizations who had sympathized with the American Railway Union in its efforts to rescue Pullman's slaves from death by starvation, the old preacher placed a crown of jeweled eulogies upon their heads and said that in all the mutations of life, in adversity or prosperity, in the vigor of youth or the infirmities of age, there would never come a time to them when like the Peri grasping a penitent's tear as a passport to heaven, they would not cherish as a valued souvenir of all their weary years that one act of sympathy of the victims of the Pullman piracy, and that when presented at the pearly gate of paradise, it would swing wide open and let them in amidst the joyous acclaims of angels.

From such reflections I turn to the practical lessons taught by this "Liberation Day" demonstration. It means that American lovers of liberty are setting in operation forces to rescue their constitutional liberties from the grasp of monopoly and its mercenary hirelings. It means that the people are aroused in view of impending perils and that agitation, organization, and unification are to be the future battle cries of men who will not part with their birthrights and, like Patrick

Henry, will have the courage to exclaim: "Give me liberty or give me death!"

I have borne with such composure as I could command the imprisonment which deprived me of my liberty. Were I a criminal; were I guilty of crimes meriting a prison cell; had I ever lifted my hand against the life or the liberty of my fellowmen; had I ever sought to filch their good name, I would not be here. I would have fled from the haunts of civilization and taken up my residence in some cave where the voice of my kindred is never heard. But I am standing here without a self-accusation of crime or criminal intent festering in my conscience, in the sunlight once more, among my fellowmen, contributing as best I can to make this "Liberation Day" from Woodstock prison a memorial day, realizing that, as Lowell sang:

"He's true to God who's true to man; wherever wrong is done,
To the humblest and the weakest, 'neath the all-beholding sun.
That wrong is also done to us, and they are slaves most base,
Whose love of right is for themselves and not for all their race."

Prison Labor

Its Effect on Industry and Trade

Address before Nineteenth Century Club at Delmonico's, New York City, March 21st, 1899.

In my early years I stood before the open door of a blazing furnace and piled in the fuel to create steam to speed a locomotive along the iron track of progress and civilization. In the costume of the craft, through the grime of mingled sweat and smoke and dust I was initiated into the great brotherhood of labor. The locomotive was my alma mater. I mastered the curriculum and graduated with the degree of D. D., not, as the lexicons interpret the letters, "Doctor of Divinity," but that better signification, "Do and Dare"—a higher degree than Aristotle conferred in his Lyceum or Plato thundered from his academy.

I am not in the habit of telling how little I know about Latin to those who have slaked their thirst for learning at the Pierian springs, but there is a proverb that has come down to us from the dim past which reads "Omnia vincit labor" and which has been adopted as the shibboleth of the American labor movement because, when reduced to English, it reads "Labor overcomes all things." In a certain sense this is true. Labor has built this great metropolis of the new world, built it as coral insects build the foundations of islands—build and die; build from the fathomless depth of the ocean until the mountain billows are dashed into spray as they beat against the fortifications beneath which the builders are forever entombed and forgotten.

Here in this proud city where wealth has built its monuments grander and more imposing than any of the seven wonders of the world named in classic lore, if you will excavate for facts you will find the remains, the bones of the toilers, buried and imbedded in their foundations. They lived, they wrought, they died. In their time they may have laughed and sung and danced to the music of their clanking chains. They married, propagated their species, and perpetuated conditions which, growing steadily worse, are today the foulest blots the imagination can conceive upon our much vaunted civilization.

And from these conditions there flow a thousand streams of vice and crime which have broadened and deepened until they constitute a perpetual menace to the peace and security of society. Jails, workhouses, reformatories and penitentiaries have been crowded with victims, and the question how to control these institutions and their unfortunate inmates is challenging the most serious thought of the most advanced nations on the globe.

The particular phase of this grave and melancholy question which we are to consider this evening is embodied in the subject assigned the speakers: "Prison Labor, Its Effects on Industry and Trade."

I must confess that it would have suited my purpose better had the subject been transposed so as to read: "Industry and Trade, Their Effect on Labor," for, as a Socialist, I am convinced that the prison problem is rooted in the present system of industry and trade, carried forward, as it is, purely for private profit without the slightest regard to the effect upon those engaged in it, especially the men, women and children who perform the useful, productive labor which has created all wealth and all civilization.

Serious as is the problem presented in the subject of our discussion, it is yet insignificant when compared with the vastly greater question of the effect of our social and economic system upon industry and trade.

The pernicious effect of prison contract labor upon "free labor," so called, when brought into competition with it in the open market, is universally conceded, but it should not be overlooked that prison labor is itself an effect and not a cause, and that convict labor is recruited almost wholly from the propertyless, wage-working class and that the inhuman system which has reduced a comparative few from enforced idleness to crime, has sunk the whole mass of labor to the dead level of industrial servitude.

It is therefore with the economic system, which is responsible for, not only prison labor, but for the gradual enslavement and degradation of all labor, that we must deal before there can be any solution of the prison labor problem or any permanent relief from its demoralizing influences.

But we will briefly consider the effect of prison labor upon industry and then pass to the larger question of the cause of prison labor and its appalling increase, to which the discussion logically leads.

From the earliest ages there has been a prison problem. The ancients had their bastiles and their dungeons. Most of the pioneers of progress, the haters of oppression, the lovers of liberty, whose names now glorify the pantheon of the world, made such institutions a necessity in their day. But civilization advances, however slowly, and there has been some progress. It required five hundred years to travel from the inquisition to the injunction.

In the earlier days punishment was the sole purpose of imprisonment. Offenders against the ruling class must pay the penalty in prison cell, which, not infrequently, was equipped with instruments of torture. With the civilizing process came the idea of the reformation of the culprit, and this idea prompts every investigation made of the latter-day problem. The inmates must be set to work for their own good, no less than for the good of the state.

It was at this point that the convict labor problem began and it has steadily expanded from that time to this and while there have been some temporary modifications of the evil, it is still an unmitigated curse from which there can be no escape while an economic system endures in which labor, that is to say the laborer, man, woman and child, is sold to the lowest bidder in the markets of the world.

More than thirty years ago Prof. E. C. Wines and Prof. Theodore W. Dwight, then commissioners of the Prison Association of New York, made a report to the legislature of the state on prison industry in which they said:

"Upon the whole it is our settled conviction that the contract system of convict labor, added to the system of political appointments, which necessarily involves a low grade of official qualification and constant changes in the prison staff, renders nugatory, to a great extent, the whole theory of our penitentiary system. Inspection may correct isolated abuses; philanthropy may relieve isolated cases of distress; and religion may effect isolated moral cures; but genuine, radical, comprehensive, systematic improvement is impossible.''

The lapse of thirty years has not affected the wisdom or logic of the conclusion. It is as true now as it was then. Considered in his most favorable light, the convict is a scourge to himself, a menace to society and a burden to industry, and whatever system of convict labor may be tried, it will ultimately fail of its purpose at reformation of the criminal or the relief of industry as long as thousands of "free laborers," who have committed no crime, are unable to get work and make an honest living. Not long ago I visited a penitentiary in which a convict expressed regret that his sentence was soon to expire. Where was he to go, and what was he to do? And how long before he would be sentenced to a longer term for a greater crime?

The commission which investigated the matter in Ohio in 1877 reported to the legislature as follows:

"The contract system interferes in an undue manner with the honest industry of the state. It has been the cause of crippling the business of many of our manufacturers; it has been the cause of driving many of them out of business; it has been the cause of a large percentage of reductions which have taken place in the wages of our mechanics; it has been the cause of pauperizing a large portion of our laborers and increasing crime in a corresponding degree; it has been no benefit to the state; as a reformatory measure it has been a complete, total and miserable failure; it has hardened more criminals than any other cause; it has made total wrecks morally of thousands and thousands who would have been reclaimed from the paths of vice and crime under a proper system of prison management, but who have resigned their fate to a life of hopeless degradation; it has not a single commendable feature. Its tendency is pernicious in the extreme. In short, it is an insurmountable barrier in the way of the reformation of the unfortunates who are compelled to live and labor under its evil influences; it enables a class of men to get rich out of the crimes committed by others; it leaves upon the fair escutcheon of the state a relic of the very worst form of human slavery; it is a bone of ceaseless contention between the state and its mechanical and industrial interests; it is abhorred by all and respected by none except those, perhaps, who make profit and gain out of it. It should be tolerated no longer but abolished at once.''

And yet this same system is still in effect in many of the states of the Union. The most revolting outrages have been perpetrated upon prison laborers under this diabolical system. Read the official reports and stand aghast at the atrocities committed against these morally deformed and perverted human creatures, your brothers and my brothers, for the private profit of capitalistic exploiters and the advancement of Christian civilization.

What a commentary on the capitalist competitive system! First, men are forced into idleness. Gradually they are driven to the extremity of begging or stealing. Having still a spark of pride and self-respect they steal and are sent to jail. The first sentence seals their doom. The brand of Cain is upon them. They are identified with the criminal class. Society, whose victims they are, has exiled them forever, and with this curse ringing in their ears they proceed on their downward career, sounding every note in the scale of depravity until at last, having graduated in crime all the way from petit larceny to homicide, their last despairing sigh is wrung from them by the hangman's halter. From first to last these unfortunates, the victims of social malformation, are made the subjects of speculation and traffic. The barbed iron of the prison contractor is plunged into their quivering hearts that their torture may be coined into private profit for their exploiters.

In the investigation in South Carolina, where the convicts had been leased to railroad companies, the most shocking disclosures were made. Out of 285 prisoners employed by one company, 128, or more than 40 per cent, died as the result, largely, of brutal treatment.

It is popular to say that society must be protected against its criminals. I prefer to believe that criminals should be protected against society, at least while we live under a system that makes the commission of crime necessary to secure employment.

The Tennessee tragedy is still fresh in the public memory. Here, as elsewhere, the convicts, themselves brutally treated, were used as a means of dragging the whole mine-working class down to their crime-cursed condition. The Tennessee Coal and Iron Company leased the convicts for the express purpose of forcing the wages of miners down to the point of subsistence. Says the official report: "The miners were compelled to work in competition with low-priced convict labor, the presence of which was used by the company as a scourge to force free laborers to its terms." Then the miners, locked out, their families suffering, driven to desperation, appealed to force and in a twinkling the laws of the state were trampled down, the authorities overpowered and defied, and almost five hundred convicts set at liberty.

Fortunately the system of leasing and contracting prison labor for private exploitation is being exposed and its frightful iniquities laid bare. Thanks to organized labor and to the spirit of prison reform, this horrifying phase of the evil is doomed to disappear before an enlightened public sentiment.

The public account system, though subject to serious criticism, is far less objectionable than either the lease, the contract or the piece-price system. At least the prisoner's infirmities cease to be the prey of speculative greed and conscienceless rapacity.

The system of manufacturing for the use of state, county and municipal institutions, adopted by the state of New York, is an improvement upon those hitherto in effect, but it is certain to develop serious objections in course of time. With the use of modern machinery the limited demand will soon be supplied and then what? It may be in order to suggest that the prisoners could be employed in making shoes and clothes for the destitute poor and school books for their children and many other articles which the poor sorely need but are unable to buy.

Developing along this line it would be only a question of time until the state would be manufacturing all things for the use of the people, and then perhaps the inquiry would be pertinent: If the state can give men steady employment after they commit crime, and manufacturing can be carried forward successfully by their labor, why can it not give them employment before they are driven to that extremity, thereby preventing them from becoming criminals?

All useful labor is honest labor, even if performed in a prison. Only the labor of exploiters, such as speculators, stock gamblers, beef-embalmers and their mercenary politicians, lawyers and other parasites—only such is dishonest labor. A thief making shoes in a penitentiary is engaged in more useful and therefore more honest labor than a "free" stonemason at work on a palace whose foundations are laid in the skulls and bones, and cemented in the sweat and blood of ten thousand victims of capitalistic exploitation. In both cases the labor is compulsory. The stonemason would not work for the trust-magnate were he not compelled to.

In ancient times only slaves labored. And as a matter of fact only slaves labor now. The millions are made by the magic of manipulation. The coal miners of West Virginia, Pennsylvania, Ohio, Indiana and Illinois receive an average wage of less than seventy-five cents a day. They perform the most useful and necessary labor, without which your homes, if possible at all, would be cheerless as caves and the great heart of industry would cease to throb. Are they free men, or are they slaves? And what is the effect of *their* labor on trade and industry and upon themselves and their families? Dante would search the realms of inferno in vain for such pictures of horror and despair as are to be found in the mining regions of free America.

To the student of social science the haggard fact stands forth that under the competitive system of production and distribution the prison problem will never be solved—and its effect upon trade and industry will never be greatly modified. The fact will remain that whatever labor is performed by prison labor could and should be performed by free labor, and when in the march of economic progress the capitalist system of industry for private profit succumbs to the socialist system of industry for human happiness, when the factory, which is now a penitentiary crowded with life convicts, among whom children often constitute the majority—when this factory is transformed into a temple of science, and the machine, myriad-armed and tireless, is the only slave, there will be no prison labor and the problem will cease to vex the world, and to this it is coming in obedience to the economic law, as unerring in its operation as the law of gravitation.

That prison labor is demoralizing in its effect on trade and industry whenever and wherever brought into competition with it, especially under the various forms of the contract system, is of course conceded, but that it has been, or is at present, a great factor in such demoralization is not admitted. There is a tendency to exaggerate the blighting effects of prison labor for the purpose of obscuring the one overshadowing cause of demoralized trade and impoverished industry.

Prison labor did not reduce the miner to a walking hunger-pang, his wife to a tear-stained rag, and his home to a lair. Prison labor is not responsible for the squares of squalor and miles of misery in New York, Chicago and all other centers of population. Prison labor is not chargeable with the sweating dens in which the victims of capitalistic competition crouch in dread and fear until death comes to their rescue. Prison labor had no hand in Cœur d'Alene, Tennessee, Homestead, Hazleton, Virdin, Pana, that suburb of hell called Pullman and other ensanguined industrial battle fields where thousands of workingmen after being oppressed and robbed were imprisoned life felons, and shot down like vagabond dogs; where venal judges issued infamous injunctions and despotic orders at the behest of their masters, enforcing them with deputy marshals armed with pistols and clubs and supported by troops with gleaming bayonets and shotted guns to drain the veins of workingmen of blood, but for whose labor this continent would still be a wilderness. Only the tortures of hunger and nakedness provoked protest, and this was silenced by the bayonet and bullet; by the club and the blood that followed the blow.

Prison labor is not accountable for the appalling increase in insanity, in suicide, in murder, in prostitution and a thousand other forms of vice and crime which pollute every fountain and contaminate every stream designed to bless the world.

Prison labor did not create our army of unemployed, but has been recruited from its ranks, and both owe their existence to the same social and economic system.

Nor are the evil effects confined exclusively to the poor working class. There is an aspect of the case in which the rich are as unfortunate as the poor. The destiny of the capitalist class is irrevocably linked with the wroking class. Fichte, the great German philosopher said, "Wickedness increases in proportion to the elevation of rank."

Prison labor is but one of the manifestations of our economic development and indicates its trend. The same cause that demoralized industry has crowded our prisons. Industry has not been impoverished by prison labor, but prison labor is the result of impoverished industry. The limited time at my command will not permit an analysis of the process.

The real question which confronts us is our industrial system and its effects upon labor. One of these effects is, as I have intimated, prison labor. What is its cause? What makes it necessary? The answer is, the competitive system, which creates wage-slavery, throws thousands out of employment and reduces the wages of thousands more to the point of bare subsistence.

Why is prison labor preferred to "free labor?" Simply because it is cheaper; it yields more profit to the man who buys, exploits and sells it. But this has its limitations. Capitalist competition that throngs the streets with idle workers, capitalist production that reduces human labor to a commodity and ultimately to crime—this system produces another kind of prison labor in the form of child labor which is being utilized more and more to complete the subjugation of the working class. There is this difference: The prison laborers are clothed and housed and fed. The child laborers whose wage is a dollar a week, or even less, must take care of themselves.

Prison labor is preferred because it is cheap. So with child labor. It is not a question of prison labor, or of child labor, but of *cheap* labor.

Tenement-house labor is another form of prison labor.

The effects of cheap labor on trade and industry must be the same, whether such labor is done by prisoners, tenement house slaves, children or starving "hoboes."

The prison laborer produces by machinery in abundance but does not consume. The child likewise produces, but owing to its small wages, does not consume. So with the vast army of workers whose wage grows smaller as the productive capacity of labor increases, and then society is afflicted with overproduction, the result of under-consumption. What follows? The panic. Factories close down, wage-workers are idle and suffer, middle-class business men are forced into bankruptcy, the army of tramps is increased, vice and crime are rampant and prisons and work-houses are filled to overflowing as are sewers when the streets of cities are deluged with floods.

Prison labor, like all cheap labor, is at first a source of profit to the capitalist, but finally it turns into a two-edged sword that cuts into and destroys the system that produced it.

First, the capitalist pocket is filled by the employment of cheap labor—and then the bottom drops out of it.

In the cheapening process, the pauperized mass have lost their consuming power.

The case may now be summed up as follows:

First. Prison labor is bad; it has a demoralizing effect on capitalist trade and industry.

Second. Child labor, tenement house and every other form of cheap labor is bad; it is destructive of trade and industry.

Third. Capitalist competition is bad; it creates a demand for cheap labor.

Fourth. Capitalist production is bad; it creates millionaires and mendicants, economic masters and slaves, thus intensifying the class struggle.

This indicates that the present capitalist system has outlived its usefulness, and that it is in the throes of dissolution. Capitalism is but a link in the chain of social and economic development. Just as feudalism developed capitalism and then disappeared, so capitalism is now developing socialism, and when the new social system has been completely evolved the last vestige of capitalism will fade into history.

The gigantic trust marks the change in production. It is no longer competitive but co-operative. The same mode of distribution, which must inevitably follow, will complete the process.

Co-operative labor will be the basis of the new social system, and this will be for use and not for profit. Labor will no longer be bought and sold. Industrial slavery will cease. For every man there will be the equal right to work with every other man and each will receive the fruit of his labor. Then we shall have economic equality. Involuntary idleness will be a horror of the past. Poverty will relax its grasp.

The army of tramps will be disbanded because the prolific womb which now warms these unfortunates into life will become barren. Prisons will be depopulated and the prison labor problem will be solved.

Each labor-saving machine will lighten the burden and decrease the hours of toil. The soul will no longer be subordinated to the stomach. Man will live a complete life, and the march will then begin to an ideal civilization.

There is a proverb which the Latin race sent ringing down the centuries which reads, "Omnia vincit amor," or "Love conquers all things." Love and labor in alliance, working together, have transforming, redeeming and emancipating power. Under their benign sway the world can be made better and brighter.

Isaiah saw in prophetic vision a time when nations should war no more—when swords should be transformed into plowshares and spears into pruning hooks. The fulfillment of the prophecy only awaits an era when Love and Labor, in holy alliance, shall solve the economic problem.

Here, on this occasion, in this great metropolis with its thousand spires pointing heavenward, where opulence riots in luxury which challenges hyperbole, and poverty rots in sweat shops which only a Shakespeare or a Victor Hugo could describe, and the transfer to canvas would palsy the hand of a Michael Angelo—here, where wealth and want and woe bear irrefutable testimony of deplorable conditions, I stand as a socialist, protesting against the wrongs perpetrated upon Les Miserables, and pleading as best I can for a higher civilization.

The army of begging Lazaruses, with the dogs licking their sores at the gates of palaces, where the rich are clothed in purple and fine linen with their tables groaning beneath the luxuries of all climes, make the palaces on the highland where fashion holds sway and music lends its charms, a picture in the landscape which, in illustrating disparity, brings into bolder relief the hut and the hovel in the hollow where want, gaunt and haggard, sits at the door and where light and plenty, cheerfulness and hope are forever exiled by the despotic decree of conditions as cruel as when the Czar of Russia orders to his penal mines in Siberia the hapless subjects who dare whisper the sacred word liberty—as cruel as when this boasted land of freedom commands that a far-away, innocent people shall be shot down in jungle and lagoon, in their bamboo huts, because they dream of freedom and independence.

These conditions are as fruitful of danger to the opulent as they are of degradation to the poor. It is neither folly nor fanaticism to assert that the country cannot exist under such conditions. The higher law of righteousness, of love and labor will prevail. It is a law which commends itself to reasoning men, a primal law enacted long before Jehovah wrote the decalogue amidst the thunders and lightnings of Sinai. It is a law written upon the tablets of every man's heart and conscience. It is a law infinitely above the creeds and dogmas and tangled disquisitions of the churches—the one law which in its operations will level humanity upward until men, redeemed from greed and every debasing ambition, shall obey its mandates and glory in its triumph.

Love and labor will give us the Socialist Republic—the Industrial Democracy—the equal rights of all men and women, and the emancipation of all from the vicious and debasing thraldoms of past centuries.

The Socialist Party and the Working Class

Opening Speech Delivered as Candidate of the Socialist Party for President, at Indianapolis, Ind., September 1, 1904

Mr. Chairman, Citizens and Comrades:

There has never been a free people, a civilized nation, a real republic on this earth. Human society has always consisted of masters and slaves, and the slaves have always been and are today, the foundation stones of the social fabric.

Wage-labor is but a name; wage-slavery is the fact.

The twenty-five millions of wage-workers in the United States are twenty-five millions of twentieth century slaves.

This is the plain meaning of what is known as

THE LABOR MARKET.

And the labor market follows the capitalist flag.

The most barbarous fact in all christendom is the labor market. The mere term sufficiently expresses the animalism of commercial civilization.

They who buy and they who sell in the labor market are alike dehumanized by the inhuman traffic in the brains and blood and bones of human beings.

The labor market is the foundation of so-called civilized society. Without these shambles, without this commerce in human life, this sacrifice of manhood and womanhood, this barter of babes, this sales of souls, the capitalist civilizations of all lands and all climes would crumble to ruin and perish from the earth.

Twenty-five millions of wage-slaves are bought and sold daily at prevailing prices in the American Labor Market.

This is the

PARAMOUNT ISSUE

in the present national campaign.

Let me say at the very threshold of this discussion that the workers have but the one issue in this campaign, the overthrow of the capitalist system and the emancipation of the working class from wage-slavery.

The capitalists may have the tariff, finance, imperialism and other dust-covered and moth-eaten issues entirely to themselves.

The rattle of these relics no longer deceives workingmen whose heads are on their own shoulders.

They know by experience and observation that the gold standard, free silver, fiat money, protective tariff, free trade, imperialism and anti-imperialism all mean capitalist rule and wage-slavery.

Their eyes are open and they can see; their brains are in operation and they can think.

The very moment a workingman begins to do his own thinking he understands the paramount issue, parts company with the capitalist politician and falls in line with his own class on the political battlefield.

The political solidarity of the working class means the death of despotism, the birth of freedom, the sunrise of civilization.

Having said this much by way of introduction I will now enter upon the actualities of my theme.

THE CLASS STRUGGLE.

We are entering tonight upon a momentous campaign. The struggle for political supremacy is not between political parties merely, as appears upon the surface, but at bottom it is a life and death struggle between two hostile economic classes, the one the capitalist, and the other the working class.

The capitalist class is represented by the Republican, Democratic, Populist and Prohibition parties, all of which stand for private ownership of the means of production, and the triumph of any one of which will mean continued wage-slavery to the working class.

As the Populist and Prohibition sections of the capitalist party represent minority elements which propose to reform the capitalist system without disturbing wage-slavery, a vain and impossible task, they will be omitted from this discussion with all the credit due the rank and file for their good intentions.

The Republican and Democratic parties, or, to be more exact, the Republican-Democratic party, represent the capitalist class in the class struggle. They are the political wings of the capitalist system and such differences as arise between them relate to spoils and not to principles.

With either of these parties in power one thing is always certain and that is that the capitalist class is in the saddle and the working class under the saddle.

Under the administration of both these parties the means of production are private property, production is carried forward for capitalist profit purely, markets are glutted and industry paralyzed, workingmen become tramps and criminals while injunctions, soldiers and riot guns are brought into action to preserve "law and order" in the chaotic carnival of capitalistic anarchy.

Deny it as may the cunning capitalists who are clear-sighted enough to perceive it, or ignore it as may the torpid workers who are too blind and unthinking to see it, the struggle in which we are engaged today is a class struggle, and as the toiling millions come to see and understand it and rally to the political standard of their class, they will drive all capitalist parties of whatever name into the same party, and the class struggle will then be so clearly revealed that the hosts of labor will find their true place in the conflict and strike the united and decisive blow that will destroy slavery and achieve their full and final emancipation.

In this struggle the workingmen and women and children are represented by the Socialist party and it is my privilege to address you in the name of that revolutionary and uncompromising party of the working class.

ATTITUDE OF THE WORKERS.

What shall be the attitude of the workers of the United States in the present campaign? What part shall they take in it? What party and what principles shall they support by their ballots? And why?

These are questions the importance of which are not sufficiently recognized by workingmen or they would not be the prey of parasites and the service tools of scheming politicians who use them only at election time to renew their masters' lease of power and perpetuate their own ignorance, poverty and shame.

In answering these questions I propose to be as frank and candid as plain-meaning words will allow, for I have but one object in this discussion and that object is not office, but the truth, and I shall state it as I see it, if I have to stand alone.

But I shall not stand alone, for the party that has my allegiance and may have my life, the Socialist party, the party of the working class, the party of emancipation, is made up of men and women who know their rights and scorn to compromise with their oppressors; who want no votes that can be bought and no support under any false pretense whatsoever.

The Socialist party stands squarely upon its proletarian principles and relies wholly upon the forces of industrial progress and the education of the working class.

The Socialist party buys no votes and promises no offices. Not a farthing is spent for whiskey or cigars. Every penny in the campaign fund is the voluntary offerings of workers and their sympathizers and every penny is used for education.

What other parties can say the same?

Ignorance alone stand in the way of socialist success. The capitalist parties understand this and use their resources to prevent the workers from seeing the light.

Intellectual darkness is essential to industrial slavery.

Capitalist parties stand for Slavery and Night.

The Socialist party is the herald of Freedom and Light.

Capitalist parties cunningly contrive to divide the workers upon dead issues.

The Socialist party is uniting them upon the living issue: Death to Wage Slavery!

When industrial slavery is as dead as the issues of the

Siamese capitalist parties the Socialist party will have fulfilled its mission and enriched history.

And now to our questions:

First, all workingmen and women owe it to themselves, their class and their country to take an active and intelligent interest in political affairs.

THE BALLOT.

The ballot of united labor expresses the people's will and the people's will is the supreme law of a free nation.

The ballot means that labor is no longer dumb, that at last it has a voice, that it may be heard and if united shall be heeded.

Centuries of struggle and sacrifice were required to wrest this symbol of freedom from the mailed clutch of tyranny and place it in the hand of labor as the shield and lance of attack and defense.

The abuse and not the use of it is responsible for its evils.

The divided vote of labor is the abuse of the ballot and the penalty is slavery and death.

The united vote of those who toil and have not will vanquish those who have and toil not, and solve forever the problem of democracy.

THE HISTORIC STRUGGLE OF CLASSES.

Since the race was young there have been class struggles. In every state of society, ancient and modern, labor has been exploited, degraded and in subjection.

Civilization has done little for labor except to modify the forms of its exploitation.

Labor has always been the mudsill of the social fabric—is so now and will be until the class struggle ends in class extinction and free society.

Society has always been and is now built upon exploitation—the exploitation of a class—the working class, whether slaves, serfs or wage-laborers, and the exploited working class in subjection have always been, instinctively or consciously, in revolt against their oppressors.

Through all the centuries the enslaved toilers have moved slowly but surely toward their final freedom.

The call of the Socialist party is to the exploited class, the workers in all useful trades and professions, all honest occupations, from the most menial service to the highest skill, to rally beneath their own standard and put an end to the last of the barbarous class struggles by conquering the capitalist government, taking possession of the means of production and making them the common property of all, abolishing wage-slavery and establishing the co-operative commonwealth.

The first step in this direction is to sever all relations with

CAPITALIST PARTIES.

They are precisely alike and I challenge their most discriminating partisans to tell them apart in relation to labor.

The Republican and Democratic parties are alike capitalist parties—differing only in being committed to different sets of capitalist interests—they have the same principles under varying colors, are equally corrupt and are one in their subservience to capital and their hostility to labor.

The ignorant workingman who supports either of these parties forges his own fetters and is the unconscious author of his own misery. He can and must be made to see and think and act with his fellows in supporting the party of his class and this work of education is the crowning virtue of the socialist movement.

THE REPUBLICAN PARTY.

Let us briefly consider the Republican party from the worker's standpoint. It is capitalist to the core. It has not and can not have the slightest interest in labor except to exploit it.

Why should a workingman support the Republican party?

Why should a millionaire support the Socialist party?

For precisely the same reason that all the millionaires are opposed to the Socialist party, all the workers should be opposed to the Republican party. It is a capitalist party, is loyal to capitalist interests and entitled to the support of capitalist voters on election day.

All it has for workingmen is its "glorious past" and a "glad hand" when it wants their votes.

The Republican party is now and has been for several years, in complete control of government.

What has it done for labor? What has it not done for capital?

Not one of the crying abuses of capital has been curbed under Republican rule.

Not one of the petitions of labor has been granted.

The eight hour and anti-injunction bills, upon which organized labor is a unit, were again ruthlessly slain by the last congress in obedience to the capitalist masters.

David M. Parry has greater influence at Washington than all the millions of organized workers.

Read the national platform of the Republican party and see if there is in all its bombast a crumb of comfort for labor. The convention that adopted it was a capitalist convention and the only thought it had of labor was how to abstract its vote without waking it up.

In the only reference it made to labor it had to speak easy so as to avoid offense to the capitalists who own it and furnish the boodle to keep it in power.

The labor platforms of the Republican and Democratic parties are interchangeable and non-redeemable. They both favor "justice to capital and justice to labor." This hoary old platitude is worse than meaningless. It is false and misleading and so intended. Justice to labor means that labor shall have what it produces. This leaves nothing for capital.

Justice to labor means the end of capital.

The old parties intend nothing of the kind. It is false pretense and false promise. It has served well in the past. Will it continue to catch the votes of unthinking and deluded workers?

What workingmen had part in the Republican national convention or were honored by it?

The grand coliseum swarmed with trust magnates, corporation barons, money lords, stock gamblers, professional politicians, lawyers, lobbyists and other plutocratic tools and mercenaries, but there was no room for the horny-handed and horny-headed sons of toil. They built it, but were not in it.

Compare that convention with the convention of the Socialist party, composed almost wholly of working men and women and controlled wholly in the interest of their class.

But a party is still better known by its chosen representatives than by its platform declarations.

Who are the nominees of the Republican party for the highest offices in the gift of the nation and what is their relation to the working class?

First of all, Theodore Roosevelt and Charles W. Fairbanks, candidates for President and Vice-President, respectively, deny the class struggle and this almost infallibly fixes their status as freinds of capital and enemies of labor. They insist that they can serve both; but the fact is obvious that only one can be served and that one at the expense of the other. Mr. Roosevelt's whole political career proves it.

The capitalists made no mistake in nominating Mr. Roosevelt. They know him well and he has served them well. They know that his instincts, associations, tastes and desires are with them, that he is in fact one of them and that he has nothing in common with the working class.

The only evidence to the contrary is his membership in the Brotherhood of Locomotive Firemen which seems to have come to him co-incident with his ambition to succeed himself in the presidential chair. He is a full fledged member of the union, has the grip, signs and passwords; but it is not reported that he is attending meetings, doing picket duty, supporting strikes and boycotts and performing such other duties as his union obligation imposes.

When Ex-President Grover Cleveland violated the constitution and outraged justice by seizing the state of Illinois by the throat and handcuffing her civil administration at the behest of the crime-stained trusts and corporations, Theodore Roosevelt was among his most ardent admirers and enthusiastic supporters. He wrote in hearty commendation of the atrocious act, pronounced it most exalted patriotism and said he would have done the same himself had he been president.

And so he would and so he will!

How impressive to see the Rough Rider embrace the Smooth Statesman! Oyster Bay and Buzzard's Bay! "Two souls with but a single thought, two hearts that beat as one."

There is also the highest authority for the statement charging Mr. Roosevelt with declaring about the same time he was lauding Cleveland that if he was in command he would have such as Altgeld, Debs and other traitors lined up against a dead wall and shot. The brutal remark was not for publication but found its way into print and Mr. Roosevelt, after he became a candidate, attempted to make denial, but the words themselves sound like Roosevelt and bear the impress of his savage visage.

Following the Pullman strike in 1894 there was an indignant and emphatic popular protest against "government by injunction," which has not yet by any means subsided.

Organized labor was, and is, a unit against this insidious form of judicial usurpation as a means of abrogating constitutional restraints of despotic power.

Mr. Roosevelt with his usual zeal to serve the ruling class and keep their slaves in subjection, vaulted into the arena and launched his tirade upon the "mob" that dared oppose the divine rule of a corporation judge.

"Men who object to what they style 'government by injunction,'" said he, "are, as regards the essential principles of government, in hearty sympathy with their remote skin-clad ancestors, who lived in caves, fought one another with stone-headed axes and ate the mammoth and woolly rhinoceros. They are dangerous whenever there is the least danger of their making the principles of this ages-buried past living factors in our present life. They are not in sympathy with men of good minds and good civic morality."

In direct terms and plain words Mr. Roosevelt denounces all those who oppose "Government by Injunction" as cannibals, barbarians and anarchists, and this violent and sweeping stigma embraces the whole organized movement of labor, every man, woman and child that wears the badge of union labor in the United States.

It is not strange in the light of these facts that the national congress, under President Roosevelt's administration, suppresses anti-injunction and eight-hour bills and all other measures favored by labor and resisted by capital.

No stronger or more convincing proof is required of Mr. Roosevelt's allegiance to capital and opposition to labor, nor of the class struggle and class rule which he so vehemently denies; and the workingman who in the face of these words and acts, can still support Mr. Roosevelt, must feel himself flattered in being publicly proclaimed a barbarian, and sheer gratitude, doubtless, impels him to crown his benefactor with the highest honors.

If the working class are barbarians, according to Mr. Roosevelt, this may account for his esteeming himself as having the very qualities necessary to make himself Chief of the Tribe.

But it must be noted that Mr. Roosevelt denounced organized labor as savages long before he was a candidate for president. After he became a candidate he joined the tribe and is today, himself, according to his own dictum, a barbarian and the enemy of civic morality.

The labor union to which President Roosevelt belongs and which he is solemnly obligated to support, is unanimously opposed to "Government by Injunction." President Roosevelt knew it when he joined it and he also knew that those who oppose injunction rule have the instincts of cannibals and are a menace to morality, but his proud nature succumbed to political ambition, and his ethical ideas vanished as he struck the trail that led to the tribe and, after a most dramatic scene and impressive ceremony, was decorated with the honorary badge of international barbarism.

How Theodore Roosevelt, the trade-unionist, can support the presidential candidate who denounced him as an immoral and dangerous barbarian, he may decide at his leisure, and so may all other union men in the United States who are branded with the same vulgar stigma, and their ballots will determine if they have the manhood to resent insult and rebuke its author, or if they have been fitly characterized and deserve humiliation and contempt.

The appointment of Judge Taft to a cabinet position is corroborative evidence, if any be required, of President Roosevelt's fervent faith in Government by Injunction. Judge Taft first came into national notoriety when, some years ago, sitting with Judge Ricks, who was later tried for malfeasance, they issued the celebrated injunction during the Toledo, Ann Arbor & North Michigan railroad strike that paralyzed the Brotherhoods of Locomotive Engineers and Firemen and won for them the gratitude and esteem of every corporation in the land. They were hauled to Toledo, the headquarters of the railroad, in a special car, pulled by a special engine, on special time, and after hastily consulting the railroad magnates and receiving instructions, let go the judicial lightning that shivered the unions to splinters and ended the strike in total defeat. Judge Taft is a special favorite with the trust barons and his elevation to the cabinet was ratified with joy at the court of St. Plutus.

Still again did President Roosevelt drive home his archenmity to labor and his implacable hostility to the trade-union movement when he made Paul Morton, the notorious union hater and union wrecker, his secretary of the navy. That appointment was an open insult to every trade-unionist in the country and they who lack the self-respect to resent it at the polls may wear the badge, but they are lacking wholly in the spirit and principles of union labor.

Go ask the brotherhood men who were driven from the C. B. & Q. and the striking union machinists on the Santa Fe to give you the pedigree of Mr. Morton and you will learn that his hate for union men is equalled only by his love for the scabs who take their places.

Such a man and such another as Sherman Bell, the military ferret of the Colorado mine owners, are the ideal patriots and personal chums of Mr. Roosevelt, and by honoring these he dishonors himself and should be repudiated by the ballot of every working man in the nation.

Mr. Fairbanks, the Republican candidate for Vice-President, is a corporation attorney of the first class and a plutocrat in good and regular standing. He is in every respect a fit and proper representative of his party and every millionaire in the land may safely support him.

THE DEMOCRATIC PARTY.

In referring to the Democratic party in this discussion we may save time by simply saying that since it was born again at the St. Louis convention it is near enough like its Republican ally to pass for a twin brother.

The former party of the "common people" is no longer under the boycott of the plutocracy since it has adopted the Wall street label and renounced its middle class heresies.

The radical and progressive element of the former Democracy have been evicted and must seek other quarters. They were an unmitigated nuisance in the conservative counsels of the old party. They were for the "common people" and the trusts have no use for such a party.

Where but to the Socialist party can these progressive people turn? They are now without a party and the only genuine Democratic party in the field is the Socialist party, and every true Democrat should thank Wall street for driving him out of a party that is democratic in name only and into one that is democratic in fact.

The St. Louis convention was a trust jubilee. The Wall street reorganizers made short work of the free silver element. From first to last it was a capitalistic convocation. Labor was totally ignored. As an incident, two thousand choice chairs were reserved for the Business Men's League of St. Louis, an organization hostile to organized labor, but not a chair was tendered to those whose labor had built the convention hall, had clothed, transported, fed and wined the delegates and whose votes are counted on as if they were so many dumb driven cattle, to pull the ticket through in November.

As another incident, when Lieutenant Richmond Hobson dramatically declared that President Cleveland had been the only president who had ever been patriotic enough to use the federal troops to crush union labor, the trust agents, lobbyists, tools and clackers screamed with delight and the convention shook with applause.

The platform is precisely the same as the Republican platform in relation to labor. It says nothing and means the same. A plank was proposed condemning the outrages in Colorado under Republican administration, but upon order from the Parryites it was promptly thrown aside.

The editor of *American Industries,* organ of the Manufacturers' Association, commented at length in its issue of

July 15 on the triumph of capital and the defeat of labor at both Republican and Democratic national conventions. Among other things he said: "The two labor lobbies, partly similar in make-up, were, to put it bluntly, thrown out bodily in both places." And that is the simple fact and is known of all men who read the papers. The capitalist organs exult because labor, to use their own brutal expression, was kicked bodily out of both the Republican and Democratic national conventions.

What more than this is needed to open the eyes of workingmen to the fact that neither of these parties is their party and that they are as strangely out of place in them as Rockefeller and Vanderbilt would be in the Socialist party?

And how many more times are they to be "kicked out bodily" before they stay out and join the party of their class in which labor is not only honored but is supreme, a party that is clean, that has conscience and convictions, a party that will one day sweep the old parties from the field like chaff and issue the Proclamation of Labor's Emancipation?

Judge Alton B. Parker corresponds precisely to the Democratic platform. It was made to order for him. His famous telegram in the expiring hour removed the last wrinkle and left it a perfect fit.

Thomas W. Lawson, the Boston millionaire, charges that Senator Patrick McCarren, who brought out Judge Parker for the nomination, is on the pay roll of the Standard Oil Company as political master mechanic at twenty thousand dollars a year, and that Parker is the chosen tool of Standard Oil. Mr. Lawson offers Senator McCarren one hundred thousand dollars if he will disprove the charge.

William Jennings Bryan denounced Judge Parker as a tool of Wall street before he was nominated and declared that no self-respecting Democrat could vote for him, and after his nomination he charged that it had been dictated by the trusts and secured by "crooked and indefensible methods." Mr. Bryan also said that labor had been betrayed in the convention and need look for nothing from the Democratic party. He made many other damaging charges against his party and its candidates, but when the supreme test came he was not equal to it, and instead of denouncing the betrayers of the "common people" and repudiating their made-to-order Wall street program, he compromised with the pirates that scuttled his ship and promised with his lips the support his heart refused and his conscience condemned.

The Democratic nominee for President was one of the Supreme Judges of the State of New York who declared the eight-hour law unconstitutional and this is an index of his political character.

In his address accepting the nomination he makes but a single allusion to labor and in this he takes occasion to say that labor is charged with having recently used dynamite in destroying property and that the perpetrators should be subjected to "the most rigorous punishment known to the law." This cruel intimation amounts to conviction in advance of trial and indicates clearly the trend of his capitalistically trained judicial mind. He made no such reference to capital, nor to those ermined rascals who use judicial dynamite in blowing up the constitution while labor is looted and starved by capitalistic freebooters who trample all law in the mire and leer and mock at their despoiled and helpless victims.

It is hardly necessary to make more than passing reference to Henry G. Davis, Democratic candidate for Vice-President. He is a coal baron, railroad owner and, of course, an enemy to union labor. He has amassed a great fortune exploiting his wage-slaves and has always strenuously resisted every attempt to organize them for the betterment of their condition. Mr. Davis is a staunch believer in the virtue of the injunction as applied to union labor. As a young man he was in charge of a slave plantation and his conviction is that wage-slaves should be kept free from the contaminating influence of the labor agitator and render cheerful obedience to their master.

Mr. Davis is as well qualified to serve his party as is Senator Fairbanks to serve the Republican party and wage-workers should have no trouble in making their choice between this pernicious pair of plutocrats, and certainly no intelligent workingman will hesitate an instant to discard them both and cast his vote for Ben Hanford, their working class competitor, who is as loyally devoted to labor as Fairbanks and Davis are to capital.

THE SOCIALIST PARTY.

In what has been said of other parties I have tried to show why they should not be supported by the common people, least of all by workingmen, and I think I have shown clearly enough that such workers as do support them are guilty, consciously or unconsciously, of treason to their class. They are voting into power the enemies of labor and are morally responsible for the crimes thus perpetrated upon their fellow-workers and sooner or later they will have to suffer the consequences of their miserable acts.

The Socialist party is not, and does not pretend to be, a capitalist party. It does not ask, nor does it expect the votes of the capitalist class. Such capitalists as do support it do so seeing the approaching doom of the capitalist system and with a full understanding that the Socialist party is not a capitalist party, nor a middle class party, but a revolutionary working class party, whose historic mission it is to conquer capitalism on the political battle-field, take control of government and through the public powers take possession of the means of wealth production, abolish wage-slavery and emancipate all workers and all humanity.

The people are as capable of achieving their industrial freedom as they were to secure their political liberty, and both are necessary to a free nation.

The capitalist system is no longer adapted to the needs of modern society. It is outgrown and fetters the forces of progress. Industrial and commercial competition are largely of the past. The handwriting blazes on the wall. Centralization and combination are the modern forces in industrial and commercial life. Competition is breaking down and co-operation is supplanting it.

The hand tools of early times are used no more. Mammoth machines have taken their places. A few thousand capitalists own them and many millions of workingmen use them.

All the wealth the vast army of labor produces above its subsistence is taken by the machine owning capitalists, who also own the land and the mills, the factories, railroads and mines, the forests and fields and all other means of production and transportation.

Hence wealth and poverty, millionaires and beggars, castles and caves, luxury and squalor, painted parasites on the boulevard and painted poverty among the red lights.

Hence strikes, boycotts, riots, murder, suicide, insanity, prostitution on a fearful and increasing scale.

The capitalist parties can do nothing. They are a part, an iniquitous part, of the foul and decaying system.

There is no remedy for the ravages of death.

Capitalism is dying and its extremities are already decomposing. The blotches upon the surface show that the blood no longer circulates. The time is near when the cadaver will have to be removed and the atmosphere purified.

In contrast with the Republican and Democratic conventions, where politicians were the puppets of plutocrats, the convention of the Socialist party consisted of workingmen and women fresh from their labors, strong, clean, wholesome, self-reliant, ready to do and dare for the cause of labor, the cause of humanity.

Proud indeed am I to have been chosen by such a body of men and women to bear aloft the proletarian standard in this campaign, and heartily do I endorse the clear and cogent platform of the party which appeals with increasing force and eloquence to the whole working class of the country.

To my associate upon the national ticket I give my hand with all my heart. Ben Hanford typifies the working class and fitly represents the historic mission and revolutionary character of the Socialist party.

CLOSING WORDS.

These are stirring days for living men. The day of crisis is drawing near and Socialists are exerting all their power to prepare the people for it.

The old order of society can survive but little longer. Socialism is next in order. The swelling minority sounds warning of the impending change. Soon that minority will be the majority and then will come the co-operative commonwealth.

Every workingman should rally to the standard of his class and hasten the full-orbed day of freedom.

Every progressive Democrat must find his way in our direction and if he will but free himself from prejudice and study the principles of Socialism he will soon be a sturdy supporter of our party.

Every sympathizer with labor, every friend of justice, every lover of humanity should support the Socialist party as the only party that is organized to abolish industrial slavery, the prolific source of the giant evils that afflict the people.

Who with a heart in his breast can look upon Colorado without keenly feeling the cruelties and crimes of capitalism! Repression will not help her. Brutality will only brutalize her. Private ownership and wage-slavery are the curse of Colorado. Only Socialism will save Colorado and the nation.

The overthrow of capitalism is the object of the Socialist party. It will not fuse with any other party and it would rather die than compromise.

The Socialist party comprehends the magnitude of its task and has the patience of preliminary defeat and the faith of ultimate victory.

The working class must be emancipated by the working class.

Woman must be given her true place in society by the working class.

Child labor must be abolished by the working class.

Society must be reconstructed by the working class.

The working class must be employed by the working class.

The fruits of labor must be enjoyed by the working class.

War, bloody war, must be ended by the working class.

These are the principles and objects of the Socialist party and we fearlessly proclaim them to our fellowmen.

We know our cause is just and that it must prevail.

With faith and hope and courage we hold our heads erect and with dauntless spirit marshal the working class for the march from Capitalism to Socialism, from Slavery to Freedom, from Barbarism to Civilization.

Craft Unionism

Speech at Chicago, November 23, 1905

We have met under the auspices and in the interests of the Industrial Workers of the World. Organized here in Chicago, less than five months ago, the Industrial Workers already number almost, if not quite, a hundred thousand workingmen and women, enrolled as dues-paying members, in a revolutionary, economic organization of the working class.

Why has this new organization been instituted? Why will not the old trade unions that already occupy the field serve the purpose? Why a new organization? These are questions that are up for consideration; that address themselves to all the workers of the country, whether they favor or oppose the new organization.

For many years I have been connected with one and another of the old trade unions. Indeed, since February, 1875, when I first joined the Brotherhood of Locomotive Firemen, I have been an active member of a trade union; and during that time I have had some experience by virtue of which I trust I have profited sufficiently to enable me to determine whether a trade union is organized for the purpose of serving the working class or not.

At the very threshold of this discussion I aver that the old form of trade unionism no longer meets the demands of the working class. I aver that the old trade union has not only fulfilled its mission and outlived its usefulness, but that it is now positively reactionary, and is maintained, not in the interests of the workers who support it, but in the interests of the capitalist class who exploit the workers who support it.

Let me cite an instance or two for illustration. The Brotherhood of Locomotive Engineers has been organized about forty years. It professes to be a trade union, an organization of and for the working class. The organization has the favor and support of practically every railroad corporation in the United States. The late P. M. Arthur was its grand chief for many years. In the beginning of his official career he was true to the working class. As the organization developed in numbers and in power, and became a menace to the corporations, they realized the necesssity of securing control of that organization. And how did they go about it? By making certain concessions to that so-called brotherhood, by flattering its grand chief, by declaring that they had no objection to a labor organization such as this brotherhood, especially while under the supervision of so conservative a leader as Mr. Arthur. Every time the corporations made a concession to the engineers it was at the expense of poorly paid employes in other departments who were unorganized; and when the men in these departments protested and finally went out on strike, the engineers have invariably been used by the corporation to defeat their fellow-workers, who were in revolt against degrading economic conditions.

Mr. Arthur was, therefore, a prime favorite with the railroad corporations. They granted him annual passes over their lines; and when the Brotherhood of Locomotive Engineers met in convention, their delegates were provided with special trains to transport them to and from the convention, free of charge, as evidence that the corporation appreciated the value of the Brotherhood of Locomotive Engineers.

Since the engineers were organized, the firemen, conductors, brakemen, switchmen, telegraphers and trackmen have also been organized, and several other departments have been partially organized, and they all have practically the same form of organization. They are all conservative. They all operate within the bounds set and approved by the railroad corporations. Are they, can they be true to the men who pay the dues, to the workingmen who support them? I answer that they cannot. Not only are they not true to the wage-workers who support them, but they are pressed into service, politically and otherwise, when occasion demands it, in the interest of these corporations, and to the detriment of their own.

Only the other day, since this much-discussed matter of rate legislation has been pending, the grand chiefs of these various brotherhoods have been convened. By whom? By the railroad corporations. For what purpose? This will appear as I proceed.

Just after the grand chiefs of these labor unions met with the railroad officials, another meeting took place. Of whom? Of the representatives of the principal of these several organizations, who, acting under the advice of their grand officers, proceeded to the city of Washington, held a conference with President Roosevelt, and protested that the labor unions they represented, consisting of the railway workers of the country, were opposed to any sort of legislation that would have a tendency to reduce railroad rates in the United States. The announcement also went forth at the same time that these brotherhoods would make their political power felt in the interests of the railroad corporations; that is to say, against the common people, the toiling millions of the land.

What a picture, indeed!

One glance proves beyond a shadow of a doubt that these unions are exceedingly useful to the corporations; and to the extent that they serve the economic and political purposes of the corporations, they are the foes—and not the friends—of the working class.

The United Mine Workers, in point of numbers a powerful labor organization, embraces a large majority of the coal miners of the country. Is this organization of any real benefit to coal miners? What has it actually done for them during the last few years? What have the miners, who have paid millions of dollars from their scant earnings in support of the organization, what have they to show in return?

These miners are well organized. They have the numbers. They ought to have real economic power. But they lack it. And why? For the simple reason that they are not organized upon the basis of the class struggle. Their union principles are not right; and it is for this reason that their organization has the hearty support of the coal operators of the country, who, by the way, are in session in Chicago at this very time, for the purpose of uniting, for the purpose of dealing with the miners, not through the rank and file of their union, but, as they themselves declare, *through their national board.*

And this is a very important point for the union miners to take into consideration. These operators, these exploiters, who are conscious of their class interests, propose to deal, not with the union at large, not with the great body of the miners, not with the rank and file, not with the common herd, not with the black beasts of burden, but with their National Executive Board. They will fix things that are out of joint and settle matters generally. They will arrive at mutually satisfactory conclusions. They will harmonize beautifully. And when they do harmonize, it will be in the interests, not of the miners who do the work, who dig the coal, who produce the wealth, but in the interests of the operators who own the mines and exploit the slaves of the pits.

Why, the most zealous supporter of the United Mine Workers is the coal operator himself. The simple fact that the coal operator collects the union dues, and discharges the miner who refuses to pay his dues, is sufficient evidence of this fact.

The coal operator does not collect the dues from the man who happens to belong to the Industrial Workers. He knows enough to know what is good for him; and he knows that the miners, organized as they are at present, can do him little harm, but can do him great good. And this is why he wants the miners organized in the pure and simple old-fashioned way. He knows that if they were totally unorganized they would spontaneously go out on strike. But they cannot strike as they are now organized without securing the sanction of their national, district and local officers; and so the operator keeps a friendly eye upon the union which fortifies and facilitates the exploitation of the coal diggers in his mines.

At stated periods the operators and representatives of the miners meet; and sometimes the sessions are very spirited, the miners insisting upon an increase, and the operators upon a decrease of wages, as was the case at the last interstate conference, when the union officials declared that under no circumstances would they accept a reduction, and the delegates voted by practically a unanimous vote not to accept any reduction, and for a while there was every indication of a strike. But the national officers met with the operators, and a reduction of wages was agreed to, and then the union officers went out among the rank and file and told them that if they were foolish enough to go out on strike they would certainly be defeated, and that the best thing they could do was to accept the reduction. So these union officials, backed by the operators, virtually forced the reduction upon the miners.

The operator can well afford to support that kind of a labor union.

The United Mine Workers, under its present policy, denies and seeks to obscure the class struggle. President Mitchell used to be quoted as saying that the interests of the miners and the operators were identical. He made an address the other day in which he claimed that he had been misquoted; he had not said that their interests were identical, but that they were reciprocal. I would like to have Mr. Mitchell show in what way the operator who fleeces the miner reciprocates to that miner. The simple fact is that the operator—and I don't know why he is called that, he doesn't operate anything—the operator takes from the miner what the miner produces. He serves him in that capacity, and no other.

The miners' union denies, in effect, the class struggle, and vainly seeks to harmonize the economic interests of these two antagonistic classes—the exploiting masters and the exploited wage-slaves; the robbers and the robbed. It cannot be done; not permanently at least; and if it be done even temporarily, it is always at the expense of the wage-slaves. Such an organization as that cannot truly serve the best interests of the working class. It is impossible.

There are many who concur in these views, yet insist that the organization must be changed from the inside; that it can only be brought to its proper position by "boring from within." I deny it. It is historically impossible. This organization has practically run its course. It has fulfilled its mission as a labor union, whatever that has been. It is now practically in charge of the mine owners; and the only way the miners can get away from that situation is to sever their relations with that capitalist-controlled union and join and build up one of their own upon the basis of the class struggle; and then they will be in position to fight the capitalist class with some chance of success.

The most important fact in all the world for workingmen to take cognizance of is the class struggle. The Industrial Workers expresses economically the interests of the working class in that struggle. The Industrial Workers declare that there can be nothing in common between the exploiting capitalist and the exploited wage-worker; that there is inevitably a struggle between them, and that this struggle cannot end until the capitalist class is overthrown, and the wage-system wiped out. Then and then only can there be an end to class rule.

Now, if you are a workingman and if you believe that you have an economic interest in common with that of the capitalist who employs you, remain in the old trade union. That is where you belong. If that is your conviction we do not want you to join the Industrial Workers. You do not properly belong to us. You do belong to the American Federation of Labor and its affiliated organizations. But, if you believe, as I believe, that the working class have economic interests of their own, separate and apart from and in conflict with the economic interests of the capitalist class, then you should, and sooner or later will have to, sever your relation with the old trade union and join the Industrial Workers, the only union organized upon the basis of class struggle.

And now, let me ask, have we a class struggle? The answer comes of itself. This struggle finds expression daily, hourly, in strikes, in boycotts, in lockouts, injunctions, riots, assaults and bloodshed. It is not an unmixed evil, however, for in this great world-wide class struggle, that is shaking the foundations of civilized society everywhere, there are being wrought out the most important problems of our modern civilization.

The working class are in an overwhelming majority. They have the numbers. They ought to have the power. And they would have the power if only they were conscious of their interests *as a class*.

Every effort is put forth by the exploiting capitalist to prevent workingmen from seeing the class struggle. The capitalist insists that there is no such struggle. The editor in the employ of the capitalist echoes "no class struggle." The teacher, professor and the minister, all of them dependent upon the capitalist for the chance to make a living, agree that there are no classes and no class struggle. In unison they declaim against class agitation and seek to obscure class rule that it may be perpetuated indefinitely.

We insist that there *is* a class struggle; that the working class must recognize it; that they must organize economically and politically upon the basis of that struggle; and that when they do so organize they will then have the power to free themselves and put an end to that struggle forever.

Now, have not the workers, especially here in Chicago, had sufficient experience during the last few years? Have they not been defeated often enough to demonstrate the inherent weakness of the old trades union movement? Haven't they been enjoined by the Courts often enough? Clubbed by the police and flung into jail often enough? Haven't they had experience of this kind enough to open their eyes to the fact that there is a mighty class struggle in progress, and that there will never be any material change in their condition until they unite their class in every department of industrial activity?

Speaking for myself, I was made to realize long ago that the old trade union was utterly incompetent to deal successfully with the exploiting corporations in this struggle. I was made to see that in craft unionism the capitalist class have it in their power to keep the workers divided, to use one part of them with which to conquer and crush another part of them. Indeed, I was made to see that the old form of unionism separates the workers and keeps them helpless at the mercy of their masters.

Object lessons are presented to you every day in the week. You have hundreds of thousands of workers organized in Chicago, in every conceivable kind of a union, and under the direction of an infinite variety of leaders. I will not say that these leaders are all incompetent or corrupt. That would not be true. But many of them are corrupt, and in that capacity have it in their power to betray and sell out the workers who trust them. In this position the workers will remain—where there is no hope for them—so long as they cling to the outgrown old trade union and its inefficient methods. We have had the proof of this over and over again. Take all the great strikes that have occurred in Chicago during the last few years. Have any of them been successful? Have they not uniformly failed?

The capitalists have not entirely stamped out the defeated unions, that is true. They have had the power to do this in the hour of the workers' defeat, but they have refrained from doing it, because they are shrewd enough to know that if they destroyed those unions, another and better one would take their places. Is it not a fact that they had the butcher workmen absolutely at their mercy, and could have compelled the members to entirely withdraw from the unions before giving them employment? They did not crush the unions out. When they had conquered they were satisfied. They had driven the unionists back to their reservations and they were perfectly satisfied that they should build up again along the same old lines.

The Employers' Association had the striking teamsters completely at their mercy, and could, had they seen fit, have utterly crushed out their union. They did not do it. In the closing part of the negotiations the settlement hinged upon the alleged privilege of the teamsters wearing their union badges, and this the Employers' Association finally conceded; and then the claim was put forth that the striking teamsters had come out victorious. The truth is that they lost everything; but the employer was not anxious to destroy their organization. He knew very well that if he did a stronger one would spring from the ruins; that a crushed union at least teaches workingmen to see its inherent defects.

The employer is shrewd enough to know that when you totally wipe out organizations you drive the workers into solidarity.

The teamsters were entirely defeated, nothing left; and yet their leaders boasted that they had served their organization. It reminded me of the dispatch once sent from a field of battle by a general who had been completely routed: "There is nothing left but honor, and d—n little of that!"

It is true that there are some employers who are supposed to be entirely opposed to unionism, even the old form of trade unionism. But the great majority of capitalists, especially the shrewder, far-seeing ones, unqualifiedly approve the pure and simple labor union. And now let me show that between these two sections of the capitalist class there is, after all, no vital difference with regard to the trade union movement.

C. W. Post, president of the Citizens' Industrial Association, and David M. Parry, president of the Manufacturers' Association, who are opposing the American Federation of Labor, have repeatedly said that they are not opposed to trade unionism if it will confine itself to its "legitimate" functions. In other words, they are not opposed to trade unionism if it does not antagonize the capitalist class. That is their position. Now, what is the position of the great body of capitalists who avow their friendship for the trade union movement? Precisely the same. They are in favor of the trade union as long as it does not menace or attack the capitalist class; that is, as long as it doesn't do anything. And in its present shape it is not doing anything; and that is why the capitalists are not opposed to it. Let these trade unions unite tomorrow; let them declare in favor of waging this fight along the lines of the class struggle, and they will soon find out whether these capitalists are in favor of trade unionism or not.

The very fact that the great majority of capitalists favor trade unionism proves that it is doing little or nothing for its members. Were it really doing something for them it would be antagonizing the capitalist class, and that class would fight it. But the capitalists are not fighting the old brand of unionism; they have, in fact, formed an alliance with it and the union is the silent partner in the firm.

You have all doubtless heard of the Civic Federation. This federation is supposed to be fair and impartial. It is organized for the one purpose of dove-tailing the interests of labor and capital, and every member of this body insists that these interests can be harmonized; that there is no necessary conflict between them. That is what Mr. Gompers says; that is what Mr. Mitchell says; that is what Archbishop Ireland and Bishop Potter say, and that is what they all say—that there is no necessary conflict between capitalists and wage-workers. If there be no necessary conflict between them, it follows that all the fighting that is going on must be unnecessary. I suppose then that ought to be very easily ended.

A gentleman named August Belmont presides over this harmonizing body. Not long ago, in an address, he claimed that there was no better trade-unionist in the country than he, and he proved it during the Interborough strike in the city of New York, when several thousand union employes of that corporation, of which he is president, went out on strike because they were driven to that extremity by his pernicious policy. He proved that he was a loyal trade-unionist when he employed James Farley, the notorious professional strike-breaker, and his army of Hessians to take the places of his former employes. Just a little while after Mr. Belmont had thus defeated his employes and disrupted their unions, he met at the hospitable banqueting board of the Civic Federation with the national officers of the American Federation of Labor and its allied unions, and there made good his claim that he was a true trades-unionist of the old school.

Do you think that a labor leader who is absolutely true to the working class could sit at such a banquet with such a capitalist as Belmont? Do you think he would be the guest of such an organization as the Civic Federation, whose only purpose is by subtle schemes to reduce the trade-union movement to harmless impotency?

It is for this and this alone that the Civic Federation has been organized. This is its real mission. The American Federation of Labor has fallen within the fatal influence of this emasculating alliance, and has thus proven that it is not organized to advance the true interests of the working class.

The American Federation of Labor is now holding its annual convention in the city of Pittsburg. What are its delegates doing there? Simply passing the same old resolutions. Once more they are going to petition Congress to enact an eight-hour law. They have done that over and over again, and their petition has been as repeatedly pigeon-holed. They have also resolved to petition Congress to restrict the powers of capitalist courts in dealing with labor. They have done that time and again, and what have they gained by it? Absolutely nothing. No attention has been paid to these servile supplications. They have been disregarded, thrown aside, treated with contempt; but the delegates solemnly meet in convention once more to pass the same hoary resolutions, to introduce the same stale petitions, with the same inevitable results. Now, is not this a perfectly stupid procedure? Are these men incapable of profiting by experience? Do they not by this time understand the nature and essential functions of capitalist-class government?

Can they not see that we have a capitalist-class Congress, and capitalist-class legislatures, elected in every instance by an ignorant working class, kept ignorant, designedly, in the name of unionism, and with the aid of the labor lieutenants of the capitalist class? And that it is the very height of folly and depth of humiliation for a committee of the working class to beg the representatives of the capitalist class to legislate in the interests of the working class?

They were elected to serve the masters. And they are serving them. And we have no right to find fault with them— at least those of us who are responsible for their being where they are.

Now, we who have organized the Industrial Workers have had enough of this kind of experience. We have quit the old unions. We have organized the Industrial Workers for the purpose of uniting the working class; the whole working class. Not only the skilled workers, not only those who are favored, but the working class, skilled and unskilled, male and female, in every department of activity, are united upon the principle of Industrial Unionism.

The old unions were built up on tools that have been discarded and upon trades that have ceased to exist.

Half a century ago the trade union was right; it was adapted to the then existing industrial conditions. For illustration, a cooper shop was a cooper shop. It contained coopers and coopers only, and the Coopers' Union was organized. That embraced the coopers who were employed at their trade in the shop. Since then there has been half a century of industrial evolution. Compare the great cooperage establishment of today with the cooper shop of fifty years ago, in which the old hand tools were used, in which the apprentice learned his trade, and having mastered this, could seize the small tools with which work was done and virtually employ himself. There has been a marvelous change since that time. A modern cooperage establishment is the result of industrial evolution; and if you will visit one you will find that scores of different kinds of labor are performed there. Indeed, you will find almost any kind of worker there except a cooper!

Now, we behold that the form of the union must correspond to the mode of industry. In other words, the union, like the trade, is subject to the inexorable laws of evolution. We want a union today that expresses all the various subdivisions of labor now engaged in a cooperage establishment. Suppose there are 500 such employes in a plant. We organize them all, and they are assigned to their various departments; and if one of them has a grievance it becomes the concern of every worker in that establishment.

How is it now? Certain departments are organized in craft unions, meet with the officials and make an agreement or contract. They do not care what becomes of the rest, if only they can get what they are after for themselves. After they are thus tied up, the employes in some other department present a grievance and are turned down and out. They go out on strike. Those tied fast in an agreement say: "We would like to help you, we are in sympathy with you, but you see we have an agreement, and that agreement is sacred; it must be preserved inviolate; and while we are in sympathy with you and hate to see you defeated and lose your jobs, we cannot go back on our agreement." And in this way one union is used to crush another, labor is defeated and scabs are made by thousands.

It is a fact that nearly all scabs and strike-breakers are ex-unionists. Go among them and interrogate them and you will find that they will tell you in almost every case that at heart they are in favor of union labor, but that they were beaten by it and found this the only way of getting even. I know of hundreds of instances, of my own knowledge, of men who have been made scabs in precisely that way. Now, the trade unions feel very bitter toward scabs, and pursue them relentlessly until the unfortunates seek escape in suicide. And yet, while they so bitterly persecute the scab, they support the union that makes the scab.

What we want today, above all things, is united economic and political action, and we can never have that while the working class are parceled out among hundreds, aye, thou-

SPEECHES.

sands, of separate unions, that keep them divided for reasons, many of which very readily suggest themselves.

Who is it that is so violently opposed to the Industrial Workers? It is not the rank and file of the trade unions. It is their officers. And why are they so fiercely opposed to the Industrial Workers? For the reason that when the working class are really united a great many labor leaders will be out of jobs.

There are at present thousands of unions. Some of them have a few members and others have a great many; and every time, in the evolution of industry, there is a new subdivision of labor, however minute, a new union must be launched, clear down to the Grand International Brotherhood of Peanut Peelers, Polishers and Packers, or whatever it may be. And they elect a staff of their own grand international officers, and their names are put upon the payroll; and let me say to you that their interests are primarily in keeping themselves there.

Why should the railroad employes be parceled out among a score of different organizations? They are all employed in the same service. Their interests are mutual. They ought to be able to act together as one. But they divide according to craft and calling, and if you were to propose today to unite them that they might actually do something to advance their collective and individual interests as workers, you would be opposed by every grand officer of these organizations. The payroll and expense account of the officers of the railroad brotherhoods alone amount to more than a quarter of a million dollars a year.

There is an army of men who serve as officers who are on the salary list who get a good living keeping the working class divided. They start out with good intentions as a rule. They really want to do something to serve their fellows. They leave the shops or the mines as common workingmen. They are elected officers of a labor organization and they change their clothes. They now wear a white shirt and a standing collar. They change their habits and their methods. They have been used to cheap clothes, coarse fare and to associating with their fellow-workers. After they have been elevated to official position, as if by magic they are recognized by those who previously scorned them and held them in contempt. They find that some of the doors that were previously barred against them now swing inward, and they can actually put their feet under the mahogany of the capitalist.

Our common workingman is now a labor leader. The great capitalist pats him on the back and tells him that he knew long ago that he was a coming man, that it was a fortunate thing for the workers of the world that he had been born, that, in fact they had been long waiting for just such a wise and conservative leader. And this has a certain effect upon our new-made leader, and unconsciously, perhaps, he begins to change—just as John Mitchell did when Mark Hanna patted him on the shoulder and said, "John, it is a good thing you are at the head of the miners. You are the very man. You have the greatest opportunity a labor leader ever had on this earth. You can immortalize yourself. Now is your time." Then John Mitchell admitted that this capitalist, who had been pictured to him as a monster, was not half as bad as he had thought he was; that, in fact, he was a genial and companionable gentleman. He repeats his visit the next day, or the next week, and is introduced to some other distinguished person he had read about, but never dreamed of meeting, and thus goes on the transformation. All his dislikes disappear and all feeling of antagonism vanishes. He concludes that they are really most excellent people and, now that he has seen and knows them, he agrees with them that there is no necessary conflict between workers and capitalists. And he proceeds to carry out this pet capitalist theory and he can only do it by betraying the class that trusted him and lifted him as high above themselves as they could reach.

It is true that such a leader is in favor with the capitalists; that their newspapers write editorials about him and crown him a great and wise leader; and that ministers of the gospel make his name the text for their sermons, and emphasize the vital point that if all labor leaders were such as he there would be no objection to labor organizations. And the leader feels himself flattered. And when he is charged with having deserted the class he was supposed to serve, he cries out that the indictment is brought by a discredited labor leader. And that is probably true. The person who brings the charge is very likely discredited. By whom? By the capitalist class, of course; and its press and pulpit and "public" opinion. And in the present state of the working class, when he is discredited by the capitalists, he is at once repudiated by their wage-slaves.

The labor leader who is not discredited by the capitalist class is not true to the working class. If he be unswervingly loyal to the working class he will not be on friendly terms with the capitalist class. He cannot serve both. When he really serves one he serves that one against the other.

The labor leader who is in high favor with the exploiters is pronounced safe, conservative, wise and honest, and the workers are appealed to to look to him for advice, for guidance and leadership. The unthinking accept the advice with enthusiasm. And so the labor leader who serves the capitalist class instead of the working class is hailed deliverer and basks in the public favor.

But let me say to you that in spite of all this the honest and discredited leaders will be lovingly remembered long after the popular ones of today are forgotten.

Now, in these matters, I am not asking you to take my advice. I am not asking you to follow me. I simply want you to think over these things for yourselves. The very first need is that you open your eyes and see for yourselves. Take nothing for granted.

So many of you are satisfied to blindly follow where others lead; and so you are deceived and betrayed; you have to pay all the penalties.

It is high time you were ceasing to depend upon someone to "lead" you; that you were opening your eyes; that you were doing your own thinking. And that is all I am asking you to do.

I have already told you that I have had some experience and that I hope I have in some measure profited by it. I have been involved in strikes enough to satisfy me. I have so often been saddened by the outcome of such strikes.

I have seen men by scores and hundreds and thousands, after striking for weeks and months, lose their jobs. I have seen the poor wretches blacklisted and I have seen them persecuted until they were in rags, and their families were upon the streets, and I have said there must be another and a better way. I have seen enough of this to satisfy me. There is a better way. But you will never find it by pursuing the old lines. You have got to unite the whole working class, and this can be done. It is not an impossible task. Every worker, however limited his mentality, ought to be able to see that there is little or nothing to be accomplished along the old lines; that, in fact, there is no hope; that you are engaged in an unequal struggle, and that the ultimate outcome is certain to be defeat, despair and death.

The capitalists have at present ten thousand advantages over us. They own and control all the sources and means of wealth production. They are the masters of the tools; they act together. They control all the powers of government. They can at their own sweet will shut down their mills and factories and mines, and they can wait patiently weeks and months and even years, until the impoverished workers become hungry and are glad to be taken back at any terms. The capitalists have all these advantages, and they never hesitate to do anything, everything, that may be required to keep the working class in subjection. And they can and will keep them there just as long as they are divided.

There is but one hope, and that is in the economic and political solidarity of the working class; one revolutionary union, and one revolutionary party. It is for this reason that the Industrial Workers, an economic organization, has been launched and now makes its appeal to you as wage-slaves aspiring to be free. You cannot be satisfied to live and die as beasts of burden; to toil unceasingly to enrich masters who hold you in contempt; to be dependent upon these masters for your jobs and crawl like sycophants at their feet. You may not be satisfied, even though you have sufficient food and clothing and shelter. You are a human, not a hog; a man, not a mere animal. You have a manhood to sustain; you have your freedom to achieve, and you have an intellect to develop; and these questions will appeal to you with ever-increasing force and compel an accounting at last, if you have the pith and purpose of a typical, self-respecting workingman.

In the capitalist system you workers are simply merchandise; your master can at his own will sentence you to idleness, your wife to want and your child, perhaps, to a brothel. You cannot be satisfied with such a slavish lot and now is the time to make up your mind to change it. In your heart you will feel the thrill of a new-born joy. You will join the Industrial Workers, the one international labor union that proposes to unite all workers, that all of them may act together in harmonious co-operation for the good of all; a union that recognizes no aristocracy, but the whole working class; that insists that each member shall have all the rights that are accorded every other; a union built upon the class struggle, appealing to all workers to get together on the right side of that struggle and achieve the emancipation of their class.

It is true that this is a stupendous task; that there are great opposing forces; that every falsehood that malignity can devise will be put in circulation to defeat the object of this industrial organization, but nevertheless, those of us who have quitted the old unions and organized the Industrial Workers have done so with the determination that no matter what opposing forces may be set in operation, we will stand together side by side in the true spirit of class-conscious solidarity; we will move forward, step by step, in one solid body; we will speak the truth as we see the truth, and defy all the opposition that may be brought to bear against the Industrial Workers by all the capitalist class and all its vassals and emissaries.

This organization has a mission as high and as noble as ever prompted workingmen, or any other men, to action in this world.

The primal need of the working class is education. By education I mean revolutionary education; the kind that enables men to see that the twenty odd millions of wage-workers in the United States are wage-slaves; that the economic interests of these many millions of human beings who do all the useful work and produce all the wealth are absolutely identical; that they must unite; that they must act together; that they must assert their collective power. When they reach this point they will cease to be slaves and become the masters of the situation; they will wipe out the wage-system and walk the earth free men.

They can do this, and only *they can* do it.

I cannot do this for you, and I want to be frank enough to say that I would not if I could. For if I could do it for you, somebody else could undo it for you. But when you do it for yourselves it will remain done forever. And until you do it you have got to pay the penalty of your ignorance, indifference and neglect. You have got to pay it to the last farthing. Nobody on earth or in heaven can relieve you of the consequences of your inaction. As long as you workers remain divided and at cross purposes, instead of closing up the ranks and acting together, you will have to pay the penalty of defeat and humiliation and slavery and all their attendant brood and festering evils.

But day by day you are increasing the sum of your revolutionary knowledge. You are becoming wiser by experience. The Industrial Workers would not have been possible a few years ago. It is an outgrowth of the very conditions I have described. It has become an imperative necessity. The workers everywhere are beginning to recognize it, and that is why they are flocking to its standard. That is why they are subscribing to its principles; why they are working for it day and night with a zeal that has never been known in the history of the organized working-class movement; and why it is rapidly spreading over the whole country, and increasing grandly in numbers and in power. Let me say to you that no matter what formidable or subtle opposition may be marshaled against it by the capitalist class the ultimate triumph of its principles is as certain as that I stand in your presence.

There are a great many workers who insist that the old unions are good enough; and as long as they are of that opinion that is where they belong. So far as I am concerned I gave the old unions a fair trial. I am sure I had no prejudice against them. I am equally sure I did all I possibly could to build them up. For fifteen years I traveled almost continuously over this country organizing railroad men, and all kinds of workingmen, under the mistaken conviction that if we could only get them into the several unions of their trades and occupations we could in some way lift them out of their slavery. My mind was disabused. We had the railroad men, especially in this part of the country, pretty thoroughly organized. We had the numbers and to some extent the power, but we didn't know about the class struggle. We had that to learn. Then came the great conflict with the combined railroad corporations. We defeated them; and then we learned that the corporations control the powers of government. We got our first vital lesson in the class struggle. All the corporations had to do was to press the judicial button in their private office and the judges acted promptly in obedience to the command of their capitalist masters; the police and militia and regular troops followed in regular order; the press and pulpit and deputy marshals did the rest—and that was enough.

I never knew exactly how it happened until I understood the meaning of economic determinism and the class struggle, and then it was perfectly clear to me. And from that time I realized the imperative necessity for a different kind of organization. I then said, we have got to organize, not only the railroad employes, but the whole body of workers for concerted economic and political action; organize them all, so that all of them shall act together and assert the full measure of their power in the interests of all. As soon as a beginning was attempted the railroad corporations said, "This vicious thing must be stamped out of existence," and so, for two years, I scarcely traveled a foot without being shadowed by detectives of the railroad corporations. No matter where I went, the detectives were there. When I would reach the end of a certain line the detectives who had followed me would go back where they came from and others would take their places.

I remember when I got to Providence, Rhode Island, one night, I was conscious that detectives were watching me very closely. I learned that the railroad officials in New England had announced that the American Railway Union should never get a foothold there. There were two or three loyal men there I knew and could trust; I sent them word not to come to the hotel and not to hold a meeting, but to come to my room at midnight, and come one at a time. And they did come to my room one at a time and I organized them in my room at midnight. I left the city early next morning, and when I got to the next point I received a telegram reporting that they were all discharged, every one of them.

Notwithstanding our secrecy the corporations knew who had entered my room and for what purpose; and the men were summarily discharged. Why was it that the railroad corporations would not allow the American Railway Union to organize? For the simple reason that the American Railway Union proposed to line up all the railroad employes as the beginning of a thorough reorganization of the working class in general, and the railroads did not propose to tolerate that kind of an organization.

They were and are entirely satisfied with the old brotherhoods, supplying their officers with annual passes and their delegates with special trains to take them to and from their conventions. To such an extent is this partiality carried on some railroads that if a member of one of the brotherhoods refuses to pay his dues and is expelled by the brotherhood, he is promptly discharged by the corporation. The corporation favors the organizations that divide, but is implacably hostile to the one that unites the workers.

For the same reason the capitalist newspapers have so ferociously denounced the Industrial Workers.

They have warned workingmen that the Industrial Workers consists of anarchists, socialists, revolutionists and chronic fault-finders and peace-disturbers, who have been kicked out of other reputable labor organizations; of discredited leaders who do not lead, in whom the workers have no confidence and for whom they can have no respect.

The capitalist press is a unit in denouncing the Industrial Workers, and practically a unit in commending the American Federation of Labor.

If you workers think that the capitalist press is a safe guide in such a matter, you properly belong with the American Federation of Labor. But if you believe, as I believe, and as every intelligent workingman must believe, that the kind of labor organization that the capitalists endorse is not the kind that is for your good—that the organization the capitalist press condemns is the one that has working class virtue and efficiency—then you will do as we have done; you will join the Industrial Workers of the World.

Think it over for yourself!

Take a backward look over the last three or four years; satisfy yourself by your own study and observation that there has been little but defeat for the workers in the struggle during all that period; that they have gained substantially nothing; that they are divided and disrupted and not organized in any true sense at all. The time has come for a real economic organization of the workers, and that organization is now in the field and makes its appeal to all workers, and its principles and purposes deserve the encouragement, the support and the loyalty of every workingman who has intelligence enough to understand his best interests and manhood enough to assert and stand by them.

I shall occupy your time no longer. I think that no great argument is required in support of our position. The preamble to the constitution states clearly and in few words the object of the Industrial Workers. You will find it written there that the workers and capitalists have nothing in common; that there are a few who have all the good things in life, while millions writhe in poverty and cry out in despair; that those who do nothing and produce nothing are rich, while those who do everything and produce everything are poor; that these two classes consist of capitalists who own tools they do not use, and of workers who use tools they do not own; that the capitalists who own the tools have it in their power to take and do take from the workers what they produce, and that the workers must organize both their economic and political power to take and hold that which they produce by their labor.

This is brief and to the point, and every workingman is capable of understanding it.

As the chairman has stated, the Industrial Workers has no object in concealing any part of its mission, and while it proposes to ameliorate the condition of the workers in every way in its power as far as that is possible in capitalist society, its ultimate object is to entirely abolish the capitalist system, by making the workers themselves the masters of their tools, that they may work freely, unrestrained and unexploited; that they may secure to themselves and enjoy all the fruit of their own labors.

This is the object of the Industrial Workers, and if it has

your approval, join it and help it to fulfill its mission, and thus hasten the emancipation of the working class, and the brighter, happier day for all humanity.

QUESTIONS.

Q. In the Industrial Workers are you going to separate the different trades, or has a man who joins the privilege of going where he chooses?

Mr. Debs: He joins the department that represents his particular trade or occupation. The Industrial Workers is organized in separate departments, so that the autonomy of the trade is preserved within the organization. Take the men of a certain trade; they belong to a certain department of the organization; they have jurisdiction over their own trade affairs. They are subject, however, to the supervision of the general organization. Take the machinists, for instance; they have a grievance; it will be adjusted, primarily, if possible, within their own department. If that is not possible then it becomes the grievance of the general organization—the concern of all. Instead of merely the machinists going out on strike as now, all their fellow-workers lay down their tools and support them to a finish.

Q. Is it true that the Industrial Workers was organized because the workers cannot gain anything by political action?

Mr. Debs: No, that is not true. The workers have never yet tried to get anything by united political action. They will some time, I do not doubt. The Industrial Workers was organized because under the old form of organization they could get little or nothing by economic action. If they had secured satisfactory concessions under the old forms there would be no Industrial Workers. It has been organized because of the failure of the old unions on the economic field. Now, if it can be shown that they have succeeded, or even measureably succeeded, then there is no necessity for the Industrial Workers. But if, on the other hand, it can be shown that they have repeatedly and wretchedly failed, then there is an unanswerable argument in favor of the Industrial Workers.

Q. What is a tradesman or a skilled worker? Why should

there be any distinction between a tradesman and any other worker in a shop?

Mr. Debs: That is not a very easy question to answer. There used to be a great many skilled mechanics who are now common workers. In proportion as machinery is improved the skill of the trade is transferred from the worker to the machine; and the skilled labor of one day becomes the common labor of the next. The locomotive engineer has always regarded himself as a skilled worker, and he has refused to affiliate with what is called the common laborer. Within the next few years the locomotive engineer will probably become a motorman and he will then come off the perch. The work will be so simple that almost any worker can perform it. I have already referred to the coopers. In the town where I live there used to be a number of cooper shops in which there were skilled men; and they had a large and strong Coopers' Union. All the coopers that worked there belonged to it. And these coopers didn't have anything to do with common labor. They flocked by themselves upon the theory that they were skilled men and could not afford to put their skill on the same level with the common labor of unskilled workers. During the last few years that trade has undergone a complete change. The skilled coopers have practically disappeared and but a shadow of the old union remains.

Now, if you will ask that old cooper, who was a skilled man and belonged to a union that represented skilled labor a few years ago—if you will ask him who the skilled man is, I think he can give you a satisfactory answer to your question. The skill of the trade is being gradually eliminated, and we are taking cognizance of that fact. We Industrial Workers recognize no aristocracy of skill. If any partiality were to be shown, however, I would give the unskilled man the benefit of it, because he needs it most. But there is no such discrimination in the Industrial Workers. The workingman, skilled or unskilled, is a worker; a man, and, whatever his occupation, has all of the wants and aspirations and is entitled to all the rights and opportunities of a human being for self-development. The machine is rapidly reducing workers to a common industrial equality, making the unskilled man the productive equal of the

27

skilled man. The machine is the skilled man, and when he gets through, that question will have answered itself.

Q. Does the Industrial Workers make any provision for a wage scale?

Mr. Debs: Yes; it is going to get all the wages for its members that it possibly can, while the wage-system lasts.

Q. How are you going to prevent the leaders from being as bad as those of the trades unions are today?

Mr. Debs: In the first place, there will be but a single organization. There will not be a hundred different and conflicting organizations and as many different sets of officers.

Q. Then they will have only one to buy; it won't cost so much.

Mr. Debs: All the chances will be reduced to the minimum. Take the railroad brotherhoods, for instance. If every locomotive engineer running into Chicago voted tomorrow to go out on strike they could not go out without the official sanction of the Grand Chief of the Brotherhood of Locomotive Engineers, and he alone could prevent the strike. That is, they might vote unanimously to strike, but the power of one single grand officer would outweigh that of the entire organization. With us it is the rank and file that decides and is the supreme power. It is not likely they will sell themselves out. Besides, the Industrial Workers is made up of a body of class-conscious industrial revolutionists, who will not be sold out. They are wide-awake workers who think for themselves, and that is why they are in the Industrial Workers. The old trade unions are mainly run by the officers. Didn't you notice in the papers this morning that the coal operators who were here in session declared that they proposed to deal, not with the rank and file, the common herd, but with the national officers of the union? They will settle things, and that is how they are generally settled in the old unions; but that is not the way they will be settled in the Industrial Workers.

This is an important point. Take a plant such as a brewery, for instance; a score of different kinds of labor represented by as many different organizations, and as many different sets of officers. Here are temptation and opportunity multiplied by twenty. Here we have wide-open chances and incentive to bribery, corruption and treachery. Suppose now, that the same plant is organized in the Industrial Workers. Instead of being parceled out among twenty different unions they are all embraced in one. The men in one department have a grievance. That plant has a general committee; and if the grievance fails of adjustment in the department in which it arises, it is referred to the general committee that has supervision of the plant, and if they fail to satisfactorily adjust it, the matter goes to all the employes, as Industrial Workers, for action. They vote to go out on strike and that settles it. In the Industrial Workers no national officer and no set of national officers have power to override the action of the rank and file. And when they vote to go out, they go out and stay out, until they vote to go back.

Class Unionism

Speech at South Chicago, November 24, 1905

The year now drawing to a close will be memorable in the annals of labor because of the organization of the Industrial Workers of the World.

For thirty years I have been connected with the labor movement. All of the years of my young manhood were devoted to the work of organizing my fellow-workingmen, that by the power of united effort they might do something to improve their condition as workers, promote their interests as citizens and advance their general welfare as men. There was a time when I believed that the trade union was in itself sufficient for this work. I have been compelled to revise my opinion and to conclude that something larger, more thorough and comprehensive in the way of organization is required to meet the demands of modern times.

The trade union, itself the product of industrial evolution, is subject to the laws of change, and the union that may have served some purpose a quarter of a century ago is now as completely out of date as the tools of industry that were then in use.

Now, I assume that most of you are more or less familiar with the history of the industrial development of the land; that you know in a general way that in the beginning of industrial society in the United States, when the tool with which work was done was a simple hand tool, made and used by an individual, the average workingman could look forward to the time when he would be an employer instead of an employe; that, having mastered his trade, he could grasp the few simple tools with which his work was done, virtually employ himself, own what he produced and enjoy the fruit of his labor.

At that time one man worked for another, not in the capacity of a wage worker as we understand that term today, but simply to learn his trade, and having become the master of this he was in a position to command most, if not all, his labor produced. It was when the simple tool of the hand laborer was supplanted by the machine and the workingman lost control of the tool with which he worked, that the modern industrial revolution had its beginning. The small employer became the capitalist and the employe became the wage worker; and there began the division of society into two distinct economic classes, and we have these classes before us today, in capitalist society, fully developed.

These two classes, consisting of relatively few capitalists who own tools in the form of great machines that they did not make and that they cannot use, and of a vast army of wage workers who did make these machines and who do use them, but who do not own them—these two classes, tool-owners and tool-users; that is to say, masters and slaves, exploiters and exploited; to put it into perfectly plain terms, robbers and robbed—these two economic forces whose interests ceaselessly clash, are pitted against each other in a mighty struggle for the mastery. It is because of this conflict of economic interests between these two classes into which modern society has been divided in the evolution of the capitalist system that we have the strike, the boycott, the lockout, the scab, the strike-breaker and slugger, and countless other evils that need not be enumerated here, all of which spring from the fundamental contradiction that inheres in capitalist society; that is, the individual ownership of the social tool of production and the individual appropriation of the social product of the working class.

Because of this, the capitalist who does no useful work has the economic power to take from a thousand or ten thousand workingmen all they produce, over and above what is required to keep them in working and producing order, and he becomes a millionaire, perhaps a multi-millionaire. He lives in a palace in which there is music and singing and dancing and the luxuries of all climes. He sails the high seas in his private yacht. He is the reputed "captain of industry" who privately owns a social utility, has great economic power, and commands the political power of the nation to protect his economic interests. He is the gentleman who furnishes the "political boss" and his swarm of mercenaries with the funds with which the politics of the nation are corrupted and debauched. He is the economic master and the political ruler; and you workingmen are almost as completely at his mercy as if you were his property under the law. It is true that he has no title to your bodies; but he is the master of your jobs; he controls the employment upon which your lives depend; he has it in his power to decide whether you shall work or not; that is to say, whether you shall live or die. And the man who has the power of life and death over you, though he may not wear a crown or be hailed a king, is as completely your master and your ruler as if you were his chattels and subject to his commands under the laws of the state.

What is your status as a workingman today? You are not in the position of your grandfather, who could work with tools of his own, and who, when he produced something, was the master of it. Work is no longer done with that kind of tools. It is done with the most intricate and costly machinery, such as you have in this great steel plant here in South Chicago. That is the twentieth century tool of production. Work is now done with that kind of gigantic social agencies, made by you workingmen and used by you workingmen. Nobody but workingmen can make them; nobody but workingmen can use them.

You have made all these marvelous machines and now your employment, your very lives, depend upon your having access to them. But these large grown tools, made by labor and used by labor, are not owned by labor in the capitalist system, but belong to a capitalist or group of capitalists who live in New York or some other remote point; and when it suits their pleasure they can order their tool houses locked up and you workingmen locked out without consulting you and without a moment's warning. You have not a word to say. At such a time it is useless for you to leave here and look for work elsewhere, for when this mill closes down so do others. You are out of employment and you begin to suffer, and most of you don't know what the trouble is. You only know that you are no longer wanted at the mill; that workers are a drug on the market. With these wonderful tools with which you now work, every few years you have produced so much that all of the markets at home and abroad are glutted, and the capitalists cannot sell what you have produced in such abundance, and so they stop their machinery, shut up their mills, lock out their "hands" and paralyze industry, and there you are, idle, helpless, hungry, hopeless, desperate. And these conditions will come upon you and become worse, no matter how well you are organized in your several trade unions; and this will continue as long as you workingmen allow the idle capitalists to own and control the tools of industry.

Has it ever occurred to you workingmen that if you could make these tools and use them you can also own them and produce wealth in plenty for yourselves?

The old trade union is organized on the basis of the identity of interests of capitalists and wage workers, and spends its time and devotes its energies to harmonizing these two classes; and it is a vain and hopeless task. When these interests can be even temporarily harmonized it is always in the interest of the capitalist class, and at the expense of the working class.

Most capitalists heartily approve the old form of trade unionism and encourage and liberally support it, for the very reason that this outgrown unionism does not truly represent and cannot actually express the economic interests of the working class.

The simple fact is that industrial conditions have undergone such a complete change that now the trade union, instead of uniting the workers, divides them, incites craft jealousy, breeds dissension and promotes strife—the very things capitalists desire; for so long as the working class is divided, the capitalists will be secure in their dominion of the earth and the seas, and the millions of toilers will remain in subjection.

Now, let me see if I can make myself perfectly clear upon this important point. In the railroad service there are various organizations of employes. Some of the departments are pretty thoroughly organized. The engineers, the firemen, conductors, brakemen, switchmen, telegraphers and some others are organized in their several craft unions. They have repeatedly tried to federate these organizations, so as to bring them into harmonious alliance with each other, but every such attempt has failed. The selfish spirit of craft autonomy, that is, the jealousy of each particular branch to organize itself, establish its own petty supremacy and look out for itself, has made it impossible to federate these organizations. The members of these brotherhoods have increasing grievances and try to have them adjusted in the old way. The railroad corporations are always shrewd enough to enter into contractual relations with unions representing two or three or four departments, so that in every emergency they can always control these departments, while refusing increases, making reductions or discharging without cause employes in other departments of the service.

It has not been long ago since the union operators on the Missouri, Kansas & Texas directed their committee to call on the railroad officials for a small wage concession that had been granted by other systems. But the company, having contracts with its engineers and firemen, conductors and brakemen, peremptorily refused the request of the telegraphers, and about 1,300 of them went out on strike—quit the service of the company, as a union, to enforce their demands. What was the result? This large body of union workingmen who thus went out on strike to enforce a righteous claim all lost their jobs, every one of them.

It was only a short time after they struck that I happened to go over the system. I met the strikers at various points and they told me the story of their defeat by their own fellow employes who belong to other unions. I understood it all before they told me. When the operators went out all the others remained at their posts, doing their usual work, and hauling and delivering scabs, wherever they were needed, to fill the places vacated by their fellow workers and fellow craft unionists. Union engineers and conductors took their train orders from scab operators; all the union men stood loyally by the company in its attack on one of their number, and so the operators were routed and scattered to the four winds and their union wiped from the system.

Here we have a perfect illustration of craft unionism in action. Another example is furnished by the Santa Fe system where but a few months ago the union machinists went out from one end of the system to the other. The engineers and firemen, conductors and brakemen, and all the rest of them holding union cards, remained faithfully at work until a new set of machinists was employed and broken in, and now everything is running as smoothly as before.

Still another case of recent date is that of the Great Northern and the Northern Pacific systems, where the telegraph operators, after having failed in securing an adjustment of their grievances, went out on strike in a body, under orders from their union. What happened there? Just what had happened on the M., K. & T. The engineers, firemen, conductors and brakemen continued at their posts and discharged their duties with fidelity while their brother unionists, the operators, were mowed down and their places filled with scabs.

It is this that is taking place before our eyes every day. Here in Chicago you have witnessed the crushing defeat of one regiment after another of the army of organized labor. Indeed, during the last two or three years all the great strikes have failed. There has not been a single exception to relieve the rule, not one.

Now, when you see such things as these; when you see workingmen in craft unions go out on strike again and again and meet with constant defeat, does it not occur to you that there is something wrong with that kind of unionism? That that kind of unionism can be improved upon? Doesn't it occur to you that instead of fighting the capitalist enemy, who are always united, who always act together—that instead of fighting them by squads and companies, the thing for us to do is to fight them as they fight us, with a united and compact army?

In this respect, if no other, we may well profit by the example set by the enemy. They unite, because they are conscious of their interests as a class. When the teamsters struck in this city last summer, the bankers subscribed $50,000 to defeat them. Now, the teamsters were not striking against the bankers; but the teamsters were striking against the capitalist class; and the bankers sprang loyally to the support of their class. And this brings an important fact to our attention, and that is that the struggle in which we are engaged today is a class struggle, and labor organization, to be of any value to the working class, must be formed, not along craft lines, but along class lines.

The Industrial Workers is a working class organization, so all-inclusive, so comprehensive, that it will embrace every man and woman who works for a livelihood. Certain departments have been established and certain subdivisions have been made, so that the identity of the trade, the autonomy of the craft may be preserved within the organization. Joining the Industrial Workers you take your place in your proper department. That department which represents your employment is organized, it has control of craft interests within its jurisdiction, so that, so far as craft autonomy is concerned, it adjusts itself within the general organization.

Suppose you join the Industrial Workers as a switchman. You belong to the transportation department. You have a grievance, as a switchman, and the switchmen have charge of that grievance. The switchmen, organized in their respective department, having supervision of their craft affairs, seek to adjust that grievance. If they fail, then, instead of having to rely upon the switchmen alone in the support of that grievance, as now happens, they can call to their aid, not only all the switchmen, but the firemen, the conductors, the brakemen and engineers. They can call to their aid the boilermakers, the machinists and the blacksmiths, the shopmen and yardmen and office men; and, if it becomes necessary, they can command the combined support of all the organized workers of that entire system.

That is the kind of unionism required to deal effectively with the industrial situation of today.

Now, I am well aware that there is tremendous opposition to this organization. I know that upon every hand you hear it said that we already have plenty of organizations in the field, and that if they are not right we ought to set them right instead of starting a new one. This kind of reasoning may have some effect with the unthinking, but if you are a student of this great question you know that it is historically impossible for an old and outgrown and out-of-date labor organization to adjust itself to a new economic mission.

Reform unions rarely, if ever, become revolutionary bodies. It is admitted that there are thousands of unions in the field. These unions all have staffs of officers, whose name is legion and on the payroll. They all draw salaries and expense money. They don't want the working class united—that would mean an army of jobless leaders. You would be amazed if you knew how many of such union officials there are; and you would be still more amazed if you knew the aggregate amount of salary and expenses, millions of dollars, they draw every year. Now, they, like you, are looking out for their jobs. It is perhaps too much to expect them to discharge themselves. It is to their personal interest to keep the workers of the country divided into a thousand different organizations, so that a thousand different sets of officials will be required; so that a thousand sets of officials may draw salary from the scant wages of the working class. You may be told that the reason I am in favor of a new union is that I am a discredited labor leader and that I am trying to create a new job for myself. The truth is that if I had been inclined to serve the corporations instead of the workers I could have been drawing a large salary and enjoying to the full the popularity of what is miscalled successful labor leadership.

You railroad men know that the late P. M. Arthur, grand chief of the Brotherhood of Locomotive Engineers, was called by the capitalist press a very successful labor leader. He was successful only in the sense that he served with far greater fidelity the corporations than he did the employes who paid his salary. I can remember the time when most of the present grand officers of the railroad brotherhoods denounced Mr. Arthur of the Engineers, because of his conservative and reactionary policy. All of these grand officers occupy today precisely the same position that he did, and which they condemned. They are now just as acceptable to the railroads as was Mr. Arthur. These corporations not only do not object to, but actually favor the leaders of these brotherhoods. In fact the corporation officials find these organizations very serviceable to them, and they would far rather have them than not. They could wipe them out—and they would if they were a menace to them—but they will not do it.

SPEECHES.   409

A little thing occurred the other day which will prove what I say. I do not know whether you happen to be aware of it, but the Brotherhood of Engineers and the Brotherhood of Firemen on the Northern Pacific a few weeks ago, clashed in the matter of jurisdiction; and that matter is becoming more and more a plague to crafts unionism. The grand officers of the two brotherhoods met at St. Paul, and they had quite a heated controversy, which had a most sensational climax, grand chief Warren Stone, of the engineers, hotly declaring to Grand Master Hannehan, of the firemen, that if it came to a "showdown" the engineers would remain at their posts and if the firemen went out on strike, the engineers would stay with the corporation and defeat the firemen. Now, the general manager of the Northern Pacific, had he been so inclined, could have encouraged these two craft unions to clash and wipe each other from the system. But the railway official was too wise to allow this to be done. He kindly interceded and told them that they ought not to quarrel with each other, that they should in truth love each other; and so he succeeded in saving the unions and restoring harmonious relations.

The general manager appreciated the value of craft organization and proposed to preserve it for future use. Note again: the railroads grant annual passes to all the grand officers of these several organizations. Why? Because they love you railroad employes? Not at all; but because they are wise enough to understand their interests as corporations, as capitalists. So you find that the grand officers of craft unions ride free over railroads; and when the several brotherhoods hold their conventions they are provided with trains and Pullman cars and transported to the convention city and back again free of charge. This is one of the best investments the railroads could make.

It costs them very little to furnish the delegates with free transportation; and every penny of it comes out of your earnings. They know that as you are now organized you can do little for yourselves, but that you can do much for them. That is why they are so partial to the old organizations.

Let me point out one of the ways they use you when they need you. President Roosevelt is championing a measure that is to empower the Interstate Commerce Commission to fix the rates of railroads in certain cases. This measure is opposed by the railroad corporations. They do not want the government to interfere with their right to fix rates to suit themselves. What do they do? They send for the grand chiefs of the several brotherhoods and a conference is held. Then the press dispatches announce that the railroad and brotherhood officials are one in their opposition to the proposed rate-fixing legislation. A few days later a joint session is held of the standing committees of the several brotherhoods and they decide to stand by the railroads; and so they call upon President Roosevelt and serve notice upon him that they and the unions they represent are opposed to rate legislation.

In this the unions appear for the railroads; the brotherhoods being the puppets of the corporations; and in the meantime the railroad magnates announce through the press that the employes are up in arms and will assert the political power of their unions in opposition to the rate-fixing measure.

Not that there is anything of interest in rate legislation so far as you are concerned, but there is a vital point involved. When the railroads find it necessary to use the brotherhoods as breastworks, or as weapons with which to fight their battles, they issue their orders and the grand officers and unions fall in line to the tune "our interests are mutual and we must stand together." The unions then are made the active allies of the corporations in robbing and defying the people.

It is just because the corporations find these organizations exceedingly useful that they make petty concessions to them. I recognized this fact a number of years ago, and concluded then that what was needed for the employes was a real working class union embracing them all. The American Railway Union was organized. There are those present who were in the great strike of 1894, and you know how bitterly we were fought by the railroad corporations. You remember that they were not satisfied with merely defeating us—and they never would have beaten us had they not been in control of the government. But for this the victory would have been won for the working class. They were defeated, completely; and when they realized this they had their 3,600 thugs and thieves and convicts sworn in as deputy United States marshals, and they incited the riots and led the mobs, and then the courts issued their injunctions, while the capitalist press flashed the lurid reports over the wires that Chicago was at the mercy of a mob. The rest followed as a matter of course.

But they were not satisfied with mere defeat of the strike. They must crush the life out of the union. For two years after I was released by the courts—after being eighteen months in their custody—I was followed by their detectives, to prevent organization; and those who were reported as joining, or even as being friendly, were instantly discharged.

They defeated us, but they didn't destroy us. We are stronger today than we ever were, and we are coming again. We are on the main track. We are not after a few pennies more a day this time. We are after the whole works.

Yes, for two years after I was finally released, they followed me from one end of the country to the other. They kept their detectives at my heels. And the order preceded me everywhere that the employes who had anything to do with Debs would be discharged.

I concluded to go into those sections where the American Railway Union had not been organized, and where there had been no strike; and I started south. When I reached Louisville, the morning paper contained press despatches with startling headlines reporting a series of resolutions passed by the railroad employes of that section, saying: "Whereas, we are advised that E. V. Debs, the anarchist, of Chicago, is on his way south to disrupt the pleasant and harmonious relations that exist between the railroad employes and the companies; therefore, be it resolved, that we hereby serve notice on said anarchist, Debs, that we repudiate him and that we have nothing to do with him nor the anarchist organization he represents."

After these resolutions appeared I had a number of letters from the poor slaves who were employed upon these railroads, apologizing for the resolutions, and saying that the railroad officials had prepared and submitted them to the employes for their signatures, and then given them to the press.

But even this was not sufficient. They discharged those

who attended our meetings. They had their special men at the doors of meeting places to take the names of those who attended. They were determined to annihilate the union and stamp out the last spark of its life. And they did succeed in crushing the organization, but they could not kill the spirit of the American Railway Union. That still lives.

A far greater organization has come to take its place—as much greater as the American Railway Union was greater than the old union—and that organization is the Industrial Workers of the World. This great union is organized on the basis of the class struggle. It makes its appeal to the intelligence of the working class. It commands you workingmen to open your eyes and see for yourselves; to use your brains, and think for yourselves; to cultivate self-reliance and learn to depend upon yourselves. That is your only safety.

You have been taught in the old union school to look to some leader; to depend upon some master. You have been trained to submit; to follow and obey orders. You have not developed your own capacity for thinking; you are lacking in the essentials of sturdy manhood. Many of you have become satisfied to blindly follow where others lead; and so you are often deceived, betrayed; and when the smoke of battle clears away you find yourselves defeated and out of jobs. You have often felt disheartened; you have quit the union in despair and disgust, and some of you have turned into scabs.

Thousands who once belonged to unions have become, not only non-union men, but scabs and strike-breakers, and in their desperation have turned upon the union and become its most bitter enemies. If you will call the roll of the strike-breakers who gather here in Chicago and elsewhere when union workers are out on strike, you will find that nearly all of them are ex-union men; men who once wore the badge of union labor, believed in it and marched proudly beneath the union banner.

What do you think of a unionism that creates an army for its own overthrow? There is something fundamentally wrong with that kind of unionism.

Long since, and after years of study and experience, I became convinced that the old unions are not fit to cope successfully with the enemy of the working class, and that a new organization was an imperative necessity.

In the Industrial Workers we have a union large enough to embrace us all; a union organized upon democratic principles recognizing the equal rights of all and extending its benefits equally to all.

Industrial unionism is the principle upon which the Industrial Workers is organized. This means actual unity of purpose and action. It means the economic solidarity of our class. It means that the grievance of one is the concern of all; and that from this time forward craft division is to be eliminated; that we are to get together and fight and win together for all. Industrial unionism means that such a plant as you have here in South Chicago, in which ten or twelve thousand men are employed, shall be thoroughly and efficiently organized.

What is the condition there today? You have innumerable unions represented there, but no unity. You have this great body of workers parceled out among scores of petty and purposeless unions, which are in ceaseless conflict with each other, jealous to preserve their craft identity. As long as this great army of workers is scattered among so many craft unions, it will be impossible for them to unite and act in harmony together.

Craft unionism is the negation of solidarity. The more unions you have, the less unity; and here, in fact, you have no unity at all. In this state you can do nothing to improve your working condition. You are substantially at the mercy of the corporation.

What you need is industrial unionism and you will have it when you get together in the Industrial Workers.

When workingmen join the one economic working class organization that unites them upon the basis of the class struggle they can do something to better their working condition; not only will they have the economic power to do this, but they will represent a new and a vital force to which they are now total strangers—the revolutionary force that industrial unionism generates in the body.

There is something far different between a strike on the part of unions in which men are ignorant, blindly striking against something that they only vaguely understand, with no comprehension of the class struggle—there is something vastly different between that kind of a strike and the strike of the body of class-conscious, revolutionary workingmen, who, while they are striking for an immediate advantage, at the same time have their eyes clearly fixed upon the goal. And what is that goal? It is the overthrow of the capitalist system and the emancipation of the working class from wage-slavery.

The Industrial Workers is essentially an educational organization—and one of the vitally important things it will teach the workers is the complete operation and control of the industry in which they are employed. Have you ever thought about that? Has it ever been brought to your attention in craft unions?

I have already reminded you that you workingmen have made all the machinery there is in operation everywhere; that only you can use it. Now, why should not you own it?

Why shouldn't you be your own employers? Why shouldn't you be the masters of your own jobs? Why depend upon the capitalist for a chance to work? Why clothe him with the power to discharge and starve you at his will? Why engage him to take from you all you produce except enough to keep you at work? That is all that remains for you.

You get a wage, and that wage suffices to keep you working for the capitalist. The tool you work with has got to be oiled, and you have got to be fed. The wage is simply your lubricant. The wage oils you and keeps you in working order.

The capitalist doesn't intend that you shall ever be anything but his wage-slave. He would scout the suggestion that you are his equal. He doesn't associate with you. He belongs to another class; and the class to which he belongs is called the upper class. You, as a workingman, belong to the lower class. The working class has always been the lower class, and is today; and you will be the lower class as long as you are content to be that class. It is in your power to make yourselves the upper class, and in fact the only class. You are in an overwhelming majority. There are only a few capitalists as compared to you. And yet, they own practically everything and rule the land; and will keep on owning and ruling the land as long as you workingmen allow them to; and you will allow them to as long as you persist in remaining divided in trade unions and being used against each other, instead of uniting and acting solidly with and for each other and against the capitalists.

The Industrial Workers is organized—and we declare it boldly—to fight the capitalist class. We want it distinctly understood that we claim nothing in common with that class. They have economic interests separate from and opposed to the economic interests of the working class. And we propose that the working class shall be organized economically and politically to retire the capitalist class from business.

Our business is to put the exploiters of labor out of business.

You, Mr. Workingman, don't need a capitalist; and if you think you do, it is because you are ignorant. It is because you don't understand your own interest. You don't need him. You imagine that he gives you a job; but he does nothing of the kind. You give him a job. You employ him to take from you what you produce; and he faithfully sticks to his job. Why, the capitalist could not exist a second without you. Can you imagine a capitalist without workingmen?

Capitalism is based upon the exploitation of the working class; and when the working class ceases to be exploited, there will no longer be any capitalists.

Now, while the capitalist could not exist without you, you would just begin to live without him. He is on your back; he rides you, and he rides you even when he rides in the automobile that you make. You make it. You never knew of a capitalist that ever made an automobile. The capitalist doesn't make it but rides in it; the workingman does make it but does not ride in it.

If it were not for you the capitalist would have to walk, and if it were not for him you would ride.

You don't need the capitalist; he is, in fact, a curse to you. What has the capitalist owner of a modern plant to do with its operation? Absolutely nothing. He might as well live in the moon, as far as you are concerned. There may be a group of them, but they have nothing to do with the mill. They simply get what is produced there, because you will have it so. You are organized on that basis. In your moss-covered old unions you say, "Our interests are mutual." Certainly, if you can stand this arrangement the capitalist can. He has no grievance.

He does nothing and gets everything, and you do everything and get nothing.

If you can stand this he can; and if you don't put an end to it he won't. And why should he? And why shouldn't you? Mr. Workingman, you are a man. You ought not to be satisfied to be a mere wealth-producing animal. You have a brain, and you ought to develop it. You should aspire to rise above the animal plane. If you can work in a mill and produce wealth for a capitalist, who holds you in contempt, you can also work in that mill as a free man and produce wealth for yourself and your wife and family to enjoy. If not, why not?

It is upon this basis that the Industrial Workers is organized. It is for this supreme mission that the Industrial Workers has entered the field.

We have declared war upon the capitalist class, and upon the capitalist system. We are of the working class. We say: Arouse, you workingmen! It is in your power to put an end to this system. It is your duty to build up this great revolutionary economic organization of your class, to seize and control the tools with which you work, and make yourselves the masters instead of being the slaves of industry.

Wipe out the wage system so that you can walk this earth free men!

Not only is it your right, not only have you the opportunity, but it is your solemn duty to do this, unless you are base enough to be guilty of treason to yourself, to your class and humanity.

Let me say to you, my fellow workers, that the hour has struck for a great change in the world of organized labor. Long enough have we been divided into quarreling factions. Long enough have we suffered ourselves to blindly and stupidly follow a leadership that has misled and deceived and betrayed. Long enough have we been clubbed by the police, and it may be pertinent to observe that when the club of a policeman descends upon the head of a workingman he hears an echo of the vote he cast at the preceding election.

SPEECHES.

It is only necessary for us to do a bit of serious reasoning on our own account to satisfy ourselves that the Industrial Workers is the only working class organization in the field. It requires but little intelligent reflection to satisfy ourselves that we have got to build up this organization, unless we have given up in the struggle and succumbed to defeat and despair. Is it possible that we could for a moment make up our minds that we and those who are to come after us are forever doomed to wage slavery? The very suggestion is abhorrent to every worker with a spark of manhood, with a drop of manly blood coursing in his veins. Why, you men, you workingmen, are more than the salt of this earth. Without you society would perish. Society does not need the idle capitalists. They are parasites. They are worse than useless. They simply take what you make, leaving you in poverty; thousands of you idle; if not now, when the times become hard. And every few years the times become hard in the capitalist system, for reasons you can easily understand, but I have not the time to fully explain this evening.

A panic comes, industry is paralyzed, because with machinery you can produce so much more than your paltry wage will allow you to consume. You make all things in great abundance, but you do not consume them. You can only consume that part of your product which your wage, the price of your labor power, will buy. If you cannot consume what you produce, it follows that in time there is bound to be overproduction, because the few capitalists cannot absorb the surplus. The market is glutted, business comes to a standstill and mills and factories shut down.

At such a time Chicago is hit, and hit hard; and you workingmen find yourselves out of employment, a drug on the market. Nobody wants your labor power, because it cannot be utilized at a profit to the capitalist who owns the tool, and when he cannot use your labor power at a satisfactory profit to himself he doesn't buy it. And if he doesn't buy your labor power you are idle, and when you are idle you don't draw any wages, and you can't buy groceries and pay rent; you can't buy clothing and shoes, and you begin to look seedy and shabby. By degrees you become a vagrant and a wanderer and lose what little self-respect you had. And then you hear that your wife has been evicted, and that is a thing that happens every day in the week. Your child is now upon the street and your former cottage home is deserted and you start out on what proves to be a never ending journey. The road you are now traveling stretches wearily on, and from the hedges bark the dogs of civilization. You are a tramp.

Are there not thousands and thousands of tramps all over this country today? There were none half a century ago. There is a great army of them now. They have been recruited in capitalist society; they are the products of the capitalist system.

A man is out of work a good while and he gets hungry; he still has a little self-respect and steals rather than beg. That is how men become tramps and thieves and criminals; that is why we have an army of tramps; that is why all the penitentiaries are crowded; why the insane asylums are overflowing and why thousands commit suicide. All these shocking evils are the outgrowth of the capitalist system, to which the Industrial Workers proposes to put an everlasting end.

If you think that these horrors ought to be; if you, as a workingman, think that you ought to have a master—just as the ignorant chattel slave on the plantation in the South used to think that he had to have a master to rob him of what he produced—if you think that you are so helpless that you would die unless you had a master to give you a job and take from you all except just enough to keep you working for him; if you think that workingmen ought to fight each other; if you think that unity, the unity of the working class, would be a bad thing for the working class; if you think that your interest is identical with the interest of the capitalist who robs you; if you think that you ought to be in slavish submission to the capitalist who does nothing and gets what you produce; if you think that, then certainly you ought to stay in the old trade union and keep out of the Industrial Workers.

But if you have a bit of intelligence, just enough to realize that you are a workingman, and that, as a workingman, you are a human being; if you are capable of understanding that you have the inherent power of self-development, that the brain you have can be developed so that you can think clearly for yourself; if you will use that intelligence just enough to satisfy yourself that you ought to be the master of your own job; then, instead of being a wage slave, you will soon be a man among men, and if you have intelligence enough to conceive and to express that thought, then let me say to you, a revolutionary light will be kindled in your eyes and you will feel the thrill of a new-born joy, and for the first time in your life you will stand perfectly erect and know what it is to be self-reliant and touch elbows with your fellow-workers throughout the world.

Remember that no matter who or what a worker may be, if he works for wages he is in precisely the same economic position that you are. He is in your class; he is your brother; he is your comrade.

As an individual worker you cannot escape from wage-slavery. It is true that one in ten thousand wage-workers may become a capitalist, to be pointed out as a man worth a million who used to be a clerk, but he is the exception that proves the rule. The wage worker in the capitalist system remains the wage worker.

There is no escape for you from wage-slavery by yourself, but while you cannot alone break your fetters, if you will unite with all other workers who are in the same position that you are; that is, if—instead of being bound up in a little union of a score, or a hundred, or a thousand, that is almost as helpless to do anything for you as you are to do anything by yourself—if you will join the organization that represents your whole class, you can develop the power that will achieve your freedom and the equal freedom of all.

The workingman who does this is a missionary in the field of sound working class organization; he wears the badge of the Industrial Workers; he has a new idea of unionism. Instead of being satisfied with ancient, out-of-date, reactionary methods he will have the advanced and progressive ideas of industrial revolutionists. That is to say, he will understand that when the workers are united in one great economic organization and one great political organization; when they strike together and vote together they can put their class in power in every council, in every legislature and in the national congress; they can abolish the capitalist system, take over the industries to themselves and rule the land forevermore.

For this great change the workers must prepare themselves through organization and education. Were it to come today it would result in collapse. It would mean a catastrophe, and why? Because if, for example, the Illinois Steel Works were turned over to the workers today they would not be fitted, trained, drilled, equipped for the operation of this mammoth industrial enterprise.

The Industrial Workers proposes to first unite all workers within one organization, classified in the various departments representing their several trades and occupation, to bring them all into harmonious economic relations with each other. The next thing is to coördinate them within their several industries with an eye to operating these industries when they secure control of them. That is the central function of the new union, and by far the most important one.

The old union never makes any reference to industrial self-control, because so far as the old union is concerned wage-slavery is to prevail forever.

The Industrial Workers declares that it is organized to put an end to the wage system, to free the workers, to make them the masters of the mills and other plants in which they are employed. In order to fit them to operate these enterprises in their own interests when they are turned over to them it is necessary that they undergo a thorough process of industrial education.

So that, after you join the Industrial Workers, when you go to your work in the morning, you will not be tied to your task blindly; you will have a thought about your relation to your fellow-workingmen in all other departments. You will understand your part in the enterprise, and your connection with and relation to the whole. You will help to fit your fellows for the new function, so that when the hour strikes you will be perfectly trained and ready to take control of industry and operate the productive enterprises in the interests of the people. To me nothing could be simpler.

Don't you think we are capable of effecting this change?

I do. I not only think it; I know it. And I know it is inevitable.

Upon the one hand the capitalists are combining. It will be but a short time until practically all the lands, railroads, telegraphs, steel mills, sugar refineries, breweries and all other great establishments will belong to practically a single syndicate, controlled by a few capitalists. But while they are combining and centralizing their capital we are organizing the workers that they may act together, economically and politically, and possibly in other ways before the struggle is ended and the victory won.

In the Industrial Workers they will vote as they strike, and strike as they vote—all together.

Do you know what I expect to see? I expect to see a general strike in the city of Chicago. I would rather see it here than in any other city in America; than any other in the world.

The capitalists are drunken with their power. They are running things to suit themselves, and they are going to keep the working class in subjection just as the remnants of the Indians are kept on their reservations out on the plains. And if you object they are so completely in control that they will club you, or they will jail you, or kill you if necessary.

I want to see the time when the workers of Chicago will be so thoroughly organized in their economic capacity that they can quit work and paralyze industry in Chicago for just twenty-four hours, and when they are organized well enough to do that they will have every capitalist in the city and nation suing for peace. When they are organized well enough to do that they will secure more economic concessions in five minutes than they can get in five years striking and boycotting along the old trade union lines.

How is it now? Why, the union butcher workmen go out on strike, and they strike bravely and loyally to the bitter end. But all other union men remain at work until the butcher workmen are used up.

The capitalists are rich; the loss of a few hundreds or thousands of dollars doesn't hurt them, because they get it all back again. So they can wait until this corps of the working army is defeated and its stanchest supporters are out of jobs. Many of these quit the union; it is no use. They tried the union and are disgusted with it, and in all probability some of them will stay at work in the next strike and help defeat the union.

Next comes the strike of the Chicago machinists, and that lasts a long time. All their fellow unionists remain at work. Here we have a large body of machinists engaged in a life and death struggle, and they hold out wonderfully well. They levy assessments on all other machinists who keep at work to help these strikers in idleness for many weary months, and then at last, when all the resources are exhausted and the men are on the point of starvation, they have got to surrender, and they go back defeated, and the open shop system is established, and the union, so far as any usefulness to the machinist is concerned, is practically wiped out of existence.

What good has the machinists' union done to these machinists? It collects high dues and pays high salaries. Hundreds of thousands of dollars are contributed by the workers with which to buy their own defeat. Now, defeat would be bad enough if it came about free of charge, but if you have to pay $174,000 for it, as the official report of the machinists show, it is time you were doing a little thinking on your own account.

Mr. James O'Connell is at the head of the machinists' union, and he is also a labor lieutenant of the capitalist class. He sits at the same banqueting table with the capitalists and is hand in glove with August Belmont—the employer of James Farley, the professional strikebreaker, who, when you go on strike, steps in and gets as much pay in a day as you get in a year.

You can hardly blame the men who get disgusted with unions as they are run in Chicago. Not alone Mr. O'Connell, but Mr. Mitchell, president of the Mine Workers; Mr. Gompers, president of the American Federation of Labor, and other pure and simple union leaders are in economic tune with the master class, and are held up as model labor leaders by capitalist newspapers.

Periodically these model leaders go to New York to attend a love feast between capitalists and wage workers, or, rather, between capitalists and leaders of wage workers.

You are only the common herd. They don't have anything to do with you, and they don't need to have anything to do with you. They deal with your leaders and between them they fix things, and all you have to do is to work and put up the money and they will attend to the rest.

Last fall, a year ago, when I was in New York, there came near being a strike on the Interborough railway lines. The employes had been outraged by the management of the Interborough under an agreement that had been shamefully violated by the company. They threatened to go out on strike. It happened to be a national election year, and under the pressure that was brought to bear upon him, Mr. Belmont, the president of the system, on the eve of the election, settled with the men and averted the strike. In a speech I made in New York that night I predicted that the settlement was temporary and for political effect, and that soon after the election was over the corporation would begin to violate agreement and goad the men to strike. And so it came to pass.

After the election was over the corporation renewed its offensive tactics until at last 6,000 of the men went out on strike. And now we behold an exhibition of the impotency, if not the crime, of outgrown unionism. When these 6,000 men went out on strike August Belmont already had James Farley and his army of professional strikebreakers on the ground; had them there weeks in advance. And they were getting their pay, $5 a day and expenses, while Farley got an advance payment, said to have been $10,000.

August Belmont, the president of the Interborough, was photographed with Farley, the strikebreaker. They were pictured side by side; they occupied the first page of the New York newspapers; they were represented as the modern strikebreakers, August Belmont, the capitalist, and James Farley, his mercenary minion.

The strike was soon defeated and the places of the men filled with scabs.

The union men who were in the power houses, who could and who should have shut off the power, kept those great plants in operation. They said, "We are in sympathy with you and would like to help you, but we cannot go out on strike without violating our contract." And so, to preserve the sanctity of their craft contract, they cut the throats of their 6,000 fellow unionists, virtually scabbing on them, so far as the effect of their action was concerned. These union men might as well have stepped out of the power houses and taken the places that were vacated by the strikers.

Now comes the closing chapter of this story, the blackest of all. A little while after the 6,000 union men had gone out on strike and had been defeated by strike-breakers under Farley, the lieutenant of Belmont, the Civic Federation held its banquet. August Belmont attended this banquet, being the president of the Federation. So also did the labor leaders. In their regular order came President Gompers, President Mitchell, President O'Connell, President Duncan and the rest of the presidents. They surrounded the banqueting board and sat and feasted and laughed and made joy together. The labor question was speedily settled, so far as they were concerned.

What do you think of the labor leader who would sit down, side by side, at the same banquet, with August Belmont, fresh from the field upon which he had slaughtered 6,000 union men? Do you think that a true union leader, a man whose heart was with the working class, could feast and make common cause with a capitalist who had just thrust the dagger of assassination into the heart of his union? Do you think that a real labor leader would fraternize with one whose hands were dripping with the blood of union labor?

I say that a labor leader who attends that kind of a banquet and who greets in social fellowship an arch-enemy of labor, is himself a Belmont at heart and the foe of the working class.

You may feel assured that there is no officer of the Industrial Workers who will ever banquet with the Civic Federation.

Could you imagine Charles O. Sherman—who has given his life to the working class—could you imagine him consorting with Belmont? Could you imagine Trautmann—the very incarnation of the revolutionary spirit of the working class—could you imagine Trautmann attending a banquet of the Civic Federation, in full fellowship with the men who live out of the blood of the working class? It is unimaginable. They would scorn to do it; they would consider this an act of basest treason to their class.

In closing, I appeal to you, as workingmen, to think for yourselves; to cut loose from those who have misled and betrayed you; to close up the ranks and unify your forces. I appeal to you to ally yourselves with the economic organization of your class; I appeal to you to join the union that truly represents you, the union that unites you, the union in which you can stand shoulder to shoulder, regardless of your occupation; the union in which you will move forward, step by step, marching proudly to the inspiring music of the new emancipation.

I appeal to you to declare yourselves here and now, to be for once true enough to yourselves to join the only industrial union that is absolutely true to you.

And if you join this union in sufficient numbers, if you build up this union and give it the power it ought to have— if you will rally to the standard of this revolutionary army— then, as certain as I stand before you, you will carry that banner to victory. Then the workers will be the sovereign citizens, the rulers of this earth. They will build houses and live in them; they will plant vineyards and enjoy the fruits thereof. The labor question will have been settled, and the working class, emancipated from the fetters of wage-slavery, will begin the real work of civilizing the human race.

Revolutionary Unionism

Speech at Chicago, November 25, 1905

The unity of labor, economic and political, upon the basis of the class struggle, is at this time the supreme need of the working class. The prevailing lack of unity implies lack of class consciousness; that is to say, enlightened self-interest; and this can, must and will be overcome by revolutionary education and organization. Experience, long, painful and dearly bought, has taught some of us that craft division is fatal to class unity. To accomplish its mission the working class must be united. They must act together; they must assert their combined power, and when they do this upon the basis of the class struggle, then and then only will they break the fetters of wage slavery.

We are engaged today in a class war; and why? For the simple reason that in the evolution of the capitalist system in which we live, society has been mainly divided into two economic classes—a small class of capitalists who own the tools with which work is done and wealth is produced, and a great mass of workers who are compelled to use those tools. Between these two classes there is an irrepressible economic conflict. Unfortunately for himself, the workingman does not yet understand the nature of this conflict, and for this reason has hitherto failed to accomplish any effective unity of his class.

It is true that workers in the various departments of industrial activity have organized trade unions. It is also true that in this capacity they have from time to time asserted such power as this form of organization has conferred upon them. It is equally true that mere craft unionism, no matter how well it may be organized, is in the present highly developed capitalist system utterly unable to successfully cope with the capitalist class. The old craft union has done its work and belongs to the past. Labor unionism, like everything else, must recognize and bow to the inexorable law of evolution.

The craft union says that the worker shall receive a fair day's pay for a fair day's work. What is a fair day's pay for a fair day's work? Ask the capitalist and he will give you his idea about it. Ask the worker and, if he is intelligent, he will tell you that a fair day's pay for a fair day's work is all the workingman produces.

While the craft unionist still talks about a fair day's pay for a fair day's work, implying that the economic interests of the capitalist and the worker can be harmonized upon a basis of equal justice to both, the Industrial Worker says, "I want all I produce by my labor."

If the worker is not entitled to all he produces, then what share is anybody else entitled to?

Does the worker today receive all he produces? Does he receive anything like a fair (?) share of the product of his labor? Will any trade-unionist of the old school make any such claim, and if he is bold enough to make it, can he verify it?

The student of this question knows that, as a matter of fact, in the capitalist system in which we live today the worker who produces all wealth receives but enough of his product to keep him in working and producing order. His wage, in the aggregate, is fixed by his living necessities. It suffices, upon the average, to maintain him according to the prevailing standard of living and to enable him to reproduce himself in the form of labor power. He receives, as a matter of fact, but about 17 per cent of what his labor produces.

The worker produces a certain thing. It goes from the manufacturer to the jobber, from the jobber to the wholesaler, and from the wholesaler to the retailer—each of these adding a profit, and when it completes the circle and comes back to the worker who produced it and he stands face to face with the product of his own labor, he can buy back, upon the average, with his paltry wage but about 17 per cent of it. In other words, he is exploited, robbed, of about 83 per cent of what his labor produces. And why? For the simple reason that in modern industry, the tool, in the form of a great machine with which he works and produces, is the private property of the capitalist, who didn't make it, and could not, if his life depended upon it, use it.

The evolution is not yet complete.

By virtue of his private ownership of the social tool—made and used by the co-operative labor of the working class—the employer has the economic power to appropriate to himself, as a capitalist, what is produced by the social labor of the working class. This accounts for the fact that the capitalist becomes fabulously rich, lives in a palace where there is music and singing and dancing, and where there is the luxury of all climes, while the workingmen who do the work and produce the wealth and endure the privations and make the sacrifices of health and limb and life, remain in a wretched state of poverty and dependence.

The exploiting capitalist is the economic master and the political ruler in capitalist society, and as such holds the exploited wage worker in utter contempt.

No master ever had any respect for his slave, and no slave ever had, or ever could have, any real love for his master.

I must beg you to indulge the hoarseness of my voice, which has been somewhat strained addressing meetings of the Industrial Workers held in and about Chicago during the last two or three evenings; but, fortunately, my eyesight has not been strained reading the accounts of these meetings in the capitalist papers of Chicago.

Alert, vigilant, argus-eyed as the capitalist dailies of Chicago are, there is not one of them that knows of this meeting of the Industrial Workers. But if this were a meeting of the American Federation of Labor and an old trade union leader were here, you would read tomorrow morning a full account of it and him in every capitalist paper in the city. There is a reason for this that explains itself.

The capitalist papers know that there is such an organization as the Industrial Workers, because they have lied about it. Just now they are ignoring it. Let me serve notice on them through you and the thousands of others who flock to our meetings everywhere, that they will reckon with the Industrial Workers before six months have rolled around.

There are those wage workers who feel their economic dependence, who know that the capitalist for whom they work is the owner of their job, and therefore the master of their fate, who are still vainly seeking by individual effort and through waning craft unions to harmonize the conflicting interests of the exploiting capitalist and the exploited wage slave. They are engaged in a vain and hopeless task. They are wasting time and energy worthy of a better cause. These interests never can and never will be harmonized permanently, and when they are adjusted even temporarily it is always at the expense of the working class.

* * * * * * *

It is no part of the mission of this revolutionary working class union to conciliate the capitalist class. We are organized to fight that class, and we want that class to distinctly understand it. And they do understand it, and in time the working class will also understand it; and then the capitalist class will have reason to understand it better still. Their newspapers understand it so well even now that they have not a single favorable comment to make upon it.

When the convention of delegates was in session here in June last for the purpose of organizing the Industrial Workers, every report that appeared in a Chicago paper—capitalist paper I mean; every single report was a tissue of perversion, misstatement and downright falsehood. They knew that we had met for a purpose, and that that purpose was to fight the class of which they are the official mouthpieces. Now, it seems to me that this uniform hostility of the capitalist press ought to be significant to even the unthinking workingman. Capitalist papers are, as a rule, quite friendly to the craft unions. They do not misrepresent them; do not lie about them; do not traduce their representatives. They are exceedingly fond of them, because they know enough about their own interests to know that the craft unions are not only not a menace to them, but are in fact bulwarks of defense to them. And why? Because, chiefly, craft unions divide and do not unite the working class. And I challenge contradiction.

There was a time when the craft union expressed in terms of unionism the prevailing mode of industry. That was long ago when production was still mainly carried on by handicraftmen with hand tools; when one man worked for another to learn his trade that he might become its master. The various trades involved skill and cunning; considerable time was required to master them. This was in the early stages of the capitalist system. Even at that early day the antagonism between employer and employed found expression, although the employer was not at that time the capitalist as he is today. The men who followed these trades found it necessary in order to protect themselves in their trade interests to band together, form a union, so that they might act together in resisting the encroachments of the "boss." So the trade union came into existence.

The mode of production since that time has been practically revolutionized. The hand tool has all but disappeared. The mammoth machine has taken its place. The hand tool was made and used by the individual worker and was largely within his own control. Today the machine that has supplanted the old tool is not owned nor controlled by the man, or rather the men, who use it. As I have already said, it is the private property of some capitalist who may live at a remote point and never have seen the machine or the wage slaves who operate it.

In other words, the production of wealth, in the evolution of industry, from being an individual act a half a century ago has become a social act. The tool, from being an individual tool, has become a social instrument. So that the tool has been socialized and production has also been socialized. But the evolution is yet to complete its work. This social tool, made socially and used socially, must be socially owned.

In the evolution of industry the trade has been largely undermined. The old trade union expresses the old form of industry, the old mode of individual production based upon the use of the individual tool. That tool has about disappeared; that mode of production has also about disappeared, but the trade union built upon that mode of production, springing from the use of the hand tool, remains essentially the same.

The pure and simple trade union, in seeking to preserve its

autonomy, is forced into conflict with other trade unions by the unceasing operation of the laws of industrial evolution. How many of the skilled trades that were in operation half a century ago are still practiced?

At the town where I live there used to be quite a number of cooper shops. Barrels were made by hand and a cooper shop consisted wholly of coopers. The coopers' union was organized and served fairly well the purposes of the coopers of that day, but it does not serve the purposes of the workers who make barrels today. They do not make barrels in the way they used to be made. Today we want a union that expresses the economic interests of all the workers in the cooperage plant engaged in making and handling barrels. But a few coopers still remain, a very few. It is no longer necessary to be a cooper to make a barrel. The machine is the cooper today. The machine makes the barrel, and almost anyone can operate the machine that makes the barrel.

You will observe that labor has been subdivided and specialized and that the trade has been dissipated; and now a body of men and boys work together co-operatively in the making of a barrel, each making a small part of a barrel. Now we want a union which embraces all the workers engaged in making barrels. We lose sight of the cooper trade as evolution has practically disposed of that. We say that since the trade has completely changed, the union which expressed that trade must also change accordingly. In the new union we shall include not only the men who are actually engaged in the making of barrels directly, but also those who are placing them upon the market. There are the typewriters, the bookkeepers, the teamsters, and all other classes of labor that are involved in the making and delivering of the barrels. We insist that all the workers in the whole of any given plant shall belong to one and the same union.

This is the very thing the workers need and the capitalist who owns the establishment does not want. He believes in labor unionism if it is the "right kind." And if it is the right kind for him it is the wrong kind for you. He is more than willing that his employes shall join the craft union. He has not the slightest objection. On the contrary, it is easily proven that capitalists are among the most active upholders of the old craft unions.

The capitalists are perfectly willing that you shall organize, as long as you don't do a thing against them; as long as you don't do a thing for yourselves. You cannot do a thing for yourselves without antagonizing them; and you don't antagonize them through your craft unions nearly as much as you buttress their interests and prolong their mastery.

* * * * * * *

The average workingman imagines that he must have a leader to look to; a guide to follow, right or wrong. He has been taught in the craft union that he is a very dependent creature; that without a leader the goblins would get him without a doubt, and he therefore instinctively looks to his leader. And even while he is looking at his leader there is someone else looking at the same leader from the other side.

You have depended too much on that leader and not enough on yourself. I don't want you to follow me. I want you to cultivate self-reliance.

If I have the slightest capacity for leadership I can only give evidence of it by leading you to rely upon yourselves.

As long as you can be led by an individual you will be betrayed by an individual. That does not mean that all leaders are dishonest or corrupt. I make no such sweeping indictment. I know that many of them are honest. I know also that many of them are in darkness themselves, blind leaders of the blind. That is the worst that can be said of them. And let me say to you that the most dangerous leader is not the corrupt leader, but the honest, ignorant leader. That leader is just as fatal to your interests as the one who deliberately sells you out for a paltry consideration.

You are a workingman! Now, at your earliest leisure look yourself over and take an inventory of your resources. Invoice your mental stock; see what you have on hand.

You may be of limited mentality; and that is all you require in the capitalist system. You need only small brains, but huge hands.

Most of your hands are calloused and you are taught by the capitalist politician, who is the political mercenary of the capitalist who fleeces you, you are taught by him to be proud of your horny hands. If that is true he ought to be ashamed of his. He doesn't have any horns on his hands. He has them on his brain. He is as busy with his brain as you are with your hands, and because he is busy with his brain and you neglect yours, he gets a goodly share of what you produce with your hands. He is the gentleman who calls you the horny handed sons of toil. That fetches you every time. I tell you that the time has come for you to use your brains in your own interest, and until you do that you will have to use your hands in the interest of your masters.

Now, after you have looked yourself over; after you have satisfied yourself what you are, or rather, what you are not, you will arrive at the conclusion that as a wage worker in capitalist society you are not a man at all. You are simply a thing. And that thing is bought in the labor market, just as hair, hides and other forms of merchandise are bought.

When the capitalist requires the use of your hands, does he call for men? Why, certainly not. He doesn't want men, he only wants hands. And when he calls for hands, that is what he wants. Have you ever seen a placard posted: "Fifty hands wanted"? Did you ever know of a capitalist to respond to that kind of an invitation?

President Roosevelt would have you believe that there are no classes in the United States. He was made president by the votes of the working class. Did you ever know of his stopping over night in the home of a workingman? Is it by mere chance that he is always sheltered beneath the hospitable roof of some plutocrat? Not long ago he made a visit here and he gave a committee representing the workers about fifteen minutes of his precious time, just time enough to rebuke them with the intimation that organized labor consisted of a set of law-breakers, and then he gave fifteen hours to the plutocrats of Chicago, being wined and dined by them to prove that there are no classes in the United States, and that you, horny handed veteran, with your wage of $1.50 a day, with six children to support on that, are in the same class with John D. Rockefeller! Your misfortune is that you do not know you are in the same class. But on election day it dawns upon you and you prove it by voting the same ticket.

SPEECHES.

Since you have looked yourself over thoroughly, you realize by this time that, as a workingman, you have been supporting, through your craft unions and through your ballots, a social system that is the negation of your manhood.

The capitalist for whom you work doesn't have to go out and look for you; you have to look for him, and you belong to him just as completely as if he had a title to your body; as if you were his chattel slave.

He doesn't own you under the law, but he does under the fact.

Why? Because he owns the tool with which you work, and you have got to have access to that tool if you work; and if you want to live you have got to work. If you don't work you don't eat; and so, scourged by hunger pangs, you look about for that tool and you locate it, and you soon discover that between yourself, a workingman, and that tool that is an essential part of yourself in industry, there stands the capitalist who owns it. He is your boss; he owns your job, takes your product and controls your destiny. Before you can touch that tool to earn a dime you must petition the owner of it to allow you to use it, in consideration of your giving to him all you produce with it, except just enough to keep you alive and in working order.

* * * * * * *

Observe that you are displaced by the surplus product of your own labor; that what you produce is of more value under capitalism than you who produce it; that the commodity which is the result of your labor is of greater value under capitalism than your own life. You consist of palpitating flesh; you have wants. You have necessities. You cannot satisfy them, and you suffer. But the product of your labor, the property of the capitalist, that is sacred; that must be protected at all hazards. After you have been displaced by the surplus product of your labor and you have been idle long enough, you become restive and you begin to speak out, and you become a menace. The unrest culminates in trouble. The capitalist presses a button and the police are called into action. Then the capitalist presses button No. 2 and injunctions are issued by the judges, the judicial allies and servants of the capitalist class.

Then button No. 3 is pressed and the state troops fall into line; and if this is not sufficient button No. 4 is pressed and the regular soldiers come marching to the scene. That is what President Roosevelt meant when he said that back of the mayor is the governor, back of the governor the President; or, to use his own words, back of the city, the state, and back of the state the nation—the capitalist nation.

If you have been working in a steel mill and you have made more steel than your master can sell, and you are locked out and get hungry, and the soldiers are called out, it is to protect the steel and shoot you who made the steel—to guard the men who steal the steel and kill the men who made it.

* * * * * * *

I am not asking you to withdraw from the craft unions simply because the Industrial Workers has been formed. I am asking you to think about these matters for yourselves.

I belonged to a craft union from the time I was nineteen years of age. I can remember the very evening I first joined the Brotherhood of Locomotive Firemen. I can recall with what zeal I went to work to organize my craft, and it was the pride of my life to see that union expand. I did what I could to build it up. In time I was made to realize that that union was not sufficient unto itself. I next did what I could to organize other branches of the service and then establish a federation of the various unions of railroad employes, and finally succeeded; but soon after the federation was formed, on account of craft jealousies, it was disrupted. I then, along with a number of others who had had the same experience and had profited by it, undertook to organize the railway men within one organization, known as the American Railway Union. The railroad corporations were the deadly enemies of that organization. They understood that its purpose was to unify all the railroad employes. They knew that the unity of the working class meant their end, and so they set their faces like flint against the American Railway Union. And while they were using all their powers to crush and to stamp out the American Railway Union, they were bestowing all their favors upon the several craft brotherhoods, the engineers and the firemen, the conductors and the brakemen. They knew that so long as these craft unions existed there could be no unification of the men employed in the railway service.

Are the railroad men of this country organized today? No! Not nearly one-half of them are organized at all. And when the railroad corporations from motives of good policy make a concession to the engineers or the conductors, it is gouged out of the poor devils who work for a dollar a day and are compelled to submit.

There are a great many engineers who are perfectly willing to be tied up in a contract. They think they can save themselves at the expense of their fellow-workers. But they are going to reap, sooner or later, just what they have sown. In the next few years they will become motormen.

While we are upon this question, let us consult industrial history a moment. We will begin with the craft union railroad strike of 1888. The Brotherhood of Engineers and the Brotherhood of Firemen on the C., B. & Q. system went out on strike. Some 2,000 engineers and firemen vacated their posts and went out on one of the most bitterly contested railroad strikes in the history of the country. When they went out, the rest of the employes, especially the conductors, who were organized in craft unions of their own, remained at their posts, and the union conductors piloted the scab engineers over the line. I know whereof I speak. I was there. I took an active part in that strike.

I saw craft union pitted against craft union, and I saw the Brotherhood of Engineers and the Brotherhood of Firemen completely wiped from the C., B. & Q. system. And now you find these men, seventeen years later, scattered all over the United States. They had to pay the penalty of their ignorance in organizing a craft instead of organizing as a whole.

In 1892 a strike occurred on the Lehigh Valley; the same result. Another on the Toledo, Ann Arbor & North Michigan. Same result. The engineers have had no strike from that time to this. Every time they have had a strike they have been defeated.

The railroad corporations are shrewd enough to recognize the fact that if they can keep certain departments in their employ in a time of emergency they can defeat all of the rest.

A manager of a railroad who can keep control of 15 per cent of the old men can allow 85 per cent to go out on strike and defeat them every time. That is why they have made some concessions to the engineers and conductors and brakemen, and now and then to the switchmen, the most militant labor union of them all.

A year and a half ago the telegraph operators on the Missouri, Kansas & Texas went out on strike. The engineer remained at his post; so did the fireman; the conductor at his; and the brakeman at his. And they hauled the scabs that flocked from all parts of the country to the several points along the line, and delivered them in good order to take the places vacated by the strikers; worked all round them and with them until they had mastered the details of their several duties; and having done this, the strike was at an end, and the 1,300 craft unionists out of jobs. You will find them scattered all over the country.

Now, were not these other craft unions scabbing on the telegraphers just as flagrantly as if they had stepped into their positions and discharged their duties? They were acting with the corporation against their union fellow workingmen, helping the corporation to defeat and crush them. Without their aid the corporation could not have succeeded. With their aid it was very easily done.

Is it possible that a craft unionist can see such an object lesson as this so plainly presented to him and still refuse to profit by it? Still close his eyes and, as it were, shut up his reason, and absolutely decline to see that this is suicidal policy and that its fruit must always be disruption and disaster?

This world only respects as it is compelled to respect; and if you workingmen would be respected you must begin by respecting yourselves. You have had enough of this sort of experience. You have had more than enough of it right here in Chicago.

Why didn't the steel trust annihilate the Amalgamated Steelworkers? Only two years ago they defeated them completely. The trust had its iron heel upon the neck of the Steelworkers' Union, and could have, had it chosen, completely crushed the life out of it. But Morgan was too wily. Schwab was too wise. They used to oppose trade unions. They don't oppose them any longer. They have discovered that a union can be turned the other way; that it can be made useful to them instead of being useful to the working class. Morgan now says he is in favor of trade unions, and Schwab agrees. They didn't crush out the Steelworkers' Union because they knew that another and a better one would spring from its ruins. They were perfectly willing that the old craft union should grow up again and block the way to real union.

* * * * * * *

You have had a machinists' strike here in Chicago. You are well aware of this without my telling you. There is something pathetic to me about every strike.

I have said and say again that no strike was ever lost; that it has always been worth all it cost. An essential part of a workingman's education is the defeats he encounters. The strikes he loses are after all the only ones he wins. I am heartily glad for myself that I lost the strike. It is the best thing that ever happened to me. I lost the strike of the past that I may win the strike of the future.

I am a discredited labor leader, but I have good staying qualities. The very moment the capitalist press credits me with being a wise labor leader, I will invite you to investigate me upon the charge of treason. I am discredited by the capitalist simply because I am true to his victim. I don't want his favors. I do not court his approbation. I would not have it. I can't afford it. If I had his respect it would be at the price of my own.

I don't care anything about what is called public opinion. I know precisely what that means. It is but the reflect of the interests of the capitalist class. As between the respect of the public and my own, I prefer my own; and I am going to keep it until I can have both.

When I pick up a capitalist newspaper and read a eulogy of some labor leader, I know that that leader has at least two afflictions; the one is mental weakness and the other is moral cowardice—and they go together. Put it down that when the capitalist who is exploiting you credits your leader with being safe and conservative and wise, that leader is not serving you.

And if you take exception to that statement, just ask me to prove it.

* * * * * * *

The rank and file of all unions, barring their ignorance, are all right. The working class as a whole is all right. Many of them are misguided, and stand in the light of their own interest.

It is sometimes necessary that we offend you and even shock you, that you may understand that we are your friends and not your enemies. And if we are against your unions it is because we are for you. We know that you have paid your dues into them for years and that you are animated by a spirit of misdirected loyalty to those unions.

I can remember that it was not a very easy matter for me to give up the union in which I had spent my boyhood and all the years of my young manhood. I remember that I felt there was something in it in the nature of a sacrifice, and yet I had to make it in the interest of the larger duty that I owed myself and the working class.

Let me say to you, if you are a craft unionist, that infinitely greater than your loyalty to your craft is your loyalty to the working class as a whole. No craft union can fight this great battle successfully alone. The craft is a part, a part only, of the great body of the working class. And the time has come for this class, numerically overwhelmingly in the majority, to follow in one respect at least the example of its capitalist masters and unite as a whole.

In this barbarous competitive struggle in which we are engaged, the workers, the millions, are fighting each other to sell themselves into slavery; the middle class are fighting each other to get enough trade to keep soul and body together, and the professional class are fighting each other like savages for practice. And this is called civilization! What a mockery! What a sham! There is no real civilization in the capitalist system.

Today there is nothing so easily produced as wealth. The whole earth consists of raw materials; and in every breath of nature, in sunshine, and in shower, hidden everywhere, are the subtle forces that may, by the touch of the hand of labor, be set into operation to transmute these raw materials into wealth, the finished products, in all their multiplied forms and in opulent abundance for all. The merest child can press a button that will set in operation a forest of machinery and produce wealth enough for a community.

Whatever may be said of the ignorant, barbarous past, there is no excuse for poverty today. And yet it is the scourge of the race. It is the Nemesis of capitalist civilization. Ten millions, one-eighth of our whole population, are in a state of chronic poverty. Three millions of these have been sunk to unresisting pauperism. The whole working class is in a sadly dependent state, and even the most favored wage-worker is left suspended by a single thread. He does not know what hour a machine may be invented to make his trade useless, displace him and throw him into the increasing army of the unemployed.

And how does labor live today? Here in Chicago you may walk along a certain boulevard, say 18th street, and you will find it lined with magnificent palaces. Beyond that you will find a larger district where the still complacent middle class abide. Beyond that is a very much larger territory where the working class exist; and still beyond that, to complete the circle, you see the red lights flickering in the distance.

Prostitution is a part, a necessary part, of capitalist society. The department store empties in the slums.

I have been here enough to know that when the daughter of a workingman is obliged to go up the street to look for employment, when she is fourteen or fifteen years of age, and ought to be in the care and keeping of a loving mother, and have all of the advantages that our civilization makes possible for all—when she is forced to go to a department store, to one of those capitalist emporiums, and there find a place, if she can, and work for a wage of $3 a week, and have to obey a code of cast-iron regulations, appear tidy and neatly dressed and be subject to a thousand temptations daily, and then takes a misstep, the first, as she is more than apt to do, especially if she has no home in any decent sense of that term—the very instant this is added to her poverty, she is doomed—damned. All the doors of capitalist society are closed in her face. The coals of contumely are poured upon her head. There is for her no redemption, and she takes the next step, and the next, until at last she ends a disgraceful career in a brothel hell.

This may be your child. And if you are a workingman, and this should fall to the lot of the innocent blue-eyed child that you love more than you do your own life—I want you to realize that if such a horror be written in the book of fate, that you are responsible for it, if you use or misuse your power to perpetuate the capitalist system and working class slavery.

You can change this condition—not tomorrow, not next week, nor next year; but in the meantime the next thing to changing it is making up your mind that it shall be changed. That is what we Industrial Unionists have done. And so there has come to us a new state of mind, and in our hearts there is the joy of service and the serenity of triumph.

We are united and we cannot be disunited. We cannot be stampeded. We know that we are confronted by ten thousand difficulties. We know that all the powers of capitalism are to be arrayed against us. But were these obstacles multiplied by a million, it would simply have the effect of multiplying our determination by a million, to overcome them all. And so we are organizing and appealing to you.

*   *   *   *   *   *   *

The workingman today does not understand his industrial relation to his fellow-workers. He has never been correlated with others in the same industry. He has mechanically done his part. He has simply been a cog, with little reference to, or knowledge of, the rest of the cogs. Now, we teach him to hold up his head and look over the whole mechanism. If he is employed in a certain plant, as an Industrial Unionist, his eyes are opened. He takes a survey of the entire productive mechanism, and he understands his part in it, and his relation to every other worker in that industry. The very instant he does that he is buoyed by a fresh hope and thrilled with a new aspiration. He becomes a larger man. He begins to feel like a collective son of toil.

Then he and his fellows study to fit themselves to take control of this productive mechanism when it shall be transferred from the idle capitalist to the workers to whom it rightfully belongs.

In every mill and every factory, every mine and every quarry, every railroad and every shop, everywhere, the workers, enlightened, understanding their self-interest, are correlating themselves in the industrial and economic mechanism. They are developing their industrial consciousness, their economic and political power; and when the revolution comes, they will be prepared to take possession and assume control of every industry. With the education they will have received in the Industrial Workers they will be drilled and disciplined, trained and fitted for Industrial Mastery and Social Freedom.

Industrial Unionism

Address at Grand Central Palace, New York, December 10, 1905

There is an inspiration in your greeting and my heart opens wide to receive it. I have come a thousand miles to join with you in fanning the flames of the proletarian revolution. (Applause.)

Your presence here makes this a vitalizing atmosphere for a labor agitator. I can feel my stature increasing, and this means that you are growing, for all my strength is drawn from you, and without you I am nothing.

In capitalist society you are the lower class; the capitalists are the upper class—because they are on your backs; if they were not on your backs, they could not be above you. (Applause and laughter.)

Standing in your presence, I can see in your gleaming eyes and in your glowing faces the vanguard; I can hear the tramp, I can feel the thrill of the social revolution. The working class are waking up. (A voice, "You bet.") They are beginning to understand that their economic interests are identical, that they must unite and act together economically and politically, and in every other way; that only by united action can they overthrow the capitalist system and emancipate themselves from wage-slavery. (Applause.)

I have said that in the capitalist society the working class are the lower class; they have always been the lower class. In the ancient world for thousands of years they were abject slaves; in the Middle Ages, serfs; in modern times, wage-workers; to become free men in socialism, the next inevitable phase of advancing civilization. (Applause.) The working class have struggled through all the various phases of their development, and they are today engaged in the last stage of the animal struggle for existence; and when the present revolution has run its course, the working class will stand forth the sovereigns of this earth.

In capitalist society the working man is not, in fact, a man at all; as a wage-worker, he is simply merchandise; he is bought in the open market the same as hair, hides, salt, or any other form of merchandise. The very terminology of the capitalist system proves that he is not a man in any sense of that term.

When the capitalist needs you as a workingman to operate his machine, he does not advertise, he does not call for men, but for "hands"; and when you see a placard posted, "Fifty hands wanted," you stop on the instant; you know that that means YOU, and you take a bee-line for the bureau of employment to offer yourself in evidence of the fact that you are a "hand." When the capitalist advertises for hands, that is what he wants.

He would be insulted if you were to call him a "hand." He has his capitalist politician tell you, when your vote is wanted, that you ought to be very proud of your hands because they are horny; and if that is true, he ought to be ashamed of his. (Laughter and applause.)

What is your status in society today? You are a human being, a wage-worker. Here you stand just as you were created, and you have two hands that represent your labor power; but you do not work, and why not? For the simple reason that you have no tools with which to work; you cannot compete against the machinery of the capitalist with your bare hands; you cannot work unless you have access to it, and you can only secure access to it by selling your labor power, that is to say, your energy, your vitality, your life itself, to the capitalist who owns the tool with which you work, and without which you are idle and suffer all of the ills that idleness entails.

In the evolution of capitalism, society has been divided mainly into two economic classes; a relatively small class of capitalists who own tools in the form of great machines they did not make and cannot use, and a great body of many millions of workers who did make these tools and who do use them, and whose very lives depend upon them, yet who do not own them; and these millions of wage-workers, producers of wealth, are forced into the labor market, in competition with each other, disposing of their labor power to the capitalist class, in consideration of just enough of what they produce to keep them in working order. They are exploited of the greater share of what their labor produces, so that while, upon the one hand, they can produce in great abundance, upon the other they can consume but that share of the product that their meagre wage will buy; and every now and then it follows that they have produced more than can be consumed in the present system, and then they are displaced by the very products of their own labor; the mills and shops and mines and quarries in which they are employed close down, the tools are locked up and they are locked out, and they find themselves idle and helpless in the shadow of the very abundance their labor has created.

There is no hope for them in this system. They are beginning to realize this fact, and so they are beginning to organize; they are no longer relying upon someone else, but they are making up their minds to depend upon themselves and to organize for their own emancipation.

Too long have the workers of the world waited for some Moses to lead them out of bondage. He has not come; he never will come. I would not lead you out if I could; for if you could be led out, you could be led back again. (Applause.) I would have you make up your minds that there is nothing that you cannot do for yourselves.

You do not need the capitalist. He could not exist an instant without you. You would just begin to live without him. (Laughter and prolonged applause.) You do everything and he has everything; and some of you imagine that if it were not for him you would have no work. As a matter of fact, he does not employ you at all; you employ him to take from you what you produce, and he faithfully sticks to his task. If you can stand it, he can; and if you don't change this relation, I am sure he won't. You make the automobile, he rides in it. If it were not for you, he would walk; and if it were not for him, you would ride.

The capitalist politician tells you on occasion that you are the salt of the earth; and if you are, you had better begin to salt down the capitalist class.

The revolutionary movement of the working class will date from the year 1905, from the organization of the INDUSTRIAL WORKERS OF THE WORLD. (Prolonged applause.) Economic solidarity is today the supreme need of the working class. The old form of unionism has long since fulfilled its mission and outlived its usefulness, and the hour has struck for a change.

The old unionism is organized upon the basis of the identity of interests of the capitalist and working classes. It spends its time and energy trying to conciliate these two essentially antagonistic classes; and so this unionism has at its head a harmonizing board called the Civic Federation. This federation consists of three parts; a part representing the capitalist class; a part supposed to represent the working class, and still another part that is said to represent the "public." The capitalists are represented by that great union labor champion, August Belmont. (Laughter and hisses.) The working class by Samuel Gompers, the president of the American Federation of Labor (hisses and cries, "sic him"), and the public, by Grover Cleveland. (Laughter.)

Can you imagine a fox and goose peace congress? Just fancy such a meeting, the goose lifting its wings in benediction, and the fox whispering, "Let us prey."

The Civic Federation has been organized for the one purpose of prolonging the age-long sleep of the working class. Their supreme purpose is to keep you from waking up. (A voice: "They can't do it.")

The Industrial Workers has been organized for an opposite purpose, and its representatives come in your presence to tell you that there can be no peace between you, the working class, and the capitalist class who exploit you of what you produce; that as workers you have economic interests apart from and opposed to their interests, and that you must organize by and for yourselves; and that if you are intelligent enough to understand these interests you will sever your relations with the old unions in which you are divided and sub-divided, and join the

Industrial Workers, in which all are organized and united upon the basis of the class struggle. (Applause.)

The Industrial Workers is organized, not to conciliate, but to fight the capitalist class. We have no object in concealing any part of our mission; we would have it perfectly understood. We deny that there is anything in common between workingmen and capitalists. We insist that workingmen must organize to get rid of capitalists and make themselves the masters of the tools with which they work, freely employ themselves, secure to themselves all they produce, and enjoy to the full the fruit of their labors. (Applause.)

The old union movement is not only organized upon the basis of the identity of interests of the exploited and exploiting classes, but it divides instead of uniting the workers, and there are thousands of unions, more or less in conflict, used against one another; and so long as these countless unions occupy the field, there will be no substantial unity of the working class. (Applause.)

And here let me say that the most zealous supporter of the old union is the capitalist himself. August Belmont, president of the Civic Federation, takes special pride in declaring himself a "union man" (laughter); but he does not mean by that that he is an Industrial Worker; that is not the kind of a union he means. He means the impotent old union that Mr. Gompers and Mr. Mitchell lead, the kind that keeps the working class divided so that the capitalist system may be perpetuated indefinitely.

For thirty years I have been connected with the organized labor movement. I have long since been made to realize that the pure and simple union can do nothing for the working class; I have had some experience and know whereof I speak. The craft union seeks to establish its own petty supremacy. Craft division is fatal to class unity. To organize along craft lines means to divide the working class and make it the prey of the capitalist class. The working class can only be unionized efficiently along class lines; and so the Industrial Workers has been organized, not to isolate the crafts but to unite the whole working class. (Applause.)

The working class has had considerable experience during

the past few years. In almost every conflict between labor and capital, labor has been defeated. Take the leading strikes in their order, and you will find that, without a single exception, the organized workers have been defeated, and thousands upon thousands of them have lost their jobs, and many of them have become "scabs." Is there not something wrong with a unionism in which the workers are always worsted? Let me review hurriedly some of this history of the past few years.

I have seen the conductors on the Chicago, Burlington & Quincy Railroad, organized in a craft union, take the place of the striking union locomotive engineers on the same system.

I have seen the employes of the Missouri, Kansas & Texas Railway, organized in their several craft unions, stand by the corporation as a unit, totally wiping out the union telegraphers, thirteen hundred of them losing their jobs.

I have seen these same craft unions, just a little while ago, on the Northern Pacific and Great Northern systems— I have seen them unite with the corporation to crush out the telegraphers' union, and defeat the strikers, their own co-unionists and fellow employes.

Just a few weeks ago, in the city of Chicago, the switchmen on the Grand Trunk went out on strike. All their fellow unionists remained at work and faithfully served the corporation until the switchmen were defeated, and now those union switchmen are scattered about looking for jobs.

The machinists were recently on strike in Chicago. They went out in a body under the direction of their craft union. Their fellow unionists all remained at work until the machinists were completely defeated, and now their organization in that city is on the verge of collapse.

There has been a ceaseless repetition of this form of scabbing of one craft union upon another until the working man, if his eyes are open, is bound to see that this kind of unionism is a curse and not a benefit to the working class.

The American Federation of Labor does not learn by experience. They recently held their annual convention, and they passed the same old stereotyped resolutions; they are going to petition Congress to restrict the power of the courts; that is to say, they are going to once more petition a capitalist Congress to restrict the power of capitalist courts. That is as if a flock of sheep were to petition a pack of wolves to extract their own fangs. They have passed these resolutions over and over again. They have been totally fruitless and will continue to be.

What good came to the working class from this convention? Put your finger upon a single thing they did that will be of any real benefit to the workers of the country!

You have had some experience here in New York. You have plenty of unionism here, such as it is, yet there is not a city in the country in which the workers are less organized than they are here. It was in March last that you had here an exhibition of pure and simple unionism. You saw about six thousand craft union men go out on strike, and you saw their fellow unionists remain at work loyally until all the strikers were defeated and sacrificed. Here you have an object lesson that is well calculated to set you thinking, and this is all I can hope to do by coming here, set you thinking, and for yourselves; for when you begin to think, you will soon begin to act for yourselves. You will then sever your relations with capitalist unions and capitalist parties (applause), and you will begin the real work of organizing your class, and that is what we of the Industrial Workers have engaged to do. We have a new mission. That mission is not merely the amelioration of the condition of the working class, but the complete emancipation of that class from slavery. (Applause.)

The Industrial Workers is going to do all for the working class that can be done in the capitalist system, but while it is engaged in doing that, its revolutionary eye will be fixed upon the goal; and there will be a great difference between a strike of revolutionary workers and a strike of ignorant trade unionists who but vaguely understand what they want and do not know how to get that. (Applause.)

The Industrial Workers is less than six months old, and already has a round hundred thousand of dues-paying members. (Applause.) This splendid achievement has no parallel in the annals of organized labor. From every direction come the applications for charters and for organizers, and when the delegates of this revolutionary economic organization meet in the city of Chicago, next year, it will be the greatest convention that ever met in the United States in the interest of the working class. (Applause.)

This organization has a world-wide mission; it makes its appeal directly to the working class. It asks no favors from capitalists.

No organization of working men has ever been so flagrantly misrepresented by the capitalist press as has been the Industrial Workers of the World; every delegate to the Chicago convention will bear testimony to this fact; and this is as it should be; the capitalist press is the mouthpiece of the capitalist class, and the very fact that the capitalist press is the organ, virtually, of the American Federation of Labor, is in itself sufficient to open the eyes of the working class.

If the American Federation of Labor were not in alliance with the capitalist class, the capitalist press would not pour its fulsome eulogy upon it.

This press has not one friendly word for the Industrial Workers, not one, and we do not expect it to have. These papers of the plutocrats know us and we know them (applause); between us there is no misunderstanding.

The workers of the country (the intelligent ones at least) readily see the difference between revolutionary and reactionary unionism, and that is why they are deserting the old and joining the new; that is why the Industrial Workers is building up so rapidly; that is why there is such a widespread demand for organizers and for literature and for all other means of building up this class-conscious economic organization. (Applause.)

As I have said, the Industrial Workers begin by declaring that there is nothing in common between capitalists and wageworkers.

The capitalists own the tools they do not use, and the workers use the tools they do not own.

The capitalists, who own the tools that the working class use appropriate to themselves what the working class produce, and this accounts for the fact that a few capitalists become fabulously rich while the toiling millions remain in poverty, ignorance and dependence.

Let me make this point perfectly clear for the benefit of those who have not thought it out for themselves. Andrew Carnegie is a type of the capitalist class. He owns the tools with which steel is produced. These tools are used by many thousands of working men. Andrew Carnegie, who owns these tools, has absolutely nothing to do with the production of steel. He may be in Scotland, or where he will, the production of steel goes forward just the same. His mills at Pittsburg, Duquesne and Homestead, where these tools are located, are thronged with thousands of toolless wage-workers, who work day and night, in winter's cold and summer's heat, who endure all the privations and make all the sacrifices of health and limb and life, producing thousands upon thousands of tons of steel, yet not having an interest, even the slightest, in the product. Carnegie, who owns the tools, appropriates the product, and the workers, in exchange for their labor power, receive a wage that serves to keep them in producing order; and the more industrious they are, and the more they produce, the worse they are off; for the sooner they have produced more than Carnegie can get rid of in the markets, the tool houses are shut down and the workers are locked out in the cold.

This is a beautiful arrangement—for Mr. Carnegie; he does not want a change, and so he is in favor of the Civic Federation, and a leading member of it; and he is doing what he can to induce you to think that this ideal relation ought to be maintained forever.

Now, what is true of steel production is true of every other department of industrial activity; you belong to the millions who have no tools, who cannot work without selling your labor power, and when you sell that, you have got to deliver it in person; you cannot send it to the mill, you have got to carry it there; you are inseparable from your labor power.

You have got to go to the mill at 7 in the morning and work until 6 in the evening, producing, not for yourself, but for the capitalist who owns the tools you made and use, and without which you are almost as helpless as if you had no arms.

This fundamental fact in modern industry you must recognize, and you must organize upon the basis of this fact; you must appeal to your class to join the union that is the true expression of your economic interests, and this union must be large enough to embrace you all, and such is the Industrial Workers of the World.

Every man and every woman who works for wages is eligible to membership.

Organized into various departments, when you join you become a member of the department that represents your craft, or occupation, whatever it may be; and when you have a grievance, your department has supervision of it; and if you fail to adjust it in that department, you are not limited to your craft alone for support, but, if necessary, all the workers in all other departments will unite solidly in your defense to the very last. (Applause.)

Take a plant in modern industry. The workers, under the old form of unionism, are parceled out to a score or more of unions. Craft division incites craft jealousy and so they are more or less in conflict with each other, and the employer constructively takes advantage of this fact, and that is why he favors pure and simple unionism.

It were better for the workers who wear craft fetters if they were not organized at all, for then they could and would spontaneously go out on strike together; but they cannot do this in craft unionism, for certain crafts bind themselves up in craft agreements, and after they have done this, they are at the mercy of the capitalist; and when their fellow unionists call upon them for aid, they make the very convenient excuse that they cannot help them, that they must preserve the sanctity of the contract they have made with the employer. This so-called contract is regarded as of vastly more importance than the jobs, aye, the very lives of the workingmen themselves.

We do not intend that certain departments shall so attach themselves to the capitalist employers. We purpose that the workers shall all be organized, and if there is any agreement, it will embrace them all; and if there is any violation of the agreement, in the case of a single employe, it at once becomes the concern of all. (Applause.) That is unionism, industrial unionism, in which all of the workers, totally regardless of occupation, are united compactly within the one organization, so that at all times they can act together in the interests of all. It is upon this basis that the Industrial Workers of the World is organized. It is in this spirit and with this object in view that it makes its appeal to the working class.

Then, again, the revolutionary economic organization has a new and important function which has never once been thought of in the old union, for the simple reason that the old union intends that the wage system shall endure forever.

The Industrial Workers declares that the workers must make themselves the masters of the tools with which they work; and so a very important function of this new union is to teach the workers, or, rather, have them teach themselves the necessity of fitting themselves to take charge of the industries in which they are employed when they are wrested, as they will be, from their capitalist masters. (Applause.)

So when you join the Industrial Workers you feel the thrill of a new aspiration; you are no longer a blind, dumb wage-slave. You begin to understand your true and vital relation to your fellow-workers. In the Industrial Workers you are correlated to all other workers in the plant, and thus you develop the embryonic structure of the co-operative commonwealth. (Applause.)

The old unionism would have you contented. We Industrial Workers are doing what we can to increase your discontent. We would have you rise in revolt against wage-slavery. The working man who is contented today is truly a pitiable object. (Applause.)

Victor Hugo once said: "Think of a smile in chains,"— that is a working man who, under the influence of the Civic Federation, is satisfied with his lot; he is glad he has a master, some one to serve; for, in his ignorance, he imagines that he is dependent upon the master.

The Industrial Workers is appealing to the working class to develop their latent powers and above all, their capacity for clear thinking.

You are a working man and you have a brain and if you do not use it in your own interests, you are guilty of treason to your manhood. (Applause.)

It is for the very reason that you do not use your brain in your interests that you are compelled to deform your body in the interests of your master.

I have already said that the capitalist is on your back; he furnishes the mouth, you the hands; he consumes, you produce. That is why he runs largely to stomach and you to hands. (Laughter.)

I would not be a capitalist; I would be a man; you cannot be both at the same time. (Applause.)

The capitalist exists by exploitation, lives out of the labor, that is to say the life, of the working man; consumes him, and his code of morals and standard of ethics justify it and this proves that capitalism is cannibalism. (Applause.)

A man, honest, just, high-minded, would scorn to live out of the sweat and sorrow of his fellow man—by preying upon his weaker brother.

We purpose to destroy the capitalist and save the man. (Applause.) We want a system in which the worker shall get what he produces and the capitalist shall produce what he gets. (Applause.) That is a square deal.

The prevailing lack of unity implies the lack of class consciousness. The workers do not yet understand that they are engaged in a class struggle, that they must unite their class and get on the right side of that struggle economically, politically and in every other way—(applause), strike together, vote together and, if necessary, fight together. (Prolonged applause.)

The capitalist and the leader of the pure and simple union do what they can to wipe out the class lines; they do not want you to recognize the *class* struggle; they contrive to keep you divided, and as long as you are divided, you will remain where you are, robbed and helpless.

When you unite and act together, the world is yours. (Prolonged applause.)

The fabled Samson, shorn of his locks, the secret of his power, was the sport and prey of the pygmies that tormented him. The modern working class, shorn of their tools, the secret of their power, are at the mercy of a small class who exploit them of what they produce and then hold them in contempt because of their slavery.

No master ever had the slightest respect for his slave, and no slave ever had the least real love for his master.

Between these two classes there is an irrepressible conflict, and we Industrial Workers are pointing it out that you may see it, that you may get on the right side of it, that you may get together and emancipate yourselves from every form of servitude.

It can be done in no other way; but a bit of sober reasoning will convince you workers of this fact.

It is so simple that a child can see it. Why can't you? You can if you will think for yourselves and see for yourselves. But you will not do this if you were taught in the old union school; you will still look to someone else to lead that you may follow; for you are trained to follow the blind leaders of the blind. You have been betrayed over and over again, and there will be no change until you make up your minds to think and see and act for yourselves.

I would not have you blindly walk into the Industrial Workers; if I had sufficient influence or power to draw you into it, I would not do it. I would have you stay where you are until you can see your way clear to join it of your own accord. It is your organization; it is composed of your class; it is committed to the interests of your class; it is going to fight for your class, for your whole class, and continue the fight until your class is emancipated. (Applause.)

There is a great deal of opposition to this organization. The whole capitalist class and all their labor lieutenants are against it (applause); and there is an army of them, and all their names are on the pay-roll and expense account. They all hold salaried positions, and are looking out for themselves.

When the working class unite, there will be a lot of jobless labor leaders. (Applause.)

In many of these craft unions they have it so arranged that the rank and file do not count for any more than if they were so many sheep. In the railroad organizations, for instance, if the whole membership vote to go out on strike, they cannot budge without the official sanction of the "Grand Chief." His word outweighs that of the entire membership. In the light of this extraordinary fact, is it strange that the workers are often betrayed? Is it strange that they continue at the mercy of their exploiters?

Haven't they had quite enough of this? Isn't it time for them to take an inventory of their own resources?

If you are a working man, suppose you look yourself over, just once; take an invoice of your mental stock and see what you have. Do not accept my word; do not depend upon anybody but yourself. Think it out for yourself; and if you do, I am quite certain that you will join the organization that represents your class (applause); the organization that has room for all your class; the organization that appeals to you to develop your own brain, to rely upon yourself and be a man among men. And that is what the working class have to do, cultivate self-reliance and think and act for themselves; and that is what they are stimulated to do in the Industrial Workers.

We have great hope and abiding faith for we know that each day will bring us increasing numbers, influences and power; and this notwithstanding all the opposition that can be arrayed against us.

We know that the principles of the Industrial Workers are right and that its ultimate triumph is assured beyond the question of a doubt; and if you believe in its conquering mission, then we ask you to be true enough to yourselves and your class to join it; and when you join it you will have a duty to perform and that duty will be to go out among the unorganized and bring them into the ranks and help in this great work of education and organization, without which the working class is doomed to continued ignorance and slavery.

Karl Marx, the profound economic philosopher, who will be known in future as the great emancipator, uttered the inspiring shibboleth a half century ago: "Workingmen of all countries unite; you have nothing to lose but your chains; you have a world to gain."

You workers are the only class essential to society; all

others can be spared, but without you society would perish. You produce the wealth, you support government, you create and conserve civilization. You ought to be, can be and will be the masters of the earth. (Great applause.)

Why should you be dependent upon a capitalist? Why should this capitalist own a tool he cannot use? And why should not you own the tool you have to use?

Every cog in every wheel that revolves everywhere has been made by the working class, and is set and kept in operation by the working class; and if the working class can make and operate this marvelous wealth-producing machinery, they can also develop the intelligence to make themselves the masters of this machinery (applause), and operate it not to turn out millionaires, but to produce wealth in abundance for themselves.

You cannot afford to be contented with your lot; you have a brain to develop and a manhood to sustain. You ought to have some aspiration to be free.

Suppose you do have a job, and that you can get enough to eat and clothes enough to cover your body, and a place to sleep; you but exist upon the animal plane; your very life is suspended by a slender thread; you don't know what hour a machine may be invented to displace you, or you may offend your economic master, and your job is gone. You go to work early in the morning and you work all day; you go to your lodging at night, tired; you throw your exhausted body upon a bed of straw to recuperate enough to go back to the factory and repeat the same dull operation the next day, and the next, and so on and on to the dreary end; and in some respects you are not so well off as was the chattel slave.

He had no fear of losing his job; he was not blacklisted; he had food and clothing and shelter; and now and then, seized with a desire for freedom, he tried to run away from his master. You do not try to run away from yours. He doesn't have to hire a policeman to keep an eye on you. When you run, it is in the opposite direction, when the bell rings or the whistle blows.

You are as much subject to the command of the capitalist as if you were his property under the law. You have got to go to his factory because you have got to work; he is the master of your job, and you cannot work without his consent, and he only gives this on condition that you surrender to him all you produce except what is necessary to keep you in running order.

The machine you work with has to be oiled; you have to be fed; the wage is your lubricant, it keeps you in working order, and so you toil and sweat and groan and reproduce yourself in the form of labor power, and then you pass away like a silk worm that spins its task and dies.

That is your lot in the capitalist system and you have no right to aspire to rise above the dead level of wage-slavery.

It is true that one in ten thousand may escape from his class and become a millionaire; he is the rare exception that proves the rule. The wage-workers remain in the working class, and they never can become anything else in the capitalist system. They produce and perish, and their exploited bones mingle with the dust.

Every few years there is a panic, industrial paralysis, and hundreds of thousands of workers are flung into the streets; no work, no wages; and so they throng the highways in search of employment that cannot be found; they become vagrants, tramps, outcasts, criminals. It is in this way that the human being degenerates, and that crime graduates in the capitalist system, all the way from petty larceny to homicide.

The working millions who produce the wealth have little or nothing to show for it. There is widespread ignorance among them; industrial and social conditions prevail that defy all language properly to describe. The working class consist of a mass of human beings, men, women and children, in enforced competition with one another, in all of the circling hours of the day and night, for the sale of their labor power, and in the severity of the competition the wage sinks gradually until it touches the point of subsistence.

In this struggle more than five millions of women are engaged and about two millions of children, and the number of child laborers is steadily increasing, for in this system profit is important, while life has no value. It is not a question of male labor, or female labor, or child labor; it is simply a question of cheap labor without reference to the effect upon the working class; the woman is employed in preference to the man and the child in preference to the woman; and so we have millions of children, who, in their early, tender years, are seized in the iron clutch of capitalism, when they ought to be upon the playground, or at school; when they ought to be in the sunlight, when they ought to have wholesome food and enjoy the fresh atmosphere they are forced into the industrial dungeons and there they are riveted to the machines; they feed the insatiate monsters and become as living cogs in the revolving wheels. They are literally fed to industry to produce profits. They are dwarfed and deformed, mentally, morally and physically; they have no chance in life; they are the victims of the industrial system that the Industrial Workers is organized to abolish in the interest, not only of the working class, but in the higher interest of all humanity. (Applause.)

If there is a crime that should bring to the callous cheek of capitalist society the crimson of shame, it is the unspeakable crime of child slavery; the millions of babes that fester in the sweat shops, are the slaves of the wheel, and cry out in their agony, but are not heard in the din and roar of our industrial infernalism.

Take that great army of workers, called coal miners, organized in a craft union that does nothing for them; that seeks to make them contented with their lot. These miners are at the very foundation of industry and without their labor every wheel would cease to revolve as if by the decree of some industrial Jehovah. (Applause.) There are 600,000 of these slaves whose labor makes possible the firesides of the world, while their own loved ones shiver in the cold. I know something of the conditions under which they toil and despair and perish. I have taken time enough to descend to the depths of these pits, that Dante never saw, or he might have improved upon his masterpiece. I have stood over these slaves and I have heard the echo of their picks, which sounded to me like muffled drums throbbing funeral marches to the grave, and I have said to myself, in the capitalist system, these wretches are simply following their own hearses to the potter's field.

In all of the horizon of the future there is no star that sheds a ray of hope for them.

Then I have followed them from the depth of these black holes, over to the edge of the camp, not to the home, they have no home; but to a hut that is owned by the corporation that owns them, and here I have seen the wife,—Victor Hugo once said that the wife of a slave is not a wife at all; she is simply a female that gives birth to young—I have seen this wife standing in the doorway, after trying all day long to make a ten-cent piece do the service of a half-dollar, and she was ill-humored; this could not be otherwise, for love and abject poverty do not dwell beneath the same roof. Here there is no paper upon the wall and no carpet upon the floor; there is not a picture to appeal to the eye; there is no statue to challenge the soul, no strain of inspiring music to touch and quicken what Lincoln called the better angels of human nature. Here there is haggard poverty and want. And in this atmosphere the children of the future are being reared, many thousands of them, under conditions that make it morally certain that they will become paupers, or criminals, or both.

Man is the product, the expression of his environment. Show me a majestic tree that towers aloft, that challenges the admiration of man, or a beautiful rose-bud that, under the influence of sunshine and shower, bursts into bloom and fills the common air with its fragrance; these are possible only because the soil and climate are adapted to the growth and culture. Transfer this flower from the sunlight and the atmosphere to a cellar filled with noxious gases, and it withers and dies. The same law applies to human beings; the industrial soil and the social climate must be adapted to the development of men and women, and then society will cease producing (cry of "down with capitalism") the multiplied thousands of deformities that today are a rebuke to our much vaunted civilization, and, above all, an impeachment of the capitalist system. (Applause.)

What is true of the miners is true in a greater or less degree of all workers in all other departments of industrial activity. This system has about fulfilled its historic mission.

Upon every hand there are the unerring signs of change, and the time has come for the education and organization of the working class for the social revolution (applause) that is to lift the workers from the depths of slavery and elevate them to an exalted plane of equality and fraternity. (Applause.)

At the beginning of industrial society men worked with hand tools; a boy could learn a trade, make himself the master of the simple tools with which he worked, and employ himself and enjoy what he produced; but that simple tool of a century ago has become a mammoth social instrument; in a word, that tool has been socialized. Not only this, but production has been socialized. As small a commodity as a pin or a pen, or a match involves for its production all of the social labor of the land; but this evolution is not yet complete; the tool has been socialized, production has been socialized, and now ownership must also be socialized; in other words, those great social instruments that are used in modern industry for the production of wealth, those great social agencies that are socially made and socially used, must also be socially owned. (Applause.)

The Industrial Workers is the only economic organization that makes this declaration, that states this fact and is organized upon this foundation, that the workers must own their tools and employ themselves. This involves a revolution, and this means the end of the capitalist system, and the rearing of a working class republic (prolonged applause), the first real republic the world has ever known; and it is coming just as certainly as I stand in your presence.

You can hasten it, or you can retard it, but you cannot prevent it.

This the working class can achieve, and if you are in that class and you do not believe it, it is because of your ignorance; it is because you got your education in the school of pure and simple unionism, or in a capitalist political party. This the working class can achieve and all that is required is that the working class shall be educated, that they shall unite, that they shall act together.

The capitalist politician and the labor lieutenant have always contrived to keep the working class divided, upon the economic field and upon the political field; and the workers have made no progress, and never will until they desert those false leaders and unite beneath the revolutionary standard of the Industrial Workers of the World. (Applause.)

The capitalists have the mills and the tools and the dollars, but you are an overwhelming majority; you have the men, you have the votes. There are not enough of them to continue this system an instant; it can only be continued by your consent and with your approval, and to the extent that you give it you are responsible for your slavery; and if you have your eyes opened, if you understand where you properly belong, it is still a fortunate thing that you cannot do anything for yourself until you have opened the eyes of those that are yet in darkness. (Applause.)

Now, there are many workers who have had their eyes opened and they are giving their time and energy to the revolutionary education of the working class (applause), and every day sees our minority increasing, and it is but a question of time until this minority will be converted into the triumphant majority (applause); and so we wait and watch and work in all of the circling hours of the day and night.

We have just begun here in New York, and with a vim and an energy unknown in the circles of unionism. In six months from this night you will find that there is a very formidable organization of Industrial Workers in New York (applause); and if you are a working man and you have convictions of your own, it is your duty to join this union and take your place where you belong.

Don't hesitate because somebody else is falling back. Don't wait because somebody else is not yet ready. Act and act now and for yourself; and if you happen to be the only Industrial Workers in your shop, or in your immediate vicinity, you are simply monumental of the ignorance of your fellow-workers, and you have got to begin to educate them. For a little while they may point you out with the finger of contempt, but you can stand this; you can bear it with patience; if they persecute you, because you are true to yourself, your latent powers will be developed, you will become stronger than you now dream, and then you will do the deeds that live, and you will write your name where it will stay.

SPEECHES. 465

Never mind what others may say, or think, or do. Stand erect in the majesty of your own manhood.

Listen for just once to the throbbing of your own heart, and you will hear that it is beating quick-step marches to Camp Freedom.

Stand erect! Lift your bowed form from the earth! The dust has long enough borne the impress of your knees.

Stand up and see how long a shadow you cast in the sunlight! (Applause). Hold up your head and avow your convictions, and then accept, as becomes a man, the consequences of your acts!

We need you and you need us. We have got to have the workers united, and you have got to help us in the work. And so we make our appeal to you tonight, and we know that you will not fail. You can arrive at no other conclusion; you are bound to join the industrial workers, and become a missionary in the field of industrial unionism. You will then feel the ecstacy of a new-born aspiration. You will do your very best. You will wear the badge of the Industrial Workers, and you will wear it with pride and joy.

The very contempt that it invites will be a compliment to you; in truth, a tribute to your manhood.

We will wrest what we can, step by step, from the capitalists, but with our eye fixed upon the goal; we will press forward, keeping step together with the inspiring music of the new emancipation; and when we have enough of this kind of organization, as Brother De Leon said so happily the other day (applause), when we are lined up in battle array, and the capitalists try to lock us out, we will turn the tables on the gentlemen and lock them out. (Applause.)

We can run the mills without them but they cannot run them without us. (Applause.)

It is a very important thing to develop the economic power, to have a sound economic organization. This has been the inherent weakness in the labor movement of the United States. We need, and sorely need, a revolutionary economic organization. We must develop this kind of strength; it is the kind that we will have occasion to use in due time, and it is the kind that will not fail us when the crisis comes. So we shall organize and continue to organize the political field; and I am of those who believe that the day is near at hand when we shall have one great revolutionary economic organization, and one great revolutionary political party of the working class. (Cheers and prolonged applause.) Then will proceed with increased impetus the work of education and organization that will culminate in emancipation.

This great body will sweep into power and seize the reins of government; take possession of industry in the name of the working class, and it can be easily done. All that will be required will be to transfer the title deeds from the parasites to the producers; and then the working class, in control of industry, will operate it for the benefit of all. The work day will be reduced in proportion to the progress of invention. Every man will work, or at least have a chance to work, and get the full equivalent of what he produces. He will work, not as a slave, but as a free man, and he will express himself in his work and work with joy. Then the badge of labor will be the only badge of aristocracy. The industrial dungeon will become a temple of science. The working class will be free, and all humanity disenthralled.

The workers are the saviours of society (applause); the redeemers of the race; and when they have fulfilled their great historic mission, men and women can walk the highlands and enjoy the vision of a land without masters and without slaves, a land regenerated and resplendent in the triumph of Freedom and Civilization. (Long, continued applause.)

Golden Wedding Anniversary

Tribute Paid to Parents, Jean Daniel Debs and Marguerite Bettrich Debs, on behalf of the family, at Golden Wedding Anniversary, Terre Haute, Ind., September 13, 1899

The celebration of a Golden wedding is a rare occurrence in the history of families; only to the favored few is such a blessing vouchsafed. It is an occasion when nuptial vows pledged at Hymen's altar take on inexpressible sacredness. A far distant day is recalled when "two souls with but a single thought" and two loving hearts that "beat as one" courageously and confidently entered upon the voyage of matrimonial life. Thomas Moore, inspired by the genius of love, rapturously sang:

> "There's a bliss beyond all that the minstrel has told,
> When two, that are linked in one heavenly tie,
> With heart never changing and brow never cold,
> Live on thro' all ills, and love on till they die."

It is not given to us, children and grandchildren, who meet today at the old home shrine to lay our offerings, consecrated by affection, upon the family altar, to know the heart and soul yearnings of our aged parents to find some favored spot, some oasis in the desert, where they could build a home and enjoy the fruitions of peace and contentment amidst a family of bright-eyed, rosy-cheeked and merry-voiced children.

In fancy's eye we see their beautiful and vine-clad native France; we see them in the bloom and strength of youth, standing at the altar and pledging to each other unchanging fidelity in storm and shine, ready to meet the future as the day unfolded their duties, their opportunities, their tasks and trials, sustained by a faith and hope which cheered them on their pilgrimage through all their married days.

Those of us who have reached years of maturity and are here with wives and husbands and children and children's children, may in fancy's telescopic vision see the youthful pair leaving the old for the new world, whispering to each other with brimful eyes and quivering lips:

> "Go where we will, this hand in thine,
> Those eyes before me smiling thus,
> Through good and ill, through storm and shine,
> The world's a world of love for us."

And such has been the world to them. Love has been their guiding star; no cloud ever obscured it, and the darker the day of adversity the brighter shone their love which bathed their home and our home in its mellow, cheering light.

In celebrating this golden wedding anniversary, all the halcyon days of our lives are included and there come to us messages from the past, under the sea and over the land, burdened with the aroma of violets and roses, caught from the flower gardens of memory, planted in youth and blooming in perennial beauty to old age.

I confess to you, my venerable parents, and to you my sisters and brothers, and to those of younger generations, to overmastering emotions of love and gratitude as I survey this family scene, never to be pictured again save upon the canvas of our memories. But I would voice no requiem note. Today our ears are not attuned to the dirge's mournful cadence. This is not the occasion for planting weeping-willows, the cypress or the ivy vine—

> "Creeping where grim death is seen."

Here the mingled cup of love and gratitude and joy, brimful, is quaffed in honor of an event which to us all is a priceless benediction; but, if from its foundation a tear mingles with the draught to sparkle on the brim of the loving cup, it bears testimony that our hearts are touched by feelings as divine as ever sanctified human affection.

The serenity, the rare loveliness of this scene create emotions which no words, however fitly chosen, can express. I can but say in the name of my sisters and my brothers and those younger in the bonds of family allegiance to our father—the patriarch of these sons and daughters—that we tender him our warmest congratulations upon this rare occasion. When we greet him our hearts are in our hands; when we kiss his time-furrowed cheeks our hearts are on our lips, and when we congratulate him upon this, his golden wedding anniversary, our hearts are in our words.

Freely do we avow the fealty of our love for his devotion to us, his children, for his watchful guardianship over our giddy footsteps on youth's flowery pathways; and this love is blended with profound veneration for his courage, which no vicissitude could dampen; for his masculine virtues which have endeared him to the home circle; for his spotless integrity of character which has given him the confidence of men, whether in poverty's vale or upon the more elevated plane of prosperity, secured by industry and frugality, and above all, for that parental ambition and self-denial to secure for us an education which should equip his children for respectable and honorable positions in life.

This, my beloved and honored sire, is the tribute of affection your children bring to you today. Your tender and unceasing devotion has won the overflowing gratitude of our hearts, and this thankfulness, this abounding sense of obligation, dearest father, we children with the fingers of our love weave today into a crown and place it on your venerable head, and though the years shall continue to whiten your locks, dim the lustre of your eyes and impair the strength of your manly form, the wealth of our affection shall ever increase, nor shall it cease when the silver cord be loosed and at the final goal you lay all your burdens down.

And now our happy family circle, rejoicing in kindred ties, will fill again the sparkling cup with the ambrosia of affection that we may drink to:

> "My mother's voice! how often creep
> Its accents on my lonely hours.
> Like healing sent on wings of sleep,
> Or dew to the unconscious flowers.
> I can forget her melting prayer
> While leaping pulses madly fly,

> But in the still, unbroken air
>   Her gentle tone comes stealing by—
> And years, and sin, and folly flee,
>   And leave me at my mother's knee."

There are two words in our language forever sacred to memory—Mother and Home! Home, the heaven upon earth, and mother its presiding angel. To us, children, here today, mother and home have realized all the longing, yearning aspirations of our souls, and now, in this blissful presence, we quaff to our mother this cup full and overflowing with the divine nectar of our love. I need not attempt to recite her deeds of devotion. There is not a page of our memory, not a table of our hearts, that is not adorned and beautified by acts of her loving care, in which her heart and her hands, her eyes and her soul, in holy alliance, ministered to our happiness.

There was never a time when there was not a song in her heart, sweeter than Æolian melody, wooing her children from folly to the blessedness, security, peace and contentment of home. Her children were her jewels in home's shining circle, and if by the fiat of death a gem dropped away, the affectionate care it had received added soulful charm to her lullaby songs when at night she dismissed us and sent us to dreamland repose.

Years of duty and trial, anxiety and care have bowed her form, whitened her hair, dimmed her eyes and robbed her cheeks of their maiden bloom; but O, our mother is still to us our beautiful mother. Her heart is as young and loving as when in infancy, in youth and in riper years it throbbed responsive to our plaints; her hands are as beautiful in our eyes as when in our childhood they were laid caressingly upon our heads, and her dimpled fingers smoothed our hair or wooded back to order our truant tresses, and her voice, though less resonant than in the years when she called us from play to duty, has the same cadence as when bending over us she sang the cradle song which lulled to sleep and to dreams.

O, our mother! beloved more than any wealth of words could express, your children on this anniversary day of your wedding fifty years ago, offer you, aye shower upon you in the name of filial devotion, all the holiest treasures of garnered affection.

> "We give thee all, we can no more,
> Though poor the offering be;
> Our hearts—our love is all the store
> And this we bring to thee."

We hear the wedding bells ringing in celebration of the nuptials of our aged parents—our ears are attuned to their merry chimes and our hearts respond with all the joyousness of a wedding march, for peace and happiness and contentment crown the hour. We do not ask what the future has in store, we only know that we have the bride and groom in our presence, and that it is an inexpressible joy to pledge them anew our unfaltering devotion and our eternal love.

The Issue

Speech at Girard, Kas., May 23, 1908

[NOTE.—Girard, Kansas, is a quiet little city built about a capacious plaza or square. This plaza is carpeted with Nature's emerald and roofed with the protecting branches of the catalpa and the elm tree. When the news came that Debs had again been chosen as the candidate of the Socialists for that station in our public affairs of most comprehensive service to the people, the citizens, without reference to political faiths, gathered upon this green out of compliment to their fellow-townsman who had been thus honored for the third time by such signal confidence on the part of so many earnest people of the nation at large. These good people of Girard had seen bevies of children following this arch "undesirable citizen" to and from his work, and about the town in his resting hours, for almost the entire period of his residence here, and now it had come to pass that he was loved by every man, woman and child here. They sent for him. Eli Richardson, the "Hot Cinders" Socialist, affectionately known for so long a time as "Baldy," explained in a few dramatic words the occasion of the gathering, and presented Debs with the remark, "You can pin your faith to a man loved by children." The address which follows, wholly impromptu, is perhaps the most remarkable ever delivered, and came hot from the foundry of his mighty genius and fresh from the loom of his kindly, loyal, loving soul.]

Comrades, Ladies and Gentlemen: When I made inquiry a few moments ago as to the cause of this assembling I was told that it was the beginning of another street fair. I am quite surprised, and agreeably so, to find myself the central attraction. Allow me in the very beginning to express my heartiest appreciation of the more than kind and generous words which have been spoken here for me this afternoon. There are times when words—mere words—no matter how fitly chosen or well expressed—are almost meaningless. As the rosebud under the influence of sunshine and shower opens, so does my heart receive your benediction this afternoon.

I am a new resident of Girard; have been here but a comparatively short time, and yet I feel myself as completely at home among you, most of whom disagree with me upon very vital questions, as I do in the town in which I was born and reared and have lived all the days of my life. Since the day I first came here I have been treated with uniform kindness. I could not have been treated more hospitably anywhere. I have met practically all of your people, and all of them have taken me by the hand and treated me as cordially as if I had been neighbor and friend with them; and to say that I appreciate this is to express myself in hackneyed and unsatisfactory terms.

AS TO THE PRESIDENCY.

The honor to which reference has been made has come to me through no fault of my own. It has been said that some men are born great, some achieve greatness, and some have greatness thrust upon them. It is even so with what are called honors. Some men have honors thrust upon them. I find myself in that class. I did what little I could to prevent myself from being nominated by the convention now in session at Chicago, but the nomination sought me out, and in spite of myself I stand in your presence this afternoon the nominee of the Socialist party for the presidency of the United States.

Long, long ago I made up my mind never again to be a candidate for any political office within the gift of the people. I was constrained to violate that vow because when I joined the Socialist party I was taught that the desire of the individual was subordinate to the party will, and that when the party commanded it was my duty to obey. There was a time in my life when I had the vanities of youth, when I sought that bubble called fame. I have outlived it. I have reached that point when I am capable of placing an estimate upon my own relative insignificance. I have come to realize that there is no honor in any real sense of that term to any man unless he is capable of freely consecrating himself to the service of his fellow men.

To the extent that I am able to help those who are unable to help themselves, to that extent, and to that extent alone, do I honor myself and the party to which I belong. So far as the presidency of the United States is concerned, I would spurn it were it not that it conferred the power to serve the working class, and he who enters that office with any other conception of it prostitutes and does not honor that office.

THE BOUNTY OF NATURE.

Now, my friends, I am opposed to the system of society in which we live today, not because I lack the natural equipment to do for myself, but because I am not satisfied to make myself comfortable knowing that there are thousands upon thousands of my fellow men who suffer for the barest necessities of life. We were taught under the old ethic that man's business upon this earth was to look out for himself. That was the ethic of the jungle; the ethic of the wild beast. Take care of yourself, no matter what may become of your fellow man. Thousands of years ago the question was asked: "Am I my brother's keeper?" That question has never yet been answered in a way that is satisfactory to civilized society.

Yes, I am my brother's keeper. I am under a moral obligation to him that is inspired, not by any maudlin sentimentality, but by the higher duty I owe to myself. What would you think of me if I were capable of seating myself at a table and gorging myself with food and saw about me the children of my fellow beings starving to death?

Allow me to say to you, my fellow men, that nature has spread a great table bounteously for all of the children of men. There is room for all and there is a plate and a place and food for all, and any system of society that denies a single one the right and the opportunity to freely help himself to nature's bounties is an unjust and iniquitous system that ought to be abolished in the interest of a higher humanity and a civilization worthy of the name. And here let me observe, my fellow men, that while the general impression is that human society is stationary—a finality as it were—it is not so for a single instant. Underlying society there are great material forces that are in operation all of the circling hours of the day and night, and at certain points in the social development these forces outgrow the forms that hold them and these forms spring apart and then a new social system comes into existence and a new era dawns for the human race.

The great majority of mankind have always been in darkness. The overwhelming majority of the children of men have always been their own worst enemies. In every age of this world's history, the kings and emperors and czars and potentates, in alliance with the priests, have sought by all the means at their command to keep the people in darkness that they might perpetuate the power in which they riot and revel in luxury while the great mass are in a state of slavery and degradation, and he who has spoken out courageously against the existing order, he who has dared to voice the protest of the oppressed and downtrodden, has had to pay the penalty, all the way from Jesus Christ of Galilee down to Fred Warren of Girard.

CORONATIONS AND CRUCIFIXIONS.

Do you know, my friends, it is so easy to agree with the ignorant majority. It is so easy to make the people applaud an empty platitude. It takes some courage to face that beast called the Majority, and tell him the truth to his teeth! Some men do so and accept the consequences of their acts as becomes men, and they live in history—every one of them. I have said so often, and I wish to repeat it on this occasion, that mankind have always crowned their oppressors, and they have as uniformly crucified their saviors, and this has been true all along the highway of the centuries. It is true today. It will not always be so. When the great mass know the truth, they will treat an honest man decently while he lives and not crucify him, and then a thousand years afterward rear a monument above the dust of the hero they put to death.

I am in revolt against capitalism (and that doesn't mean to say, my friends, that I am hating you—not the slightest). I am opposed to capitalism because I love my fellow men, and if I am opposing you I am opposing you for what I believe to be your good, and though you spat upon me with contempt I should still oppose you to the extent of my power.

NEW SYSTEM NEEDED.

I don't hate the workingman because he has turned against me. I know the poor fellow is too ignorant to understand his self-interest, and I know that as a rule the workingman is the friend of his enemy and the enemy of his friend. He votes for men who represent a system in which labor is simply merchandise; in which the man who works the hardest and longest has the least to show for it.

If there is a man on this earth who is entitled to all the comforts and luxuries of this life in abundance it is the man whose labor produces them. If he is not, who is? Does he get them in the present system?

And, mark you, I am not speaking in a partisan sense this afternoon. I appreciate the fact that you have come here as republicans and democrats as well as Socialists to do me a personal honor, and I would be ungrateful, indeed, if I took advantage of such an occasion to speak to you in an offensive partisan sense. I wish to say in the broadest possible way that I am opposing the system under which we live today because I believe it is subversive of the best interests of the people. I am not satisfied with things as they are, and I know that no matter what administration is in power, even were it a Socialist administration, there will be no material change in the condition of the people until we have a new social system based upon the mutual economic interests of the whole people; until you and I and all of us collectively own those things that we collectively need and use.

That is a basic economic proposition. As long as a relatively few men own the railroads, the telegraph, the telephone, own the oil fields and the gas fields and the steel mills and the sugar refineries and the leather tanneries—own, in short, the sources and means of life—they will corrupt our politics, they will enslave the working class, they will impoverish and debase society, they will do all things that are needful to perpetuate their power as the economic masters and the political rulers of the people. Not until these great agencies are owned and operated by the people can the people hope for any material improvement in their social condition.

Is the condition fair today, and satisfactory to the thinking man?

THE UNEMPLOYED.

According to the most reliable reports at our command, as I speak here this afternoon there are at least four millions of workingmen vainly searching for employment. Have you ever found yourself in that unspeakably sad predicament? Have you ever had to go up the street, begging for work, in a great city thronged with humanity—and, by the way, my friends, people are never quite so strange to each other as when they are forced into artificial, crowded and stifled relationship.

I would rather be friendless out on the American desert than to be friendless in New York or Chicago. Have you ever walked up one side of the street and come back on the other side, while your wife, Mary, was waiting at home with three or four children for you to report that you had found work? Quite fortunately for me I had an experience of similar nature quite early in my life. Quite fortunately because, had I not known from my own experience just what it is to have to beg for work, just what it is to be shown the door as if I were a very offensive intruder, had I not known what it is to suffer for the want of food, had I not seen every door closed and barred in my face, had I not found myself friendless and alone in the city as a boy looking for work, and in vain, perhaps I would not be here this afternoon. I might have grown up, as some others have who have been, as they regard themselves, fortunate. I might have waved aside my fellowmen and said, "Do as I have done. If you are without work it is your own fault. Look at me; I am self-made. No man is under the necessity of looking for work if he is willing to work."

Nothing is more humiliating than to have to beg for work, and a system in which any man has to beg for work stands condemned. No man can defend it. Now the rights of one are as sacred as the rights of a million. Suppose you happen to be the one who has no work. This republic is a failure so far as you are concerned.

Every man has the inalienable right to work.

EVOLUTION OF INDUSTRY.

Here I stand, just as I was created. I have two hands that represent my labor power. I have some bone and muscle and sinew and some energy. I want to exchange the use of these for food and clothing and shelter. But between me and the tools with which work is done there stands a man artificially created. He says, "No, no!" Why not? "Because you cannot first make a profit for me."

Now, there has been a revolution in industry during the last fifty years, but the trouble with most people is that they haven't kept pace with it. They don't know anything about it and they are especially innocent in regard to it in the small western cities and states, where the same old conditions of a century ago still largely prevail. Your grandfather could help himself anywhere. All he needed was some cheap, simple primitive tools and he could then apply his labor to the resources of nature with his individual tools and produce what he needed. That era in our history produced our greatest men. Lincoln himself sprang from this primitive state of society. People have said, "Why, he had no chance. See how great he became." Yes, but Lincoln had for his comrades great, green-plumed forest monarchs. He could put his arms about them and hear their heart-throbs, as they whispered: "Go on, Abe, a great destiny awaits you." He was in partnership with nature. He associated with birds and bees and flowers, and he was in the fields and heard the rippling music of the laughing brooks and streams. Nature took him to her bosom and nourished him, and from his unpolluted heart there sprang his noble aspirations.

Had Lincoln been born in a sweatshop he would never have been heard of.

How is it with the babe that is born in Mott street, or in the lower Bowery, or in the east side of New York City? That is where thousands, tens of thousands and hundreds of thousands of babes are born who are to constitute our future generations.

I have seen children ten years of age in New York City who had never seen a live chicken. The babes there don't know what it is to put their tiny feet on a blade of grass. It is the most densely populated spot on earth.

You have seen your bee-hive—just fancy a human bee-hive of which yours is the miniature and you have the industrial hive under capitalism. If you have never seen this condition you are excusable for not being a Socialist. Come to New York, Chicago, San Francisco with me; remain with me just twenty-four hours, and then look into my face as I shall look into yours when I ask: "What about Socialism now?" These children by hundreds and thousands are born in sub-cellars, where a whole grown family is crowded together in one room, where modesty between the sexes is absolutely impossible. They are surrounded by filth and vermin. From their birth they see nothing but immorality and vice and crime. They are tainted in the cradle. They are inoculated by their surroundings and they are doomed from the beginning. This system takes their lives just as certainly as if a dagger were thrust into their quivering little hearts, and let me say to you that it were better for many thousands of them if they had never seen the light.

Now I submit, my friends, that such a condition as this is indefensible in the twentieth century. Time was when everything had to be done in a very primitive way, and most men had to work all their days, all their lives, to feed and shelter themselves. They had no time, they had no opportunity for higher development, and so they were what the world calls "illiterate." They had little chance. It took all their time and energy to feed the animal; but how is it today? Upon the average twenty men can today, with the aid of modern machinery, produce as much wealth as a thousand did a half century ago. Can you think of a single thing that enters into our daily existence that can not be easily produced in abundance for all? If you can I wish you would do me the kindness to name it.

WHY SUFFER AMID ABUNDANCE?

I don't know it all. I am simply a student of this great question, and I am serving as best I can and I know my eyes are ready for the light, and I thank that man, no matter what he be, who can add to the flame of the torch I bear. If there is a single thing that you can think of that cannot be produced in abundance, name it. Bread, clothing, fuel—everything is here.

Nature's storehouse is full to the surface of the earth. All of the raw materials are deposited here in abundance. We have the most marvelous machinery the world has ever known. Man has long since become master of the natural forces and made them work for him. Now he has but to touch a button and the wheels begin to spin and the machinery to whirr, and wealth is produced on every hand in increasing abundance.

Why should any man, woman or child suffer for food, clothing or shelter? Why? The question cannot be answered.

Don't tell me that some men are too lazy to work. Suppose they are too lazy to work, what do you think of a social system that produces men too lazy to work? If a man is too lazy to work don't treat him with contempt. Don't look down upon him with scorn as if you were a superior being. If there is a man who is too lazy to work there is something the matter with him. He wasn't born right or he was perverted in this system. You could not, if you tried, keep a normal man inactive, and if you did he would go stark mad. Go to any penitentiary and you will find the men there begging for the privilege of doing work.

I know by close study of the question exactly how men become idle. I don't repel them when I meet them. I have never yet seen the tramp I was not able to receive with open arms. He is a little less fortunate than I am. He is made the same as I am made. He is a child of the same Father. Had I been born in his environment, had I been subjected to the same things to which he was I would have been where he is.

TOOLS AND TRAMPS.

Can you tell me why there wasn't a tramp in the United States in 1860? In that day, if some one had said "tramp," no one would have known what was meant by it. If human nature is innately depraved and men would rather ride on brake-beams and sleep in holes and caves instead of comfortable beds, if they would do that from pure choice and from natural depravity, why were they not built that way fifty years ago? Fifty years ago capitalism was in its earlier stages. Fifty years ago work was still mainly done by hand, and every boy could learn a trade and every boy could master the tools and go to work. That is why there were no tramps. In fifty years that simple tool has become a mammoth machine. It gets larger and larger all the time. It has crowded the hand tool out of production. With the machine came the capitalist.

There were no capitalists, nor was there such a thing as capital before the beginning of the present system. Capitalists came with machinery. Up to the time that machinery supplanted the hand tool the little employer was himself a workingman. No matter what the shop or factory, you would find the employer working side by side with his men. He was a superior workman who got more orders than he could fill and employed others to help him, but he had to pay them the equivalent of what they produced because if he did not they would pack up their tools and go into business for themselves.

Now, the individual tool has become the mammoth machine. It has multiplied production by hundreds. The old tool was individually owned and used. The modern tool, in the form of a great machine, is social in every conception of it. Look at one of these giant machines. Come to the Appeal office and look at the press in operation. Here the progressive conception of the ages is crystallized. What individual shall put his hand on this social agency and say, "This is mine! He who would apply labor here must first pay tribute to me."

The hand tool has been very largely supplanted by this machine. Not many tools are left. You are still producing in a very small way here in Girard, but your production is flickering out gradually. It is but a question of time until it will expire entirely. In spite of all that can be said or done to the contrary production is organizing upon a larger and larger scale and becoming entirely co-operative. This has crowded out the smaller competitor and gradually opened the way for a new social order.

WILL MAKE HOME POSSIBLE.

Your material interest and mine in the society of the future will be the same. Instead of having to fight each other like animals, as we do today, and seeking to glorify the brute struggle for existence—of which every civilized human being ought to be ashamed—instead of this, our material interests are going to be mutual. We are going to jointly own these mammoth machines, and we are going to operate them as joint partners and we are going to divide all the products among ourselves.

We are not going to send our surplus to the Goulds and Vanderbilts of New York. We are not going to pile up a billion of dollars in John D. Rockefeller's hands—a vast pyramid from the height of which he can look down with scorn and contempt upon the "common herd." John D. Rockefeller's great fortune is built upon your ignorance. When you know enough to know what your interest· is you will support the great party that is organized upon the principle of collective ownership of the means of life. This party will sweep into power upon the issue of emancipation just as republicanism swept into power upon the abolition question half a century ago.

In the meantime, don't have any fear of us Socialists. We don't mean any harm! Many of you have been taught to look upon us as very dangerous people. It is amazing to what extent this prejudice has struck root. The capitalist press will tell you of a good many evil things that we Socialists are going to do that we never intend to do. They will tell you we are going to break up the home. Great heaven! What about the homes of the four million tramps that are looking for work today? How about the thousands and thousands of miserable shacks in New York and every great city where humanity festers? It would be a good thing if they were torn down and obliterated completely, for they are not fit for human habitation. No, we are not going to destroy the home, but we are going to make the home possible for the first time in history.

PROGRESS BORN OF AGITATION.

You may think you are very comfortable. Let me make you a little comparison. You may not agree with me. I don't expect you to and I don't ask you to. I am going to ask you to remember what I say this afternoon and perhaps before I am elected president of the United States you will believe what I say is true. Now there are those of you who are fairly comfortable under the present standard. Isn't it amazing to you how little the average man is satisfied with? You go out here to the edge of town and you find a small farmer who has a cabin with just room enough to keep himself and wife and two or three children, which has a mortgage on it, and he works early and late and gets just enough in net returns to keep him in working order, and he will deliver a lecture about the wonderful prosperity of the country.

He is satisfied, and that is his calamity.

Now, the majority of you would say that is his good fortune.

"It is a blessing that he is satisfied." I want to see if I can show you that it is a curse to him and to society that he is satisfied.

If it had not been for the discontent of a few fellows who have not been satisfied with their condition you would still be living in caves. You never would have emerged from the jungle. Intelligent discontent is the mainspring of civilization.

Progress is born of agitation. It is agitation or stagnation. I have taken my choice.

This farmer works all day long, works hard enough to produce enough to live the life of a man; not of an animal, but of a man. Now there is an essential difference between a man and an animal. I admire a magnificent animal in any form except in the human form. Suppose you had everything that you could possibly desire, so far as your physical wants are concerned. Suppose you had a million to your credit in the bank, a palatial home and relations to suit yourself, but no soul capacity for real enjoyment. If you were denied knowing what sorrow is, what real joy is, what music is, and literature and sculpture, and all of those subtle influences that touch the heart and quicken the pulses and fire the senses, and so lift and ennoble a man that he can feel his head among the stars and in communion with God himself—if you are denied these, no matter how sleek or fat or contented you may be, you are still as base and as corrupt and as repulsive a being as walks God's green earth.

THE FARMER'S NEED.

You may have plenty of money. The poorest people on this earth are those who have most money. A man is said to be poor who has none, but he is a pauper who has nothing else. Now this farmer, what does he know about literature? After his hard day's work is done, here he sits in his little shack. He is fed, and his animal wants are satisfied. It is at this time that a man begins to live. It is not while you work and slave that you live. It is when you have done your work honestly, when you have contributed your share to the common fund, that you begin to live. Then, as Whitman said, you can take out your soul; you can commune with yourself; you can take a comrade by the hand and you can look into his eyes and down into his soul, and in that holy communion you live. And if you don't know what that is, or if you are not at least on the edge of it, it is denied you to even look into the promised land.

Now this farmer knows nothing about the literature of the world. All its libraries are sealed to him. So far as he is concerned, Homer and Dante and Dickens might as well not have lived; Beethoven, Liszt and Wagner, and all those musicians whose art makes the common atmosphere blossom with harmony, never have been for this farmer. He knows nothing about poetry or art. Never rises above the animal plane upon which he is living. Within fifteen minutes after he has ceased to live he is forgotten; the next generation doesn't know his name, and the world doesn't know he ever lived. That is life under the present standard.

You tell me that is all the farmer is fit for? What do I propose to do for that farmer? Nothing. I only want him to know that he is robbed every day in the week, and if I can awaken him to the fact that he is robbed under the capitalist system he will fall into line with the Socialist movement, and will march to the polls on election day, and instead of casting his vote to fasten the shackles upon his limbs more firmly, he will vote for his emancipation. All I have to do is to show that farmer, that day laborer, that tramp, that they are victims of this system, that their interests are identical, that they constitute the millions and that the millions have the votes. The Rockefellers have the dollars, but we have the votes; and when we have sense enough to know how to use the votes we will have not only the votes but the dollars for all the children of men.

WHO WILL SAVE US FROM CONGRESS?

This seems quite visionary to some of you, and especially to those of you who know nothing about economics. I could not begin to tell you the story of social evolution this afternoon; of how these things are doing day by day, of how the world is being pushed into Socialism, and how it is bound to arrive, no matter whether you are for it or against it. It is the next inevitable phase of civilization. It isn't a scheme, it isn't a contrivance. It isn't anything that is made to order. The day is coming when you will be pushed into it by unseen hands whether you will or not. Nothing can be introduced until the people want it, and when the majority want it they will know how to get it.

I venture the prophecy that within the next five years you will be completely dispossessed. You are howling against the trusts, and the trusts are laughing at you. You keep on voting in the same old way and the trusts keep on getting what you produce. You say congress will give you some relief. Good heavens! Who will save us from congress? Don't you know that congress is made up almost wholly of trust lawyers and corporation attorneys? I don't happen to have the roll of this one, but with few exceptions they are all lawyers. Now, in the competitive system the lawyer sells himself to the highest bidder the same as the workingman does. Who is the highest bidder? The trust and corporation, of course. So the trust buys the best lawyer and the common herd gets the shyster.

POLITICS REFLEX OF ECONOMICS.

Now it is a fact that politics is simply the reflex of economics. The material foundation of society determines the character of all social institutions—political, educational, ethical and spiritual. In exact proportion as the economic foundation of society changes the character of all social institutions changes to correspond to that basis. Half of this country was in favor of chattel slavery, and half was opposed to it, geographically speaking. Why was the church of the south in favor of chattel slavery? Why was the church of the north opposed to chattel slavery? The northern capitalist wasn't a bit more opposed to chattel slavery from any moral sense than was the southern plantation owner. The south produced cotton for the market by the hand labor of negro slaves. On the other hand, the north wasn't dependent upon cotton—could raise no cotton. In the north it was the small capitalist at the beginning of capitalism, who, with the machine, had begun to manufacture, and wanted cheap labor; and the sharper the competition the cheaper he could buy his labor. Now, chattel slavery to the southern plantation owner was the source of his wealth. He had to have slaves, and what the plantation owner had to have in economics the preacher had to justify in religion. As long as chattel slavery was necessary to the southern plantation owner, as long as that stage of the economic condition lasted, the preachers stood up in the pulpits of the south and said it was ordained of God, and proved it by the Bible. I don't know of any crime that the oppressors and their hirelings have not proven by the Bible.

ANALOGIES FROM HISTORY.

Then competition between workers began as machines took the place of hand labor. Manufacturers wanted larger and larger bodies of labor and that competition spread out here to Kansas, and I have always felt when in Kansas that I stood on sacred soil. When I hear the name of Kansas I doff my hat in reverence. The free soilers came here, despised, hated and persecuted. They were the enemies of the human race. Why? Because they had hearts throbbing within their breasts. Because they looked with compassion upon the negro slave who received his wages in lashes applied to his naked back; who saw his crying wife torn from him and his children, pleading, snatched from his side and sold into slavery, while the great mass looked on just as the great mass is looking on today, and the preachers stood up in their pulpits and said: "It is all right. It is God-ordained." And whenever an abolitionist raised his head he was persecuted and hounded as if he had been a wild beast.

I heard this story from Wendell Phillips one evening. I never can forget it. How I wish he were here this afternoon! We sat together and he said: "Debs, the world will never know with what bitter and relentless persecution the early abolitionists had to contend."

Wendell Phillips was the most perfect aristocrat in the true sense I have ever seen; came nearest being a perfect man. And yet he was treated as if he had been the worst felon on earth. They went to his house one night to mob him, and why? Because he protested against sending a young negro girl back into slavery. They came to take her back, and the whole commonwealth of Massachusetts said, "Take her back! Obey the law!" That is what they are everlastingly saying to us—"Obey the law!" Just above the door of the state house there was an inscription: "God bless the Commonwealth of Massachusetts." Wendell Phillips said: "If Massachusetts has become a slave hunter, if Massachusetts is in alliance with the slave catchers of the south, the inscription over that portal should be changed, and in place of 'God Bless the Commonwealth of Massachusetts' it should be: 'God Damn the Commonwealth of Massachusetts!'" God smiled in that same instant.

GROWTH OF SOCIALISM.

All of the slave catchers and holders, all of the oppressors of man, all of the enemies of the human race, all of the rulers of Siberia, where a large part of this earth's surface has been transformed into a hell—all have spoken in the name of the Great God and in the name of the Holy Bible.

There will be a change one of these days. The world is just beginning to awaken, and is soon to sing its first anthem of freedom. All the signs of the times are cheering. Twenty-five years ago there was but a handful of Socialists; today there are a half million. When the polls are closed next fall you will be astounded. The Socialist movement is in alliance with the forces of progress. We are today where the abolitionists were in 1858. They had a million and a quarter of votes. There was dissension in the whig, republican and free soil parties, but the time had come for a great change, and the republican party was formed in spite of the bickerings and contentions of men. Lincoln made the great speech in that year that gave him the nomination and afterward made him president of the United States.

If you had said to the people in 1858, "In two years from now the republican party is going to sweep the country and seat the president," you would have been laughed to scorn. The Socialist party stands today where the republican party stood fifty years ago. It is in alliance with the forces of evolution, the one party that has a clear-cut, overmastering, overshadowing issue; the party that stands for the people, and the only party that stands for all the people. In this system we have one set who are called capitalists, and another set who are called workers; and they are at war with each other.

WILL ESTABLISH PRIVATE PROPERTY.

Now, we Socialists propose that society in its collective capacity shall produce, not for profit, but in abundance to satisfy human wants; that every man shall have the inalienable right to work, and receive the full equivalent of all he produces; that every man may stand fearlessly erect in the pride and majesty of his own manhood.

Every man and every woman will then be economically free. They can, without let or hindrance, apply their labor, with the best machinery that can be devised, to all the natural resources, do the work of society and produce for all; and then receive in exchange a certificate of value equivalent to that of their production. Then society will improve its institutions in proportion to the progress of invention. Whether in the city or on the farm, all things productive will be carried forward on a gigantic scale. All industry will be completely organized. Society for the first time will have a scientific foundation. Every man, by being economically free, will have some time for himself. He can then take a full and perfect breath. He can enjoy life with his wife and children, because then he will have a home.

We are not going to destroy private property. We are going to establish private property—all the private property necessary to house man, keep him in comfort and satisfy his wants. Eighty per cent of the people of the United States have no property today. A few have got it all. They have dispossessed the people, and when we get into power we will dispossess them. We will reduce the workday and give every man a chance. We will go to the parks, and we will have music, because we will have time to play music and desire to hear it.

Is it not sad to think that not one in a thousand knows what music is? Is it not pitiable to see the poor, ignorant, dumb human utterly impervious to the divine influences of music? If humanity could only respond to the higher influences! And it would if it had time.

Release the animal, throw off his burden; give him a chance and he rises as if by magic to the plane of a man. Man has all of the divine attributes. They are in a latent state. They are not yet developed. It does not pay now to love music.

Keep your eye on the almighty dollar and your fellowman. Get the dollar and keep him down. Make him produce for you. You are not your brother's keeper. Suppose he is poor! Suppose his wife is forced into prostitution! Suppose his child is deformed! And suppose he shuffles off by destroying himself! What is that to you?

But you ought to be ashamed. Take the standard home and look it in the face. If you know what that standard means, and you are a success, God help the failure!

Our conduct is determined by our economic relations. If you and I must fight each other to exist, we will not love each other very hard. We can go to the same church and hear the same minister tell us in good conscience that we ought to love each other, and the next day we approach some business transaction. Do we remember what the minister told us? No; it is gone until next Sunday. Six days in the week we are following the Golden Rule reversed. Now, when we approach a business transaction in competition, what is more natural than that we should try to get the better of it?—get the better of our fellowman?—cheat him if we can?

And if you succeed that fixes you as a business man. You have all the necessary qualifications. Don't let your conscience disturb you—that would interfere with business.

HUMANITY AND THE FUTURE.

Competition was natural enough at one time, but do you think you are competing today? Many of you think you are competing. Against whom? Against Rockefeller? About as I would if I had a wheelbarrow and competed with the Santa Fe from here to Kansas City. That is about the way you are competing; but your boys will not have even that chance—if capitalism lives that long. You hear of the "late" panic. It is very late. It is going to be very late. This panic will be with us five years from now, and will continue till then.

I am not a prophet. I can no more penetrate the future than you can. I do study the forces that underlie society and the trend of evolution. I can tell by what we have passed through about what we will have in the future; and I know that capitalism can be abolished and the people put in possession. Now, when we have taken possession, and we jointly own the means of production, we will no longer have to fight each other to live; our interests, instead of being competitive, will be co-operative. We will work side by side. Your interest will be mine and mine will be yours. That is the economic condition from which will spring the humane social relation of the future.

When we are in partnership and have stopped clutching each other's throats, when we have stopped enslaving each other, we will stand together, hands clasped, and be friends. We will be comrades, we will be brothers, and we will begin the march to the grandest civilization the human race has ever known.

I did not mean to keep you so long this afternoon. I am sure I appreciate the patience with which you have listened to me. From the very depths of my heart I thank you, each of you—every man, woman and child—for this splendid testimonial, this beautiful tribute, which I shall remember with gratitude and love until memory empties its urn into forgetfulness.

APPRECIATIONS

FREDERIC AUGUSTE BARTHOLDI

The great sculptor who modeled the colossal statue, "Liberty Enlightening the World," in New York harbor, wrote of Debs:

"He is endowed with the most precious faculty to which one can aspire—the gift of language, and he uses it for the proclamation of the most beautiful and generous thoughts. His beautiful language is that of an apostle."

Appreciations

Mr. Debs an Artist in Expression

If the use of language to express thought is an art, Mr. Debs is an artist. If oratory is a science, he is a master of the science. If eloquence reaches and takes hold of the hearts and emotions of mankind, Mr. Debs has that which will make his auditors stand and deliver the goods. His address lasted over two hours and at its close, not only men, but women, surged to the platform to grasp his hand and congratulate him. This is something unique, for while it is customary for men to do so with labor leaders, women generally stay in the background if they attend these meetings at all.—*Detroit Times.*

From Woodstock to Boise

Walter Hurt in Appeal to Reason, November 23, 1907

Capitalism made its first great mistake when it put Eugene V. Debs in jail. It made its second great mistake when it put William D. Haywood in jail. And it adds to its mistakes every time it wrongfully imprisons any member of the working class.

Woodstock was plutocracy's Waterloo and Boise was its Bull Run.

Debs entered jail a labor agitator and emerged therefrom a Social Revolutionist.

Haywood went to prison defeated and left it victorious.

In each case it was a transformation and a triumph.

It should be understood that the word "defeat" is here used merely as a term of convenience. No man is truly defeated unless he is conquered, and Debs and Haywood are unconquerable.

Moreover, whatever its reverses, there can be no defeat for

a righteous cause, for in the eternal equipoise of social conservation—

> "Ever will right come uppermost
> And ever will justice be done."

And these celebrated cases are not exceptional, for history proves that, despite the purpose for which they were designed, prisons have always been the instruments of progress—unfailing agencies of human advancement.

The path of progress extends undeviating from Woodstock to Boise. The experience of a Debs was necessary to the evolvement of a Haywood.

In their effort to destroy Debs the money-masters overreached themselves. They crushed the American Railway Union—crushed it into the cohesion of the Social Democracy.

It is interesting to observe this operation—to watch the metamorphosis of Debs and trace the evolution of the industrial movement from the date of his imprisonment; in this process we find the philosophy of progress, the development of the social purpose.

Both Debs and his persecutors were involuntary instruments of sovereign economic forces; the latter an unconscious agency, responding blindly to conservatory impulsion, the former obedient to an intelligent enthusiasm logically directed toward a definite and an attainable object.

Under the pressure of prison walls Debs' dynamic being developed until its expanding forces found expression in the Socialist idea, of which his own potent personality was the informing influence.

From the corporate wreck of the A. R. U. the Social Democracy was organized. Debs reformed this disintegration, he was the atom of attraction; his irresistible individuality was the core to which the others cohered—the compelling factor that drew to an integrative coalescence the shattered, scattered remnants of a vast industrial organism as surely as a magnet draws the metal.

The Pullman strike was not lost. It was won decisively and completely. A movement for industrial liberation as magnificent in its scope as any campaign of the immortal Corsican, had succeeded. For the first time in history Plutocracy was

APPRECIATIONS. 497

paralyzed in the clutch of Toil, directed by a man of intelligence and integrity.

But victory was plucked from the grasp of the strikers by the strong hand of federal power. They were robbed of the sweet fruits of their bitter struggle by the wealth-won favor of presidential authority.

This result puzzled Debs. He couldn't understand how such a tremendous triumph could be turned into defeat.

He had to go to jail to find the solution of the problem.

In jail he studied Socialism. And straightway a great illumination burst upon his intelligence.

He turned from craft-consciousness to class-consciousness.

It was revealed to him that the entire theory of industrial organization as it existed was fundamentally false. He realized that any social benefit to be large and lasting must be also universal.

Moreover, he came to know the reason for the failure of the Pullman strike after it had been fairly and fully won; and he understood then that revolution was the only remedy for economic ills and that the only hope for government protection of proletarian interests lay in the capture of governmental power.

From the narrow confines of his cell and the not less narrow confines of craft interest he simultaneously stepped into physical freedom and into the world-wide sweep of the Social Revolution.

Debs had been so dangerous that the masters deemed it advisable to send him to jail. He left that prison a thousand times more dangerous than when he entered it.

For Debs *is* dangerous. This is the one truth plutocracy tells about him. He's as dangerous as dynamite—to capitalistic interests.

Capitalism thought it had destroyed Debs. It merely had made him.

His cell was a chrysalis, from which his soul came forth with unfurled wings.

Defeat cannot come to such a man as Debs. His triumphal return to Chicago after his release from Woodstock jail is neither paralleled nor approximated in all history except by

Napoleon's victorious march upon Paris after his escape from Elba.

The kindest thing ever done to Debs was the act of his enemies. The greatest blessing mankind has received was bestowed by those who sought to enslave it.

When it sentenced Debs to jail, Capitalism signed its own death warrant.

Debs' career from November 22, 1895, to July 28, 1907, spanning the years from Woodstock to Boise, forms the seven-hued bow of proletarian promise.

Here Comes a Man

By George B cknell

Here comes a man with one free call;
   He shouts aloud nor does he fear
   The foolish threat of deafened ear;
Nor does he heed who would enthrall.

Here comes a man with love for men
   As pure and broad as boundless space;
   He gathers light from every race,
And sheds it on the world again.

His joy is not alone for self;
   His life makes gladsome whom he meets
   By turning bitter galls to sweets
And shaming every show of pelf.

Here comes a man whose like is rare;
   A kindred heart for hearts that bleed;
   A refuge in dark hours of need;
A burdened world his greatest care;

His call the call to Love and Faith,
   To Love and Faith and Liberty;
   But some decry, and some there be
Who say: "A Dream;" "A soulless wraith."

Yet, though his call be but a dream,
   The love he sheds in spreading this
   Will give the world much lasting bliss
And purify a Hate-filled stream.

Then hail to him who loves so well!
   The Brother of the Poor; the Friend
   Of them that labor without end.
And hail the dawn he dares foretell!

Without Guile

No man ever looked into the frank, blue eyes of Eugene V. Debs but felt the thrill of seeing the open soul of a man without guile. In two years' daily intercourse with him I never saw him change in mental attitude. He has won the love of every person who has met and talked with him. His soul takes in the universe. He is one of the great men who will leave his footprints on the sands of the road of human uplift. Like all men who have higher ideals than their time and generation, he will be better appreciated in the time to come. It is not that he is the peer of any orator who ever addressed an American public, but that what he says goes to the root of things. It is what he says more than the beautiful way he says it. It always reaches the heart, reaches the deep-hidden good that is in every creature. He is the same in the ordinary conversation that he is on the platform. No man can look into his frank soul and refuse to love him. His name will live in letters of light on the pages of the history of this nation. And his star will grow brighter as humanity better perfects its telescopes of perception. We love him for what he is.

J. A. WAYLAND.

Eugene V. Debs as an Orator

By Max Ehrmann

TERRE HAUTE, IND., August, 1907.

No man in America has been more hated, and few have been so much loved as Eugene V. Debs. His name is known and his face is familiar where the city of his birth was never heard of. His opinions are considered by men in high places as the countersign of bloodshed, anarchy and riot, and by millions of others they are regarded as the beacon light that is to lead humanity to a better life and a higher civilization. Whatever may be said of his philosophy, one thing is certain, that he has won a place in American history as one of its greatest orators; and in my opinion, there is not a man on the American platform today who is his equal. His is a new and different kind of oratory. He resorts to no tricks of rhetoric, no claptrap and stage effects, no empty pretense of deep emotion; but he stands frankly before his audiences and opens the doorways of his mind and heart that seem ever to be overflowing with terrible invective or the sweet waters of human kindness.

This style is very different from that of such speakers as Senator Beveridge. Mr. Beveridge's orations on occasions and in the Senate are finished, modeled, filed and practiced. Intonation and gesture are carefully arranged to fit the sentiment. It is a piece of good workmanship. But the whole effect lacks sincerity. You feel that Mr. Beveridge is secretly using you for his personal ends. None of these elements enter the oratory of Mr. Debs, and his sincerity is almost terrible in its reality. You feel that he will tell you what he thinks regardless of consequence.

The first time I heard Mr. Debs was more than ten years ago, when I was a student at Harvard. He was booked to lecture at Prospect Union, Cambridge. This was shortly after the great Chicago strike; and a good many Harvard students and some instructors came out to see the "monster." Mr. Debs was late; but the audience waited. When he came there was no applause. He began to speak, and for more than two hours he held that audience as if riveted to the seats; and they who had come to scorn, hovered around him for more than an hour, and went away his friends. It was more than half an hour before I could get to the speaker's stand and shake hands with him.

The night before that he had spoken to one of the largest audiences that had ever crowded into Faneuil Hall, Boston. And so generously was his message received that, as Dr. John Clarke Ridpath afterwards told me, he feared the audience would "tear him to pieces trying to shake his hand." Dr. Ridpath was at that time editor of the *Arena* and believed then that Mr. Debs was one of the most masterful orators that had ever been reared on American soil and that he had then already a secure place in American history.

The next time I tried to hear Mr. Debs was in Denver. The crowd was so great that I could not get within fifty feet of the door of the largest public hall in that city, and it was then said that up to that time there had never been such an audience in that hall.

I did, however, get to hear Mr. Debs the next Sunday, in the same city, where the day was celebrated as Debs-Day at Manhattan Beach Gardens—at that time a prominent summer garden of Denver. He spoke in the theater, and after the speech an opera was given by the splendid stock company playing there that summer. Everybody wore Debs badges and the day was generally observed in Denver as given to the great Socialist.

And Mr. Debs has gone on and on and spoken to more and larger audiences than any other speaker except Mr. Bryan, until every great rostrum in America has supported his tall figure, and the walls of every great public hall have resounded his words.

In some ways our distinguished fellow-townsman has wandered a stranger in the city of his birth. Here we have been the last to acknowledge his power and influence. We see him often, recognize him as a quiet, respected citizen, possessing those domestic virtues that all men and women admire; but the great Debs, the Debs who first arraigned the trust abuses in this country, who broke the first ground for the harvest of modern popular reforms—that Debs we have never yet recognized, nor that power of his—whatever one may think of his doctrines—which is the type that has made the names of men undying.

Lincoln, 1860 — Debs, 1894

By John Swinton

NEW YORK, September, 1895.

When Eugene Victor Debs came to New York from Chicago last year he made a speech in Cooper Union which I heard. I sat near a spot at which I had sat at another meeting held in the same place thirty-four years previously, which was addressed by another speaker who came to New York from Chicago. The western speaker who stood on that platform in August, 1894, was to me a reminder of the other western speaker who stood there in February, 1860. Both men were tall and spare in figure; the complexion of each rather dark—darker in the one than in the other; the face of each was rather gaunt, that of the earlier speaker much more gaunt than that of the later; both were men of good and strong features; there was something intense about the facial expression of each; both were men of commanding and impressive manners.

I recall the somewhat peculiar and shrill voice of the speaker of 1860; I heard another voice in 1894 which resembled it. As they spoke, it was easy for a New Yorker to discern that they were both men of the west.

The man to whose speech I listened in Cooper Union in February, of 1860, was Abraham Lincoln, of Illinois—born in Kentucky; the man who spoke from the same platform within my hearing last year was Eugene Victor Debs, of Illinois—born in Indiana.

I recalled the appearance, the manner, the voice and the speech of Lincoln as Debs stood before me thirty-four years afterwards.

It seemed to me that both men were imbued with the same spirit. Both seemed to me as men of judgment, reason, earnestness and power. Both seemed to me as men of free, high, genuine, generous manhood. I "took" to Lincoln in my early life, as I took to Debs a third of a century later.

In the speeches of both westerners there was cogent argument; there were apt illustrations; there were especially emphatic passages; there were moments of lightning; there were touches of humor, and there were other qualities which produce conviction or impel to action. Each speaker was as free as the other from gross eloquence. I confess that I was as much impressed with the closing words of Debs' speech as I was with those of Lincoln, when he exclaimed, "Let us have faith that right makes might, and in that faith let us to the end dare to do our duty, as we understand it."

As Lincoln stands in my memory while looking far back, Debs stands in it as I saw him in Cooper Union a year ago.

Lincoln spoke for man; so spoke Debs. Lincoln spoke for

APPRECIATIONS. 503

right and progress; so spoke Debs. Lincoln spoke for the freedom of labor; so spoke Debs. Lincoln was the foe of human slavery; so is Debs.

I was in the deepest sympathy with Lincoln when he came here, as I was also with Debs when he came here. I had striven for Fremont in my youth, as I have striven in later years for principles that are the logical sequence of those of Lincoln and are represented by Debs.

Let no admirer of Abraham Lincoln—I do not mean the apotheosized emancipator, but the Lincoln of 1860—offer objection to aught that has been here said. At the time I have spoken of Lincoln was regarded by millions of people as a cross between a crank and a monster. In hundreds of papers and by hundreds of speakers he was called the "Illinois baboon." Every epithet that hate could invent was applied to him; every base purpose that malice could conceive was imputed to him. To the "Satanic press" of New York Lincoln was an object of loathing and derision, a "nigger lover," a clown, a subverter of the constitution and the law; and above all, he was a blatant fool who would destroy that indestructible "system of labor" which had existed of old, which was upheld by the supreme court and the lynch law court, the church, the army, the press and the capitalist, as also by congress—both houses. Why, the Debs whom we have with us in our country today is a harmless citizen compared with the Lincoln of 1860, as he had been described before he came to New York. It looks to me as though the newspaper slubberdegullions and plutocracy in our time had lost that power of cantankerous invective which was possessed by their contemporaries of 1860, now mostly dead and forgotten. I have read some assaults upon Debs, but all of them were poorly done.

Lincoln's name was less familiar to New York masses at the opening of 1860 than Debs' was in 1894. Lincoln had campaigned in the west, but the west was much farther away then than it is now, and western men were less known in the east than they are now. Lincoln drew a crowd to Cooper Union, but not as large a crowd as Debs drew.

Well, when I heard Debs' speech here I had half a notion that it might be the prelude to an incident like that which followed Lincoln's speech. There were few people, at least in New York, who could have believed that within three months from the day of Lincoln's speech here, Lincoln would be a candidate for the office of President of the United States. "Some say," he said while in New York then, "some say they may make me Vice-President with Seward."

It was always the opinion of my old friend Raymond, the founder of the *New York Times*, whom I long served as chief of his editorial staff, that it was the Cooper Union speech of Lincoln that made it possible for him to be a candidate for the presidency, and that it was most potent in making him acceptable to the Republican party in the east. It certainly was a factor of influence in the nomination in Chicago the following May.

No matter about that now. When, in Cooper Union, a year ago, I heard the speech of Eugene V. Debs, which, in so many ways reminded me of that of Abraham Lincoln long ago, I felt sure that nobody could deny that here again, in this new western leader in the struggle for labor's emancipation, there might be the stuff for a presidential candidate.

And this suggestion would have been made by me at the New York meeting but for the jam of perversity on the platform.

Debs in Cooper Union reminded me of Lincoln there. As Lincoln, of Illinois, became an efficient agent for freedom, so, perchance might Debs, of Indiana, become in the impending conflict for the liberation of labor. Let us never forget Lincoln's great words, "Liberty before property; the man before the dollar."

Eugene V. Debs, Incarnate Spirit of Revolt

John Spargo, June, 1908

To be chosen standard bearer of the Socialist party in three successive electoral campaigns is to receive a unique tribute. For the candidates of the Socialist movement are not chosen by a few bosses, free to reward their favorite servitors with honors, place and pelf: they are chosen by the nearest approach to ideal democratic methods yet devised by any political party.

No man who had unworthily borne the Socialist banner in one campaign, or who had disappointed the hopes of his comrades, could possibly be nominated a second time. One act of cowardice or dishonor would be enough to make the renomination of any man impossible, no matter how gifted he might be.

Demos is a hard taskmaster. Some have said that Demos is ungrateful and unappreciative of loyal service. The annals of the Socialist movement certainly furnish some support to the charge. And yet, though its appreciation is not shouted from housetops, nor symbolized by golden crowns and hero-worship, those who have served longest and hardest in the ranks know that service to the Cause of Liberty is not unappreciated; that love and faithful comradeship are showered upon the true and brave soldiers in the great army of Labor.

No man in America has done nobler service for the cause of Socialism than Eugene V. Debs; no man has given more freely of his strength to keep the altar fires of the Revolution bright. And no man has been more richly and warmly loved than Debs has been. The love of his comrades has been his constant reward and inspiration.

And Debs has given love for love. How much the outpouring of his love upon the hearts of his comrades has meant to the Socialist movement will never be measured. To many a wearied fighter in the ranks his words of cheer, vibrant with love and appreciative sympathy, has been as a cooling draught from the deep fountains of life. To many a comrade walking in the dark and silent places his strong handclasp has brought strength and assurance. To many a soul swept from its moorings he has given the anchorage of a new faith. He has mingled his tears with the tears of many of his stricken comrades and borne upon his strong shoulders the burdens which bore too heavily upon them. Debs draws love from a million hearts as a well draws from showers and springs; and like a well he gives it back to all who thirst for love as they cross the desert of life.

Our love for Eugene V. Debs, the greatest lover of us all, entered into our choice of him as the bearer of our standard, the scarlet banner of the sacred cause, the symbol of a world-brotherhood to be. But it was not our love alone. Into our choice there entered another element than our love for Debs, namely, our consciousness that he was splendidly equipped for the task. Nature and Destiny seemed to have joined to dower Debs with the qualities of mind and soul needed for the task we gave him.

Inscrutable are the ways of Nature's working, and we may not understand the fashioning of a human life in her mysterious workshop. Was it a father's independence and pride which infused the son's being with a rebel spirit? Was it the mother's passion for beauty and freedom in life during the long days and nights when her unborn son stirred within her which caused the boy so soon to seek the companionship of the flowers and the stars, to envy the freedom of the birds and to shudder at all the ugly in life?

To such questions Science can give no answer. We only know that there was such a child, worshipping beauty and loving freedom; hating ugliness and pain. And this we know only as we know the man. The man must have been in the boy.

We know that there can be no living Socialist movement in any country which is not a product of its own life and experience. The Socialist movement is born anew out of the womb of capitalistic conditions In every country. And as with the Socialist movement itself, so must it be with the apostles of its faith. The greatest apostles of the emancipation must likewise be the products of the life and experience from which the movement springs. No amount of intellectual training can take the place of that proletarian psychology which is expressed in the irresistible passion for liberty of that great red army whose tread onward shakes the world.

The psychology and passion of the proletariat are incarnated in Eugene V. Debs. Life, Fate, Destiny—call it what you will!—added to Nature's contribution the elements which made him the Genius of the Revolution. The little comrade of the stars and the flowers grew to be the human embodiment of the Spirit of the revolt of the Disinherited and Despoiled, the living Voice of the Doomed and Damned.

But first of all he must suffer. To voice the cry of Labor he must first endure its agony; to speak the protest of the Doomed he must first endure the doom. Led by Destiny, he went the weary way of toil and tragedy, the way along which the dumb millions march in pain to their Golgotha. Each footfall tore his heartstrings; each fallen human wreck woke in his soul a yearning to speak their curse to the driving Power he could not see. Each human cry sank into his heart, each tortured curse he nourished as his own.

He heard voices and saw visions. Voices called him to a service he could not understand. As Joan of Arc listened to the unseen voices, so he listened. But he understood not. They cried out to him, bidding him voice the wrong. "Speak! Speak for the Dumb who cannot speak! Speak their protest! Speak their curse!"

He saw visions where other men saw only a black void. For him the blackness was peopled with tragic human shapes. He saw the Victims of the Centuries. He saw Labor bound to wheels. He saw Hunger rob the Cradle. He saw Death dance to the cries of Mocked Motherhood. And far off, like the Prisoner of Patmos, he saw a New Earth in which all human beings were comrades of the flowers and the stars, and sharers of the freedom of the birds.

He obeyed the voices. He spoke in the Assembly of the Law-makers—spoke for Labor and against Labor's wrongs. He spoke for the Dumb, for the Doomed and Damned. He spoke their protest and their curse. He spoke for Childhood and for Motherhood—spoke for the Makers of Laws. And when he spoke they answered with the howl of the Beast.

But Labor heard him speak its own Protest; heard him hurl at the Makers of Laws and the Masters of Bread the curse its heart had fashioned and its lips failed to speak. Labor knew that Debs voiced its own dumb agony and cheered him on by glad applause and by its love. But while he spoke there was sadness in his heart, each speech was answered in his own soul by a sense of sadness and of shame. Perhaps it was vain to speak to the Makers of Laws and the Masters of Bread! Perhaps it was better to speak to the Slaves of Bread! Better to speak to Labor and to teach it speech!

But the new speech brought no heartease. Ever the sense of Failure shamed him and tore his soul. And yet the voices bade him speak. "Speak of the visions! Speak of the New Earth! Speak and lead the way!" they cried. And his tortured soul answered in agony: "I cannot show the way, for I know it not!"

The Masters of Bread knew nothing of the struggle of his soul; they knew not that his speech which woke their fears was but his whisper! They could not know that the things their Fear and their Hate bade them do would loosen his tongue and give it speech like thunder. In their ignorance they forged a thunderbolt with which the barriers to the pathway to the land of the vision would be shattered. They cast Debs into prison. And in his prison cell Debs was to find Freedom —the Freedom of his Soul.

When they prisoned Debs they unprisoned his soul. When they drew the bolts that pent his body in Woodstock jail they made Eugene V. Debs a free man. In the silences of that prison cell his tongue was loosed and his eyes saw the vision of the Comrade-world and the way by which it must be reached. In the prison cell the Angel of Freedom touched his lips with fire from the altar and set him free to proclaim the Revolution. In their rage the Masters of Bread thought that they could silence Debs, but instead they broke the only fetter upon his soul and upon his speech.

Thus was Debs trained to be our standard bearer. Thus did he become the Voice of the Revolution whose call to Labor was destined to shake the hemisphere. He bore the people's banner as one marked for the mission by Inexorable Destiny. He bore it proudly, nobly, wherever the fight was fiercest, and when he shouted the battle cry of Socialism it echoed through the land from sea to sea, from snow-capped mountain and deepest valley. And Labor heard the battle cry and answered in speech both clear and strong. And when he took the banner and went forth a second time, louder and stronger grew the answering cry, so that the Masters of Bread trembled in their seats of power and privilege.

And now, once more, speeded by the love of fifty thousand comrades in the organized movement, and by half a million in the larger army, Debs goes forth bearing the banner and proclaiming the message of Socialism. Once more he goes forth to voice the cry of the Disinherited, the curse of the Doomed and Damned. Once more the Incarnate Spirit of the Revolution goes forth to point men to the Vision of a world rich with the glory of comradeship, throbbing with the joy of freedom, radiant with love—the New Earth, resonant with the mingled songs of free and happy human beings; resplendent with the beauty of unfettered life.

And a million workingmen will answer with their cheers and pledge their faith with their votes!

A Companion to Truth

By Robert Hunter

I remember as a little lad of eight or nine years, walking with my father in one of the streets of Terre Haute. A tall, slender, handsome young man stopped to talk with my father. At first I was fascinated by the way they grasped hands and looked into each other's eyes. I was then impressed by their animated conversation. But they talked on and on until it seemed to me hours in length; and finally I began to tug at my father's coat-tails, urging him to come on. After a while they parted, and my father said to me very seriously, "You should not interrupt me, Robert, when I am talking. That young man is one of the greatest souls of this earth, and you should have listened to what he said."

From time to time afterwards I heard of 'Gene, and many were the stories told of him. Everyone spoke of his friendship for the poor. He could never keep money in his pocket. His wife says he always gives away his clothes to those who come to his door; and he gives his best suits, never his old ones.

Once I was told he had a gold watch of considerable value which had been given to him, and a fireman who had been out of work for some time stopped him to say that he had a job offered on the railroad, but he would have to have a watch before he could go to work. Immediately 'Gene took out his gold watch and give it to the man, telling him to return it when he was able to buy one for himself.

These and countless other stories are told by his fellow-citizens. Many of them do not understand 'Gene. His views and his work they cannot comprehend, but every man, woman and child in that town loves him with a devotion quite extraordinary.

They say that a prophet is without honor in his own country, but in Terre Haute you will find that however much they misunderstand the work that 'Gene is doing there is not one who does not honor and love him.

Ask anyone. Go to the poor, the vagrant, the hobo. Go to the churches, to the rich, to the banker, to the traction magnate. You will find that every single one will say that 'Gene has something which other men do not possess. Some will say he is rash, unwise, and too radical. Others will say that he is too good for this world, and that his visions and dreams are the fanciful outpourings of a generous but impractical soul. But ask them about his character, his honesty, his sincerity, and unconsciously many of them will remove their hats.

Some of these statements will seem an exaggeration. But one cannot avoid that in speaking of 'Gene. When one who knows him makes any statement, no matter how moderate, it will seem to others who do not know him an exaggeration.

'Gene has followed Truth wherever she has led. He does not ask what is politic, what is wise, what is expedient; he only asks what is truth. He loves Truth beyond all things. She is his absolute mistress, and he has gone with her from riches to poverty, from popularity to unpopularity. He has gone with her out of great positions into small positions. He has stood up for her against all men. For her he has seemed at times to sacrifice all earthly gain, and to accept without one pang of regret misunderstanding, misrepresentation, and almost universal condemnation. For her he has been momentarily one of the most popular men in the country, and for her he has been momentarily one of the most unpopular men in the country. He has been her companion when everyone believed in her, and he has been her companion when to believe in her meant to go into prison stripes, behind iron bars.

Sometimes I have differed with 'Gene. I have said to him that what he was doing was unwise, impolitic, dangerous. At such times, under such criticism, he is always kindly but undeterred; and it is his conscience that answers you back and asks, "But is it right? Is it true?"

Shortly after I left college I went to live in one of the most poverty-stricken districts of Chicago. One Sunday it was announced that Eugene would come there to speak. Thousands came to hear him, and overflowing the hall a multitude waited outside to hear him speak from a truck. After waiting for two hours perhaps, 'Gene came out and began to speak. Most of the audience were foreigners who could hardly understand a word of English, and as I heard his beautiful words and saw their wistful, earnest faces I felt that something more powerful, penetrating and articulate than mere words was passing between the audience and the speaker. For a moment it seemed to me that a soul was speaking from the eyes and frame of 'Gene, and that, regardless of differences of language and all the traditional barriers that separated him from the multitude about him, they understood and believed all he said. I remember how my heart beat, and how tears began to flow from my boyish eyes. I was ashamed for fear someone would see me. And it was not because of anything that 'Gene was saying. It was solely because of something back of the man, something greater than the man, something bigger, more powerful, and more moving than any words or expression. And after the thing was over I went to him, helped him on with his coat, and fondled him as I would my own father or brother. And as we went away together there kept coming into my heart the words of Ruth:

"Entreat me not to leave thee or to return from following after thee. For whither thou goest I will go, and whither thou lodgest I will lodge. Thy people shall be my people, and thy God my God."

Greater Love Hath No Man

To me the name of Eugene V. Debs means this—loyalty absolute, unswerving, incorruptible to the Cause of Labor, the Cause of Humanity itself. Where that Cause is at stake, Debs sinks his personality with utter self-abnegation; he fears nothing, he dares all in defense of that splendid ideal. No threat deters him; nor is there gold enough in all the swollen purses of Plutocracy to turn this man one hair's-breadth aside from his fidelity to Labor. Greater love than his hath no man. All honor to 'Gene Debs, say I.—GEORGE ALLAN ENGLAND, Bryant's Pond, Maine.

Agitator and Poet

Eugene V. Debs is an agitator with the heart of a poet. The combination is rare, and Socialism in America is to be congratulated on having a leader of his caliber. I think of Debs as preëminently the voice of the working class. The proletarian spirit has found in him its loyalest and bravest exponent. But he is much more than that. He is a dreamer as well as a fighter. He leads men because he *loves* them. If Walt Whitman could return, he would surely recognize in Debs a man who believes with all the intensity of his nature in "the dear love of comrades." LEONARD D. ABBOTT.

A Love Shared by Lincoln and Debs

Forty-six years ago the hand of the martyred LINCOLN rested gently upon the head of a child, who looked into the rugged, kindly face made beautiful by the divinity of the SAVIOR OF THE SLAVE, and gave instant and unquestioning love to the MAN "with charity for all." Time came when the boy, with crepe on his arm and the ache of childhood in his throat, watched the sad and solemn pageant for the Nation's dearest dead.

Fifteen years ago EUGENE VICTOR DEBS stretched out two generous hands and "the warmest heart that ever beat," to clasp as his own the hands and heart of a man that loved, trusted and honored him at first sight.

And in the close intimacy of our brother-comradehood I have found no fault in GENE; for he is as faithful and tender as my dear old Mother, who loves him, blessed him and bade him kiss her, as brave as a lion, as gentle as a woman, as honest and straightforward as a little child, as white, clean and sweet of soul as his elder brothers, LINCOLN and CHRIST—and these three are Nature's noblest noblemen.

W. E. P. FRENCH, U. S. Army.
Cornwall-on-Hudson, New York, Saturday, June 27, 1908.

A Righteous Cause Must Win

If I were keenly ambitious for the future acclaim of my countrymen I would rather lead the Socialist party to defeat in the campaign of 1908 than to win as the candidate either of the Republican or Democratic parties. Taft and Bryan look forward only to the power and the doubtful honor of dispensing patronage. Both stand on platforms which are barren of promise or hope. With all the world pressing on to the solution of great social and economic questions we are confronted with the lamentable spectacle of the dominant political parties of the United States beating a cowardly retreat, and we see their candidates rival one another in the timidity of their assaults on obvious and admitted wrongs.

There is no higher honor than that bequeathed with the leadership of a great moral principle. Socialism is the greatest moral principle yet discovered by humanity. It can be put into effect only by education and political action, and the Socialists of the United States have in three campaigns intrusted the leadership to Eugene V. Debs. In coming years, when some future leader will sweep the field, and when no voice will be raised against the fundamental equity and practicability of Socialism, the historian will dwell on the pioneer work of the men and women who placed Eugene V. Debs at their head, and the verdict of the historian will be far different from that of the thoughtless critics of today.

A righteous cause always wins in the end, and there is imperishable glory for those who stand at the front in the years when men's eyes are blinded to the truth. No man is great enough as a Socialist to make himself greater than his party. Bryan looms great because the Democratic party is a dull level of ignorant mediocrity; Taft is looked up to because of the belief that the great monied interests have accepted his leadership and will bring about his election; Eugene V. Debs is simply the unselfish representative of an idea which will prevail despite all which can be arrayed against it.

FREDERICK UPHAM ADAMS.

Hastings-on-Hudson, N. Y.

Love's Inter-Racial Pan-Human Language

In January, 1897, Debs joined the international Socialist movement.

Six weeks later the present writer, amid the jeers and gibes and some hisses of many old comrades, publicly hailed our Gene's adhesion to the ranks as symbolizing the Awakening of Labor.

After awhile the S. D. A. was founded, and I met Debs in this city as a member of the new party.

On that occasion he addressed an audience including hundreds of my countrymen. They hardly understood one word out of every five he spoke, but they nevertheless clearly grasped the meaning of his message as a whole, which they applauded to the echo.

Well, it was Love's inter-racial, pan-human language which had reached the hearts almost unaided by the use of words.

And ever since then they, like myself, have loved him as their big brother, their comrade, the foremost champion of their great Cause.

M. WINCHEVSKY.

APPRECIATIONS.

Eugene V. Debs! This is one of the great names of the century. No one—not even a political enemy—has ever said that Debs is not sincere to the core of his heart. It is an event to meet this courageous friend of man. The grasp of his hand is comforting, the look of his lighted face is an inspiration. In that one look you are taken into the door of his home, seated at his table, warmed at his chimney-fire!

EDWIN MARKHAM.

www.ingramcontent.com/pod-product-compliance
Lightning Source LLC
Chambersburg PA
CBHW030253100426
42812CB00002B/413